T0212714

Lecture Notes in Computer Science 9385

Commenced Publication in 1973
Founding and Former Series Editors:
Gerhard Goos, Juris Hartmanis, and Jan van Leeuwen

More information about this series at http://www.springer.com/series/7409

Elisa Fromont · Tijl De Bie
Matthijs van Leeuwen (Eds.)

Advances in Intelligent Data Analysis XIV

14th International Symposium, IDA 2015
Saint Etienne, France, October 22–24, 2015
Proceedings

 Springer

Editors
Elisa Fromont
Université de Saint Etienne
Saint Etienne
France

Tijl De Bie
Intelligent Systems Lab
University of Bristol
Bristol
UK

Matthijs van Leeuwen
Informatics Section
Katholieke Universiteit Leuven
Leuven
Belgium

ISSN 0302-9743   ISSN 1611-3349 (electronic)
Lecture Notes in Computer Science
ISBN 978-3-319-24464-8   ISBN 978-3-319-24465-5 (eBook)
DOI 10.1007/978-3-319-24465-5

Library of Congress Control Number: 2015948773

LNCS Sublibrary: SL3 – Information Systems and Applications, incl. Internet/Web, and HCI

Springer International Publishing AG Switzerland is part of Springer Science+Business Media
(www.springer.com)

Preface

We are proud to present the proceedings of IDA 2015, the 14th International Symposium on Intelligent Data Analysis, which was held from October 22 to October 24, 2015, in Saint-Etienne, France.

The series started in 1995 and was held biennially until 2009. In 2010, the symposium re-focused to support papers that go beyond established technology and contain genuinely novel and game-changing ideas, while not always being as fully realized as papers accepted at other conferences. To further support this unique focus, IDA 2015 additionally included a so-called "Horizon Track", which contained contributed talks about research that may be too preliminary for archival publication, but with a potentially very high impact. The IDA symposium is an interdisciplinary meeting that solicits contributions on all aspects of intelligent data analysis, including papers on intelligent support for modeling and analyzing data from complex, dynamical systems. Intelligent support for data analysis goes beyond the usual algorithmic offerings in the literature. Papers about established technology were only accepted if the technology was embedded in intelligent data analysis systems, or was applied in novel ways to analyzing and/or modeling complex systems.

The conventional reviewing process, which tends to favor incremental advances on established work, can discourage the kinds of papers that IDA 2015 has published. The reviewing process adopted for IDA addressed this issue explicitly: referees evaluated papers against the stated goals of the symposium, and an informed, thoughtful, positive review written by a Program Committee advisor could outweigh other, negative reviews and result in acceptance of the paper. Indeed, it was noted that this had a notable impact on the selection of papers included in the program. In addition, the new "Horizon Track" allowed researchers to present their most ground breaking research at the symposium without publishing it in the proceedings, stimulating discussions about the most exciting research ideas and visions at an early stage.

We were pleased to have a very strong program. We received 65 submissions in total. In all, 59 papers were submitted to the regular proceedings track, of which 29 were accepted for inclusion in this volume. Six papers were submitted to the Horizon Track, of which three were accepted for presentation at the symposium. The IDA Frontier Prize was awarded to the most visionary contribution. As in previous years, we included a poster and video track for PhD students to promote their work. The best 2-minute video, as decided by the participants of the symposium, was awarded the Video Prize.

We were honored to have three distinguished invited speakers at IDA 2015:

– Tony Veale from University College Dublin, Ireland, talked about "The Shape of Tweets to Come" and how Twitter presents a generative opportunity of another kind to the computationally-minded language researcher, to study how algorithmic models might impose linguistic hypotheses onto large data sources to compose novel and meaningful micro-texts of their own.

- Nick Heard from Imperial College London, UK, talked about "Combining Weak Statistical Evidence in Cyber Security" and how statistical modelling (and the use of p-values) of nodes and edges in a computer network can build up a picture of normal behavior in a system.
- Pascal Van Hentenryck from National ICT (NICTA), Australia, talked about "Evidence-Based Optimization". He showed some case studies in disaster management, energy systems, high-performance computing, and market optimization and presented some emerging architectures for evidence-based optimization.

The conference was held in the buildings of Telecom Saint-Etienne Engineering School in front of the Hubert-Curien Laboratory. All those buildings were part of the new "Manufacture d'armes de Saint-Étienne" (MAS, known for example for the FAMAS assault rifle), built in 1864 and closed in 2001. They are now part of a new university campus dedicated to computer science and physics (and in particular, optics).

We wish to express our gratitude to all authors of submitted papers for their intellectual contributions; to the Program Committee members and the additional reviewers for their effort in reviewing and commenting on the submitted papers; to the members of the IDA Steering Committee for their ongoing guidance and support; and to the Program Committee advisors for their active involvement. Special thanks go to the poster and video chair, Jesse Read; the local chair, Baptiste Jeudy; the publicity chair, Edward Cohen; the sponsorship chair, François Jacquenet; the Frontier Prize chairs, Michael Berthold and Elizabeth Bradley; and the webmaster, Leonor Becerra-Bonache. We gratefully acknowledge those who were involved in the local organization of the symposium: Romain Deville, Rémi Emonet, Damien Fourure, Matthias Gery, Amaury Habrard, Christine Largeron, and Emilie Morvant.

Finally, we are grateful to our sponsors and supporters: KNIME, for funding the IDA Frontier Prize for the most visionary contribution presenting a novel and surprising approach to data analysis; the French Artificial Intelligence Association (AFIA), for funding the IDA Video Prize for the best video presented in the PhD poster and video track; the IT company Eura Nova; Jean Monnet University (UJM); the Artificial Intelligence journal; Télécom Saint-Etienne (for sharing their building); and Springer.

August 2015

Tijl De Bie
Elisa Fromont
Matthijs van Leeuwen

Organization

General Chair

Matthijs van Leeuwen   Leiden University, Netherlands and KU Leuven, Belgium

Program Chairs

Tijl De Bie   Ghent University, Belgium
University of Bristol, UK
Elisa Fromont   University of Lyon, St-Etienne, France

Poster and Video Chair

Jesse Read   Aalto University, Finland

Local Chair

Baptiste Jeudy   University of Lyon, St-Etienne, France

Publicity Chair

Edward Cohen   Imperial College London, UK

Sponsorship Chair

François Jacquenet   University of Lyon, St-Etienne, France

Frontier Prize Chairs

Elizabeth Bradley   University of Colorado, USA
Michael Berthold   University of Konstanz, Germany

Advisory Chairs

Joost Kok   Universiteit Leiden, Netherlands
Paul Cohen   University of Arizona, USA
Nada Lavrač   Jožef Stefan Institute, Slovenia

Webmaster

Leonor Becerra-Bonache   University of Lyon, St-Etienne, France

Local Organization Committee

Romain Deville   University of Lyon, INSA de Lyon, France
Rémi Emonet   University of Lyon, St-Etienne, France
Damien Fourure   University of Lyon, St-Etienne, France
Matthias Gery   University of Lyon, St-Etienne, France
Amaury Habrard   University of Lyon, St-Etienne, France
Christine Largeron   University of Lyon, St-Etienne, France
Emilie Morvant   University of Lyon, St-Etienne, France

Program Committee Advisors

Michael Berthold   University of Konstanz, Germany
Hendrik Blockeel   KU Leuven, Belgium
Liz Bradley   University of Colorado, USA
Paul Cohen   University of Arizona, USA
Jaakko Hollmén   Aalto University School of Science, Finland
Frank Klawonn   Ostfalia University of Applied Sciences, Germany
Joost Kok   Leiden University, The Netherlands
Nada Lavrač   Jožef Stefan Institute, Slovenia
Matthijs van Leeuwen   KU Leuven, Belgium
Xiaohui Liu   Brunel University, UK
Arno Siebes   Universiteit Utrecht, Netherlands
Stephen Swift   Brunel University, UK
Hannu Toivonen   University of Helsinki, Finland
Allan Tucker   Brunel University, UK

Program Committee

Fabrizio Angiulli   DEIS, University of Calabria, Italy
Alexandre Aussem   GAMA, Université Lyon 1, France
José L. Balcázar   Universitat Politècnica de Catalunya, Spain
Elena Bellodi   ENDIF-University of Ferrara, Italy
Maria Bielikova   Slovak University of Technology in Bratislava,
                       Slovakia
Christian Borgelt   European Centre for Soft Computing, Spain
Henrik Bostrom   Stockholm University, Sweden
Marc Boullé   Orange Labs, France
Toon Calders   Université Libre de Bruxelles, Belgium
Andre Carvalho   USP-Universidade de São Paulo, Brazil
Loïc Cerf   Universidade Federal de Minas Gerais, Brazil
Edward Cohen   Imperial College London, UK

Maguelonne Teisseire	Cemagref - UMR Tetis, France
Melissa Turcotte	LANL, USA
Antti Ukkonen	Helsinki Institute for Information Technology, Finland
Maarten Van Someren	University of Amsterdam, Netherlands
Veronica Vinciotti	Brunel University, UK
Jilles Vreeken	Max-Planck Institute for Informatics and Saarland University, Germany
Zidong Wang	Brunel University, UK
Leishi Zhang	Middlesex University, UK
Indre Zliobaite	Aalto University, Finland

Additional Reviewers

Braune, Christian	Gossen, Tatiana	Nair Benrekia,
Cerri, Ricardo	Guy, Michelle	Yacine Noureddine
Cule, Boris	Held, Pascal	Palopoli, Luigi
D'Ambrosio, Antonio	Ienco, Dino	Pio, Gianvito
Doell, Christoph	Liu, Renhao	Zhang, Jianpeng
Fassetti, Fabio	Madjarov, Gjorgji	Zhou, Mu
Fortino, Vittorio	Muelas, Santiago	Ševcech, Jakub
Freitas, Alex		

Invited Talks Abstracts

The Shape of Tweets to Come

Tony Veale

University College Dublin, Ireland
tony.veale@ucd.ie
https://www.csi.ucd.ie/users/tony-veale

Abstract. Twitter has proven itself a rich and varied source of language data for linguistic analysis. For Twitter is more than a popular new platform for social interaction via language; in many ways Twitter constitutes a whole new genre of text, as users adapt to its limitations (140 character *"tweets"*) *and* its novel conventions (e.g. re-tweeting, hashtags). Language researchers can thus harvest Twitter data to study how users convey meaning with affect, and how they achieve stickiness and virality with the texts they compose. But Twitter presents an opportunity of another kind to the computationally-minded language researcher, a *generative* opportunity to study how algorithmic models might impose linguistic hypotheses onto large data sources to compose novel and meaningful micro-texts of their own. This computational turn allows researchers to go beyond merely descriptive models of playful uses of language such as metaphor, sarcasm and irony. It allows researchers to test whether their models embody a sufficiently algorithmic understanding of a phenomenon to facilitate the construction of a fully-automated computational system, one that can generate wholly novel examples that are deemed acceptable to humans. This talk presents and evaluates one such system, a *Twitterbot* named *@MetaphorMagnet* that generates, expresses and shares its own playful insights on Twitter. I shall show how *@MetaphorMagnet*s tweets are inspired by data but shaped by knowledge, and consider how the outputs of this hybrid data/knowledge-driven bot may be usefully anchored in another source of data – the news stream.

Combining Weak Statistical Evidence in Cyber Security

Nicholas A. Heard

Imperial College London, UK
n.heard@imperial.ac.uk
http://wwwf.imperial.ac.uk/~naheard/

Abstract. Cyber attacks on government and industry computer networks are now commonplace and no system can be made invulnerable to intrusion. Instead, much importance is placed on reducing the impact of cyber attacks when they occur, which first means quickly detecting their presence amongst the flow of cyber traffic. However, sophisticated hackers and cyber criminals will act carefully to hide their presence, and so any hard detection rules (signatures) can be circumnavigated. Nonetheless, if an intrusion has a malign purpose, then at least some unusual behaviour will be hidden within the network traffic data. Statistical modelling of nodes and edges in a computer network can build up a picture of normal behaviour in the system. Typical institutional computer networks produce high volume data streams and so, from time to time, surprising but benign behaviour will be observed. The task is to detect the significance of genuine intrusion events against this background. In statistical modelling, p-values are the fundamental quantities for measuring the significance of observed data against a null hypothesis. This talk will review methods of combining p-values to accumulate evidence, investigating their properties in depth. Some new approaches will then be proposed which are better suited for detecting subsets of significant p-values. Finally, the advantages of the proposed approach will be illustrated on a cyber authentication problem, stemming from collaborative work with Los Alamos National Laboratory.

Evidence-Based Optimization

Pascal Van Hentenryck

National ICT (NICTA), Australia
pascal.vanhentenryck@nicta.com.au
http://org.nicta.com.au/people/phentenryck/

Abstract. For the first time in the history of mankind, we are accumulating data sets of unprecedented scale and accuracy about physical infrastructures, natural phenomena, man-made processes, and human behavior. These developments, together with progress in high-performance computing, machine learning, and operations research, offer exciting opportunities for the evidence-based optimization of global systems. This talk reviews some case-studies in disaster management, energy systems, high-performance computing, and market optimization to showcase these unique opportunities and their associated challenges, and presents some emerging architectures for evidence-based optimization.

Horizon Track Abstracts

Towards a Data Science Collaboratory

Joaquin Vanschoren[1], Bernd Bischl[2], Frank Hutter[3], Michele Sebag[4],
Balazs Kegl[4], Matthias Schmid[5], Giulio Napolitano[5],
Katy Wolstencroft[6], Alan R. Williams[7], and Neil Lawrence[8]

[1] Eindhoven University of Technology
j.vanschoren@tue.nl
[2] Ludwig-Maximilians-University Munich
bernd.bischl@stat.uni-muenchen.de
[3] Albert-Ludwigs-Universität Freiburg
fh@informatik.uni-freiburg.de
[4] Université Paris Sud
michele.sebag@lri.fr, balazs.kegl@gmail.com
[5] Universität Bonn
{matthias.schmid,giulio}@imbie.meb.uni-bonn.de
[6] Universiteit Leiden
k.j.wolstencroft@liacs.leidenuniv.nl
[7] University of Manchester
alan.r.williams@manchester.ac.uk
[8] University of Sheffield
n.lawrence@dcs.shef.ac.uk

1 The Fragmented Data Science Ecosystem

Data-driven research requires an ecosystem of people fulfilling many different roles: domain scientists collect and analyze data to study or discover phenomena; data scientists design and evaluate algorithms, and computer scientists implement and maintain these techniques to be used throughout science and industry.

However, there exist large gaps between these communities that slow down the rate of discovery. First, because domain scientists have a more limited view on the state of the art in data science, they are often unsure about the latest and most appropriate techniques. There exist extensive algorithms libraries, but it is often not clear how to optimally use them. Hence, they either spend a lot of time on research and experimentation, or make suboptimal choices. Data scientists, on the other hand, often don't speak the language of domain scientists, hence missing opportunities to work interactively with them and innovate in their respective fields. While there exist many wonderful open data repositories, it is far from obvious how to access, understand and use this data. Hence, much research still uses datasets that are of little scientific or industrial interest today. Knowledge transfer through the literature is inefficient, as findings are spread over millions of papers based on tacit domain-specific knowledge and community-specific jargon. Moreover, while scientific papers are being produced at a tremendous rate, reproducible and readily applicable major discoveries are far fewer [1]. Empirical evaluations of algorithms on known datasets are typically not organized online, but confined to papers with varying levels of detail, making them virtually impossible to build on. In short, while it is *theoretically* possible for these communities to build on each other's work, in practice there is a lot of friction involved, such as handling myriad data formats, studying source code, emailing authors, and running complex experiments. As a result, many scientists spend vast amounts of time on tasks that others could do in a fraction of that time, that could be done much better using novel/better techniques, or that could be automated altogether.

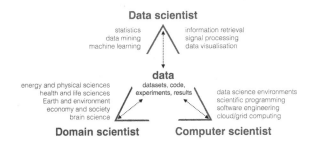

Fig. 1. Roles within the data science ecosystem and the gaps between them.

2 An Online Collaboratory

We propose to create an online *collaboratory*, where data scientists, domain scientists and computer scientists can easily interact and build directly on each other's work, transforming the practice of data science from small-scale local collaborations to massive, real-time, *online* collaborations.

First, we can extract actionable datasets from large scientific databases, identify key software components, and (auto-)annotate them with a practical base vocabulary to create a 'search engine for data science'. This helps scientists find useful tools (e.g. scalable clustering algorithms), and test algorithms on many recent datasets. Next, scientists can challenge the community to solve problems, yielding experiments showing how well each particular solution works. Crucially, experiments and results (e.g., predictive models) should be open and linked to the underlying data sets and workflows, ensuring reproducibility and creating a single, organized body of research: a 'data telescope' that can be wielded by scientists, industry and students alike. The collaboratory should support social networking to protect preliminary research, and track the impact of all contributions (reuse, downloads, altmetrics) to help scientist build their reputation.

The collaboratory can be seamlessly integrated into the tools that scientists already use, to automatically download and upload data, code and experiments [2]. Moreover, it offers unprecedented opportunities to intelligently recommend algorithms or optimize large parameter spaces, thus saving time.

We hope to bring together data scientists, computer scientists, and domain scientists from many domains to see how current tools can be connected, and best practices can be shared. We expect that this *networked* approach to data science will strongly contribute to speeding up data-driven science in the near future. Indeed, if we are all part of the same 'experimentation system in the sky', we can all become more productive and efficiently learn from each other.

References

1. Ioannidis, J.: Why most published research findings are false. PLoS Med. **2**(8), e214 (2005)
2. Vanschoren, J., van Rijn, J.N., Bischl, B., Torgo, L.: OpenML: networked science in machine learning. SIGKDD Explor. **15**(2), 49–60 (2013)

When Learning Indeed Changes the World: Diagnosing Prediction-Induced Drift

Georg Krempl, Dávid Bodnár, Anita Hrubos

Knowledge Management & Discovery, Otto-von-Guericke University,
Universitätsplatz 2, 39106 Magdeburg, Germany
georg.krempl@iti.cs.uni-magdeburg.de
http://kmd.ovgu.de/res/driftmining

Abstract. A fundamental assumption underlying many prediction systems is that they act as an invisible observer without interfering with the evolution of the population under study. More formally, their distribution is assumed to be independent of the system's previous predictions. Nevertheless, this is violated when, for example, the predictor faces intelligent and malevolent adversaries who counteract its classification rules, or when the classification as high-risk might become a self-fulfilling prophecy. The former has received some attention in adversarial machine learning [10, 12] in the context of hardening classifiers against such an adversary, and indications for the latter have been reported for recommender systems [3, 5] and financial applications [9, 13]. However, the problems of *self-defeating* and *self-fulfilling* prophecies in prediction systems have not been studied in an unified framework yet, leaving questions such as how to detect them in drift open.

We address this by presenting a first approach to assess the presence of such *prediction-induced drift* in datasets. Our work complements literature on change detection [11], change and drift mining [2, 6, 7], and concept drift [4, 8], which is based on the assumption that the observed drift is independent of the system's predictions. We illustrate and evaluate our approach on data generated with and without self-defeating and self-fulfilling prophecies. While prediction-induced drift is not limited to classification problems, but might also occur in other fields of machine learning, we focus this initial analysis on the classification task.

Our preliminary results on synthetic datasets are promising but highlight two major challenges: First, while the majority of prediction-induced drifts is correctly detected, detection of self-fulfilling prophecies seems more difficult, requiring further research. Second, this analysis requires knowing the labels that were actually assigned by prediction systems, which are currently not published in real-world benchmark datasets such as the ones in the UCI Machine Learning Repository [1].

Thus, this contribution also aims to motivate the community to collect, to share, and to analyse data with the system's actual predictions in order to allow an assessment of prediction-induced drift in real-world applications.

Keywords: prediction-induced drift, concept drift, dataset shift, population drift, nonstationarity, change mining, drift mining, change detection, self-fulfilling prophecy, self-defeating prophecy, adversarial machine learning.

Acknowledgments. We thank Daniel Kottke, Myra Spiliopoulou, Julia Hempel and Marcus Kamieth from University of Magdeburg, Battista Biggio from University of Cagliari, and Michele Sebag and Marc Schoenauer from INRIA Saclay for the insightful discussions on change mining, adversarial machine learning and ways of assessing prediction-induced drift in data.

References

1. Asuncion, A., Newman, D.J.: UCI machine learning repository (2015). http://archive.ics.uci.edu/ml/
2. Böttcher, M., Höppner, F., Spiliopoulou, M.: On exploiting the power of time in data mining. ACM SIGKDD Explor. Newsl. **10**(2), 3–11 (2008)
3. Fleder, D., Hosanagar, K.: Blockbuster culture's next rise or fall: the impact of recommender systems on sales diversity. Manag. Sci. **55**(5), 697–712 (2009)
4. Gama, J., Zliobaitė, I., Bifet, A., Pechenizkiy, M.: A survey on concept-drift adaptation. under review (2013)
5. Hagen, S.t., Someren, M.v., Hollink, V.: Exploration/exploitation in adaptive recommender systems. In: Proceedings of the European Symposium on Intelligent Technologies, Hybrid Systems and their implementation on Smart Adaptive Systems (2003)
6. Hofer, V., Krempl, G.: Drift mining in data: A framework for addressing drift in classification. Comput. Stat. Data Anal. **57**(1), 377–391 (2013)
7. Krempl, G.: Temporal density extrapolation. In: Douzal-Chouakria, A., Vilar, J.A., Marteau, P.F., Maharaj, A., Alonso, A.M., Otranto, E. (eds.) Proceedings of the ECML/PKDD 2015 Workshop on Advanced Analytics and Learning on Temporal Data (AALTD 2015), Porto, Portugal, September 11, 2015. CEUR Workshop Proceedings (2015)
8. Krempl, G., Zliobaitė, I., Brzeziński, D., Hüllermeier, E., Last, M., Lemaire, V., Noack, T., Shaker, A., Sievi, S., Spiliopoulou, M., Stefanowski, J.: Open challenges for data stream mining research. SIGKDD Explor. **16**(1), 1–10 (2014), special Issue on Big Data
9. Larsen, F.: Automatic stock market trading based on technical analysis (2007), masterthesis, Institutt for dateteknikk og informasjonsvitenskap, Norges teknisk-naturvitenskapelige universitet
10. Laskov, P., Lippmann, R.: Machine learning in adversarial environments. Mach. Learn. **81**(2), 115–119 (2010)
11. Sebastião, R., Gama, J.: A study on change detection methods. In: Proceedings of the 4th Portuguese Conference on Artificial Intelligence, Lisbon (2009)
12. Tygar, J.D.: Adversarial machine learning. IEEE Internet Comput. **15**(5), 4–6 (2011)
13. Wisniewski, T.P., Lambe, B.: The role of media in the credit crunch: The case of the banking sector. J. Econ. Behav. Organ. **85**, 163–175 (2013)

The Data Problem in Data Mining

Albrecht Zimmermann

INSA de Lyon
albrecht.zimmermann@insa-lyon.fr

Abstract. Computer science is essentially an applied or engineering science, creating tools. In Data Mining, those tools are supposed to help humans understand large amounts of data, and produce actionable insight. In this talk, I argue that for all the progress that has been made in Data Mining, in particular Pattern Mining, we are lacking understanding of key aspects of the performance and results of pattern mining algorithms. I will focus particularly on the difficulty of deriving actionable knowledge from patterns. I trace the lack of progress regarding those questions to a lack of data with varying, controlled properties, and argue that we will need to make a science of digital data generation, and use it to develop guidance to data practitioners.

1 Short-Comings in Evaluation

Data Mining, and in particular Pattern Mining, have been around for about two decades and the work in the field has led to a large number of techniques, which have been applied to pattern domains as diverse as itemsets, attribute-value data, sequences, trees, and graphs, and tasks ranging from finding associations to describing interesting subpopulations, to predicting unseen class labels.

In this talk, I will focus on the unsupervised pattern mining setting, i.e. finding unexpected, interesting and useful patterns that are not related to a variable of interest - nominal or otherwise. As I will argue, the *qualitative* evaluation of proposed techniques, i.e. how "good" the resulting patterns are, has been given short thrift in comparison to *quantitative* evaluation, i.e. how efficiently the output is found.

But also the latter has arguably not been given the attention it deserved. This case has been made convincingly early on by Zheng *et al.* [2], who showed that the evaluations performed in itemset mining up to that point in time had led to an over-fitting on the artificially generated data used. The reported performance did not transfer to real-life data, which showed different characteristics than the artificially generated data. Remarkably enough, the situation has barely improved since then, with quantitative evaluations focused on a small number of data sets, of which typically only few are used in a given evaluation.

The situation is worse for qualitative evaluations, which are rarely performed in the first place. This is understandable since the lack of a target variable corresponds to missing ground truth in the data. But at the same time, it means that even if we knew how to set parameters appropriately[1], we would not know how found patterns relate to the processes that generated the data. Since pattern mining is supposed to give us insight into those processes, and allow us to act based on found patterns, this is a serious short-coming.

2 Generating Data (and Understanding Pattern Mining)

When there is no ground truth available for real-life data (or when there is little real-life data available in the first place), generating artificial data is a promising alternative. This is not only the case in computer science, where, for instance, the SAT solving community has chosen this direction, but also in "hard sciences" like physics, see for instance [1].

Data generation allows us to both break the bottleneck of too few data sets (or data sets with a too narrow range of characteristics), and to understand how found patterns relate to the processes that generated the data. As Zheng *et al.* showed, however, and others have demonstrated since, approaching this task without forethought and an understanding of the data we aim to generate will lead to unrealistic data sets. Furthermore, limiting ourselves to a narrow selection of generative processes, e.g. generating itemset mining data only by combining itemsets, will restrict the lessons to be learned from matching patterns to processes, and carries the risk of biasing qualitative evaluations.

Fortunately, we do not have to start from scratch. More-or-less successful attempts at data generation have been made, and some infrastructure exists to support this task. Additionally, some researchers have attempted to relate patterns to different processes to evaluate their quality, especially in recent years. Finally, researchers and practitioners in other fields have developed theories of their own that, while necessarily taken with a grain of salt, can be built on to simulate real-life processes. By combining and building on this existing knowledge, we can fill in the current data gaps and start to understand those aspects of pattern mining that escape us so far.

References

1. Cern software development for experiments - Simulation. http://ph-dep-sft.web.cern.ch/project/simulation
2. Zheng, Z., Kohavi, R., Mason, L.: Real world performance of association rule algorithms. In: KDD, pp. 401–406 (2001)

---

[1] Another area in which there is too little guidance.

Contents

Data Analytics and Optimisation for Assessing a Ride Sharing System   1
Vincent Armant, John Horan, Nahid Mabub, and Kenneth N. Brown

Constraint-Based Querying for Bayesian Network Exploration   13
Behrouz Babaki, Tias Guns, Siegfried Nijssen, and Luc De Raedt

Efficient Model Selection for Regularized Classification by Exploiting
Unlabeled Data.   25
*Georgios Balikas, Ioannis Partalas, Eric Gaussier, Rohit Babbar,
and Massih-Reza Amini*

Segregation Discovery in a Social Network of Companies   37
Alessandro Baroni and Salvatore Ruggieri

A First-Order-Logic Based Model for Grounded Language Learning   49
*Leonor Becerra-Bonache, Hendrik Blockeel, María Galván,
and François Jacquenet*

A Parallel Distributed Processing Algorithm for Image Feature Extraction . . .   61
Alexander Belousov and Joel Ratsaby

Modeling Concept Drift: A Probabilistic Graphical Model Based Approach . . .   72
*Hanen Borchani, Ana M. Martínez, Andrés R. Masegosa,
Helge Langseth, Thomas D. Nielsen, Antonio Salmerón,
Antonio Fernández, Anders L. Madsen, and Ramón Sáez*

Diversity-Driven Widening of Hierarchical Agglomerative Clustering   84
Alexander Fillbrunn and Michael R. Berthold

Batch Steepest-Descent-Mildest-Ascent for Interactive Maximum
Margin Clustering.   95
Fabian Gieseke, Tapio Pahikkala, and Tom Heskes

Time Series Classification with Representation Ensembles   108
Rafael Giusti, Diego F. Silva, and Gustavo E.A.P.A. Batista

Simultaneous Clustering and Model Selection for Multinomial Distribution:
A Comparative Study   120
Md. Abul Hasnat, Julien Velcin, Stéphane Bonnevay, and Julien Jacques

On Binary Reduction of Large-Scale Multiclass Classification Problems   132
*Bikash Joshi, Massih-Reza Amini, Ioannis Partalas, Liva Ralaivola,
Nicolas Usunier, and Eric Gaussier*

Probabilistic Active Learning in Datastreams 145
Daniel Kottke, Georg Krempl, and Myra Spiliopoulou

Implicitly Constrained Semi-supervised Least Squares Classification 158
Jesse H. Krijthe and Marco Loog

Diagonal Co-clustering Algorithm for Document-Word Partitioning......... 170
Charlotte Laclau and Mohamed Nadif

I-Louvain: An Attributed Graph Clustering Method.................. 181
David Combe, Christine Largeron, Mathias Géry,
and Előd Egyed-Zsigmond

Class-Based Outlier Detection: Staying Zombies or Awaiting
for Resurrection?... 193
Leona Nezvalová, Luboš Popelínský, Luis Torgo, and Karel Vaculík

Using Metalearning for Prediction of Taxi Trip Duration Using Different
Granularity Levels.. 205
Mohammad Nozari Zarmehri and Carlos Soares

Using Entropy as a Measure of Acceptance for Multi-label Classification.... 217
Laurence A.F. Park and Simeon Simoff

Investigation of Node Deletion Techniques for Clustering Applications
of Growing Self Organizing Maps............................. 229
Thilina Rathnayake, Maheshakya Wijewardena, Thimal Kempitiya,
Kevin Rathnasekara, Thushan Ganegedara, Amal S. Perera,
and Damminda Alahakoon

Exploratory Topic Modeling with Distributional Semantics............. 241
Samuel Rönnqvist

Assigning Geo-relevance of Sentiments Mined from Location-Based Social
Media Posts.. 253
Randall Sanborn, Michael Farmer, and Syagnik Banerjee

Continuous and Discrete Deep Classifiers for Data Integration 264
Nataliya Sokolovska, Salwa Rizkalla, Karine Clément,
and Jean-Daniel Zucker

A Bayesian Approach for Identifying Multivariate Differences
Between Groups 275
Yuriy Sverchkov and Gregory F. Cooper

Automatically Discovering Offensive Patterns in Soccer Match Data 286
Jan Van Haaren, Vladimir Dzyuba, Siebe Hannosset,
and Jesse Davis

Fast Algorithm Selection Using Learning Curves 298
Jan N. van Rijn, Salisu Mamman Abdulrahman, Pavel Brazdil,
and Joaquin Vanschoren

Optimally Weighted Cluster Kriging for Big Data Regression............ 310
Bas van Stein, Hao Wang, Wojtek Kowalczyk, Thomas Bäck,
and Michael Emmerich

Slower Can Be Faster: The iRetis Incremental Model Tree Learner........ 322
Denny Verbeeck and Hendrik Blockeel

VoQs: A Web Application for Visualization of Questionnaire Surveys...... 334
Xiaowei Zhang, Frank Klawonn, Lorenz Grigull, and Werner Lechner

Author Index 345

Data Analytics and Optimisation for Assessing a Ride Sharing System

Vincent Armant[(✉)], John Horan, Nahid Mabub, and Kenneth N. Brown

Insight Centre for Data Analytics, Department of Computer Science,
University College Cork, Cork, Ireland
vincent.armant@insight-centre.org

Abstract. Ride-sharing schemes attempt to reduce road traffic by matching prospective passengers to drivers with spare seats in their cars. To be successful, such schemes require a critical mass of drivers and passengers. In current deployed implementations, the possible matches are based on heuristics, rather than real route times or distances. In some cases, the heuristics propose infeasible matches; in others, feasible matches are omitted. Poor ride matching is likely to deter participants from using the system. We develop a constraint-based model for acceptable ride matches which incorporates route plans and time windows. Through data analytics on a history of advertised schedules and agreed shared trips, we infer parameters for this model that account for 90 % of agreed trips. By applying the inferred model to the advertised schedules, we demonstrate that there is an imbalance between riders and passengers. We assess the potential benefits of persuading existing drivers to switch to becoming passengers if appropriate matches can be found, by solving the inferred model with and without switching. We demonstrate that flexible participation has the potential to reduce the number of unmatched participants by up to 80 %.

1 Introduction

Road traffic is one of the main generators of carbon emissions, and traffic congestion is a significant contributor to pollution around major cities and urban areas. Partly motivated by these issues, there has been recent strong growth in ride-sharing schemes (e.g. Blabla car, Carma, BLyft, Sidecar, Uber), where participants post details of intended trips, and the system then proposes possible matches between drivers and prospective passengers. As more matches are agreed, the number of car journeys decreases, and the total driven distance also decreases, helping to reduce congestion, emissions and energy consumption. Increasing participation in such schemes is thus considered both a benefit for society and a commercial objective for the system operators.

Deployed schemes focus on proposing a set of possible matches for each request, leaving the participants to contact each other, negotiate ride details, and to agree the match. In order to generate these offers quickly, the ride sharing systems typically propose matches using heuristics that are fast to compute,

E. Fromont et al. (Eds.): IDA 2015, LNCS 9385, pp. 1–12, 2015.
DOI: 10.1007/978-3-319-24465-5_1

based on Euclidean distance between locations and on fixed time windows. This means that the set of proposed matches may include some that are infeasible given the road network, and may omit some that would be a user's preferred match. However, users who receive few offers, or who are given offers that are a poor match for their travel plans, are unlikely to continue with the system. There is a need to assess the performance of the current matching schemes, identify ways in which performance could be improved, and assess the improvements that could be gained. To do this, we employ data analytics to infer constraints on possible matches, and to assess current performance. We then use the inferred constraints to build optimisation models and to evaluate proposed improvements.

Specifically, (i) we use shortest path routing algorithms to determine the impact of a driver being matched with a passenger; (ii) by mining records of previously agreed matches, we infer constraints on the departure and arrival time windows for drivers, and on deviations from the shortest routes, that capture 90 % of agreed matches; (iii) we compare the inferred constraint model with the heuristic matching algorithm, and assess the discrepancies between the two approaches; (iv) we analyse histories of proposed trip schedules and show an imbalance between drivers and passengers that may be hampering participation in the scheme; and (v) we propose and evaluate the potential of persuading drivers to be flexible in their roles in the scheme, showing a reduction in unmatched participants of up to 80

2   Related Work

The dial-a-ride problem has been long studied in the OR community [6]. Dial-a-ride typically assumes a single vehicle, picking up and dropping off riders at specified locations within time windows, although multiple vehicle problems have also been studied [4,5]. In [10], the authors compare different scenarios of dial-a-ride problems and show that these scenarios can be solved extending the variable neighborhood search algorithms. The dial-a-ride drivers have no journey requirements of their own. For ride-sharing schemes [7], both the drivers and the riders have their own objectives. Specific schemes vary as to whether the drivers move to the riders locations or the riders move to and from the driver routes, and whether or not drivers take single or multiple riders on a trip. One extension includes participants known as *shifters*, who may either drive or ride as a rider [1]. Armant *et al.* [3] also include shifters, but also assume that each pure rider who is not served in the matching has a probability of driving on their own, included as a penalty in the objective function. Computing an optimal matching is hard [2], and the complexity increases as the number of shifters increases. Kamar and Horvitz [8] model the problem as one of collaborative planning, where agents must balance competing goals. Yousaf *et al.* [13] model the problem as multi source-destination path planning, with a wide range of competing objectives including privacy and incentives. Schilde *et al.* [11] and Manna and Prestwich [9] consider stochastic problems, in which trip requests arrive during the execution of the solution, using scenario-based methods to minimise expected delays or unserved requests. Simonin and O'Sullivan [12] focus on the matching problem, assuming an input graph of all feasible pairings, and establishes the complexity of a number of two variations, showing that in some cases polynomial time solutions are possible. In this study, from the analysis of agreed rideshare trips advertised by real users, we model the users' behaviour and infer a Constraint Programming problem. The last problem allows us to assess the quality and the potential improvement of the heuristics used in deployed applications when answering to users' queries. A comparison of different ride-sharing problem formulations or algorithms to improve the solving time is beyond the scope of the study.

3   Euclidean-Distance Ride Matching

In the basic ride sharing scheme, drivers and riders post their start and end locations, and an expected start time, and the system proposes possible matches to the participants. The participants then select from the possible matches and contact each other to agree the details of the trip, which involves establishing a pick-up and drop-off location, and a time for the pick up. The agreed values might differ from the original values posted by the participants. When the actual ride takes place, both the driver and rider use a smartphone app to inform the system, with the driver informing the system on first departure and final arrival, and each rider notifying the system on pick-up and drop-off. The app reports GPS readings and times, from which payments are computed.

When a driver or rider posts their trip request, the ride sharing system should return in real-time a list of potential users with which the poster can share their journey. To ensure a real-time response ($< 1s$), a Euclidean distance heuristic is typically used to find the possible matches. First, for each driver, a straight line path is drawn from the driver start location to the driver destination. Secondly, for all possible riders, the euclidean distances between the rider start and destination and the driver line are computed. Only riders with distances to and from the driver line below a threshold are considered as potential matches. These are further filtered by restricting (i) rider start and destination locations to be within a threshold angle of deviation from the driver line, and (ii) rider start times to lie within a fixed threshold of the driver's start time. This simple heuristic is fast to compute, and can be more or less accurate in large cities having a road network similar to a grid. Without this particular road network configuration the heuristics frequently return infeasible matches, and also omit some high quality potential matches. The main cause of inappropriate matches is the use of straight line paths and distances, since in many circumstances the shortest or fastest route is significantly different from the straight line path. In the Fig. 1, we show an extreme example. $T45$ denotes the fixed threshold heuristic that we investigate. It fits to regular grid road maps and is similar to some heuristics used by deployed applications for fast computation of the matches. The subfigure on the left shows the standard heuristic, with trips starting and finishing in the grey zone being offered as potential matches. The subfigure on

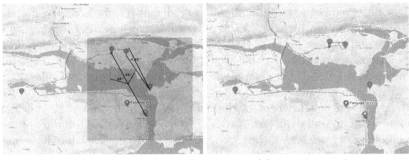

(a) matches returned by the heuristic   (b) feasible matches

Fig. 1. Example of feasible and infeasible ride matches

the right shows that fastest path for the driver, and of the two passenger request, the only feasible match is the one which was not previously offered. Secondly, the system requires each user to post a preferred start time, and then applies a fixed time window around start times to match participants. However, individual users may have different flexibility over their start or arrival times, and these are also likely to vary with the expected travel time for the journey. Repeated offering of matches which would require significant deviation from a route, or which are infeasible because of the length of time required for the journey, are liable to act as a disincentive for users to continue with the system. Similarly, if well matched participants are not offered rides, there is a reduced incentive to continue with the system.

4   Ride Sharing Optimisation Model

To describe the trip schedules and the users' constraints we introduce the following notation. D denotes the set of possible drivers, R is the set of possible riders, and $U = D \cup R$ represents the set of all users. To generate the time and geographical constraints, we use Open Street Map data to deduce minimal path distances and times between two locations. $L = \{l_1, \ldots, l_n\}$ denotes the set of road node locations identified by their GPS coordinates. A path $\pi = (l_i, \ldots, l_j)$ is an ordered list of locations, and $time(\pi)$ (resp. $dist(\pi)$) returns the driving path time (resp distance) for π. The path $\pi^*_{l_i,l_j}$ (resp. $\pi^\diamond_{l_i,l_j}$) denotes a minimal time (resp. distance) path from l_i to l_j. A trip schedule is a tuple $ts_u = (t_d^{start}, l_d^{start}, l_d^{dest})$ describing user u's intended start time t_u^{start}, start location l_u^{start}, and destination l_u^{dest}. $TS = \{ts_{u_1}, \ldots, ts_{u_n}\}$ denotes the set of user trip schedules sent to the system. To simplify the notation we consider one trip schedule per user, but the approach remains valid for multiple schedules per user. For a trip schedule ts_u, the inferred time window $tw_u = (et_u^{start}, lt_u^{dest})$ describes an earliest start time et_u^{start} and a latest arrival time lt_u^{dest}. Intuitively, the driver trip time window tw_d is consistent with a rider trip time window tw_r when there exists a time interval intersecting both tw_r and tw_d in which the rider can be picked-up and dropped-off by the driver. For a driver trip schedule ts_d, $\pi^*_{l_d^{start}, l_d^{dest}}$ denotes the inferred minimal time path from l_d^{start} to l_d^{dest}. For a rider trip schedule ts_r, m_r^{pick} denotes the inferred maximal path distance r is willing to walk from his intended start l_r^{start} to a pick-up location l_r^{pick} on the driver path $\pi^*_{l_d^{start}, l_d^{dest}}$. Similarly m_r^{drop} denotes the inferred maximal path distance the rider is willing to walk from a drop-off location l_r^{drop} to his destination l_r^{dest}.

Given the above we define the feasible matches relaying both on the users' inferred path constraints and the users' inferred time constraints.

Definition 1 (inferred feasible ride match). *A driver trip schedule and a rider trip schedule, ts_d and ts_r, represent a likely feasible ride match if:*

1. *their inferred time windows tw_d, tw_r are consistent with the rider pick-up and drop-off time:*
   (a) *$lt_d^{dest} - et_r^{start} > \pi^*_{l_{pick}, l_{drop}}$, the interval between the driver latest arrival and the rider earliest start is greater than the fastest path from the rider's inferred pick-up to his inferred drop-off, or,*
   (b) *$lt_r^{dest} - et_d^{start} > \pi^*_{l_{pick\diamond}, l_{drop\diamond}}$, the interval between the earliest driver start and the latest rider arrival is greater than the fastest path from the rider inferred pick-up to the inferred drop-off.*
2. *The expected driving path intersects the rider's possible pick-up and drop-off points.*
   (a) *$dist(\pi^\diamond_{l_r^{start}, \pi_d}) < m_r^{pick}$, the shortest path distance between the rider intended start and the expected driver path is lower than the maximal distance for the rider's pick-up.*
   (b) *$dist(\pi^\diamond_{l_r^{start}, \pi_d}) < m_r^{drop}$, the shortest path distance between the rider intended destination and the expected driver path is lower than the maximal distance for the rider's drop-off.*

Given a set of trip schedules, by iteratively checking if each pair of trip schedules are likely feasible, we incrementally discover a bipartite graph of feasible ride matches $G = (TSD, TSR, E)$ s.t. $TSD \subseteq TS$ is the set of drivers' trip schedules, $TSR \subseteq TS$ is the set of riders' trip schedules, and every edge $(ts_d, ts_r) \in E$ is a feasible ride match. G is the input parameter of the constraint programming model we build to assess the potential of a ride-sharing scheme. For each feasible match between a rider trip schedule ts_r and a driver trip schedule ts_d in $G = (TSD, TSR, E)$ is associated to a ride share trip y_{ts_d, ts_r} encoded as a collection of decision variables s.t.:

$y_{ts_d, ts_r}.start$ represents the pick-up time of r,

$y_{ts_d, ts_r}.end$ denotes a the drop-off time of r,

$y_{ts_d, ts_r}.duration$ is the time duration of the rideshare trip,

$y_{ts_d, ts_r}.presence$ denotes presence of the ride share trip in the optimal solution.

We model a served rider using $x_{,ts_r}$ s.t. $x_{,ts_r}$ equal 1 when the rider is allocated to exactly one of feasible share ride y_{ts_d, ts_r}. To assess the potential of a ride-sharing scheme, our objective is to maximize:

$$\sum_{(ts_d, ts_r) \in E} x_{,ts_r} \tag{1}$$

subject to:

$$y_{ts_d, ts_r}.start \geq max(t_d^{early}, t_r^{early}), \ \forall (ts_d, ts_r) \in E \tag{2}$$

$$y_{ts_d, ts_r}.end \leq min(t_d^{latest}, t_r^{latest}), \ \forall (ts_d, ts_r) \in E \tag{3}$$

$$y_{ts_d, ts_r}.duration = y_{ts_d, ts_r}.end - y_{ts_d, ts_r}.start, \ \forall (ts_d, ts_r) \in E \tag{4}$$

$$y_{ts_d, ts_r}.duration \geq \pi *_{l^{start}, l^{dest}}, \ \forall (ts_d, ts_r) \in E \tag{5}$$

$$CUMULATIVE(\{y_{ts_d, ts_r}\}, nbSeats_d, \leq), \ \forall ts_d \in TSD \tag{6}$$

$$ALTERNATIVE(x_{ts_r}, \{y_{ts_d, ts_r} | (ts_d, ts_r) \in E\}), \ \forall ts_r \in TSR \tag{7}$$

$$(x_{ts_c}.presence \Rightarrow y_{tr_c, ts_r}.presence), \ \forall (ts_d, ts_r) \in E \tag{8}$$

The aim is to maximize the total number of served riders (1). The constraints (2) force each rideshare trip to start after the earliest rider start and the earliest driver start. Similarly, the constraints (3) force each rideshare trip to end before the latest rider arrival and the latest driver arrival. The duration of the rideshare trip is the difference between the end and the start (4) and it is greater than the rider shortest path (5). The cumulative constraints (6) restrict each driver car occupancy to not exceed the number of available seats at any moment of the trip. When a rideshare trip is chosen in a solution, i.e., $y_{ts_d, ts_r}.presence = 1$, it corresponds to one occupied seat in a driver's car, it is equal to 0 otherwise. At any time, the driver's car occupancy corresponds to the following definition $\sum_{(ts_d, ts_r) \in E} y_{ts_d, ts_r}.presence \leq nbSeats_d, \forall ts_d \in TSD$. The alternative constraints (7) enforce that at most one y_{ts_d, ts_r} rideshare trip is chosen. In the successful case of the rider rideshare trip x_{ts_r} is equal to the chosen rideshare y_{ts_d, ts_r} otherwise the rider is not chosen. The constraints (8) state that a shifter assigned to be a rider does not drive.

5   Inferring Constraints from Users' Behaviour

The raw data maintained in the ride-sharing scheme is not enough to establish the parameters of the optimisation model. Participants do not post time windows for their trips, and their advertised locations may be inaccurate (to protect privacy). Similarly, details of actual shared rides are subject to errors and missing data, as they are reliant on participants reporting GPS coordinates at the time of departure and arrival; in particular, drivers have no need to start the system until the first pickup. Finally, although we have records of advertised trips, we only have confirmed data on positive examples of acceptable ride shares; a pair of schedules which did not result in a trip might not have been feasible, but equally might not have been proposed to the participants, or might have been rejected in preference to another trip for either distance or personal factors. To assess the potential of the ride-sharing scheme, we need to infer the parameters of the model from the set of positive examples.

For a trip schedule ts_u, inferring the time window tw_u involves inferring the earliest start time t_u^{early} and the latest arrival time t_u^{latest} in which a user expect the journey to happen. For this purpose, we extract from the trip records three parameters: the maximal positive start time delay, δ^+, the maximal negative start time delay, δ^-, and the estimated travel time f_1 and, as explained in Fig. 2, we add them together to infer the earliest start and the latest arrival time of the inferred time window tw_u.

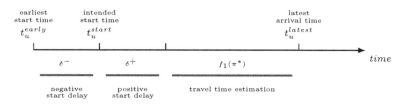

Fig. 2. Time Window Parameters

The positive and negative start time delay represents the user's time flexibility for advancing or delaying the intended start. In Fig. 3 we observe the difference between the riders' intended start time t_r^{start} and their reported pick-ups time t_r^{pick} while observing the trip duration between the riders' pick-ups and drop off. We observe no correlation between the ride share duration and the user's delayed times. Riders appear to be willing to change their start times by an amount greater than the duration of their journey in order to find a ride. To extract the maximal positive and negative time changes, δ^+ and δ^-, we determine the minimal change which encompasses almost all (90 %) accepted ride shares. The horizontal lines show the maximal positive start time (left) and negative start time delay (right) observed for the riders in region 4. We compute similarly the maximal positive and negative time delay for the drivers.

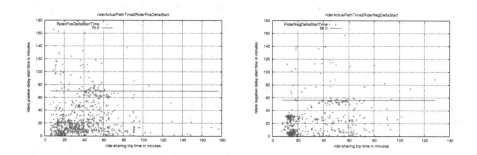

Fig. 3. Positive and negative time delay for riders in region 4

The estimated travel time represents the approximate time a user can expect to spend on the road. In Fig. 4 (left) we plot the duration of the riders' travel time from the reported pick-up t_r^{pick} to the reported drop-off t_r^{drop} against the minimal path time computed between these locations. There is a clear correlation, with linear regression indicating a factor of approximately 1.5 for the increase in travel time over the minimal path. This increase may be due to many factors, including traffic congestion and the presence of multiple passengers in a single trip, and will be the subject of further study. Moreover, one can notice few points below the diagonal (fastest path time = recorded path time). These represent cases where the driver was faster than the faster path time respecting to the speed limit indicated in OSM map.

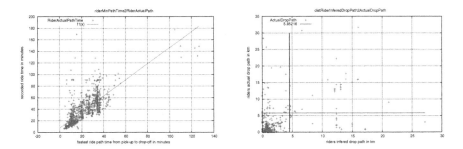

Fig. 4. Observed trip time compared to minimal path time, for region 4 (Colour figure online)

The Riders' Maximal Meeting Path Distances represent the maximal pick-up path distance, m^{pick}, from the rider intended start to the driver path, and the maximal drop off path distance, m^{drop} from the driver path to the rider intended destination. In Fig. 4 (right) we plot the path distance between the riders intended destination and reported drop-off against the minimal path distance between the destination and drop-off. Here there exists no clear correlation between the observed and minimal drop off path distances. Again, our aim is to find the minimal threshold on the meeting path distance within which 90 % of the users accepted a ride. Based on the inferred path times (which would be used in deciding whether or not to accept a ride), a limit of 4.5km (black line) includes 90 % of all accepted rides. For comparison, we show (blue line) a similar derived threshold of 5.8 km on the observed times.

We summarize the optimisation model parameters extracted from the trip records in the following table. Times are described in minutes and the distances in kilometers. We recall that given a trip schedule ts_u, we infer its time-window parameter using the following formulae: the infered earliest start time $t_u^{early} = t_u^{start} - \delta^-$ while the latest arrival time $t_u^{latest} = t_u^{start} + \delta^- + f_1(x)$. We notice that in all the regions studied, riders are more flexible than drivers, but both are willing to start early. The estimated travel time varies from 1.4 to twice the minimal path time computed using OSM Street Map, and varies depending on the region.

	drivers δ^+	drivers δ^-	riders δ^+	riders δ^-	$f_1(x)$	riders m^{pick}	riders m^{drop}
region 1	63	56	74	94	2x+11.2	2.2	1.7
region 2	31	60	57	46	1.15x+13.2	2.0	1.0
region 3	45	45	56	60	1.4x+9.7	11.3	14.3
region 4	45	54	70	56	1.4x+7.5	2.4	4.5

6   Assessing the Ride-Match Models

We now use the inferred model described in previous section to assess the quality of the existing matching heuristics for the 4 regions in the study.

The basic Euclidean heuristic is augmented with a 45 degree sweep angle, and allows up to 2 hours variation in the start times. In the following table we evaluate the precision and the recall of this heuristic with respect to inferred feasible ride match model represented as the graph G. The recall rate (the percentage of feasible matches from G returned by the heuristic) is relatively high, ranging between 90 % and 95 %, although this still indicates that between 5 and 10 % of feasible matches are not being considered. The precision rate (percentage of matches returned by the heuristic that are feasible in G) however varies from 58 % to 90 %, indicating that many infeasible matches are being proposed. The heuristic is most effective on region 3, with poor performance on region 1 and region 2. The appears to be a consequence of the geography of the regions - region 3 is a large urban area with a regular road network, while region 2 has a mix of urban and rural roads, and an irregular road network around harbours and coastal areas. Relatively low precision and recall (regions 1 and 2) indicate many inappropriate match suggestions and missing proposal, which are believe to act as a disincentive for potential users.

T45	nb edges	# feasible	# feasible found	# unfeasible found	# feasible not found	precision	recall
region 1	802	647	588	214	59	0.733	0.909
region 2	559	364	326	233	38	0.583	0.896
region 3	1678	1691	1616	62	75	0.963	0.956
region 4	4223	3590	3326	897	264	0.788	0.926

To assess the potential of the ride-sharing scheme, we use the inferred CP model to compute the maximum number of assignments of riders to drivers' cars. In next table, we compare the number of matched users found in G, with number of matched users found among the feasible matches for the typical heuristic T45FM. Note that T45FM is a filtered version of the typical heuristic, removing those matches considered infeasible in G, since those matches would be rejected by the optimisation model. The first thing to note is the percentage of unmatched participants is higher in each case for the T45FM filtered heuristic compared to the inferred model, although the losses are relatively small. However, perhaps more importantly, the ratio column shows that there is a significant imbalance in the participants in the scheme; a healthy scheme should have a ratio of at least 1, and ideally should be higher, allowing multiple passengers per car. A low ratio means many drivers will be unmatched, and thus will drive with empty seats. In addition, frequent failed attempts to find a match are likely to deter those users from participating. The current optimisation model prioritises riders, and thus some drivers may have multiple passengers. Changing the criterion to balance driver utilisation may encourage drivers to continue with the system, but cannot increase the total number of matched participants, and thus is likely to reduce the society benefits of sharing journeys. Therefore, we consider a different approach, and evaluate the effect of persuading all drivers to become shifters, and to accept an offer to be a passenger rather than remain exclusively as a driver. The results of running these flexible models are shown in the rows FMS and T45FMDS. We note that FMDS is still providing a benefit over the (filtered) heuristic, but more importantly, the increased flexibility allows us to match significantly more participants. The number of unmatched participants drops by a factor of 0.33 in the poorest case (region 2) and by a factor of 5 in the best case (region 3). We conclude that, where there is a participant imbalance, the focus of the ride sharing scheme operators should be to persuade drivers to be flexible in their roles, as this appears to offer the biggest potential for continued participation in the scheme and for removing vehicles from the road network.

region 1	users	ratio R/D	matched riders	matched drivers	% unmatch	region 2	users	ratio R/D	matched riders	matched drivers	% unmatch
FM	992	0.55	246	133	61.79	FM	658	0.7	142	79	66.41
T45FM			223	124	65.02	T45FM			132	81	67.61
FMDS	992	1.55	488	196	31.05	FMDS	658	1.7	258	99	45.74
T45FMDS			446	176	37.30	T45FMDS			248	98	47.42
region 3						region 4					
FM	1871	0.67	656	328	47.41	FM	4784	0.82	1592	758	50.88
T45FM			630	332	48.58	T45FM			1521	774	52.03
FMDS	1871	1.67	1392	321	8.44	FMDS	4784	1.82	2876	864	21.82
T45FMDS			1340	316	11.49	T45FMDS			2741	880	24.31

7   Conclusion

Ride-sharing is a rapidly growing practice for reducing the number of cars on the road in urban regions. Successful ride sharing schemes require committed users, and they in turn require the scheme to provide them with feasible ride matches in real-time. In current systems, the emphasis has been on the real-time requirement rather than the feasibility of the matches. We have developed a model which uses route planning and time windows to describe feasible matches as a constraint satisfaction problem, and the ultimate goal of the ride-matching scheme as constraint optimisation. Through analysis of data sets of advertised schedules and agreed trips, we infer the parameters of the these constraint models, chosen to accept 90 % of all agreed matches. By applying the model to the data sets of advertised trips, we identify the errors in the current heuristics, and find an imbalance among participants in the ride sharing schemes. We consider the benefits that might be obtained if drivers can be persuade to switch roles and act as passengers, and by re-running the optimisation model we show that there is potential to reduce the number of unmatched participants by up to 80 %. Such flexible switching would have a societal benefit, of reducing the number of vehicles on the road and reducing the total driven distance, and would also benefit the companies concerned, by allowing more matches and encouraging sustained user participation. Future work will focus on validating the hypothesis through field trial with user in the scheme, and on developing real-time response to the users which respects the constraints on feasible matches.

Acknowledgements. This work is funded by Science Foundation Ireland (SFI) under Grant Number SFI/12/RC/2289. Moreover, we would like to acknowledge our industrial partner Carma, and the reviewers for their fruitful remarks.

References

1. Agatz, N., Erera, A., Savelsbergh, M., Wang, X.: Optimization for dynamic ride-sharing: a review. Eur. J. Oper. Res. **223**(2), 295–303 (2012)
2. Agatz, N.A., Erera, A.L., Savelsbergh, M.W., Wang, X.: Dynamic ride-sharing: a simulation study in metro atlanta. Transp. Res. Part B Methodol. **45**(9), 1450–1464 (2011)
3. Armant, V., Brown, K.N.: Minimizing the driving distance in ride sharing systems. In: 26th IEEE International Conference on Tools with Artificial Intelligence, ICTAI 2014, Limassol, November 10–12, 2014, pp. 568–575 (2014)
4. Attanasio, A., Cordeau, J.F., Ghiani, G., Laporte, G.: Parallel tabu search heuristics for the dynamic multi-vehicle dial-a-ride problem. Parallel Comput. **30**(3), 377–387 (2004)
5. Berbeglia, G., Cordeau, J.F., Laporte, G.: Dynamic pickup and delivery problems. Eur. J. Oper. Res. **202**(1), 8–15 (2010)
6. Cordeau, J.F., Laporte, G.: The dial-a-ride problem: models and algorithms. Ann. Oper. Res. **153**(1), 29–46 (2007)

7. Furuhata, M., Dessouky, M., Ordóñez, F., Brunet, M.E., Wang, X., Koenig, S.: Ridesharing: the state-of-the-art and future directions. Transp. Res. Part B Methodol. **57**(C), 28–46 (2013). http://ideas.repec.org/a/eee/transb/v57y2013icp 28-46.html

8. Kamar, E., Horvitz, E.: Collaboration and shared plans in the open world: Studies of ridesharing. In: Proceedings of the 21st International Jont Conference on Artifical Intelligence, IJCAI 2009, pp. 187–194. Morgan Kaufmann Publishers Inc., San Francisco (2009)

9. Manna, C., Prestwich, S.: Online stochastic planning for taxi and ridesharing. In: 26th IEEE International Conference on Tools with Artificial Intelligence, ICTAI 2014, Limassol, November 10–12, 2014, pp. 906–913 (2014)

10. Muelas, S., LaTorre, A., Pena, J.M.: A variable neighborhood search algorithm for the optimization of a dial-a-ride problem in a large city. Expert Syst. Appl. **40**(14), 5516–5531 (2013)

11. Schilde, M., Doerner, K.F., Hartl, R.F.: Metaheuristics for the dynamic stochastic dial-a-ride problem with expected return transports. Comput. Oper. Res. **38**(12), 1719–1730 (2011)

12. Simonin, G., O'Sullivan, B.: Optimisation for the ride-sharing problem: a complexity-based approach. In: ECAI 2014–21st European Conference on Artificial Intelligence, 18–22 August 2014, Czech Republic - Including Prestigious Applications of Intelligent Systems (PAIS 2014), pp. 831–836 (2014)

13. Yousaf, J., Li, J., Chen, L., Tang, J., Dai, X., Du, J.: Ride-Sharing: a multi source-destination path planning approach. In: Thielscher, M., Zhang, D. (eds.) AI 2012. LNCS, vol. 7691, pp. 815–826. Springer, Heidelberg (2012)

Constraint-Based Querying for Bayesian Network Exploration

Behrouz Babaki[1]([✉]), Tias Guns[1], Siegfried Nijssen[1,2], and Luc De Raedt[1]

[1] KU Leuven, Celestijnenlaan 200A, 3000 Leuven, Belgium
{Behrouz.Babaki,Tias.Guns}@cs.kuleuven.be
[2] Universiteit Leiden, Niels Bohrweg 1, 2333 Ca Leiden, The Netherlands

Abstract. Understanding the knowledge that resides in a Bayesian network can be hard, certainly when a large network is to be used for the first time, or when the network is complex or has just been updated. Tools to assist users in the analysis of Bayesian networks can help. In this paper, we introduce a novel general framework and tool for answering exploratory queries over Bayesian networks. The framework is inspired by queries from the constraint-based mining literature designed for the exploratory analysis of data. Adapted to Bayesian networks, these queries specify a set of constraints on explanations of interest, where an explanation is an assignment to a subset of variables in a network. Characteristic for the methodology is that it searches over different subsets of the explanations, corresponding to different marginalizations. A general purpose framework, based on principles of constraint programming, data mining and knowledge compilation, is used to answer all possible queries. This CP4BN framework employs a rich set of constraints and is able to emulate a range of existing queries from both the Bayesian network and the constraint-based data mining literature.

1 Introduction

Understanding a Bayesian network is not always easy. In particular users who are faced with a large network for the first time, or with networks that are dynamically updated when new data arrives, may not understand the knowledge encoded in such a network. It has been argued that BN's (especially those used for diagnosis) should be extensively evaluated before being used in practice [15].

While the Bayesian network literature already provides a set of queries and corresponding inference techniques that are helpful in gaining a better understanding of a network, most of the standard queries specify (and fix) the variables of interest, and then either ask for a most likely assignment to the variables or the computation of a particular probability.

This contrasts with common practice in the field of exploratory data mining, where one aims at understanding data by discovering and analyzing patterns. Since the seminal work on frequent itemset mining by Agrawal et al. [1], numerous techniques for exploratory mining of patterns under constraints have been developed [14]. The notions of frequency and pattern in constraint-based pattern

© Springer International Publishing Switzerland 2015
E. Fromont et al. (Eds.): IDA 2015, LNCS 9385, pp. 13–24, 2015.
DOI: 10.1007/978-3-319-24465-5_2

mining actually correspond to the notions of probability and explanation in a Bayesian network. In pattern mining, one typically searches over a space of possible patterns. In Bayesian networks, this corresponds to searching over subsets of variables and their values. In this paper, we exploit the similarities between these two fields and introduce constraint-based queries for Bayesian networks.

The contribution of this paper is three-fold. First, inspired by constraint-based mining, we introduce an expressive set of exploratory queries for Bayesian networks. Secondly, we identify how these queries can be expressed as constraints over the variables and joint distribution of the Bayesian network. Finally, we show how these constraints can be expressed as a generic constraint program, combining ideas from constraint programming, itemset mining and knowledge compilation, in particular CP4IM [9] and arithmetic circuits (AC) [5]. Our method operates on the arithmetic circuit directly and can hence be applied to any graphical model that can be compiled into an AC. By doing so, we bridge the gap between constraint-based pattern mining and graphical models and contribute towards more intelligent analysis of Bayesian networks.

2 Examples of Bayesian Network Exploration

After introducing a Bayesian Network and BN pattern, we show examples of exploratory queries over a Bayesian network in an illustrative scenario.

Bayesian Network Pattern. A *Bayesian network* $\mathcal{G}$ is a directed acyclic graph where each node represents a random variable X_i in $\mathcal{X} = \{X_1, \ldots, X_n\}$. Let $\text{Pa}_{X_i}^{\mathcal{G}}$ denote the parents of X_i in $\mathcal{G}$. A joint distribution P over the set of variables $\mathcal{X}$ is said to factorize according to $\mathcal{G}$ if $P(X_1, \ldots, X_n)$ can be expressed as the product $\prod_{i=1}^{n} P(X_i | \text{Pa}_{X_i}^{\mathcal{G}})$. We denote such a distribution by $P_{\mathcal{G}}$. We denote by $D(X_i)$ the *domain* of variable X_i, that is, the possible values the variable can take. An assignment of value x_i to variable X_i is denoted by $(X_i = x_i)$.

Definition 1 (BN pattern). *A pattern A over $P_{\mathcal{G}}$ is a partial assignment, that is, an assignment to a subset of the variables $\mathcal{X}$ in $\mathcal{G}$: $A = \{(X_1 = x_1), \ldots, (X_m = x_m)\}$, where the X_i are different variables and x_i is a possible value in $D(X_i)$.*

The probability of a pattern A, denoted by $P_{\mathcal{G}}(A)$, is $P((X_1 = x_1), \ldots, (X_m = x_m))$, that is, the marginal probability of the assignment. Our queries below will enumerate all satisfying BN patterns.

Example Constraint-Based Queries. Assume the manager of a New York car insurance company has just obtained a Bayesian network that describes the factors influencing cost claims of customers, cf. the in Fig. 1. She wants to analyze the network to be able to assess costs, get more insight and provide recommendations to her personnel. In order to do so, she is interested in exploring patterns of interest in the network and poses a number of queries.

Q1. What are likely patterns given the evidence **PropertyCost = Million**? These claims impose high costs on the company. Using a minimum probability of 0.015, she obtains 12 patterns, most of which contain either **SeniorTrain = False** or **Theft = False**. She is not interested in these and excludes them while lowering the threshold in the next query.

Q2. What are likely patterns that do not contain **SeniorTrain=False** *and* **Theft=False** *given the evidence* **PropertyCost = Million** *(with threshold $\theta = 0.0105$)?* She now gets 76 patterns, among which the pattern **A = {PropertyCost = Million, DrivingSkill = Substandard, DrivQuality = Poor, LiabilityCost = Thousand}**, which she finds interesting as it indicates a con-

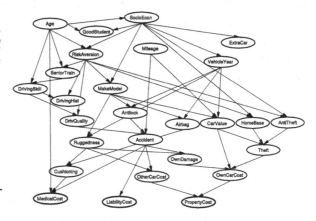

Fig. 1. The car insurance network [2].

nection between high property cost, the driving capabilities of the customer, and the liability cost incurred. However, she wonders whether the pattern cannot be simplified.

Q3. Is there a simplification of pattern **A** *with the same probability?* She finds a variant of pattern **A** in which **DrivingSkill=Substandard** is removed, indicating that this assignment was implied and that there is some determinism in the network.

Now, turning her attention to the variable "Age", our manager wonders:

Q4. Are there any patterns that would allow to distinguish the age groups **Adolescent** *and* **Senior**? She queries for patterns that have widely varying conditional probabilities when conditioned on each of these. After excluding the variables **SeniorTrain** and **GoodStudent**, which she already knows about, one of the top patterns is {**RiskAversion = Cautious, OtherCarCost = Thousand**}. Indeed the probability of having a cautious personality and incurring low third-party costs is nearly 6 times higher in senior customers.

Finally, a machine learning expert suggests to use a network trained on the company data instead (a simple naïve Bayes model). She wonders:

Q5. What are the patterns that have different probabilities according to the original and learned network? It turns out that the pattern {**Airbag=False, AntiLock=False, VehicleYear=Older**} has the largest difference of probabilities, hence the naïve Bayes model ignores the well-known relation between these three variables (namely older cars are rarely equipped with these safety components).

Table 1. The example queries expressed using constraints over pattern A.

Q1: $probability(A, \mathcal{G}, \theta)$, $superset(A, \{\text{PropertyCost=Million}\})$

Q2: $probability(A, \mathcal{G}, \theta)$, $superset(A, \{\text{PropertyCost=Million}\})$,
     $exclude(A, \{\text{SeniorTrain, Theft}\})$

Q3: $maxprobability(A, \mathcal{G}, \theta')$, $free(A, \mathcal{G})$, $subset(A, \{\text{PropertyCost} = \text{Million},$
     $\text{DrivingSkill} = \text{Substandard, DrivQuality} = \text{Poor, LiabilityCost} = \text{Thousand}\})$

Q4: $exclude(A, \{\text{SeniorTrain, GoodStudent}\})$,
     $ev\text{-}difference(A, \mathcal{G}, \{\text{Age=Adolescent}\}, \{\text{Age=Senior}\}, \beta)$

Q5: $difference(A, \mathcal{G}^1, \mathcal{G}^2, \beta)$

3 BN Query Framework

We now formalize the queries above using constraints over patterns. Many other queries can be formulated this way, leading to a general querying framework.

Definition 2 (BN Pattern Query). *Consider a joint probability distribution $P_\mathcal{G}$ represented by a Bayesian network $\mathcal{G}$. We denote the set of all patterns of $P_\mathcal{G}$ by $\mathcal{I}$. A BN pattern query $\mathcal{Q}$ is a tuple $(P_\mathcal{G}, \mathcal{C})$ where $\mathcal{C} : \mathcal{I} \rightarrow \{0, 1\}$ is a conjunction of constraints over a pattern. Pattern A is a solution for $\mathcal{Q}$ if $\mathcal{C}(A) = 1$. The result of a query consists of all patterns that satisfy the constraints.*

The queries used in the examples in Sect. 2 are given in Table 1. Most constraints have close counterparts in the constraint-based pattern mining literature. The main difference is that the notion of *(relative) frequency* of a pattern in a database is replaced by the *probability* of the pattern in the BN. The constraints and their definitions are listed in Table 2 and explained below.

Probability constraint. Query Q1 requires that the probability of a pattern A according to $P_\mathcal{G}$ should be larger than a threshold θ. We call this constraint *probability*$(A, \mathcal{G}, \theta)$ and a pattern that respects it θ-*probable*. This definition is similar to the definition of a *frequency* constraint in frequent pattern mining.

Sub/superset and exclusion constraints. Query Q1 also requires that patterns include given assignments. We enforce this with a superset constraint. Similarly, we can use $exclude(A, V)$ to exclude variables from the pattern as in query Q2. The definition is given in Table 2, where vars(A) are the variables occurring in A.
     Note that a superset constraint is conceptually similar to adding *evidence* in Bayesian networks, only that in our setting the computed probabilities will need to be normalized by the probability of the evidence to obtain the conditional probability.

Freeness, maximality and closedness constraint. Query Q3 requires that a pattern does not contain redundant variable assignments. This is similar to the well-studied problem of simplifying explanations by excluding irrelevant variables [18], e.g. because of deterministic relations between assignments [7].

Table 2. constraints for BN pattern queries over patterns A, B, and C and network $\mathcal{G}$. Constraints are represented by three-letter codes PRB: *probability(A,$\mathcal{G}$,θ)*; MXP: *maxprobability(A,$\mathcal{G}$,θ)*; SBS: *subset(A, B)*; SPS: *superset(A,B)*; EXC: *exclude(A,B)*; FRE: *free(A,$\mathcal{G}$)*; MAX: *maximal(A,$\mathcal{G}$,θ)*; CLS: *closed(A,$\mathcal{G}$)*; DIF: *difference(A,$\mathcal{G}^a$,$\mathcal{G}^b$,β)*; DDF: *DB-difference(A,$\mathcal{G}$,$\mathcal{D}$,β)*; and VDF: *ev-difference(A,$\mathcal{G}$,B,C,β)*.

code	mathematical notation	CP formulation
PRB	$P_{\mathcal{G}}(A) \geq \theta$	$\mathsf{F}_1 \geq \theta$
MXP	$P_{\mathcal{G}}(A) \leq \theta$	$\mathsf{F}_1 \leq \theta$
SBS	$A \subseteq B$	$\forall i : \mathsf{Q}_i \neq 0 \implies (X_i = \mathsf{Q}_i) \in B$
SPS	$B \subseteq A$	$\forall (X_i = x_i) \in B : \mathsf{Q}_i = x_i$
EXC	$B \cap \text{vars}(A) = \emptyset$	$\forall X_i \in \text{vars}(B) : \mathsf{Q}_i = 0$
FRE	$\forall(X = x) \in A : P_{\mathcal{G}}(A\backslash(X = x)) > P_{\mathcal{G}}(A)$	$\forall i : \mathsf{Q}_i \neq 0 \rightarrow \left(\sum_j \mathsf{D}_{i,j}\right) > \mathsf{F}_1$
MAX	$\forall X \notin \text{vars}(A), \forall x \in D(X) :$ $P_{\mathcal{G}}(A \cup \{(X = x)\}) < \theta$	$\forall i : \mathsf{Q}_i = 0 \rightarrow \bigwedge_j (\mathsf{D}_{i,j} < \theta)$
CLS	$\forall X \notin \text{vars}(A), \forall x \in D(X) :$ $P_{\mathcal{G}}(A \cup \{(X = x)\}) < P_{\mathcal{G}}(A)$	$\forall i : \mathsf{Q}_i = 0 \rightarrow \bigwedge_j (\mathsf{D}_{i,j} < \mathsf{F}_1)$
DIF	$|P_{\mathcal{G}^a}(A) - P_{\mathcal{G}^b}(A)| \geq \beta$	$|\mathsf{F}_1{}^a - \mathsf{F}_1{}^b| \geq \beta$
DDF	$|P_{\mathcal{G}}(A) - r_{\mathcal{D}}(A)| \geq \beta$	$|\mathsf{F}_1 - \mathsf{R}| \geq \beta$
VDF	$|P_{\mathcal{G}}(A \cup B)/P_{\mathcal{G}}(B) - P_{\mathcal{G}}(A \cup C)/P_{\mathcal{G}}(C)| \geq \beta$	$|\mathsf{F}_1{}^a/c_a - \mathsf{F}_1{}^b/c_b| \geq \beta$

For pattern $A = B \cup C$ (where $B \cap C = \emptyset$), if variable assignments in B determine those in C, i.e., $P_{\mathcal{G}}(A) = P_{\mathcal{G}}(B)$, we consider those in the set C irrelevant. We call a pattern *free* if none of its assignments is irrelevant. This definition is similar to the definition of free patterns in data mining [3]. In the presence of a *superset* constraint, the *free* constraint should only consider variables that are not required by the *superset* constraint.

Inspired by the related notions of maximality and closedness in frequent itemset mining, we introduce these for BN patterns too. They enforce that a pattern A does not have any superset that is θ-probable (i.e. *maximal(A,$\mathcal{G}$,θ)*) or has the same probability as A (i.e. *closed(A,$\mathcal{G}$)*).

Difference constraints. Queries Q4 and Q5 both ask for patterns that demonstrate a difference between two probabilistic models. Let $P_{\mathcal{G}_1}(A)$ and $P_{\mathcal{G}_2}(A)$ be the probability of pattern A according to networks $\mathcal{G}_1$ and $\mathcal{G}_2$. The constraint *difference(A,$\mathcal{G}_1$,$\mathcal{G}_2$,β)* requires that the difference of the probability of a pattern in these two networks is larger than β. In Q4, the two networks are obtained by assigning a variable in the original network to different values (B={Age=Adolescent} and C={Age=Senior} respectively). This can be formulated over network $\mathcal{G}$ using the constraint *ev-difference(A,$\mathcal{G}$,B,C,β)*. This constraints compares the conditional probability of A given evidence B or C.

Another variation can be used for testing the correlations between a Bayesian network and an actual dataset. This constraint compares the probability of a pattern in network $\mathcal{G}$ with the relative frequency of the corresponding itemset in the database $\mathcal{D}$. We call this constraint *DB-difference(A,$\mathcal{G}$,$\mathcal{D}$,β)*.

4 Formulating BN Pattern Queries as Constraint Programming Problems

In the Bayesian network literature, typically algorithms that search in the space of assignments are developed for specific constraints and scoring functions, which limits their general applicability (see Sect. 6 for a discussion of related work). In data mining, a recent trend is the use of generic solvers for handling a wide range of constraints in a uniform way.

We observe that there is a relationship between itemsets and BN patterns, as each variable assignment $(X_i = x_i)$ can be seen as one *item*, and hence a BN pattern can be seen as an itemset. Using this insight, we adapt the constraint programming for itemset mining framework [9] to reason over Bayesian networks. This framework has proven to support a wide range of constraints and exploratory queries over itemsets. Building on this framework, and hence the use of CP solvers, enable us to address a wide range of queries without the need to develop multiple specialized algorithms.

We first introduce the basics of constraint programming (CP), and explain how Bayesian networks can be encoded in CP in the form of an arithmetic circuit. We then explain how the constraints identified in Table 2 can be expressed in this framework.

Constraint Programming. Constraint programming is used to solve Constraint Satisfaction Problems (CSP) [17]. Constraint programming systems use generic solvers that search for solutions to a given CSP specification.

A CSP specification $\mathcal{P} = (\mathcal{V}, \mathcal{D}, C)$ consists of a set $\mathcal{V}$ of variables; $\mathcal{D}$ is the domain and maps every variable $V \in \mathcal{V}$ to a range of values $\mathcal{D}(V)$; and C is a set of constraints over subsets of $\mathcal{V}$. Generic solvers can be used to find all solutions that satisfy the constraints. These solvers use a combination of search (assigning a variable to a value) and propagation (per constraint, removing assignments from the domain that would violate that constraint) [17]. Many such generic yet efficient solvers exist.

BN Pattern in Constraint Programming (CP). We can encode a BN pattern $A = \{(X_1 = x_1), \ldots, (X_m = x_m)\}$ in CP by introducing a CP variable Q_i for every network variable X_i. The domain of the CP variable Q_i consists of $|D(X_i)| + 1$ values, where $D(X_i)$ is the set of possible values the BN variable X_i can take: value 0 to represent that X_i is not part of the pattern, e.g. it is marginalized over, and values $1 \ldots |D(X_i)|$ that each represent a possible assignment to the BN variable X_i.

BN Pattern Queries in CP. Each of the constraints $\mathcal{C}$ of a BN pattern query $(\mathcal{P}_\mathcal{G}, \mathcal{C})$ can be formulated through CP constraints over the Q_i variables. We discuss this for each of the constraints in turn.

Probability constraint. We will need to repeatedly compute the probability of a pattern, hence, we want this computation to be fast and ideally incremental. For this reason, we choose to first compile the BN into an Arithmetic Circuit (AC) [5]. Computing the probability of a partial assignment takes time polynomial to the size of the AC, though that size is exponential to the BN size in the worst case. Nevertheless, using ACs is generally recognized as one of the most effective techniques for exact computation of probabilities [5], especially when doing so repeatedly.

Figure 2 shows an example AC, consisting of product nodes, sum nodes, constants and *indicator variables* (ignore the square boxes for now). The Boolean indicator variables $\lambda_{i,j}$ indicate whether $(X_i = j)$. For ease of notation we will assume that the domain of the Bayesian variables is represented by consecutive integers starting from 1. To compute the probability of a partial assignment $\{(X_2 = 1), (X_3 = 2)\}$ we set $\lambda_{2,1} = 1, \lambda_{2,2} = 0, \lambda_{3,1} = 0, \lambda_{3,2} = 1$. X_1 is not in the pattern and needs to be marginalized away, so we set $\forall k \in D(X_1) : \lambda_{1,k} = 1$. Then, one computes the values

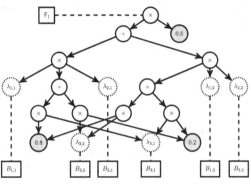

Fig. 2. Arithmetic circuit for a BN with 3 variables with domain $\{1, 2\}$ with X_1 the parent of X_2 and X_3. Square boxes represent CP variables.

of the internal AC nodes bottom-up, according to their operation ($\times$ or $+$). The value of the root node is the requested probability.

This can be encoded in CP for arbitrary ACs: for each indicator variable $\lambda_{i,j}$ in the AC, we introduce a Boolean CP variable $B_{i,j}$; the relation between the indicator variables and the CP variables Q_i is then modeled by the following constraints (recall that $Q_i = 0$ means variable X_i is not in the pattern):

$$Q_i = 0 \rightarrow \wedge_j (B_{i,j} = 1) \qquad\qquad \forall i$$
$$Q_i = k \rightarrow (B_{i,k} = 1) \wedge (\wedge_{j \neq k}(B_{i,j} = 0)) \qquad \forall i, \forall k \neq 0$$

We then introduce real-valued variable P, which will represent the computed probability. For this, we introduce an auxiliary real-valued variable F_v for each node in the circuit (round circles in Fig. 2). Assume each node has a unique identifier v, with the root node having identifier 1. Leaf nodes are either constants or indicator variables. The constants assign their corresponding F_v variable to a fixed value. For the indicator variables $\lambda_{i,j}$, the corresponding F_v variables are *channeled* to their Boolean counterparts $B_{i,j}$ meaning they must take the same value (either 0 or 1). The internal nodes are then simply encoded by their operation, namely constraint $F_v = \prod_{w \in Ch(v)} F_w$ for product nodes and constraint

$F_v = \sum_{w \in Ch(v)} F_w$ for sum nodes, where $Ch(v)$ are the identifiers of the children of node v in the AC.

Because of these constraints, when all Q_i (and hence B_i) variables are assigned, each F_v represents the value of that node of the AC, and the root node F_1 is the probability of the BN pattern. F_1 can then be used in a minimum probability constraint, see Table 2, right column.

Subset, superset and exclusion constraints. Including evidence and excluding assignments in the pattern is done by constraining the relevant Q_i variables appropriately, as indicated in Table 2.

Freeness constraint. To enforce this constraint, as explained in Sect. 3, we need to reason over the probability of subsets of a pattern. To do so, we use the observation that for an assignment $(X_i = k) \in A$: $P_\mathcal{G}(A \backslash \{(X_i = k)\}) = \sum_j P_\mathcal{G}(A \backslash \{(X_i = k)\}) \cup \{(X_i = j)\}$. Fortunately, using ACs we can efficiently compute these terms, as they correspond to *derivatives* of the function f encoded by the AC [5]. The latter work shows that for partial assignment A we have $P_\mathcal{G}(A \backslash \{(X_i = k)\}) \cup \{(X_i = j)\} = \frac{\partial f}{\partial \lambda_{i,j}}(A)$. It was also shown that this can be computed for all nodes (and hence variables X) simultaneously using the derivatives of its parents in the AC, together with the values that we store in F_v variables.

To compute these derivatives, we introduce a real-valued CP variable D_v for every node v in the circuit. The value of D_v's corresponding to leaves $\lambda_{i,j}$, denoted by $D_{i,j}$ for ease of notation, will represent the derivative of AC w.r.t $\lambda_{i,j}$: $\forall i, j\ D_{i,j} = \frac{\partial f}{\partial \lambda_{i,j}}(A)$. Hence $D_{i,j} = P_\mathcal{G}((A \backslash \{(X_i = k)\}) \cup \{(X_i = j)\})$.

Following the formulation in [5], the constraints below encode the computation of the D variables, where we denote by $Pa^+(v)$ the identifiers of summation parents and by $Pa^*(v)$ those of multiplication parents;

$$D_v = \sum_{w \in Pa^+(v)} D_w + \sum_{w \in Pa^*(v)} (D_w \prod_{\substack{v' \in Ch(w) \\ v' \neq v}} F_v) \qquad \forall v$$

$$D_1 = 1$$

To formulate the *free* constraint from Table 2 over the CP variables, we use the fact that given $(X_i = k) \in A$: $P_\mathcal{G}A \backslash (X_i = k)) = \sum_j D_{i,j}$ and that $P_\mathcal{G}A = F_1$.

Maximality and closedness constraints can be formulated using the same building blocks (c.f. Table 2).

Difference constraints. Comparing the probability of two networks over the same variables can be done by encoding the two ACs and formulating a mathematical constraint over the respective F_1 root node variables (Table 2).

Using CP allows us to easily mix different problems, such as combining the constraints of itemset mining in databases and BN's in a single CP model.

The variable F_1 can be computed as before, while the relative frequency of a database over the same variables can be computed using a constraint programming for itemset mining formulation [9]. In Table 2 we materialize the relative frequency through a CP variable R.

As we have shown, many constraints over the pattern and the network can be readily formulated in CP. Furthermore, as these are standard CP constraints, existing CP solvers can be used to enumerate the satisfying BN patterns.

5 Experiments

We used the ACE^1 compiler (version 2) for generating arithmetic circuits from Bayesian networks. The networks were compiled with parameters " -noTabular -cd06 -dtBnMinfill". We used the *Gecode* [2] CP solver version 4.2.1. Experiments were run on Linux PCs with Intel 2.83 GHz processors and 8 GB of RAM.

Execution Times for Example Queries. To give an indication of execution times, we report the runtimes for the example queries of Sect. 2 in Table 4a. The value of β for queries Q4 and Q5 was 0.08 and 0.25, respectively. The compilation time (not included in the reported runtimes) was 0.374 secs.

To investigate the influence of size of BN and AC, we ran a simple query with only a $probability(A, \mathcal{G}, \theta)$ constraint on three benchmark networks[3]. Table 3 reports BN and AC size, θ threshold and runtimes. AC compilation time is small. Observe that in Table 3 the two larger networks have smaller AC's, because of their other structural properties (see [5] for more details). While bigger ACs require more runtime, the number of solutions has a major impact on runtime too. This can be controlled up to some extend by adding extra constraints.

Table 3. Probability queries over three benchmarks network, with **#BN-n**: number of BN nodes; **c.Time**: compilation time; **#AC-n/e**: number of AC nodes/edges; θ: probability threshold; **#Sols**: number of solutions, and **s.Time**: solving time.

Network	#BN-n	c.Time(s)	#AC-n	#AC-e	θ	#Sols	s.Time(s)
HeparII	70	0.701	6963	13272	0.9	664	9.96
					0.8	24025	341.83
Win95pts	76	0.528	2786	6184	0.99	65	0.61
					0.95	214645	444.1
Insurance	27	0.374	34742	113788	0.9	12	2.76
					0.4	6662	383.66

---

[1] http://reasoning.cs.ucla.edu/ace/.
[2] http://www.gecode.org.
[3] available at http://www.bnlearn.com/bnrepository/.

Comparison with Sampling. An obvious alternative to our proposed method for executing itemset queries is to first sample a database from the joint distribution and then perform constraint-based itemset mining queries on the sampled database. Using this approach, one can execute the BN pattern queries using a constraint-based itemset mining system such as [9].

We investigate how this compares to our proposed method. We used two BNs: the first was the *insurance* network, which we will call BN1. The network BN2 is a naïve Bayes version of BN1 (With **PropertyCost** as root, and all non-cost observed variables as children) which we trained on 10000 samples from BN1. Compilation time for BN1 was 0.374 and 0.212 seconds for BN2. We then sampled a database of size 500 from BN2, which we call DB2.

In the approximate method, we sampled databases of varying sizes from BN1. We then searched for itemsets for which the relative frequency in the database and DB2 had a difference larger than 0.1. Table 4b presents the precision and recall of BN patterns found by the approximate method, compared to those found by our exact method. The results indicate that for a decent approximation, one needs to sample a large database which in turn leads to high computational costs. In comparison, the runtime of the exact method was 5.63 seconds.

Table 4. (a) Execution times of example queries, and (b) Quality of results of sampling method as compared against the solutions of exact method.

Query	Q1	Q2	Q3
Time(s)	1.63	11.7	11.67
Query	Q4	Q5	
Time(s)	58.41	12.11	

(a)

#Samples	Precision	Recall	Time(s)
100	0.39	0.76	7.59
1000	0.73	0.94	20.08
10000	0.97	0.93	375.95

(b)

6   Related Work

Much attention in the Bayesian network literature has gone to the problem of finding explanations given some evidence. These *explanation queries* typically use a scoring function to find the best explanation. In contrast to queries like MAP and MPE, we do *not* fix which variables must be in or not in the pattern, instead we conceptually search over all possible marginalizations. There are other explanation queries that share this feature. These typically use specific scoring functions, such as the generalized Bayes factor of [19]. The explanation queries are constrained optimisation problems instead of enumeration problems. Our framework on the other hand is made for exploration queries and enumerates all satisfying BN patterns instead of computing the 'optimal' one.

There is also a body of work on discarding irrelevant variables from explanations [6,11,18,19], as the *free* constraint does in our framework. In [6] each explanation found by a K-MPE algorithm is simplified by removing assignments that are considered irrelevant; [11] makes a trade-off between high probability and specificity. [18] proposes a definition for *relevance* and gives an algorithm that excludes irrelevant variables from the MAP assignments. This is a specific optimization query which is solved by a best-first-search algorithm.

Related to discriminating a BN network from a database, in [10] the authors search for subsets of variables rather than partial assignments. These *attribute sets* are then used to modify the BN to better reflects the correlations present in the data. In other studies, a Bayesian network is used to *filter* itemsets or association rules found in a database. In [8], first an itemset mining algorithm is applied to a database to find a number of association rules, and then these rules are scored using the probability in the Bayesian and the concept of D-separation. In [12] the itemsets found by the well-known *apriori* algorithm are scored according to a Bayesian network, and the itemsets and attribute sets with highest scores are obtained in a post-processing step. The main difference with the discriminative setting considered in our work is that we compare patterns in the database and the network during search instead of post-processing them.

Our framework combines constraints with probabilistic computations. In similar spirit, there has been work on combining (deterministic) constraint networks with probabilistic networks [13]. The main difference is that in the resulting networks, all satisfying assignments are aggregated to compute a single probability value; on the other hand, we enumerate all possible *partial* assignments and compute their (marginal) probability.

7   Conclusions

We have investigated the problem of *exploring* Bayesian networks by querying for BN patterns (partial assignments) under constraints. The work is inspired by all the work on exploring data using constraint-based pattern mining techniques. We have shown that similar queries and constraints as used in the constraint-based pattern mining community can be used. This results in novel querying abilities for BNs. The proposed execution strategy is to compile the BN into an arithmetic circuit, and formulate and reason over that in a constraint programming framework. Such an approach supports a wide range of queries and constraints in a flexible and declarative manner.

Our work currently focusses on enumeration queries, as is typical in pattern mining. However, it could also be used in an optimisation setting over a scoring function, where its generality would allow one to add arbitrary constraints on top of the scoring function. In future work, the approach could also be adapted to problems beyond enumerating BN pattern queries, such as verifying monotonicity of Bayesian networks [16] or computing same-decision probability [4]. Our method may also be valuable for mining patterns over data, when evaluating the interestingness of the patterns using a BN (in our case, *during* search). Given the generality of the method, efficiency can be a concern though. Efficiency could be improved by using *global* constraints that can reason over the AC more efficiently, instead of using a decomposition over auxiliary variables F.

Acknowledgment. This work was supported by the European Commission under the project "Inductive Constraint Programming" contract number FP7-284715 and by the Research Foundation–Flanders by means of two Postdoc grants

References

1. Agrawal, R., Imielinski, T., Swami, A.N.: Mining association rules between sets of items in large databases. In: Buneman, P., Jajodia, S. (eds.) SIGMOD Conference, pp. 207–216. ACM Press (1993)
2. Binder, J., Koller, D., Russell, S.J., Kanazawa, K.: Adaptive probabilistic networks with hidden variables. Mach. Learn. **29**(2–3), 213–244 (1997)
3. Boulicaut, J.-F., Jeudy, B.: Mining free itemsets under constraints. In: Proceeding IDEAS 2001, pp. 322–329. IEEE Computer Society (2001)
4. Chen, S.J., Choi, A., Darwiche, A.: Algorithms and applications for the same-decision probability. J. Artif. Intell. Res. **49**, 601–633 (2014)
5. Darwiche, A.: A differential approach to inference in Bayesian networks. J. ACM **50**(3), 280–305 (2003)
6. de Campos, L.M., Gámez, J.A., Moral, S.: Simplifying explanations in Bayesian belief networks. Int. J. Uncertainty Fuzziness Knowl. Based Syst. **9**(4), 461–490 (2001)
7. Druzdzel, M.J., Suermondt, H.J.: Relevance in probabilistic models: "backyards" in a "small world". In: Working notes of the AAAI-1994 Fall Symposium Series: Relevance, pp. 60–63 (1994)
8. Fauré, C., Delprat, S., Boulicaut, J.-F., Mille, A.: Iterative Bayesian network implementation by using annotated association rules. In: Staab, S., Svátek, V. (eds.) EKAW 2006. LNCS (LNAI), vol. 4248, pp. 326–333. Springer, Heidelberg (2006)
9. Guns, T., Nijssen, S., De Raedt, L.: Itemset mining: a constraint programming perspective. Artif. Intell. **175**(12–13), 1951–1983 (2011)
10. Jaroszewicz, S., Scheffer, T., Simovici, D.A.: Scalable pattern mining with Bayesian networks as background knowledge. Data Min. Knowl. Discov. **18**(1), 56–100 (2009)
11. Kwisthout, J.: Most Inforbable explanations: finding explanations in Bayesian networks that are both probable and informative. In: van der Gaag, L.C. (ed.) ECSQARU 2013. LNCS, vol. 7958, pp. 328–339. Springer, Heidelberg (2013)
12. Malhas, R., Aghbari, Z.A.: Interestingness filtering engine: mining Bayesian networks for interesting patterns. Expert Syst. Appl. **36**(3), 5137–5145 (2009)
13. Mateescu, R., Dechter, R.: Mixed deterministic and probabilistic networks. Ann. Math. Artif. Intell. **54**(1–3), 3–51 (2008)
14. Nijssen, S., Zimmermann, A.: Constraint-based pattern mining. In: Aggarwal, C.C., Han, J. (eds.) Frequent Pattern Mining, pp. 147–163. Springer, Switzerland (2014)
15. Przytula, K.W., Dash, D., Thompson, D.: Evaluation of Bayesian networks used for diagnostics, vol. 60 pp. 1–12 (2003)
16. Rietbergen, M.T., van der Gaag, L.C., Bodlaender, H.L.: Provisional propagation for verifying monotonicity of Bayesian networks. ECAI **263**, 759–764 (2014)
17. Rossi, F., van Beek, P., Walsh, T.: Handbook of constraint programming. Elsevier (2006)
18. Solomon Eyal Shimony: The role of relevance in explanation I: irrelevance as statistical independence. Int. J. Approx. Reasoning **8**(4), 281–324 (1993)
19. Yuan, C., Lim, H., Tsai-Ching, L.: Most relevant explanation in Bayesian networks. J. Artif. Intell. Res. (JAIR) **42**, 309–352 (2011)

Efficient Model Selection for Regularized Classification by Exploiting Unlabeled Data

Georgios Balikas[1](✉), Ioannis Partalas[2], Eric Gaussier[1], Rohit Babbar[3], and Massih-Reza Amini[1]

[1] University of Grenoble, Alpes, Saint-Martin-d'Hères, France
georgios.balikas@imag.fr
[2] Viseo R&D, Grenoble, France
[3] Max-Planck Institute for Intelligent Systems, Tübingen, Germany

Abstract. Hyper-parameter tuning is a resource-intensive task when optimizing classification models. The commonly used k-fold cross validation can become intractable in large scale settings when a classifier has to learn billions of parameters. At the same time, in real-world, one often encounters multi-class classification scenarios with only a few labeled examples; model selection approaches often offer little improvement in such cases and the default values of learners are used. We propose bounds for classification on accuracy and macro measures (precision, recall, F1) that motivate efficient schemes for model selection and can benefit from the existence of unlabeled data. We demonstrate the advantages of those schemes by comparing them with k-fold cross validation and hold-out estimation in the setting of large scale classification.

1 Introduction

Model selection is an essential step in the pipeline of data analysis tasks. Having decided on the algorithm to be used, one should proceed to parameter selection that is the process of selecting a value for the model's hyper-parameter(s) expected to obtain the optimal performance on unseen examples. For instance, when using Support Vector Machines (SVM) or Logistic Regression (LR) in a classification task, one has to tune the regularization parameter λ which controls the complexity of the model.

The fundamental idea of parameter estimation methods is to validate the model's performance in fractions of the training data. In several learning scenarios however, except few labeled data, a larger set of unlabeled data may be available (for example in text classification) as the cost of assigning labels is high. This is the case for example of the transductive learning framework [7], where the data to be classified are available beforehand and can be leveraged during the training or inference procedures.

The situation we are investigating in this paper is when unlabeled data are available during the step of parameter selection in a classification problem. The

---

R. Babbar — This work was done when the author was at University of Grenoble, Alpes.

E. Fromont et al. (Eds.): IDA 2015, LNCS 9385, pp. 25–36, 2015.
DOI: 10.1007/978-3-319-24465-5_3

challenge is to come up with a method that is able to leverage the information in the unlabeled data, instead of ignoring them as traditional model selection strategies such as k-fold cross validation (k-CV) do. To tackle this problem, we incorporate quantification techniques in order to infer the distribution of the examples on unlabeled data, which in turn is used to calculate upper bounds (Sect. 3) on the performance of a model that motivate an efficient model selection scheme (Sect. 4).

We place ourselves in the supervised learning paradigm where the i.i.d. assumption holds. Note that unlike semi-supervised and transductive learning paradigms that make use of the unlabeled data in the training process to improve the performance, we use the unlabeled data for *hyper-parameter selection* and, hence, the obtained performance in the test set depends on the amount of the available labeled data. Our method, which is an alternative to k-CV, motivates the selection of the optimal value for the model's hyper-parameter(s) from a finite set that in turn results in the optimal performance (again from a finite set of possible performances). In this work, we propose a hyper-parameter selection method that (i) benefits from unlabeled data, (ii) performs on par with k-CV but it is k times faster and (iii) has the same complexity as hold-out estimation but performs better due to the use of unlabeled data. We demonstrate the efficiency and the effectiveness of the proposed method in Sect. 5 where we present multi-class text classification results on several datasets with a large number of classes.

2   Related Work

Several approaches have been proposed for selecting the hyper-parameters of learning algorithms. The goal is always to select the hypothesis that minimizes the generalization error, which is approximated by the estimated error [13]. A popular method to calculate the estimated error is the hold-out procedure that splits the data in a training and a validation set; the estimated error is calculated on the latter.

The k-CV technique repeats k times the hold-out procedure: in each round the available training data are partitioned into two complementary subsets, one for training and one for validation. To reduce variability, multiple rounds of cross-validation are performed using different partitions and the validation results are averaged over the rounds. At the end, an hypothesis is selected e.g. by retraining the classifier on all data using the best values found for the hyper-parameters, or by averaging the hypotheses [5]. A variant of this method is proposed by Blum et al. [6] with a progressive cross-validation procedure that begins by splitting the data in training and test. At each step, it tests an example which in the next round is used for training, resulting in as many hypotheses as the available test examples. To label an example, a hypothesis is randomly selected. This method has the advantage of using more examples for training than the hold-out and was shown to select a better hypothesis. In addition, the study in [12] reviews accuracy estimation and model selection methods based on cross-validation and bootstrap. The former is shown to be better than the latter in different datasets, especially in terms of accuracy estimation (for which a stratified approach may be preferred).

The hold-out estimation and the k-CV when k is small are known to have large variance, a problem that can be partially compensated in k-CV by selecting high values for k (like 5 or 10) [1,2]. However, k-CV and its variants are computationally expensive and may be intractable in practice if one wants to search for the appropriate values in large-scale scenarios.

We propose here a different method that can select an appropriate model on unlabeled datasets. The advantages compared to the above-mentioned methods concern its efficiency and its ability to be applied when few labeled examples are available. It dispenses with the use of validation sets which can be cumbersome to produce in unbalanced or small datasets. It is, however, intended for model selection only, whereas cross-validation and hold-out estimation can be used for performance evaluation as well.

3 Accuracy and Macro-F1 Quantification Bounds

In this section, we propose an upper bound on several performance measures (accuracy and macro-F1) of a given classifier C on a dataset S which doesn't need to be labeled. We then use this bound, which is based on the class distribution induced by C on S, to perform model selection.

We consider mono-label multi-class classification problems, where observations $\mathbf{x}$ lie in an input space $\mathcal{X} \subseteq \mathbb{R}^d$. Each observation $\mathbf{x}$ is associated with a label $y \in \mathcal{Y}$, where $|\mathcal{Y}| > 2$. We suppose that examples consist of pairs of $(\mathbf{x}, y)$ identically and independently distributed (i.i.d) according to a fixed, but unknown probability distribution $\mathcal{D}$ over $\mathcal{X} \times \mathcal{Y}$ ($\mathcal{D}_{\mathcal{X}}$ will denote the marginal probability for $\mathbf{x}$ in $\mathcal{X}$). In the context of text classification, $\mathbf{x}^{(i)} \in \mathcal{X}$ denotes the vector representation of document i and its label $y^{(i)} \in \mathcal{Y}$ represents the category associated with $\mathbf{x}^{(i)}$. We further assume to have access to a training set $S_{train} = \{(\mathbf{x}^{(i)}, y^{(i)})\}_{i=1}^N$ also generated i.i.d with respect to $\mathcal{D}$.

Quantification. As explained below, our analysis makes use of $M_y^{C(S)}$, the number of documents in the unlabeled set S assigned by classifier C to class y. Many classifiers do not directly assign a category to documents, but rather produce scores (probabilistic or not) for each category, from which a categorization decision can be made. The task of determining the number of instances of each target category in a set S is called *quantification* and was first proposed by Forman et al. [10,11]. Contrary to classification that identifies in which target categories an observation belongs, quantification is solely concerned with the estimation of the number of observations belonging to a target category (the positive examples). Note that a good quantifier is not necessarily a good classifier, and vice versa. For example, in a binary problem with 40 observations, a learner that outputs 20 False Positives and 20 False Negatives is a perfect quantifier but a really bad classifier.

Given a set of instances in S, quantifiers output, for each target category y of S, a number denoting the prediction of the relative frequency of category y in S. Quantification methods using general purpose learners are usually split [8] in *aggregative* and *non aggregative* methods based on whether the quantification step requires the classification of the individual instances as a basic step or not. Quantification has been mainly used to estimate distribution drifts. We make a different use of it here, in the context of model selection, and rely on two popular quantification methods, namely: (a) *Classify and Count (CC)* and (b) *Probabilistic Classify and Count (PCC)* [8]. In *CC*, given a classifier C trained on a set S_{train}, the relative frequency of a class y in a set S, denoted by $\overline{p}_y^{C(S)}$, is obtained by counting the instances of S that classifier C assigns the target category y, that is $\overline{p}_y^{C(S)} = \frac{M_y^{C(S)}}{|S|}$, where $|S|$ denotes the size of S. *PCC* extends *CC* using the posterior probabilities of an instance belonging to a category, leading to $\overline{p}_y^{C(S)} = \frac{1}{|S|} \sum_{\mathbf{x} \in S} p(y|\mathbf{x})$, where $p(y|\mathbf{x})$ is the posterior probability that an instance $\mathbf{x}$ of S belongs to y. We do not consider the adjusted version of those two approaches proposed in [4] because they require the expensive k-fold cross-validation in the training set which is undesirable in large scale settings. Lastly, having a trained classifier, the computational complexity of quantification reduces to the prediction cost of a trained classifier.

Quantification-based Bounds. We now present our main result which consists of quantification-based upper bounds on the accuracy (denoted $A^{C(S)}$), the macro-precision (denoted $MaP^{C(S)}$), the macro-recall (denoted $MaR^{C(S)}$) and the macro-F1 (denoted $MaF^{C(S)}$) of a classifier C on a dataset S which does not need to be labeled.

Theorem 1. *Let $S = \{(\boldsymbol{x}^{(j)})\}_{j=1}^M$ be a set generated i.i.d. with respect to $\mathcal{D}_\mathcal{X}$, p_y the true prior probability for category $y \in \mathcal{Y}$ and $\frac{N_y}{N} \triangleq \hat{p}_y$ its empirical estimate obtained on S_{train}. We consider here a classifier C trained on S_{train} and we assume that the quantification method used is accurate in the sense that:*

$$\exists \epsilon, \epsilon \ll \min\{p_y, \hat{p}_y, \overline{p}_y^{C(S)}\}, \forall y \in \mathcal{Y} : |\overline{p}_y^{C(S)} - \frac{M_y^{C(S)}}{|S|}| \le \epsilon$$

Let $B_A^{C(S)}$, $B_{MaP}^{C(S)}(\epsilon)$ and $B_{MaR}^{C(S)}(\epsilon)$ be defined as:

$$\frac{\sum_{y \in \mathcal{Y}} \min\{\hat{p}_y \times |S|, \overline{p}_y^{C(S)} \times |S|\}}{|S|} \triangleq B_A^{C(S)}$$

$$\frac{1}{|\mathcal{Y}|} \sum_{y \in \mathcal{Y}} \frac{\min\{\hat{p}_y \times |S|, \overline{p}_y^{C(S)} \times |S|\} + |S|\epsilon}{\overline{p}_y^{C(S)} \times |S| + |S|\epsilon} \triangleq B_{MaP}^{C(S)}(\epsilon)$$

$$\frac{1}{|\mathcal{Y}|} \sum_{y \in \mathcal{Y}} \frac{\min\{\hat{p}_y \times |S|, \overline{p}_y^{C(S)} \times |S|\} + |S|\epsilon}{\hat{p}_y^{C(S)} \times |S| + |S|\epsilon} \triangleq B_{MaR}^{C(S)}(\epsilon)$$

Then for any $\delta \in]0, 1]$, with probability at least $(1 - \delta)$:

$$A^{C(S)} \leq B_A^{C(S)} + |\mathcal{Y}|(\sqrt{\frac{\log |\mathcal{Y}| + \log \frac{1}{\delta}}{2N}} + \epsilon) \tag{1}$$

$$MaP^{C(S)} \leq B_{MaP}^{C(S)}(\epsilon) + \sqrt{\frac{\log |\mathcal{Y}| + \log \frac{1}{\delta}}{2N}}, \quad MaR^{C(S)} \leq B_{MaR}^{C(S)}(\epsilon) + \sqrt{\frac{\log |\mathcal{Y}| + \log \frac{1}{\delta}}{2N}} \tag{2}$$

$$MaF^{C(S)} \leq \frac{2B_{MaP}^{C(S)}(\epsilon) B_{MaR}^{C(S)}(\epsilon)}{B_{MaP}^{C(S)}(\epsilon) + B_{MaR}^{C(S)}(\epsilon)} + \sqrt{\frac{\log |\mathcal{Y}| + \log \frac{1}{\delta}}{2N}} \tag{3}$$

Proof (SKETCH). We first consider the case where $S \neq S_{train}$. Using Hoeffding's inequality for random variables bounded in the interval $[0, 1]$, we have the standard result that, for any $\delta \in]0, 1]$, with probability at least $(1 - \delta)$:

$$\forall y \in \mathcal{Y}, p_y \leq \hat{p}_y + \sqrt{\frac{\log |\mathcal{Y}| + \log \frac{1}{\delta}}{2N}}$$

The $\log |\mathcal{Y}|$ factor is a result of the fact that the bound should hold simultaneously for all categories. This implies, using the quantification assumption, that, for any $\delta \in]0, 1]$, with probability at least $(1 - \delta)$, $\forall y \in \mathcal{Y}$:

$$| \min\{p_y \times |S|, M_y^{C(S)}\} - \min\{\hat{p}_y \times |S|, \overline{p}_y^{C(S)} \times |S|\}|$$
$$< |S|(\sqrt{\frac{\log |\mathcal{Y}| + \log \frac{1}{\delta}}{2N}} + \epsilon) \tag{4}$$

$\min\{p_y \times |S|, M_y^{C(S)}\}$ corresponds to an upper bound on the number of documents of S correctly classified by C in class y. Hence, the accuracy of C on S is upper bounded by:

$$\frac{\sum_{y \in \mathcal{Y}} \min\{p_y \times |S|, M_y^{C(S)}\}}{|S|}$$

which leads, using Inequality 4, to Inequality 1. The other bounds can be derived in the same way. □

The above theorem is inspired by a previous result we have developed in the context of multi-class classification [3]. We have generalized and extended it here through the consideration of macro measures and quantification. Even though this extension renders the developments more complex, it is crucial for model selection using unlabeled datasets.

When the *Classify and Count (CC)* quantification method is used, then, by definition, $\overline{p}_y^{C(S)} = \frac{M_y^{C(S)}}{|S|}$, and ϵ can be set to 0. This leads to stricter bounds for all the measures. Furthermore, the condition $\epsilon \ll \min\{p_y, \hat{p}_y, \overline{p}_y^{C(S)}\}$ in the quantification assumption implies that the term $|S|\epsilon$ is negligible compared to $|S| \times \hat{p}_y$ or $|S| \times \overline{p}_y^{C(S)}$, so that $B_{MaP}^{C(S)}(\epsilon)$ and $B_{MaR}^{C(S)}(\epsilon)$ are close to $B_{MaP}^{C(S)}(0)$ and $B_{MaR}^{C(S)}(0)$. Lastly, it can be noted that the quality of the bound is better for the macro measures than for the accuracy as the multiplying $|\mathcal{Y}|$ factor is dropped.

Theorem 1 states that the accuracy, macro-precision, macro-recall and macro-F1 of a classifier can be upper-bounded by quantities that are related to the behavior of the classifier on an unlabeled dataset, and that the quality of the bound depends on the number of classes, the size of the training set, the quality of the quantification method and the precision desired. These bounds represent necessary conditions for a classifier C to have high accuracy/macro-F1[1]. They can nevertheless be exploited, within a given family of classifiers obtained through *e.g.* different regularization parameters, to select good classifiers.

Model Selection Using Quantification Bounds. We consider here a standard regularization setting in which one aims at minimizing a combination of the empirical error and the model complexity using the following template of the objective function:

$$\hat{w} = \arg\min R_{emp}(w) + \lambda Reg(w)$$

where $Reg(w)$ is the regularization term to avoid overfitting and $R_{emp}(.)$ represents the empirical error.

The parameter λ controls the trade-off between the empirical error and the regularization term. As mentioned before, λ is typically estimated through hold-out estimation or k-fold cross-validation. We propose here to estimate it on the basis of the upper bounds presented in Theorem 1, as described in Algorithm 1. As one can note, for each value of λ, a classifier is trained and quantified on the unlabeled set S. If the quantification assumption of Theorem 1 is not valid, then one falls back on the *Classification and Count* method for quantification. The bounds, as computed by Inequalities 1 and 3 are used to select the "best" classifier. Tuning the hyper-parameter is, therefore, reduced to the problem of finding a classifier which yields the highest value of the bounds on a given set. In contrast with other selection methods, the set used to select the classifier can be an unlabeled set from the same distribution (unlabeled data is usually readily available, contrary to labeled data) or the test set in a transductive-like scenario.

In terms of complexity, the quantification cost is reduced to the prediction for the already trained classifier, which is linear in the cardinality of the set S on which quantification is performed. The computational cost for Algorithm 1 is thus the same as 1-fold cross-validation. Additionally, as only one hypothesis is generated for each parameter value by training to the whole set of labeled data one has just to select the hypothesis with the highest bound without the need of retraining the model in contrast to hold-out or k-fold

---

[1] They do not provide a sufficient condition since it is possible, in an adversarial setup, to achieve an upper bound of 1 on the accuracy by simply assigning instances to categories in the same proportion as in the training set.

Algorithm 1. Model selection using the proposed bounds

Require: Training data $S_{train} = \{(\mathbf{x}^{(i)}, y^{(i)})\}_{i=1}^{N}$, unlabeled data $S = \{(\mathbf{x}^{(j)})\}_{j=1}^{M}$ and learning algorithm (SVM, Logistic Regression, ...)

1: **for** each value of λ (typically $\lambda \in \{10^{-4}, 10^{-3}, \ldots, 10^{2}, 10^{3}\}$ **do**)
2:    Train a classifier C_λ using S_{train}
3:    Perform quantification of C_λ on S using method M_q (typically CC or PCC)
4:    If $M_q = CC$, set $\epsilon = 0$
5:    If $M_q \neq CC$, set $\epsilon = \max_{y \in \mathcal{Y}} \min\{\hat{p}_y, \overline{p}_y^{C(S)}\} - |\overline{p}_y^{C(S)} - \frac{M_y^{C(S)}}{|S|}|$
6:    If $\epsilon < 0$, go back to step 4 with $M_q = CC$
7:    Compute the accuracy bound using Inequality 1
8:    Compute the macro-F1 bound $\left(\frac{2B_{MaP}^{C_\lambda(S)}(\epsilon)B_{MaR}^{C_\lambda(S)}(\epsilon)}{B_{MaP}^{C_\lambda(S)}(\epsilon) + B_{MaR}^{C_\lambda(S)}(\epsilon)}\right)$ using Inequality 3
9: **end for**
10: Select C_λ with the highest accuracy/macro-F1 bound

cross-validation. More precisely, the complexity of our approach for m values of λ is O([Tr(N) + Pr(M)]×m), which is k times lower than the complexity of k-CV with re-training the learner for the selected λ value, given by O([Tr(($\frac{k-1}{k}$) × N)+Pr($\frac{1}{k}$ × N)] × k×m+T(N)), where Tr(N), Pr(N) are the training and predicting costs for N examples.

4   Experimental Framework

To empirically evaluate the model selection method presented above we use the publicly available datasets of the LSHTC 2011 (*Large Scale Hierarchical Text Classification*) challenge [14]. Specifically, we make use of the Dmoz and Wikipedia datasets containing 27,875 and 36,504 categories respectively. The datasets are provided in a pre-processed format using stop-word removal and stemming while we transformed the term-frequency vectors to the tf*idf representation. For each of the datasets we randomly draw several datasets with increasing number of classes.

Table 1 presents the important statistics of the different datasets. As one can note, the number of categories in our datasets ranges from 250 to 2,500, and the number of features from 26,000 to 212,000. An interesting property of the instances of those datasets is the fit to the power law distribution. As a result, there are several under-represented classes having a few labelled examples. Thus, model selection approaches using only a fraction of the labeled instances, such as hold out, may lead to sub-optimal decisions.

The classification problems defined from our datasets are multi-class, and we adopt a standard one-vs-rest approach to address them (the large datasets considered prevents one from using more complex multi-class approaches). The Dmoz dataset is single-labeled, *i.e.* each training/test instance is associated to a single target category. On the other hand, the Wikipedia dataset is multi-labeled with the average labels per instance in the training set being 1.85. We transformed the multi-label problem to single label, both in the training and the test phase, by replicating the multi-labeled instances according to the number of their labels.

Table 1: The properties of the datasets we used. The dataset name denotes the collection we sampled it from; its subscript denotes the number of categories.

Dataset	#Training inst.	#Quantification inst.	#Test inst.	#Features	# Parameters
dmoz$_{250}$	1,542	2,401	1,023	55,610	13,902,500
dmoz$_{500}$	2,137	3,042	1,356	77,274	38,637,000
dmoz$_{1000}$	6,806	10,785	4,510	138,879	138,879,000
dmoz$_{1500}$	9,039	14,002	5,958	170,828	256,242,000
dmoz$_{2500}$	12,832	19,188	8,342	212,073	530,182,500
wiki$_{250}$	1,917	3,095	1,003	26,699	6,674,750
wiki$_{500}$	4,912	8,190	2,391	46,556	23,278,000
wiki$_{1000}$	7,887	12,790	4,067	60,788	60,788,000
wiki$_{1500}$	12,156	19,776	6,160	79,973	110,959,500
wiki$_{2500}$	22,642	37,398	11,171	109,694	274,235,000

In order to empirically measure the effectiveness of model selection, we compare the following three methods: (i) **k-CV**, using $k = 5$ folds, (ii) **hold-out** estimation with a split of 70 % and 30 % for the training and the validation sets, and (iii) our method using as quantification set (i) an unlabeled set denoted "quantification set" in Table 1, and (ii) the test set which may be available during training in a transductive alike scenario. The corresponding methods are called **Bound$_{\text{UN}}$** and **Bound$_{\text{Test}}$** respectively.

Evaluation of the Quantification Methods. We first discuss the performance of the quantification methods presented above (*CC* and *PCC*), prior to comparing the results obtained by the different model selection methods (*k*-fold cross-validation, hold-out estimation, Bound$_{\text{UN}}$ and Bound$_{\text{Test}}$). Recall that Theorem 1 is based on the assumption that the quantity Max$_\epsilon = \max_{y \in \mathcal{Y}} |\overline{p}_y^{C(S)} - \frac{M_y^{C(S)}}{|S|}|$ is small. As mentioned above, this quantity is null for the quantification method *CC*, which thus agrees with our theoretical developments. The other quantification method considered, *PCC*, is based on the probabilities that an instance belongs to a class. When using LR, those probabilities are directly produced by the model. For SVMs, however, one needs to transform the confidence scores into probabilities, which can be done in several ways, as using a logistic function, a multivariate logistic regression function or neural networks based on logistic activation functions and without hidden layers (the latter two settings can be seen as generalizations of Platt's scaling for the multi-class problem). We obtained the best results with a simple logistic function defined as $\frac{1}{1+e^{-\sigma t}}$, varying σ from 1 to 10. Table 2 displays the values of Max$_\epsilon$ obtained for *PCC* for each of the dataset and for each classifier (the default hyper-parameter values of the classifiers are used), using the value of σ leading to the lowest value of Max$_\epsilon$. As one can note, although the values obtained are small in most cases (except for Dmoz$_{1000}$ and Dmoz$_{1500}$), there are not negligible compared to the class prior probabilities, which are in the range of 1 divided by the number of classes. Thus,

Table 2: Evaluation of the assumption of Theorem 1 concerning the quantification step. For each dataset, we present Max_ϵ for the PCC quantification method.

	dmz_{250}	dmz_{500}	dmz_{1000}	dmz_{1500}	dmz_{2500}	wiki_{250}	wiki_{500}	wiki_{1000}	wiki_{1500}	wiki_{2500}
SVM	0.0728	0.0967	0.1067	0.1125	0.0345	0.0287	0.0754	0.0310	0.0425	0.0365
LR	0.0942	0.0674	0.0889	0.1111	0.0530	0.0219	0.0517	0.0481	0.0310	0.0294

the quantification method PCC does not fully agree with our theoretical development. It turns out that it also performs worse than CC in practice. We thus rely on this latter method for the rest of our experiments.

Model Selection Evaluation. We evaluate model selection methods for two families of classifiers: (i) SVMs, and (ii) LR which are among the best performing models in text classification. We explore for both classifiers the value for the regularization parameter $\lambda \in \{10^{-3}, 10^{-2}, \ldots, 10^4\}$. We used the implementations in Python's scikit-learn [15] that are wrappers of the LibLinear package [9].

We report the scores obtained in Accuracy and Macro-F (MaF) measure when a classifier is applied on the test set. In particular, for each dataset of Table 1 the model selection methods are used only for selecting the regularization parameter λ when optimizing for the repsective measure. After the selection of λ, the classifier is retrained on the entire training set, and we report its performance in the test set. This last step of retraining is not required for our method since the classifier is trained in the overall labeled set from the beginning. Also, as hold-out estimation may be sensitive to the initial split, we perform 10 different random splits training/validation and report the mean and the standard deviation of the scores obtained for both evaluation measures.

Figure 1 illustrates the model selection decisions for the different methods using an SVM on the Wikipedia dataset with $1,500$ classes for the MaF measure. The curve MaF corresponds to the actual MaF on the test set. Although each parameter estimation method selects the value for λ that seems to maximize

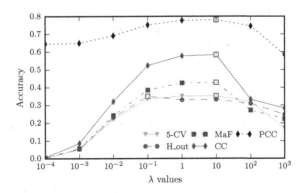

Fig. 1: Model selection process for SVM on the wiki_{1500} for MaF. The squares denote the best performance for each method.

Table 3: The performance of the model selection methods for SVM and Logistic Regression on the test set. For held out, we report the mean and in parenthesis the standard deviation of 10 rounds of the method.

	Dataset	Bound$_{Un}$ Acc	MaF	Bound$_{Test}$ Acc	MaF	Hold-out Acc	MaF	5-CV Acc	MaF
SVM	wiki$_{250}$	.7747	.5889	.7747	.5927	.7663 (±.0158)	.5746 (±.0183)	.7747	.5927
	wiki$_{500}$	.7445	.5257	.7449	.5254	.7440 (±.0006)	.5228 (±.0031)	.7445	.5254
	wiki$_{1000}$	.7000	.4737	.6993	.4732	.6996 (±.0009)	.4584 (±.0274)	.7000	.4737
	wiki$_{1500}$	.6360	.4278	.6354	.4283	.6343 (±.0049)	.4230 (±.0126)	.6360	.4278
	wiki$_{2500}$	.5808	.3763	.5811	.3762	.5822 (±.0023)	.3759 (±.0004)	.5832	.3763
	dmoz$_{250}$	.8260	.6242	.8270	.6243	.8260 (±.0000)	.6242 (±.0000)	.8260	.6242
	dmoz$_{500}$	.7227	.5584	.7227	.5584	.7221 (±.0005)	.5558 (±.0022)	.7220	.5562
	dmoz$_{1000}$	.7302	.4883	.7302	.4892	.7301 (±.0001)	.4835 (±.0155)	.7299	.4883
	dmoz$_{1500}$	.7132	.4715	.7132	.4715	.6958 (±.0457)	.4065 (±.0998)	.7132	.4715
	dmoz$_{2500}$	.6352	.4301	.6350	.4306	.6350 (±.0001)	.3949 (±.0686)	.6352	.4301
Logistic Regression	wiki$_{250}$	.7527	.5423	.7527	.5423	.7464 (±.0078)	.5335 (±.0134)	.7527	.5423
	wiki$_{500}$	.7302	.4709	.7302	.4709	.7266 (±.0056)	.4633 (±.0116)	.7302	.4709
	wiki$_{1000}$	.6836	.4354	.6836	.4354	.6836 (±.0000)	.4354(±.0000)	.6836	.4354
	wiki$_{1500}$	.6166	.3801	.6166	.3801	.6166 (±.0000)	.3801 (±.0000)	.6166	.3801
	wiki$_{2500}$	.5802	.3506	.5802	.3506	.5802 (±.0000)	.3506 (±.0000)	.5802	.3506
	dmoz$_{250}$	.7742	.4724	.7742	.4724	.7718 (±.0047)	.4692 (±.0096)	.7742	.4724
	dmoz$_{500}$	.6608	.4513	.6608	.4513	.6586 (±.0064)	.4488 (±.0076)	.6608	.4513
	dmoz$_{1000}$	.6845	.3681	.6845	.3681	.6845 (±.0000)	.3681 (±.0000)	.6845	.3681
	dmoz$_{1500}$	.6678	.3616	.6678	.3616	.6678 (±.0000)	.3616 (±.0000)	.6678	.3616
	dmoz$_{2500}$	.5959	.3351	.5959	.3351	.5959 (±.0000)	.3351(±.0000)	.5959	.3351

the performance, the goal in this example, ultimately, is to select the value that maximizes the performance of MaF.

For instance, *hold-out*, by selecting $\lambda = 10^{-1}$, fails to select the optimal λ value, while all other the methods succeed. Here, the 5-CV approach requires 1310 sec., whereas the bound approach only requires 302 sec. (the computations are performed on a standard desktop machine, using parallelized implementations on 4-cores). The bound approach is thus 4.33 times faster, a result consistent over all experiments and in agreement with the complexity of each approach (Sect. 3). Lastly, we notice that the curve for Bound$_{UN}$ with the quantification method *CC* follows the MaF curve more strictly than the curve with the quantification method *PCC*.

Table 3 presents the evaluation of the three model selection methods using as classifiers SVM and LR respectively. As one can note, the performance of the method proposed here is equivalent to the one of cross-validation, for all datasets, and for both classifiers and performance measures (accuracy and MaF). The performance of SVM is furthermore higher than the one of LR on all datasets, and for both evaluation measures, the difference being more important for the MaF. The performance of cross-validation however comes with the cost of extra processing time, as our method achieves a k speed-up compared to cross-validation. If both methods can easily be parallelized (at least on the basis of the number of values of the hyper-parameter to be tested), k-fold cross validation requires k times more computing resources than our method.

Unlike cross-validation, hold-out estimation fails to provide a good model in many instances. This is particularly true for SVMs and the MaF measure, for which the model provided by hold-out estimation lies way behind the ones provided by $Bound_{UN}$ and $Bound_{Test}$ on several collections as $Dmoz_{1500}$ and $Dmoz_{2500}$. The difference is less important for LR, but the final results in that case are not as good as in the SVM case.

5   Conclusions

We have presented in this work a new method for model selection that is able to exploit unlabeled data (this is in contrast with current model selection methods). To do so, we have introduced quantification-based bounds for accuracy and macro performance measures. We have then shown how to apply this bound in practice, in the case where unlabeled data is available in conjunction with labeled data, and in a transductive-like setting where the instances to be classified are known in advance. The experimental results, obtained on 10 datasets with different number of classes ranging from 250 to 2,500, show that the method proposed here is equivalent, in terms of the quality of the model selected, to k-fold cross-validation, while being k times faster. It furthermore consistently outperforms hold-out estimation for SVM classification, for both accuracy and macro-F1, the difference being more important for macro-F1. Furthermore, and contrary to hold-out estimation, our method needs neither a validation/train splitting procedure nor a retraining procedure.

In our future work we plan to investigate the application of a generalized versino of the proposed model selection approach in cases where more than one hyper-parameters have to be tuned. In this framework, we also plan to research the extension of the theoretical and experimental findings to multi-label classification problems i.e., multi-class classification problems where each instance can be given more than one categories at once.

Acknowledgements. This work is partially supported by the CIFRE N 28/2015 and by the LabEx PERSYVAL Lab ANR-11-LABX-0025.

References

1. Arlot, S., Lerasle, M.: Why V=5 is enough in V-fold cross-validation. ArXiv e-prints (2012)
2. Arlot, S., Celisse, A.: A survey of cross-validation procedures for model selection. Stat. Surv. **4**, 40–79 (2010)

3. Babbar, R., Partalas, I., Gaussier, E., Amini, M.r.: Re-ranking approach to classification in large-scale power-law distributed category systems. In: Proceedings of the 37th International ACM SIGIR Conference on Research & Development in Information Retrieval, SIGIR 2014 (2014)

4. Bella, A., Ferri, C., Hernández-Orallo, J., Ramírez-Quintana, M.J.: Quantification via probability estimators. In: 2010 IEEE 10th International Conference on Data Mining, (ICDM), pp. 737–742. IEEE (2010)

5. Bengio, Y., Grandvalet, Y.: No unbiased estimator of the variance of k-fold cross-validation. J. Mach. Learn. Res. **5**, 1089–1105 (2004)

6. Blum, A., Kalai, A., Langford, J.: Beating the hold-out: bounds for k-fold and progressive cross-validation. In: Proceedings of the Twelfth Annual Conference on Computational Learning Theory, pp. 203–208 (1999)

7. Chapelle, O., Schölkopf, B., Zien, A. (eds.): Semi-Supervised Learning. MIT Press, Cambridge (2006). http://www.kyb.tuebingen.mpg.de/ssl-book

8. Esuli, A., Sebastiani, F.: Optimizing text quantifiers for multivariate loss functions. Technical report 2013-TR-005, Istituto di Scienza e Tecnologie dellInformazione, Consiglio Nazionale delle Ricerche, Pisa, IT (2013)

9. Fan, R.E., Chang, K.W., Hsieh, C.J., Wang, X.R., Lin, C.J.: LIBLINEAR: A library for large linear classification. J. Mach. Learn. Res. **9**, 1871–1874 (2008)

10. Forman, G.: Counting positives accurately despite inaccurate classification. In: Gama, J., Camacho, R., Brazdil, P.B., Jorge, A.M., Torgo, L. (eds.) ECML 2005. LNCS (LNAI), vol. 3720, pp. 564–575. Springer, Heidelberg (2005)

11. Forman, G.: Quantifying counts and costs via classification. Data Min. Knowl. Discov. **17**(2), 164–206 (2008)

12. Kohavi, R.: A study of cross-validation and bootstrap for accuracy estimation and model selection. In: Proceedings of the 14th International Joint Conference on Artificial Intelligence, IJCAI 1995 (1995)

13. Mohri, M., Rostamizadeh, A., Talwalkar, A.: Foundations of Machine Learning. The MIT Press, Cambridge (2012)

14. Partalas, I., Kosmopoulos, A., Baskiotis, N., Artieres, T., Paliouras, G., Gaussier, E., Androutsopoulos, I., Amini, M.R., Galinari, P.: Lshtc: A benchmark for large-scale text classification. CoRR abs/1503.08581, March 2015

15. Pedregosa, F., Varoquaux, G., Gramfort, A., Michel, V., Thirion, B., Grisel, O., Blondel, M., Prettenhofer, P., Weiss, R., Dubourg, V., Vanderplas, J., Passos, A., Cournapeau, D., Brucher, M., Perrot, M., Duchesnay, E.: Scikit-learn: machine learning in python. J. Mach. Learn. Res. **12**, 2825–2830 (2011)

Segregation Discovery in a Social Network of Companies

Alessandro Baroni and Salvatore Ruggieri[✉]

Dipartimento di Informatica, Università di Pisa, Largo B. Pontecorvo 3,
56127 Pisa, Italy
{baroni,ruggieri}@di.unipi.it

Abstract. We introduce a framework for a data-driven analysis of segregation of minority groups in social networks, and challenge it on a complex scenario. The framework builds on quantitative measures of segregation, called segregation indexes, proposed in the social science literature. The segregation discovery problem consists of searching sub-graphs and sub-groups for which a reference segregation index is above a minimum threshold. A search algorithm is devised that solves the segregation problem. The framework is challenged on the analysis of segregation of social groups in the boards of directors of the real and large network of Italian companies connected through shared directors.

1 Introduction

Social networking services record our connections to friends, colleagues, collaborators. The analysis of those digital traces can create new comprehensive pictures of individual and group behaviour, through the discovery of patterns and models, with the potential to transform the understanding of our lives, organizations, and societies. In this paper, we will consider th social problem of group *segregation* in social networks [8], which is an unjustified separation or distance in social environments (physical, working, or on-line) of individuals on the basis of any physical or cultural trait. We present theory and tools, based on data mining and network science, for data-driven *segregation discovery*, with two main goals. First, we aim at providing a deeper understanding of segregation phenomena through the design of analytical processes that proactively support policy makers and control authorities in discovering and in anticipating potential segregation problems. Second, we aim at studying the applicability of proposed methodology in a complex scenario through the analysis of segregation of minority groups in the network of Italian companies linked through shared directors in their boards.

The paper is structured as follows. Section 2 provides an overview of segregation indexes from the social science literature. Section 3 introduces the problem of segregation discovery and provides a solution using concepts from itemset mining. Section 4 challenges the solution on the network of Italian companies by tackling a few issues arising from the case study. Section 5 concludes and presents directions for future work.

© Springer International Publishing Switzerland 2015
E. Fromont et al. (Eds.): IDA 2015, LNCS 9385, pp. 37–48, 2015.
DOI: 10.1007/978-3-319-24465-5_4

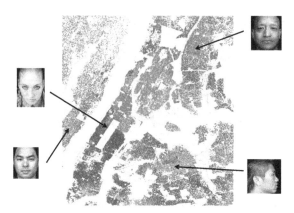

Fig. 1. Racial spatial segregation in New York City, based on Census 2000 data [7]. One dot for each 500 residents. Red dots are Whites, blue dots are Blacks, green dots are Asian, orange dots are Hispanic, and yellow dots are other races (Color figure online).

2   Segregation Indexes

2.1   On the Notion of Segregation

The term *segregation* refers to restrictions on the access of people to each other. People are partitioned into two or more groups on the grounds of personal or cultural traits that can foster discrimination, such as gender, age, ethnicity, income, skin color, language, religion, political opinion, membership of a national minority, etc. Contact, communication, or interaction among groups are limited by their physical, working or socio-economic distance. Members of a group tend to cluster together when dissecting the society into organizational units (neighborhoods, schools, job types).

In spatial segregation, groups are set apart in neighborhoods where they live in, in schools they attend to, or in companies they work at. As sharply pointed out in Fig. 1, racial segregation very often emerges in most cities characterized by ethnic diversity. Schelling's segregation model [19] shows that there is a natural tendency to spatial segregation, as a collective phenomenon, even if each individual is relatively tolerant – in his famous abstract simulation model, Schelling assumed that a person changes residence only if less than 30 % of the neighbors are of his/her own race.

Recently, [13] argued that segregation is shifting from ancient forms on the grounds of racial, ethnic and gender traits to modern socio-economic and cultural segregation on the basis of income, job position, and political-religious opinions. For instance, it has been warned that the personalization of online social networks may foster segregation and lack of consensus between different social groups, because people are only reinforced in what they already believe and lack exposure to alternative viewpoints and information [16] or because they are led to self-censorship acts [6] for fear of public opinion on personal thoughts.

2.2   Segregation Indexes

A segregation index provides a quantitative measure of the degree of segregation of social groups (e.g., Blacks and Whites) among units of social organization (e.g., schools). Many indexes have been proposed in the literature. [10] represents the earliest attempt to categorize them. Afterward, the survey [12] provided a shared classification with reference to five key dimensions: evenness, exposure, concentration, centralization, and clustering. We restrict ourselves to binary indexes, which assume a partitioning of people into two groups, say majority and minority (but could be Blacks/Whites, women/men, etc.). Let T be size of the total population, M be the size of the minority group, and $P = M/T$ be the overall fraction of the minority group. Assume that there are n units, and that for $i \in [1, n]$, t_i is the population in unit i, m_i is the minority population in unit i, and $p_i = m_i/t_i$ is the fraction of the minority group in unit i.

Evenness Indexes. *Evenness* indexes measure the difference in the distributions of social groups among the units. They are widely adopted in the social science literature on segregation. The mostly referenced indexes are dissimilarity and entropy. The *dissimilarity index* D is the weighted mean absolute deviation of every unit's minority proportion from the global minority proportion:

$$D = \frac{1}{2 \cdot P \cdot (1 - P)} \sum_{i=1}^{n} \frac{t_i}{T} \cdot |p_i - P| \tag{1}$$

The normalization factor $2 \cdot P \cdot (1 - P)$ is to obtain values in the range $[0, 1]$. Since D measures dispersion of minorities over the units, higher values of the index mean higher segregation. Dissimilarity is minimum when for all $i \in [1, n]$, $p_i = P$, namely the distribution of the minority group is uniform over units. It is maximum when for all $i \in [1, n]$, either $p_i = 1$ or $p_i = 0$, namely every unit includes members of only one group (complete segregation).

A second widely adopted index is the *information index*, also called the *Theil index* [15] in social science, and normalized mutual information in machine learning. Let the population entropy be: $E = -P \cdot \log P - (1 - P) \cdot \log (1 - P)$, and the entropy of unit i be: $E_i = -p_i \cdot \log p_i - (1 - p_i) \cdot \log (1 - p_i)$. The information index is the weighted mean fractional deviation of every unit's entropy from the population entropy:

$$H = \sum_{i=1}^{n} \frac{t_i}{T} \cdot \frac{(E - E_i)}{E} \tag{2}$$

Information index ranges in $[0, 1]$. Since it denotes a relative reduction in uncertainty in the distribution of groups after considering units, higher values mean higher segregation of groups over the units. Information index reaches the minimum when all the units respect the global entropy (full integration) and the maximum when all units contain only one group (complete segregation).

Exposure Indexes. *Exposure* indexes measure the degree of potential contact, or possibility of interaction, between members of different groups.

The most used measure of exposure is the *isolation index* [4], defined as the likelihood that a member of the minority group is exposed to another member of the same group in a unit. For a unit i, this can be estimated as the product of the likelihood that a member of the minority group is in the unit (m_i/M) by the likelihood that she is exposed to another minority member in the unit (m_i/t_i, or p_i) – assuming that the two events are independent. In formula:

$$I = \frac{1}{M} \cdot \sum_{i=1}^{n} m_i \cdot p_i \qquad (3)$$

The isolation index ranges over $[P, 1]$, with higher values denoting higher segregation. The minimum value is reached when for $i \in [1, n]$, $p_i = P$, namely the distribution of the minority group is uniform over the units. The maximum value is reached in the same conditions of the previous two indexes. The differences between indexes are the following: (a) H and I are insensitive to units i where $m_i = 0$, whilst D is not; (b) D and H are symmetric, i.e., by inverting the minority and majority groups the index remains unchanged, whilst I is not.

Other Indexes. The other three classes of indexes are specifically concerned with spatial notions of segregation. Concentration measures the relative amount of physical space occupied by social groups in an urban area. Centralization measures the degree to which a group is spatially located near the center of an urban area. Finally, clustering measures the degree to which group members live disproportionately in contiguous areas. We refer the reader to [12] for details.

3   Segregation Discovery

Traditional data analysis approaches from social science typically rely on formulating an hypothesis, i.e., a possible context of segregation against a certain social group, and then in empirically testing such an hypothesis. For instance, a suspect case of segregation of black female students in high schools from NYC is studied first by collecting data on race and gender of all high school students in NYC (reference population), and then by computing and analysing segregation indexes over black females (minority group). The formulation of the hypothesis, however, is not straightforward, and it is potentially biased by the expectations of the data analyst of finding segregation in a certain context. In this process, one may overlook cases where segregation is present but undetected. We propose a data-driven approach, which complements hypothesis testing, by driving the search (the "discovery") of contexts and social groups where a-priori unknown segregation factors are quantitatively prominent. Recall the previous example. The analyst has to collect data on gender, age, race of students (called segregation attributes), and on city location, school type, and annual fees (called context attributes). Although no segregation may be apparent in the overall data, it may turn out that for a specific combination of context attributes (e.g., high schools located in NYC), a specific minority group denoted by a combination of segregation attributes (e.g., black women) is at risk of segregation. We quantify such a risk through a reference segregation index, and assume that a value of the index above a given threshold denotes a situation worth for further scrutiny.

We call the problem of discovering a-priori unknown minority groups and reference populations for which segregation indexes are above a given threshold, the *segregation discovery problem*. The problem statement will be formalized using notation and concepts from itemset mining [9]. This allows for re-using methods and tools from this widely investigated research area. In particular, itemsets will serve to define the search space of segregation discovery. Let $\mathcal{R}$ be a relational table (or, simply, a table or a dataset). Tuples in the table denote individuals, and attribute values denote information about individuals and units they belong to. Attributes are partitioned into *segregation attributes* (SA), such as sex, age, and race, which denote minority groups potentially exposed to segregation; *context attributes* (CA) attributes, such as city and job type, which denote contexts where segregation may appear; and an attribute unit, which is an ID of the unit the tuple/individual belongs to. For a discrete attribute A, an A-*item* is a term $A = v$, where $v \in dom(A)$, the domain of A. We assume that continuous attributes are discretized into bins [11]. An *itemset* $\mathbf{X}$ is a set of items. As usual in the literature, we write $\mathbf{X}, \mathbf{Y}$ for $\mathbf{X} \cup \mathbf{Y}$. A tuple σ from $\mathcal{R}$ *supports* $\mathbf{X}$ if for every $A = v$ in $\mathbf{X}$, we have $\sigma[A] = v$, where $\sigma[A]$ is the value of the attribute A in the tuple σ. The *cover* of $\mathbf{X}$ is the set of tuples that support $\mathbf{X}$: $cover_{\mathcal{R}}(\mathbf{X}) = \{\sigma \in \mathcal{R} \mid \sigma \text{ supports } \mathbf{X}\}$. We omit the subscript $\mathcal{R}$ if it is clear from the context. E.g., $cover(\text{sex=female, age=[20--29]})$ is the set of women in their 20 s included in the dataset. The (absolute) *support* of $\mathbf{X}$ is the size of its cover, namely $supp(\mathbf{X}) = |cover(\mathbf{X})|$.

We write $\mathbf{A}, \mathbf{B}$ to denote an itemset where $\mathbf{A}$ is non-empty and it includes only SA-items, and $\mathbf{B}$ includes only CA-items. We call $\mathbf{A}$ a non-empty SA-itemset, and $\mathbf{B}$ a CA-itemset. We are now in the position to extend the notation of the segregation indexes to a reference population, which is the cover of $\mathbf{B}$, and to a reference minority group, which is the cover of $\mathbf{A}$.

Definition 1. *Let $s()$ be a segregation index. For an itemset $\mathbf{A}, \mathbf{B}$ we denote by $s(\mathbf{A}, \mathbf{B})$ the segregation index calculated for the population in $cover(\mathbf{B})$ considering as minority population those in $cover(\mathbf{A}, \mathbf{B})$.*

As an example, $D(\mathbf{A}, \mathbf{B})$ is the dissimilarity index, where $T = supp(\mathbf{B})$, $M = supp(\mathbf{A}, \mathbf{B})$, $t_i = supp(\mathbf{B}, \text{unit}=i)$, and $m_i = supp(\mathbf{A}, \mathbf{B}, \text{unit}=i)$. Reconsidering the example above, we would fix $\mathbf{A}$ as race=black,sex=female and $\mathbf{B}$ as city=NYC. $D((\text{race=black,sex=female}), \text{city=NYC})$ is then the dissimilarity index of segregation of black females in the high schools of NYC.

We introduce now the problem of segregation discovery.

Definition 2. *Let $s()$ be a segregation index, and α a fixed threshold.*
An itemset $\mathbf{A}, \mathbf{B}$ is α-integrative w.r.t. $s()$ if $cover(\mathbf{B}) = \emptyset$ or $s(\mathbf{A}, \mathbf{B}) \leq \alpha$. Otherwise, $\mathbf{A}, \mathbf{B}$ is α-segregative. The problem of segregation discovery consists of computing the set of α-segregative itemsets.

Input: relational table $\mathcal{R}$ with context attributes (CA), segregation attributes (SA), unit attribute `unit` with a total of n units.

Output: segregation index values $s(\mathbf{A}, \mathbf{B})$.

```
 1 foreach B CA-itemset do
 2    T = 0;
 3    foreach i ∈ [1,n] do
 4       tᵢ = supp(B, unit=i);
 5       T += tᵢ
 6    end
 7    foreach A non-empty SA-itemset do
 8       M = 0;
 9       foreach i ∈ [1,n] with tᵢ > 0 do
10          mᵢ = supp(A, B, unit=i);
11          M += mᵢ
12       end
13       sum = 0
14       foreach i ∈ [1,n] with tᵢ > 0 do
15          sum += fₛ(mᵢ, tᵢ, M, T)
16       end
17       s(A, B) = gₛ(sum, M, T)
18    end
19 end
```

Algorithm 1: Segregation index computation.

Intuitively, we are interested in finding itemsets $\mathbf{A}, \mathbf{B}$ denoting a minority sub-group (non-empty $\mathbf{A}$) and a non-trivial context ($\mathbf{B}$ with non-empty cover) where the segregation index $s()$ is above the α threshold.

Algorithm 1 is a solution to the problem of computing $s(\mathbf{A}, \mathbf{B})$ for a segregation index $s()$ and all itemsets $\mathbf{A}, \mathbf{B}$. It can readily solve the segregation problem by filtering itemsets whose index is lower or equal than the threshold α. We assumes that the support counting function $supp()$ is available. We implemented it by storing the subset of $\mathcal{R}$ at each unit as an array of bitmaps, one bitmap per each CA and SA item. Position i of a bitmap is set to 1 iff the ith tuple of the unit supports the item associated to the bitmap. Support counting consists then of bitmap and-operations. An alternative way of implementing $supp()$ is through the construction of an FP-tree, a compressed representation of a dataset used for frequent itemset mining [9]. The outer loop (lines 1–19) of the algorithm iterates over all CA-itemsets $\mathbf{B}$. For each of them, the total population size T is calculated at lines 3–6. The inner loop (lines 7–18) iterates over all non-empty SA-itemsets $\mathbf{A}$. First, the size M of the minority is calculated at lines 9–12. We accumulate the results of a function $f_s()$ over each unit, and then pass it to the normalization function $g_s()$. These two functions depend on the segregation index $s()$. For the information index, we observe that $H = 1 - (\sum_{i=1}^{n} t_i \cdot E_i)/(T \cdot E)$. Hence, $f_s(m_i, t_i, M, T) = t_i \cdot E_i$ and $g_s(sum, M, T) = 1 - sum/(T \cdot E)$, where E_i and E are clearly calculable from m_i, t_i and from M, T respectively.

Let $\delta = \sum_A |dom(A)|$ be the sum of the sizes of domains of context and segregation attributes, and $\pi = \prod_A |dom(A)|$ be their product. Algorithm 1 has worst-case time complexity of $O(\pi|\mathcal{R}|)$. Our bitmap-based implementation has space complexity of $\Theta(\delta|\mathcal{R}|)$. We will present actual performances on a large dataset later on. Notice that Apriori-like optimizations in the index calculations are not possible since D and H are not anti-monotonic, and I is monotonic only w.r.t $\mathbf{A}$ – i.e., $I(\mathbf{A} \cup \mathbf{A}', \mathbf{B}) \leq I(\mathbf{A}, \mathbf{B})$.

4 Segregation Discovery in Social Networks of Companies

We will challenge the framework for segregation discovery in a complex scenario with a real and large dataset. We are interested in studying segregation of minority groups (youngsters, seniors, females) in the boards of companies. The social segregation question we intend to study is: *which minority groups are segregated in the boards of companies and for which type of companies?* A possible answer may lead to the discovery that, e.g., for IT companies, females in a certain age-range appear frequently together in boards and rarely with members of the majority group (men or individuals in other age-ranges). In the following, we first introduce the notion of social network of companies, then report some basic facts on the running case study of the network of Italian companies, and finally challenge the segregation discovery framework on such a case study.

4.1 Social Networks of Companies

The *board of directors* (BoD) is a body of elected or appointed members who jointly oversee the activities of the company. The *presence* of a director is the number of BoDs the director belongs to. If presence is two or higher, the director is called a *bridge director*. As an example, the board of a controlled company typically includes directors from the board of the controlling company. Other reasons for multiple presence include partnership consolidation, collusion, cooptation, monitoring, political influence, friendship, kinship, etc. The presence of a same director in the boards of two companies (*interlocking directorate*) can then be considered a signal of business, personal, or other forms of relationship and information exchange between the two companies [14]. Under this "social tie" assumption, we model a social network of companies by linking those companies that share at least one director [3].

Let $\mathcal{N} = \{1, \ldots, N\}$ be a set of company IDs, and for $i \in \mathcal{N}$, let $BoD(i) \subseteq \mathcal{D}$ be the board of directors of company i, where $\mathcal{D} = \{1, \ldots, D\}$ is the set of directors IDs. A *social network of companies* is a weighted undirected graph $\mathcal{G} = \langle \mathcal{N}, \mathcal{E} \rangle$ where a weighted edge (i, j, w) is in $\mathcal{E} \subseteq \mathcal{N} \times \mathcal{N} \times \mathbb{R}$ iff $w = |BoD(i) \cap BoD(j)| > 0$, i.e., if companies i and j share at least one director. Intuitively, w is a measure of the strength of ties between the boards of directors of i and j. We write $e_{ij} = 1$ if $(i, j, w) \in \mathcal{E}$, and $e_{ij} = 0$ otherwise. We denote by L the number of edges, i.e., $L = |\mathcal{E}|$, and by k_i the degree of node i, i.e., $k_i = \sum_{j=1}^{N} e_{ij}$. A node is called *isolated* if its degree is 0. A connected component (CC) is a maximally connected subgraph of $\mathcal{G}$.

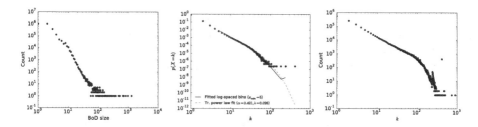

Fig. 2. Distrib.: BoD size (left), director presence (center), node degree (right).

4.2   The Social Network of Italian Companies

The Italian Business Register records information on all Italian companies and directors. We had a unique access to a complete 2012 snapshot of the registry. A company can be structured as a partnership, a corporation, or other national forms. For corporations, the BoD is elected by shareholders, while for a partnership the BoD includes all partners.

There is a total of $N \simeq 2.2 \cdot 10^6$ registered companies, and $D \simeq 3.7 \cdot 10^6$ directors. The network has $L \simeq 5.9 \times 10^6$ edges. Around $0.7 \cdot 10^6$ nodes are isolated (i.e., degree is 0). This amounts at 35.2 % of the total number of nodes, and it is quite representative of the Italian scenario, where tiny/family businesses are widespread. Figure 2 reports the distributions of BoD size, director presence, and node degree. Distributions are heavily tailed (notice the log-log plot), but only for director presence there is a good fit by a truncated powerlaw (we used the software from [2]). A few directors appear in hundreds of boards (one of them appears in as many as 404 boards). We investigated the reasons of such impressively high numbers, and found two explanations. First, when a company is winding-up because of bankruptcy, an official receiver is appointed by the court as an interim receiver and manager of the company. Such directors are independent experts appointed in many boards and for a possibly long period. Second, there are groups of companies with a pyramidal structure [1] sharing the same directors. An example is the outlier in Fig. 2 (right), representing a clique of 250 companies having a same person as the unique director in their boards. In order to reduce the impact of the two special cases above on the density of the social network of companies, we removed from the set of directors the 0.01 % with the highest presence. The age distribution of directors is shown in Fig. 3 (left). The plot sadly highlights the glass-ceiling reality for women, who suffer from a under-proportional representativeness in top-level job positions.

4.3   Segregation Discovery

We aim at exploiting the segregation discovery framework and algorithm of Sect. 3 to the case study of the social network of Italian companies. The dataset under analysis will contain one tuple for each director. Available segregation attributes include: gender, age (discretized into 5 equal-frequency bins). Context attributes include the company sector (the top level of a hierarchical classification

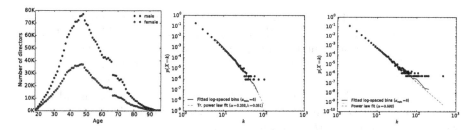

Fig. 3. Left: age distribution. Center: distribution of size of CCs before (center, without the giant component) and after (right) splitting the giant component.

used by the Italian official statistics institute), with 21 possible values, and the region of residence of the director (north-east, north-west, center, south, islands, abroad). In this section, we discuss three issues that challenge the framework of Sect. 3, and devise solutions for overcoming them.

Segregation index definitions assume a partitioning of individuals into units of social organization (schools, neighborhoods, communities). *The first challenge* in the context of social networks of companies is then to define how such units are defined. Intuitively, a unit is a set of companies within which directors can get in contact, either directly (because they belong to a same BoD) or indirectly (e.g., through a bridge director connecting two BoDs).

Our approach is to consider a structural decomposition of the social network graph into groups of companies, i.e., sub-graphs, each one representing a unit. A natural candidate is to consider the decomposition based on connected components (CCs). The distribution of the size of CCs, shown in Fig. 3 (center), is fitted by a truncated powerlaw. In addition to the isolated nodes, there are $251 \cdot 10^3$ other CCs with size in the range [2–99], and one giant component consisting of $642 \cdot 10^3$ nodes (not shown in the figure). The number of directors in the giant component amounts at 20 % of the total. This means that the giant component weights 20 % in the calculation of dissimilarity and information gain segregation indexes (for the isolation index, the weight depends also on the size of minority m_i). This may prevent segregation from being discovered, because the giant component may hide segregated finer-grained units within it. We claim that the giant component need to be further split. Observe that our assumption that bridge directors represent signals of relationships between two companies does not account for the strength of such signals. We exploit this intuition to split the giant component into components by removing edges in it that represent "weaker ties". Recall that the weight of an edge between nodes i and j is $w = |BoD(i) \cap BoD(j)|$, i.e., the number of shared directors. We remove edges from the giant component whose weight is lower or equal than a threshold. The selected threshold ($w \leq 3$) is the lowest that leads to no giant component. The resulting distribution of CCs, shown in Fig. 3 (right), is fitted by a powerlaw with exponent close the original distribution without the giant component. The total number of CCs is now $\simeq 1.6 \cdot 10^6$.

The *second challenge* in segregation discovery originates by the splitting of the giant component. In fact, a side effect of *any* splitting is that in the resulting network a bridge director may appear in two or more units. This is not accounted for in the framework of Sect. 3, which assumes that an individual belongs to only one unit. We will consider multiple instances of bridge directors in different units as distinct individuals. With reference to the notation of Sect. 2.2, we revise the definitions of the size of population T and minority group M by setting $T = \sum_i^n t_i$ and $M = \sum_i^n m_i$, i.e., by counting every *occurrence* of an individual in any unit, not every individual. Algorithm 1 remains unchanged because it already computes T and M as above.

The *third challenge* is motivated by the need of including characteristics of companies among the context attributes, so that segregation, e.g., in the subnetwork of IT companies, can be discovered. However, bridge directors may appear in BoDs of companies with different characteristics. How do we model this in our framework? We use multi-valued attributes, by admitting that, for an attribute A and a tuple σ, $\sigma[A] \subseteq dom(A)$ (instead of simply, $\sigma[A] \in dom(A)$). As an example, the industry sector of a director is defined as the set of industry sectors of companies where the director appears, e.g., $\sigma[\texttt{sector}] = \{\texttt{IT}, \texttt{Banks}\}$. Our framework can be extended to admit multi-valued tuples by simply extending the notion of support as follows: a tuple σ *supports* $\mathbf{X}$ if for every $A = v$ in $\mathbf{X}$, we have $v \in \sigma[A]$ if A is multi-valued, and $\sigma[A] = v$ otherwise. On the implementation side, this extension does not require drastic changes. The support counting method has to be initialized with a set of transaction items $A = v_1, \ldots, A = v_k$ for $\{v_1, \ldots, v_k\} = \sigma[A]$ instead of simply with $A = v$ for $v = \sigma[A]$. In our bitmap based implementation, for a multi-valued attribute A, a tuple σ will lead to set to 1 all the bitmaps of the values in $\sigma[A]$.

4.4   Segregation Discovery: Findings

The dataset processed as described in the previous section consists of $4.6 \cdot 10^6$ tuples, 2 context attributes (residence, sector), 2 segregation attributes (age, sex), and the $\texttt{unit}$ attribute. We have applied Algorithm 1 on the dataset to calculate the D, H, and I segregation indexes. The total running time of the algorithm was of 110 seconds, on a commodity PC with Intel Core i5-2410@2.30GHz with 16 Gb of RAM, Windows 7 OS, and Java 8 as programming language.

The affordable running time allows for more advanced data analysis than the one stated by the definition of segregation discovery, namely selecting/ranking itemsets $\mathbf{A}, \mathbf{B}$ whose index is above a given threshold. We are in the position of providing the segregation analyst with a data cube of indexes for exploratory analysis in the style of OLAP cubes. Here, indexes play the role of metrics, and context and segregation attributes play the role of dimensions. Also, constraints on the sizes T (resp., M) of the population (resp., minority group) can be provided to guide the analysis.

Let us present here three real cases. By setting a minimum $M \geq 10^3$, the itemset with the highest dissimilarity index:

   $\texttt{sector='agriculture'}$, $\texttt{age='<=38'}$, $\texttt{sex='F'}$ ($D = 0.916$, $H = 0.605$, $I = 0.431$)

regards the population of directors of in the agriculture sector, with women up to 38 years old as minority population. Segregation in agriculture is a well-known phenomenon. Excluding such a sector, the highest information index is for:

residence='abroad', age='>=53' ($D = 0.75$, $H = 0.675$, $I = 0.805$)

the population of directors with residence abroad, and for the minority of directors with age of 53 years or more. Finally, excluding foreign directors, the highest isolation index is for:

sector='electricity', sex='M' ($D = 0.625$, $H = 0.411$, $I = 0.907$)

directors of companies producing or supplying electric power or gas, with minority population the male directors. In this case, segregation of males means they have 90.7% of likelihood of getting in contact with other males in their board or through bridge directors.

5   Conclusions and Future Work

We have formulated the problem of segregation discovery in social networks, devised a solution that provides the data analyst with a data cube of segregation indexes for exploratory analysis, and challenged the approach on a complex scenario with a real and large dataset regarding segregation in boards of directors.

Several issues remain open for future investigation.

First, relations with research streams that appear closely linked must be explored. One related field is community discovery in attributed graphs [5], where graph clustering algorithms exploit both the structural dimension of the social graphs as well as a compositional dimension represented by features of nodes. Another related field is discrimination discovery [18], where the objective is to search for contexts with a disproportionate distribution of socially sensitive decisions (granting of a loan, admission to school, hiring, etc.) among social groups.

Second, the proposed framework need to be further validated, e.g., on whether it is able to cover more complex segregation index definitions and application scenarios, and on whether Algorithm 1 scales to a large number of attributes. The impact of different segregation indexes on the top segregative itemsets should also be evaluated, as done in [17] for discrimination indexes. The final objective will be a complete framework and working system for OLAP analysis of segregation in social networks.

Finally, we argue that segregation discovery is half way towards the more challenging objective of segregation-aware data mining and social network analysis. The objective here is the development of *segregation-aware* data analysis and data mining models that, by design, can provide a guarantee about the impact of computer-supported decisions (e.g., link predictions, group recommendation) on individuals and social groups, about the possibilities of interaction between them, and about the increase of social cohesion of society at large.

References

1. Almeida, H.V., Wolfenzon, D.: A theory of pyramidal ownership and family business groups. J. Finance **61**(6), 2637–2680 (2006)
2. Alstott, J., Bullmore, E., Plenz, D.: Powerlaw: a Python package for analysis of heavy-tailed distributions. PLoS ONE **9**(1), e85777 (2004)
3. Battiston, S., Catanzaro, M.: Statistical properties of corporate board and director networks. Euro. Phys. J. B **38**(2), 345–352 (2004)
4. Bell, W.: A probability model for the measurement of ecological segregation. Soc. Forces **32**, 357–364 (1954)
5. Bothorel, C., Cruz, J.D., Magnani, M., Micenková, B.: Clustering attributed graphs: models, measures and methods. Network Science FirstView, 1–37 (2015)
6. Das, S., Kramer, A.D.I.: Self-censorship on Facebook. In: Proceedings of the International Conference on Weblogs and Social Media (ICWSM 2013). The AAAI Press (2013)
7. Fischer, E.: Distribution of race and ethnicity in US major cities (2011) (published on line at http://www.flickr.com/photos/walkingsf under Creative Commons licence, CC BY-SA 2.0)
8. Freeman, L.C.: A set of measures of centrality based on betweenness. Sociometry **40**, 35–41 (1977)
9. Han, J., Cheng, H., Xin, D., Yan, X.: Frequent pattern mining: current status and future directions. Data Min. Knowl. Disc. **15**(1), 55–86 (2007)
10. James, D.R., Tauber, K.E.: Measures of segregation. Sociol. Methodol. **13**, 1–32 (1985)
11. Liu, H., Hussain, F., Tan, C.L., Dash, M.: Discretization: an enabling technique. Data Min. Knowl. Disc. **6**(4), 393–423 (2002)
12. Massey, D.S., Denton, N.A.: The dimensions of residential segregation. Soc. Forces **67**(2), 281–315 (1988)
13. Massey, D.S., Rothwell, J., Domina, T.: The changing bases of segregation in the United States. Ann. Am. Acad. Polit. Soc. Sci. **626**, 74–90 (2009)
14. Mizruchi, M.S.: What do interlocks do? An analysis, critique, and assessment of research on interlocking directorates. Annu. Rev. Sociol. **22**(1), 271–298 (1996)
15. Mora, R., Ruiz-Castillo, J.: Entropy-based segregation indices. Sociol. Methodol. **41**, 159–194 (2011)
16. Pariser, E.: The Filter Bubble: What the Internet is Hiding from you. Penguin, UK (2011)
17. Pedreschi, D., Ruggieri, S., Turini, F.: A study of top-k measures for discrimination discovery. In: Proceedings of ACM International Symposium on Applied Computing (SAC 2012), pp. 126–131. ACM (2012)
18. Romei, A., Ruggieri, S.: A multidisciplinary survey on discrimination analysis. Knowl. Eng. Rev. **29**(5), 582–638 (2014)
19. Schelling, T.C.: Dynamic models of segregation. J. Math. Sociol. **1**(2), 143–186 (1971)

A First-Order-Logic Based Model for Grounded Language Learning

Leonor Becerra-Bonache[1]([⊠]), Hendrik Blockeel[2,3], María Galván[1],
and François Jacquenet[1]

[1] Laboratoire Hubert Curien, Université Jean Monnet, Saint-Etienne, France
leonor.becerra@univ-st-etienne.fr
[2] Department of Computer Science, KU Leuven, Leuven, Belgium
[3] Leiden Institute of Advanced Computer Science, Leiden University,
Leiden, Netherlands

Abstract. Much is still unknown about how children learn language,
but it is clear that they perform "grounded" language learning: they learn
the grammar and vocabulary not just from examples of sentences, but
from examples of sentences in a particular context. Grounded language
learning has been the subject of much research. Most of this work focuses
on particular aspects, such as constructing semantic parsers, or on particular types of applications. In this paper, we take a broader view that
includes an aspect that has received little attention until now: learning
the meaning of phrases from phrase/context pairs in which the phrase's
meaning is not explicitly represented. We propose a simple model for this
task that uses first-order logic representations for contexts and meanings,
including a simple incremental learning algorithm. We experimentally
demonstrate that the proposed model can explain the gradual learning
of simple concepts and language structure, and that it can easily be used
for interpretation, generation, and translation of phrases.

1 Introduction

Despite the complexity of natural languages, children are able to acquire their
native language quite easily, efficiently and without any specific training. This
human ability is not yet fully understood, even though it has been studied by
researchers from many different areas: psychology, linguistics, ...

In computer science, grammatical inference (GI) deals with the learning of
grammars and languages from data. Although historically this task has been
associated with that of children acquiring their native language, most research
in GI reduces the language learning problem to syntax learning, and does not use
semantic information in this process [6]. Children, however, do have additional
information, derived from the context in which utterances are made, and they
learn not only the syntax but also the semantics of utterances. This type of
learning is often called *grounded language learning*.

Grounded language learning is a broad research area. Most of this research
focuses on particular aspects of the problem, such as semantic parsing (which

© Springer International Publishing Switzerland 2015
E. Fromont et al. (Eds.): IDA 2015, LNCS 9385, pp. 49–60, 2015.
DOI: 10.1007/978-3-319-24465-5_5

maps sentences to their semantics), or on specific types of applications. In this paper, we propose a model for grounded language learning that uses a first-order logic representation of contexts and meanings. We present a learning algorithm that analyzes utterances and the context in which they are produced to create a language model that can be used to map sentences onto meanings and vice versa. An important difference with earlier work [3,4,9,11,13] is that our learner learns from sentence/context pairs, whereas earlier work requires the meaning, or a set of candidate meanings, to be provided for each example sentence. That is, earlier work used examples of the form (x, y), with $y = f(x)$, or (x, Y) with $f(x) \in Y$, to learn the function f that maps sentences to their meaning; our work uses examples of the form (x, C) with a more complex relationship between the context description C and the meaning $f(x)$.

2   Background and Related Work

Our work is mainly inspired by Angluin and Becerra-Bonache [1,2], who present, for the first time in the field of GI, a computational model that takes into account semantics for language learning. Their main goal was to investigate the effects of semantics and meaning-preserving corrections on the language learning process. Our work mainly differs from their work in the type of methods adopted to solve the problem. Instead of using a variety of techniques such as transducers, co-occurrence graphs, decision trees, etc., we use a single model represented in first order logic. Language comprehension and generation are then achieved with a simple query to this model. The simplicity of our approach is appealing from a cognitive point of view.

Within computational linguistics, much research exists on grounded language learning. Different from GI, most of this work does not aim to learn the grammar itself or understand the learning process, but to develop systems that can deal with natural language data in a particular application. Much of it focuses on semantic parsing. Semantic parsers are often learned from a *supervised* corpus containing sentences with their meaning representation [15,20,21], but constructing such a corpus is expensive, difficult and time-consuming.

In order to avoid this limitation, researchers have investigated grounded learning from *ambiguous* training data, where each sentence is associated with a small set of candidate meanings. In seminal work on grounded language learning, Siskind [19] focused on learning word meaning, but not grammatical structure. In a series of work, Mooney and colleagues [3,4,9,11] learn to match phrases to elements of a context. Their goals are similar to ours, but an essential difference is that they only map a phrase to a single element in the context; that is, the meaning of the phrase must be a single element of the context. Chen et al. [3] acknowledge this limitation, and mention inductive logic programming (ILP) as a possible approach to learning more complex meanings, to be explored in future work. This work partially fills that gap.

Our learner is incremental, which is interesting from a cognitive point of view; apart from Angluin and Becerra-Bonache, the only other incremental learner we know of was proposed by Kwiatkowski et al. [13]. Our approach differs substantially from Kwiatkowski's in that the latter requires a parallel corpus: it can learn from ambiguous supervision (multiple candidate meanings per sentence), but for each sentence the correct meaning must still be constructed in advance and made available to the learner, whereas our approach construes meanings from scratch. Our context descriptions are motivated by how the learner perceives the world, not by what meanings might look like.

3   A Logic-Based Approach

3.1   Terminology

We assume familiarity with first-order logic and Prolog. We here briefly review the main concepts; for an extensive introduction, see [14].

First-order predicate logic allows us to make statements about objects in some universe U. A *constant* always refers to one and the same object from U. A *variable* may refer to any object. A *term* is a variable or a constant. A *predicate* refers to a relation over U^n for some $n \geq 0$; n is the *arity* of the predicate.

An *atom* is of the form $p(t_1, t_2, \ldots, t_n)$ where p is a predicate symbol and the t_i are terms. A *literal* is of the form A or $\neg A$, with A an atom. A *clause* is a set of literals. A *fact* is a clause with exactly one, positive, literal. An atom, literal or clause is *ground* if it does not contain variables. A *variable substitution* $\{X_1/t_1, X_2/t_2, \ldots, X_n/t_n\}$ is an operation that, applied to a structure, simultaneously replaces each occurrence of variable X_i in that structure by term t_i. An *instantiation* is a substitution that changes all variables into ground terms.

A ground atom $p(t_1, t_2, \ldots, t_n)$ evaluates to true if the tuple denoted by its arguments is in the relation denoted by p, and false otherwise; literal $\neg A$ evaluates to true if and only if A evaluates to false and vice versa; a clause evaluates to true if for each of its instantiations, at least one of its elements evaluates to true (so it represents a universally quantified disjunction).

We use Prolog syntax: predicates and constants start with a lowercase letter, variables with an uppercase letter, and a clause of the form $\{H, \neg B_1, \ldots, \neg B_m\}$ is written as H :- B_1, ..., B_m. The meaning of such a clause is equivalent to "if all B_i hold, then H holds" (for each instantiation of the variables). The symbol _ denotes an anonymous variable occurring in only that position.

In Prolog, clauses can be added dynamically to a knowledge base using assert, and removed using retract.

Example 1. father(joseph, hendrik) is a ground atom. When stated as a fact, it expresses that the entities referred to by the constants joseph and hendrik are in a relationship referred to as father; or, briefly: "Joseph is the father of Hendrik". The clause ancestor(adam,X) :- human(X) expresses that Adam is an ancestor of all humans ("for all X it holds that if X is human, Adam is an ancestor of X").

3.2   Representation

In our learning setting, an example is a pair (C, S) where C is a context and S is a phrase (a sentence or a part of it). A phrase is represented as a sequence of

Table 1. Constants used in context descriptions, and their interpretation.

Category	Constants	Interpretation
Color	`bl, re, gr, ye, or, pu`	blue, red, green, yellow, orange, purple
Shape	`sq, di, tr, he, st, el`	square, disc, triangle, hexagon, star, ellipse
Size	`sm, me, bg`	small, medium-sized, big
Position	`ab, be, lo, ro`	above, below, left of, right of

words, a context as a set of ground facts. Our model assumes that everything a phrase refers to is in the context, but not everything in the context is necessarily referred to in the phrase.

In our examples and experiments, we use a simplified world model with colorful figures, inspired by Feldman et al. [7]. In context descriptions, we use predicates of which it is reasonable to assume that a child, observing the world, has some notion. For instance, we assume that a child recognizes that being green and being red are two properties that describe the same aspect of the visual appearance of an object, and that being square or being round are a different aspect of that appearance; in other words, it recognizes the concepts "color" and "shape", even if it has no word for these (nor for their possible values). In line with this assumption, we use the following predicates: $object(x)$ (x is an object), $color(x,y)$, $shape(x,y)$, $size(x,y)$ (the color/shape/size of x is y), $relpos(x,r,y)$ (the position of x relative to y is r). Constants used for specific colors, shapes and sizes are shown in Table 1. Note that neither constants nor predicates are hard-coded in our model; if a new example contains constants or predicates not seen before, our learner can handle it without any change.

Example 2. A context in which a big red square is to the left of a small green triangle is represented as {object(o1), shape(o1, sq), color(o1, re), size(o1, bg), object(o2), shape(o2, tr), color(o2, gr), size(o2, sm), relpos(o1, lo, o2)}.

3.3   Learning the Meaning of Specific n-grams

The "meaning" of a sentence, phrase or word is difficult to define [5]. In this work, we use a pragmatic definition: the meaning of an n-gram (a sequence of n words) is "whatever is in common among all contexts where the n-gram can be used".[1] We formalize this as follows.

A *pattern* is an existentially quantified set of atoms (one can think of it as a Prolog query). Note that a context description can be seen as a variable-free pattern. A pattern Q *subsumes* another pattern Q' if there is a variable substitution that turns it into a subset of Q'. Two patterns are *equivalent* if they subsume each other. Given a set of contexts, their *most specific common pattern* is a pattern Q that subsumes all of them and for which no other pattern exists

---

[1] This is in line with the work by Mooney et al. and with Wittgenstein's views on the meaning of language.

that subsumes all of them and is subsumed by Q. The *meaning* of an n-gram is the most specific common pattern of all the contexts where it can be used.

The most specific common pattern can be computed using Plotkin's lgg ("least general generalization") operator [17], which is intensively used in inductive logic programming [16].

Example 3. The lgg of the following pair of contexts:

{ object(o1), color(o1, re), shape(o1, sq) }
{ object(o2), color(o2, gr), shape(o2, tr), object(o3), color(o3,re), shape(o3,tr) }

is {object(X), color(X, re), shape(X,Y)}. It captures everything that is in common among these two contexts, which is: there is an object that is red and that has some shape.

Example 4. The most specific common pattern in

{ obj(o1), clr(o1,re), shp(o1,sq), obj(o2), clr(o2,gr), shp(o2,tr), relpos(o1,lo,o2) }
{ obj(o3), clr(o3,gr), shp(o3,tr), obj(o4), clr(o4,re), shp(o4,tr), relpos(o3,lo,o4) }

is

{ obj(B), clr(B,re), shp(B,D),   obj(E), clr(E,gr), shp(E,tr),
obj(A), clr(A,C), shp(A,D),   relpos(A,lo,F),   obj(F), clr(F,G), shp(F,tr) }.

It captures that, in both contexts, there is a red object (B), a green triangle (E), and an object (A) to the left of a triangle (F). It may seem strange that this clause refers to four objects, when each context had only two, but note that different variables do not have to refer to different objects. In the first clause, $A = B$ and $E = F$, but in the second clause $A = E$ and $B = F$. Identifying all commonalities between the two contexts cannot be done with fewer than four object references, because they unify differently in both contexts.

Our algorithm incrementally learns the meaning of specific n-grams. Whenever it sees a new example with context C and phrase S, it iterates over all the n-grams in S, and for each n-gram, it replaces the currently stored meaning of the n-gram by the lgg of that meaning and the new context. Pseudocode is shown in Algorithm 1 (main algorithm and UPDATE procedure). For reasons made clear below, the algorithm also remembers the category of each constant (e.g., a constant that occurs as the second argument of color is a color), UPDATE also keeps track of how long ago the meaning of an n-gram was last changed (stability counter), and UPDATE may assert or retract mrf ("may refer to") facts.

3.4   Generalizing n-grams

There is often a relationship between the meaning of an n-gram and that of k-grams with $k < n$ it is composed of. For instance, compare:

"red triangle": there is an object that is both triangular and red
"red": there is an object that is red
"triangle": there is an object that is triangular

This particular relationship is common to all bigrams of the form "color shape". A learner that recognizes the concepts "color" and "shape" may detect this. We try to give our learner this capacity in the following manner.

When the meaning of a 1-gram w seems to have converged (that is, it has not changed for the last s updates, with s a parameter called the *stability threshold*) to a context that contains only one constant c, the learner assumes that the 1-gram refers to that constant. The fact mrf(w, c) is then asserted. (Should w's meaning change anyway later on, it is retracted again, since this implies it was asserted prematurely.)

The learner tries to generalize n-grams for $n > 1$ using this mrf mapping by constructing a more general rule, as follows (see also GENERALIZE in Algorithm 1). A word w in the n-gram is turned into a variable X_w if a corresponding mrf(w,c) is available; in the n-gram's meaning, each occurrence of c is then turned into a variable X_c, and the condition mrf(X_w, X_c) is added to the body of the rule. The category of c is also added to the body as a condition; this guarantees "cautious" generalization: everything we know about the word is added so that a maximally specific rule is obtained.

For instance, after mrf(red,re) and mrf(triangle, tr) have been learned, the fact

meaning(ngram(2, [red, triangle]), [object(O), color(O, re), shape(O,tr), size(O,_)])

can be generalized into the rule

meaning(ngram(2, [X,Y]) , [object(O), color(O, C), shape(O,S), size(O,_)]) :-
        mrf(X,C), mrf(Y,S), category(C,color,2), category(S,shape,2).

This rule essentially generalizes the meaning of the 2-gram "red triangle" into an equivalent meaning for any 2-gram of the type "color shape".

Any n-gram can be generalized in this manner, but the resulting rule is not necessarily correct. To evaluate the rule, we define two criteria: *evidence* (how much evidence is there that the rule is correct?) and *coverage* (how many separate facts could be replaced if we introduced this rule in the knowledge base?).

Let C be the set of all previously observed n-grams for which a meaning is predicted by rule R. Let $S \subseteq C$ contain all n-grams whose (currently stored) meaning is *subsumed* by the meaning predicted by R, and $E \subseteq S \subseteq C$ all n-grams whose meaning is *equivalent* to the one predicted by R. Every n-gram in E is predicted correctly by R. Every n-gram in $S - E$ is *compatible* with R, in the sense that its meaning may still converge to the predicted meaning after seeing more examples. Any n-gram in $C - S$ contradicts the rule: further updates cannot lead to a meaning equivalent to the prediction. We call a rule *valid* if $S = C$, and we call $|C|$ the *coverage* of the rule.

The fact that a rule is valid does not provide strong evidence for its correctness. A rule that predicts an empty pattern is automatically valid, but does not capture any meaning. The n-grams in E, however, do provide evidence: the larger E is, the less likely it is that the rule accidentally predicts all the meanings of all these n-grams correctly. $|E|$ is called the *evidence* for the rule.

The utility of the rule is related to $|C|$, but our confidence in its correctness is related to $|E|$. In practice, it seems reasonable to only consider valid rules whose

---

Algorithm 1. The learning algorithm

Input: stability threshold s, evidence threshold e, stream of context/phrase examples $\mathcal{D}$
Output: predicate definition for meaning

whenever a new example $(C, S) \in \mathcal{D}$ is presented:
    for each constant c occurring as the i'th argument of a predicate p in C:
        assert category(c,p,i) (if not asserted yet)
    for each n-gram G in S, with n=1, 2, ...
        UPDATE(C, G)
        GENERALIZE(G)

UPDATE(context C, n-gram G):
    if meaning(G, M) **then**
        if lgg$(M,C) = M$ **then**
            increase stability(G) by 1
            if G is a 1-gram, stability(G)=s, and M contains one constant c
            then assert mrf(G,c); CLEANUP
        else
            retract meaning(G, M); assert meaning$(G, \text{lgg}(M, C))$; stability(G)=0
            retract mrf$(G, \_)$;
    else assert meaning(G, C); stability(G)=0

GENERALIZE(n-gram G) :
    call meaning(G,M)
    $Ref = \{(w,c) | w \in G \wedge \text{mrf}(w,c)\}$
    $Cat = \{(c,x,i) | (\_,c) \in Ref \wedge \text{category}(c,x,i)\}$
    $R = \text{meaning(G, M)} :\!\!- \bigwedge_{(w,c)\in Ref} \text{mrf}(w,c), \bigwedge_{(c,x,i)\in Cat} \text{category}(c,x,i)$
    introduce for each w and c in Ref a different variable X_w, X_c
    replace in R each w and c by the corresponding X_w or X_c
    if R is valid and has evidence $\geq e$ **then** assert R; CLEANUP

CLEANUP : retract each meaning(G,M) fact covered by a rule R

$|E|$ is above some threshold, which is what our current algorithm does. Note that when R gets introduced, it replaces not only the previously stored meanings of the n-grams in E, but also those in $S - E$. For the latter, the currently stored meaning gets replaced by what the rule predicts will be their converged meaning; in other words, the rule boosts their convergence.

4 Experiments

To evaluate our model and learning algorithm, we made an example generator that generates random contexts and for each context a random phrase that describes (part of) it in English, Dutch or Spanish. Each context consists of one or two objects with a shape, color, size, and relative position. The phrases

Table 2. Some examples of contexts and relevant phrases.

`object(11),shape(11,tr),color(11,re),size(11,me),`	a red triangle to the
`object(12),shape(12,he),color(12,pu),size(12,bg),`	left of the big hexagon
`rel_pos(11,lo,12)`	
`object(52), shape(52,he), color(52,ye), size(52,sm)`	the hexagon

are generated using a simple probabilistic grammar and are surrounded by the markers $start and $stop, so that n-grams can refer to the beginning and ending of a phrase. For phrases referring to two objects, the format is the same as that used by Angluin and Becerra-Bonache [2]. Table 2 shows a few representative examples. We have generated three corpora (one for each language) of 1000 examples each. The two parameters of the learner, stability threshold and evidence threshold, were both set to 5.

4.1 Learning Meanings

Running the learning algorithm on the corpora led to the following observations about the learning process.

It is known from ILP that the size of an lgg can grow exponentially in the number of instances generalized (see, e.g., [10]). In our experiments, this behavior was indeed observed. Eventually, meanings always converge to a relatively simple pattern, but intermediate patterns can be very complex due to accidental similarities among contexts. As subsumption testing is exponential in the length of clauses, this slows down the system unacceptably. We solved this problem by simply not updating the meaning of an n-gram if the new meaning is too complex (specifically, lggs containing over 15 literals were not stored). Such behavior is in fact cognitively plausible: children are unlikely to discover such complex commonalities. Better ways of controlling the complexity of lggs exist, but for our experiments, this simple method worked well.

For English, a learning curve was observed with (among other) the following "milestones" (the number indicates the number of examples seen at this point):

79 the "*color shape*" generalized bigram is learned. The mrf map at this point contains 4 colors and 5 shapes, hence the rule predicts the meaning of 20 combinations. 5 predictions are equivalent to the stored meaning, 14 generalize it (boosting convergence), 1 is for a bigram not seen before.

85 mrf(to,bg) is retracted. Apparently, the system had earlier concluded that "to" means bg (big), because that was the only constant common in all its contexts and it remained present in the next 5 contexts. When finally a context for "to" without a big object is seen, bg disappears from the meaning; it is then clear that mrf(to,bg) was added prematurely, and it is retracted.

86 mrf(disc,di) is added. The meanings of "red disc" and "blue disc" are retracted, as they are now subsumed by the color-shape rule.

89 the "*size shape*" generalized bigram is learned.

102 mrf(yellow,ye) is added. All colors and shapes have now been learned.

165 the "*size color*" generalized bigram is learned.

188 "$start the *color shape* $stop" is learned (this pattern forms a full phrase)

416 the "*size color shape*" generalized trigram is learned.

664 "*shape* to the *relpos* of" is learned. This is an overgeneralization: it correctly covers the words "left" and "right", but incorrectly also "above", "below" and "under", all of which are associated with relative positions.

The learning curves for Dutch and Spanish are similar. However, due to the inflection of adjectives in these languages (and the fact that our representation does not express morphological structure), some forms occur less frequently and get generalized later than in English. Further, more rules overgeneralize because they do not impose, for instance, gender correspondence. This leads to the important observation that our model categorizes in the physical world, but not in the language world (it distinguishes color and shape as difference kinds of properties, but does not categorize words for shapes into masculine and feminine because these are syntactic, not physical, properties).

Retraction of an mrf fact happened only twice: the word "to" in English and "van" in Dutch. There are also incorrect mrf facts that are not retracted. Most notably, the definite article "het" in Dutch is believed to refer to a square. The reason is that among 6 shapes, only the Dutch word for square, "vierkant", uses this article. Thus, "het" only occurs when a square is present, and its meaning is indistinguishable to that of "vierkant". This mistake has dire consequences: as "het" is assumed to refer to a shape, "het oranje vierkant" is seen as an example of the pattern *shape color shape*, and generalized. Because there are 6 examples of such trigrams (for 6 different colors), and all have the same meaning as the one predicted by the rule, the system finds the evidence sufficient for introducing the generalized rule.

To some extent, this problem is an artifact of the fact that we have only one shape that uses that article: it would disappear if we had at least two. But it still points to at least two opportunities for improving our learning model. First, the fact that "het" occurs in positions where other shapes do not occur should be an indication that it is not a shape at all. Again, this would require analyzing the sentence structure when categorizing words, which our algorithm currently does not do. Second, our method for evaluating evidence (just counting the number of n-grams in E) assumes that that evidence is statistically independent. This is not the case here: all evidence for the incorrect pattern has "het" for the first word, not just any shape. Our evidence criterion needs to be refined.

4.2 Using the Model

Until now, we have mostly focused on the learning process, but the proposed model representation also makes a variety of inferences very easy to perform. We illustrate a few of these. All inferences are made using a model learned from the full corpus, and performed on the context {object(90), shape(90,tr), color(90,re),

size(90,me), object(91), shape(91,he), color(91,pu), size(91,bg), rel_pos(90,lo,91)},
which states that a medium-sized red triangle is to the left of a big purple
hexagon.

Generating Relevant *n*-grams and Phrases. The model can generate
n-grams that are relevant in some context, by simply checking which *n*-grams
have a meaning that matches part of the context. By chaining such *n*-grams,
we can produce complete phrases that in principle could be grammatically or
semantically incorrect, but in practice work well for the simple contexts here
provided. Chaining English 3-grams (with 2 words of overlap) gives 24 phrases
for our running context, all of which are correct; they include: "the big hexagon";
"a big purple hexagon"; "the red triangle to the left of the big hexagon"; etc.

For the same context, generated Spanish phrases include "el hexagono pur-
pura y grande", "un triangulo rojo", but also the incorrect "un triangulo roja".
Dutch phrases produced for this context are all correct; they include, e.g., "de
grote driehoek naast een grote paarse zeshoek".[2]

Identifying Objects. We can easily ask which part of a given context, if any,
matches the meaning of a given *n*-gram. For the *n*-gram "purple hexagon",
the system returns {object(91),shape(91,he),color(91,pu),size(91,bg)}, correctly
identifying the big purple hexagon as an object matching the description.

Producing Denoting Phrases. A phrase is denoting if it uniquely identifies
one object in a context. The ability to denote objects is important because it
is one of the main purposes of using language. Our system can easily produce
denoting phrases for some context by generating a phrase, finding what it identifies, and returning it if it identifies exactly one object. In the running context,
the following denoting phrases (among others) are returned: "a big hexagon",
"the hexagon", "a big purple hexagon", "the red triangle", ...

Note that our approach could be useful in the Referring Expression Generation domain, which concerns with how to produce a description that identifies an
specific entity in a given context [12]. It could also have interesting implications
for the field of Computer Vision, for example, by providing semantic connections
between different objects detected in a concrete context.

Translating Sentences. Meaningful *n*-grams can be translated simply by ask-
ing for an *n*-gram in another language with an equivalent meaning. E.g.:

?- meaning(ngram(4, [the, big, blue, triangle]), _, C1), meaning(L, spanish, C2),
equiv(C1,C2).

(where equiv tests equivalence) gives as possible answers for *L* the 5-gram
ngram(5, [el,triangulo,azul,y,grande]), but also versions with un, la, una instead
of el. Translations are only correct insofar the system understands the phrases
(it has not learned the meaning of articles, and therefore cannot distinguish the

---

[2] With a model learned from 2000 examples, the incorrect phrase "driehoek rode
driehoek" was produced; this is a consequence of the belief that "het" is a shape,
and the construction of a rule for *shape color shape* as a consequence.

meanings of "the red triangle" and "a red triangle"), and as said before the system currently does not learn gender correspondence.

It is worth noting that most work in Machine Translation focuses on syntactic-based approaches, but their limitations to preserve meaning structures across languages have motivated research on semantic-based machine translation (e.g., [8,18]). Our approach mainly differs from these semantic approaches in that we do not use a parallel corpus consisting of sentence/meaning pairs. Moreover, it can be viewed as a first step towards systems that are able to use the context to translate sentences from one language to another, while preserving the meaning.

5   Conclusions and Future Work

We have presented a simple model for grounded language learning that uses a first-order logic representation of contexts and meanings. Our system learns to understand and generate simple natural language utterances, from pairs consisting of utterances and the context in which these utterances are produced. In contrast to other approaches, a context is a description of what the learner can see in the world, and not a set of candidates meanings for that utterance; our system constructs all candidate meanings itself. It does not require any prior language-specific knowledge and learns incrementally. Experiments with three different languages show that our system learns a language model that can easily be used to understand, generate and translate utterances.

This paper describes a simple proof of concept. Opportunities for further work include: learning from more complex contexts (which may include actions), learning more complex languages, categorizing also n-grams (as opposed to only context elements), controlling the lgg complexity in a more principled manner, experimenting with other inductive inference methods known from inductive logic programming, robust learning in noisy environments (probabilistic logics may be useful for this), and much more.

It is worth noting that the development of computational approaches such as this one can help obtain insight into how children build a model of language and make connections between utterances and contexts. It can also help understand how language developed from its origins, since the observation of the world and the intention to communicate were crucial for the development of language.

Acknowledgements. Part of this work was done while HB was visiting Laboratoire Hubert Curien.

References

1. Angluin, D., Becerra-Bonache, L.: A model of semantics and corrections in language learning. Technical report YALE/DCS/TR1425, Yale University (2010)
2. Angluin, D., Becerra-Bonache, L.: Effects of meaning-preserving corrections on language learning. In: CoNLL, pp. 97–105 (2011)

3. Chen, D.L., Kim, J., Mooney, R.J.: Training a multilingual sportscaster: Using perceptual context to learn language. JAIR **37**, 397–435 (2010)
4. Chen, D.L., Mooney, R.J.: Learning to sportscast: a test of grounded language acquisition. In: ICML, pp. 128–135 (2008)
5. Harnad, S.: Symbol grounding problem. Scholarpedia **2**(7), 2373 (2007)
6. de la Higuera, C.: Grammatical Inference, Learning Automata and Grammars. Cambridge University Press, New York (2010)
7. Feldman, J., Lakoff, G., Stolcke, A., Weber, S.: Miniature language acquisition: A touchstone for cognitive science. In: CogSci, pp. 686–693 (1994)
8. Jones, B., Andreas, J., Bauer, D., Hermann, K.M., Knight, K.: Semantics-based machine translation with hyperedge replacement grammars. In: COLING 2012, pp. 1359–1376 (2012)
9. Kate, R.J., Mooney, R.J.: Learning language semantics from ambiguous supervision. In: AAAI, pp. 895–900 (2007)
10. Kietz, J.U.: A comparative study of structural most specific generalizations used in machine learning. In: Third International Workshop on Inductive Logic Programming, pp. 149–164 (1993)
11. Kim, J., Mooney, R.J.: Generative alignment and semantic parsing for learning from ambiguous supervision. In: COLING, pp. 543–551 (2010)
12. Krahmer, E., van Deemter, K.: Computational generation of referring expressions: A survey. Comput. Linguist. **38**(1), 173–218 (2012)
13. Kwiatkowski, T., Goldwater, S., Zettlemoyer, L.S., Steedman, M.: A probabilistic model of syntactic and semantic acquisition from child-directed utterances and their meanings. In: EACL, pp. 234–244 (2012)
14. Lloyd, J.W.: Foundations of Logic Programming, 2nd edn. Springer, Berlin (1987)
15. Lu, W., Ng, H.T., Lee, W.S., Zettlemoyer, L.S.: A generative model for parsing natural language to meaning representations. In: EMNLP, pp. 783–792 (2008)
16. Muggleton, S., Raedt, L.D.: Inductive logic programming: Theory and methods. J. Logic Program. **19**(20), 629–679 (1994)
17. Plotkin, G.D.: A note on inductive generalization. In: Melter, B., Michie, D. (eds.) Machine Intelligence 5, pp. 153–163. Edinburgh University Press, Edinburgh (1970)
18. Pust, M., Hermjakob, U., Knight, K., Marcu, D., May, J.: Using syntax-based machine translation to parse english into abstract meaning representation, CoRR abs/1504.06665 (2015)
19. Siskind, J.: A computational study of cross-situational techniques for learning word-to-meaning mappings. Cognition **61**, 39–61 (1996)
20. Wong, Y.W., Mooney, R.J.: Learning synchronous grammars for semantic parsing with lambda calculus. In: ACL, pp. 960–967 (2007)
21. Zettlemoyer, L.S., Collins, M.: Learning context-dependent mappings from sentences to logical form. In: ACL, pp. 976–984 (2009)

A Parallel Distributed Processing Algorithm for Image Feature Extraction

Alexander Belousov and Joel Ratsaby[(✉)]

Electrical and Electronics Engineering Department, Ariel University,
Ariel, Israel
ratsaby@ariel.ac.il
http://www.ariel.ac.il/sites/ratsaby/

Abstract. We present a new parallel algorithm for image feature extraction. which uses a distance function based on the LZ-complexity of the string representation of the two images. An input image is represented by a feature vector whose components are the distance values between its parts (sub-images) and a set of prototypes. The algorithm is highly scalable and computes these values in parallel. It is implemented on a massively parallel graphics processing unit (GPU) with several thousands of cores which yields a three order of magnitude reduction in time for processing the images. Given a corpus of input images the algorithm produces labeled cases that can be used by any supervised or unsupervised learning algorithm to learn image classification or image clustering. A main advantage is the lack of need for any image processing or image analysis; the user only once defines image-features through a simple basic process of choosing a few small images that serve as prototypes. Results for several image classification problems are presented.

1 Introduction

Image classification research aims at finding representations of images that can be automatically used to categorize images into a finite set of classes. Typically, algorithms that classify images require some form of pre-processing of an image prior to classification. This process may involve extracting relevant features and segmenting images into sub-components based on some prior knowledge about their context [1,2]. In [3] we introduced a new distance function, called Universal Image Distance (UID), for measuring the distance between two images. The UID first transforms each of the two images into a string of characters from a finite alphabet and then uses the string distance of [4] to give the distance value between the images. According to [4] the distance between two strings x and y is a normalized difference between the complexity of the concatenation xy of the strings and the minimal complexity of each of x and y. By complexity of a string x we mean the Lempel-Ziv complexity [5]. In [6] we presented a serial algorithm to convert images into feature vectors where the ith dimension is a feature that measures the UID distance between the image and the ith feature category. One of the advantages of the UID is that it can compare the distance between two

ⓒ Springer International Publishing Switzerland 2015
E. Fromont et al. (Eds.): IDA 2015, LNCS 9385, pp. 61–71, 2015.
DOI: 10.1007/978-3-319-24465-5_6

images of different sizes and thus the prototypes which are representative of the different feature categories may be relatively small. For instance, a prototype of *airplane* category can be a small image of an airplane over a simple background such as blue sky.

In this paper we introduce a parallel distributed algorithm which is based on the serial algorithm of [6]. Compared to [6] the current version of the algorithm offers a very large acceleration in processing speed which allows us to test the algorithm on more challenging image classification tasks. On a standard graphics processing unit (GPU) it improves the execution speeds relative to [6] by more than three orders of magnitude. The algorithm converts an input image into a labeled case and doing this for the corpus of images, each labeled by its class, yields a data set that can be used to train any 'off-the-shelf' supervised or unsupervised learning algorithm. After describing our method in details we report on the speed and accuracy that are achieved by this method.

It is noteworthy that our process for converting an image into a finite dimensional feature vector is very straightforward and does not involve any domain knowledge or image analysis expertise. Compared to other image classification algorithms that extract features based on sophisticated mathematical analysis, for instance, analyzing the texture, or checking for special properties of an image, our approach is very basic and universal. It is based on the complexity of the 'raw' string-representation of an image. Our approach is to extract features automatically just by computing distances from a set of prototypes images that are selected once at the first stage.

The algorithm that we present here is designed with the main aim of *scalable* distributed computations. Building on recent ideas [7], we designed it to take advantage of relatively cheap and massively-parallel processors that are ubiquitous in today's technology. Our method extracts image features that are unbiased in the sense that they do not employ any heuristics in contrast to other common image-processing techniques [1,2]. The features that we extract are based on information implicit in the image and obtained via a complexity-based UID distance which is an information-theoretic measure.

2   Distance

The UID distance function [3] is based on the LZ- complexity of a string. The definition of this complexity follows [4,5]: let S, Q and R be strings of characters that are defined over the alphabet $\mathcal{A}$. Denote by $l(S)$ the length of S, and $S(i)$ denotes the ith element of S. We denote by $S(i,j)$ the substring of S which consists of characters of S between position i and j (inclusive). An extension $R = SQ$ of S is reproducible from S (denoted as $S \rightarrow S$) if there exists an integer $p \leq l(S)$ such that $Q(k) = R(p+k-1)$ for $k = 1, \ldots, l(Q)$. For example, $aacgt \rightarrow aacgtcgtcg$ with $p = 3$ and $aacgt \rightarrow aacgtac$ with $p = 2$. R is obtained from S (the seed) by first copying all of S and then copying in a sequential manner $l(Q)$ elements starting at the pth location of S in order to obtain the Q part of R.

A string S is *producible* from its prefix $S(1, j)$ (denoted $S(1, j) \Rightarrow S$), if $S(1, j) \rightarrow S(1, l(S) - 1)$. For example, $aacgt \Rightarrow aacgtac$ and $aacgt \Rightarrow aacgtacc$ both with pointers $p = 2$. The production adds an extra 'different' character at the end of the copying process which is not permitted in a reproduction.

Any string S can be built using a *production process* where at its ith step we have the production $S(1, h_{i-1}) \Rightarrow S(1, h_i)$ where h_i is the location of a character at the ith step. (Note that $S(1, 0) \Rightarrow S(1, 1)$). An m-step production process of S results in parsing of S in which $H(S) = S(1, h_1) \cdot S(h_1 + 1, h_2) \cdots S(h_{m-1} + 1, h_m)$ is called the *history* of S and $H_i(S) = S(h_{i-1} + 1, h_i)$ is called the ith component of $H(S)$. For example for $S = aacgtacc$ we have $H(S) = a \cdot ac \cdot g \cdot t \cdot acc$ as the history of S. If $S(1, h_i)$ is not reproducible from $S(1, h_{i-1})$ then the component $H_i(S)$ is called *exhaustive* meaning that the copying process cannot be continued and the component should be halted with a single character *innovation*. A history is called exhaustive if each of its components is exhaustive. Every string S has a unique exhaustive history [5]. Let us denote by $c_H(S)$ the number of components in a history of S. The LZ complexity of S is $c(S) = \min \{c_H(S)\}$ where the minimum is over all histories of S. It can be shown that $c(S) = c_E(S)$ where $c_E(S)$ is the number of components in the exhaustive history of S.

A distance for strings based on the LZ-complexity was introduced in [4] and is defined as follows: given two strings X and Y of any finite alphabet, denote by XY their concatenation then define

$$d(X, Y) := \max \{c(XY) - c(X), c(YX) - c(Y)\}$$

(see several normalized versions of d in [4]). In [3,6] we have found that the following normalized distance

$$\mathsf{d}(X, Y) := \frac{c(XY) - \min \{c(X), c(Y)\}}{\max \{c(X), c(Y)\}} \tag{1}$$

is useful for image classification.

In [7] we introduced a parallel distributed processing algorithm (LZMP) for computing the complexity $c(X)$ of a string X. Let us denote by $\mathsf{dp}(X, Y)$ the distance between X and Y where the complexity c is computed by the LZMP algorithm. Thus (1) is now represented by its parallel counterpart

$$\mathsf{dp}(X, Y, a, b) := \frac{LZMP(XY) - \min \{a, b\}}{\max \{a, b\}} \tag{2}$$

where a, b are the LZ-complexity values of the string X, Y, respectively, and for efficiency they are pre-computed as seen for instance in Procedure DMat, step 2(IV).

3 The Algorithm

We describe the parallel algorithm for image feature extraction, starting with a listing of several procedures followed by the main part which is split into several

Procedure LZMP. computes LZ complexity of a string (parallel processing over all symbols of string)

1. **Input**: string $S = \{S[i]\}_{i=1}^n$
2. **Initialize**:
   - I. H history buffer
   - II. $m := 0$, length of history buffer
   - III. $d := 0$ number of components in exhaustive history
   - IV. SM shared memory variable common to all threads
   - V. Q number of computing threads
   - VI. $\{T_q\}_{q=1}^Q$, T_q is a single computing thread
3. **Launch threads** T_q , $1 \le q \le Q$, in parallel, each executes the code below
   - I. **while**$(m < n)$
     - A. $SM := 0$
     - B. **for**$(l = 0$ **to** $\lfloor m/Q \rfloor)$
       - i. initialize variable $j^{(q)} = q + l \cdot Q$
       - ii. **if**$(j^{(q)} < m)$
         - a. initialize variable $i_{j^{(q)}} := 0$
         - b. initialize variable $k_{j^{(q)}} := j^{(q)}$
         - c. initialize variable $h_{j^{(q)}} := m - j^{(q)}$
         - d. **while**$(H[k_{j^{(q)}}] = S[m + i_{j^{(q)}}])$
           - 1. $i_{j^{(q)}} := i_{j^{(q)}} + 1$
           - 2. $k_{j^{(q)}} := k_{j^{(q)}} + 1$
           - 3. $h_{j^{(q)}} := h_{j^{(q)}} - 1$
           - 4. **if**$(h_{j^{(q)}} = 0$ **or** $m + i_{j^{(q)}} = n)$
             - I. **break;**
           - 5. **end if;**
         - e. **end while;**
         - f. **if**$(h_{j^{(q)}} = 0$ **and** $m + i_{j^{(q)}} < n)$
           - 1. initialize $z_{j^{(q)}} := m$
           - 2. **while**$(S[z_{j^{(q)}}] = S[m + i_{j^{(q)}}])$
             - I. $z_{j^{(q)}} := z_{j^{(q)}} + 1$
             - II. $i_{j^{(q)}} := i_{j^{(q)}} + 1$
             - III. **if**$(m + i_{j^{(q)}} = n)$
               - A. **break;**
             - IV. **end if;**
           - 3. **end while;**
         - g. **end if;**
         - h. **if** $(i_{j^{(q)}} > SM)$
           - 1. $SM := i_{j^{(q)}}$, // winner thread overrides
         - i. **end if;**
       - iii. **end if;**
     - C. **end for;**
     - D. synchronize all threads T_q, $1 \le q \le Q$
     - E. **if**$(q = 1)$
       - i. $H := H + \text{substring}(S[m], S[m + SM + 1])$
       - ii. $d := d + 1$
       - iii. $m := m + SM + 1$
     - F. **end if;**
     - G. synchronize all threads T_q, $1 \le q \le Q$
   - II. **end while;**
4. **Output**: $LZMP(S) = d$, the LZ-complexity of string S

sub-algorithms. Procedure LZMP computes the LZ-complexity of a given string. It runs in parallel over the symbols that comprise the string. The procedure appears in [7] and we enclose it here for completeness. Procedure VLZMP computes the LZ-complexity of a set of input strings in parallel. Procedure DMat computes the UID distance of every pair of strings from two given input lists, in parallel. The variable $i_{p,q}$ denotes an index variable of the computing block $B_{p,q}$ (each block has its own local memory and set of variables). The main algorithm is split into sub-algorithms (as done in [6]) which are numbered from 2 to 4 and the letter P denotes that it is a parallel computing algorithm. Algorithm 2P selects the prototype images (its serial version is Algorithms 1 and 2 of [6]).

Algorithm 2P. Prototypes selection

---

1. **Input**: M image feature categories, and a corpus $\mathcal{C}_N$ of N unlabeled colored (RGB) images $\{I_j\}_{j=1}^{N}$.
2. **for** $(i := 1$ to $M)$ **do**
     I. Based on *any* of the images I_j in $\mathcal{C}_N$, let the user **select** L_i prototype images $\left\{P_k^{(i)}\right\}_{k=1}^{L_i}$ and set them as feature category i. Each prototype is contained by some image, $P_k^{(i)} \subset I_j$, and the size of $P_k^{(i)}$ can vary, in particular it can be much smaller than the size of the images I_j, $1 \le j \le N$.
     II. Transform each of the images of feature category i into grayscale. Each pixel is now a single numeric value in the range of 0 to 255. We refer to this set of values as the alphabet and denote it by $\mathcal{A}$.
     III. Scan each of the grayscale images from top left to bottom right and form a string of symbols from $\mathcal{A}$. Denote the string of grayscale image I as $X^{(I)}$.
3. **end for**;
4. **Enumerate** all the prototypes into a single *unlabeled* set $\{P_k\}_{k=1}^{L}$, where $L = \sum_{i=1}^{M} L_i$.
5. Vector of strings that corresponds to the set of all prototypes be, $v = \left[X^{(P_k)}\right]_{k=1}^{L}$.
6. Calculate the distance matrix $H = DMat(v, v)$
7. **Run** hierarchical clustering on H and obtain the associated dendrogram (note: H does not contain any 'labeled' information about feature-categories, as it is based on the unlabeled set).
8. **If** there are M clusters with the ith cluster consisting of the prototypes $\left\{P_k^{(i)}\right\}_{k=1}^{L_i}$ **then** terminate and **go to** step 10.
9. **Else go to** step 2.
10. **Output**: the set of labeled prototypes $\mathcal{P}_L := \left\{\left\{P_k^{(i)}\right\}_{k=1}^{L_i}\right\}_{i=1}^{M}$ where L is the number of prototypes.

Algorithm 3P computes the set of cases (feature vectors) for images in the input corpus. The algorithm utilizes a number of computing blocks which begin to run in parallel in step 12. Steps 6 to 11 which run in serial are responsible for converting the input images into strings of symbols.

Procedure VLZMP. computes a vector of LZ complexities for multiple input strings in parallel

---

1. **Input:** vector $v := \{v[i]\}_{i=1}^{k} = [S_1, S_2, S_3, \ldots, S_k]$ where S_i is a string
2. **Initialize:**
   I. $u = \{u[i]\}_{i=1}^{k}$
   II. n number of parallel computing blocks
   III. $\{B_q\}_{q=1}^{n}$, B_q is block of multiple computing cores (threads)
3. **Launch blocks** B_q , $1 \leq q \leq n$, in parallel, each executes the code below
   I. **for**$(l = 0$ **to** $\lfloor k/n \rfloor)$
      A. initialize index vector $i = [i_1, \ldots, i_n]$ where $i_q = q + l \cdot n$
      B. **if** $(i_q \leq k)$
         i. $u[i_q] = LZMP(v[i_q])$
      C. **end if;**
   II. **end for;**
4. **Output:** $VLZMP(v) = u$

Procedure DMat. computes dp distance for all pairs of input strings in parallel

---

1. **Input:**
   I. $v := \{v[i]\}_{i=1}^{m} = [S_1, S_2, ..., S_m]$, where S_i is a string
   II. $u := \{u[j]\}_{i=1}^{n} = [S_1', S_2', ..., S_n']$, where S_j' is a string
2. **Initialize:**
   I. D matrix of $m \times n$ elements, $D := \{D[i,j]\}_{i=1,j=1}^{m,n} = \begin{pmatrix} d_{11} & d_{12} & d_{13} & ,.., & d_{1n} \\ d_{21} & d_{22} & d_{23} & ,.., & d_{2n} \\ d_{31} & d_{32} & d_{33} & ,.., & d_{3n} \\ ,.., & ,.., & ,.., & ,.., & ,.., \\ d_{m1} & d_{m2} & d_{m3} & ,.., & d_{mn} \end{pmatrix}$
   II. $M \cdot N$ number of parallel computing blocks
   III. $\{B_{p,q}\}_{p=1,q=1}^{M,N}$, $B_{p,q}$ is a block of multiple computing cores (threads)
   IV. $a := \{a[i]\}_{i=1}^{m} = VLZMP(v)$, $b := \{b[i]\}_{i=1}^{n} = VLZMP(u)$, LZ-complexity vectors
3. **Launch** blocks $B_{p,q}$, $1 \leq p < M$, $1 \leq q < N$, in parallel, each executes the code below
   I. **for** $(x = 0$ **to** $\lfloor n/N \rfloor)$
      A. initialize index $i_{p,q} = q + x \cdot N$
      B. **for** $(y = 0$ **to** $\lfloor m/M \rfloor)$
         i. initialize index $j_{p,q} = p + y \cdot M$
         a. **if** $(i_{p,q} \leq m$ **and** $j_{p,q} \leq n)$
            1. $D[i_{p,q}, j_{p,q}] = dp(v[i_{p,q}], u[j_{p,q}], a[i_{p,q}], b[j_{p,q}])$
         b. **end if;**
      C. **end for;**
   II. **end for;**
4. **Output:** $DMat(v, u) = D$

Algorithm 3P. produces a set of cases from input images (in parallel)

---

1. Input set $\mathcal{P} := \left\{ \left\{ P_k^{(i)} \right\}_{k=1}^{L_i} \right\}_{i=1}^{M}$ of labeled prototype images, where $P_k^{(i)}$ is k^{th} prototype of feature category i (obtained from Algorithm 2P).

2. Let $L := |\mathcal{P}|$ be the total number of prototypes

3. Input the set of all images $\mathcal{I} := \{I_l\}_{l=1}^{N}$ to be represented as cases of feature vectors

4. Q is number of parallel computing blocks

5. $\{B_q\}_{q=1}^{Q}$, B_q is a block of multiple computing cores (threads)

6. Let W be a rectangle of size equal to the maximum prototype size

7. **for** $(i := 1$ to $N)$

    I. Scan a window W across I_i from top-left to bottom-right in a non-overlapping way, and let the sequence of obtained sub-images of I be denoted by $\left\{ I_j^{(i)} \right\}_{j=1}^{m_i}$ (m_i is the number of windows W inside I_i).

    II. **for** $(j := 1$ to $m_i)$

        A. Transform $I_j^{(i)}$ into grayscale. Each pixel is represented by a single numeric value in the range of 0 to 255. Denote by $\mathcal{A}$ the alphabet of these values (same as $\mathcal{A}$ of Algorithm 2P).

        B. Scan grayscale of $I_j^{(i)}$ from top left to bottom right to form a string of symbols from $\mathcal{A}$.

        C. Denote the string by $X_{i,j}$

    III. **end for;**

    IV. $v_i = [X_{i,1}, \ldots, X_{i,m_i}]$

8. **end for;**

9. **for** $(l := 1$ to $M)$

    I. **for** $(k := 1$ to $L_l)$

        A. Transform $P_k^{(l)}$ into grayscale. Each pixel is represented by a single numeric value in the range of 0 to 255. Denote by $\mathcal{A}$ the alphabet of these values (same as $\mathcal{A}$ of Algorithm 2P).

        B. Scan grayscale image of $P_k^{(l)}$ from top left to bottom right to form a string of symbols from $\mathcal{A}$

        C. Denote the string by $Y_{l,k}$

    II. **end for;**

10. **end for;**

11. $u := [Y_{1,1}, Y_{1,2}, \ldots, Y_{1,L_1} \ldots, Y_{M,1}, \ldots Y_{M,L_M}]$

Algorithm 4 is identical to that of [6] and we present it for completeness. It uses the training cases that are produced in Algorithm 3P and uses any off-the-shelf supervised learning algorithm to produce a classifier.

4 Results

The following hardware was used: a 2.8 Ghz AMD Phenom©II X6 1055T Processor with number of cores $n = 6$ and a Tesla K20C board with a single GK110 GPU from nVIDIA. This GPU is based on the Keppler architecture

Algorithm 3P. continued...

12. **Launch** blocks B_q, $1 \leq q < Q$, in parallel, each executes the code below
    1. **for** $(x = 0$ **to** $\lfloor N/Q \rfloor)$
        I. initialize index vector $i = [i_1, \ldots, i_Q]$ where $i_q = q + x \cdot Q$
        II. **if** $(i_q \leq N)$
            A. $D_q = \mathtt{DMat}\left(v_{i_q}, u\right)$
              i. **for** $(j := 1$ **to** $m_{i_q})$ **do**
                  a. **for** $(l := 1$ **to** $M)$ **do**
                      1. $temp := 0$
                      2. **for** $(k := 1$ **to** $L_l)$ **do**
                          I. $temp := temp + (D_q[j,k])^2$
                      3. **end for;**
                  b. $temp = (1/L_l) \cdot temp$
                  c. $r_l^{(q)} := \sqrt{temp}$
                  d. **end for;**
                  e. Let $l_q^*(j) := \mathrm{argmin}_{1 \leq l \leq M} r_l^{(q)}$, this is the decided feature category
                    for sub-image $I_j^{(i_q)}$
                  f. **Increment** the count, $c_{l_q^*(j)}^{(q)} := c_{l_q^*(j)}^{(q)} + 1$
              ii. **end for;**
            B. **Normalize** the counts, $V_l^{(q)} := \dfrac{c_l^{(q)}}{\sum_{z=1}^{M} c_z^{(q)}}$, $1 \leq l \leq M$
            C. $V^{(q)} = \left[V_1^{(q)}, \ldots V_M^{(q)}\right]$ as the feature-vector (case) representation for
              image I_{i_q}
            D. $W[i_q] = V^{(q)}$
    2. **end for;**
13. Output: the array W of cases corresponding to the set $\mathcal{I}$ of input images

(with compute capabilities of 3.5). The CUDA is release 6.0 and the operating system is Ubuntu Linux 2.6.38-11-generic.

We tested the algorithm on several two-category image classification problem obtained from the CALTECH-101 corpus [1]. Due to the lack of space, we present one such problem which has as categories, *airplane* and *ketch* (yacht). We chose 10 prototypes of each category simply by collecting small images of airplanes and boats. The prototypes of *airplane* are of size 150×70 pixels and the prototypes of *ketch* are of size 150×130. Figure 1 shows a few examples of such prototypes.

The corpus of input images consist of 74 images of airplanes of size 420×200 and 100 images of yachts of size 300×300. It takes 345 seconds for Algorithm 3P to produce the 174 cases starting from the image corpus. Figure 2 displays two examples of input images, one from category *airplane* and one from *ketch* and their corresponding divisions into sub-images of size 150×150 (obtained in Algorithm 3P, step 7). Note that the algorithm permits the size of prototypes to differ and the size (or number) of sub-images to differ from one feature category to another. We ran four learning algorithms, multi-layer perceptrons, decision

---

Algorithm 4. Image classification learning

---

1. **Input**: (1) a target class variable T taking values in a finite set $\mathcal{T}$ of class categories, (2) a set $\mathcal{D}_T$ of labeled cases which is based on the M-dimensional cases in array $\mathcal{D}$ obtained from Algorithm 3P and labeled with target values in $\mathcal{T}$ (3) any supervised learning algorithm $\mathcal{L}$
2. Partition $\mathcal{D}_T$ using n-fold cross validation into Training and Testing sets of cases
3. Train and test algorithm $\mathcal{L}$ and produce a classifier C which maps the feature space $[0, 1]^M$ into $\mathcal{T}$
4. Define Image classifier as follows: given any image I the classification is $F(I) := C(v(I))$, where $v(I)$ is the M-dimensional feature vector of I
5. **Output**: classifier F

Fig. 1. Three prototypes from category *airplane*

Fig. 2. Input images from category *airplane* and *ketch* and their respective sub-images

trees J48, naive-Bayes and lazy IB1, on a ten-fold cross validation using the 174 input images. Table 1 presents the accuracy results versus the baseline algorithm (rules.ZeroR) which classifies based on the prior class probability. The configuration parameter values of the learning algorithms used in WEKA [8] are displayed under the accuracy result. As can be seen, the $J48$ decision tree learner achieves the highest accuracy of 96.54 % (relative to the baseline accuracy of 57.52 %).

Table 1. Classification result for *airplane* v.s. *ketch* problem

Dataset	(1)	(2)	(3)	(4)	(5)
airplane-ketch	57.52	83.65 ∘	93.82 ∘	96.54 ∘	86.75 ∘

∘, • statistically significant improvement or degradation

(1) rules.ZeroR " 48055541465867954
(2) functions.MultilayerPerceptron '-L 0.3 -M 0.2 -N 500 -V 0 -S 0 -E 20 -H a' -5990607817048210779
(3) lazy.IB1 " -6152184127304895851
(4) trees.J48 '-C 0.25 -M 2' -217733168393644444
(5) bayes.NaiveBayesMultinomialUpdateable " -7204398796974263186

Next, we considered a more challenging problem of recognizing different image textures. We obtained the 1000 images of the Texture Database [2] which has 25 categories of various types of real textures, for instance, glass, water, wood, with 40 images each of size 640×480 per category. We chose as feature categories the categories themselves and selected five small prototypes of size 150×150 from each one without using Algorithm 2P (just picking parts of images in a random way to be prototypes). It takes about 25 h for Algorithm 3P to produce the 1000 cases starting from the image corpus. We ran the following classification learning algorithms: lazy IB1, decision trees J48, multi-layer perceptrons, naive Bayes, random forest. Ten fold cross validation accuracy results are displayed in Table 2 (parameter settings are displayed under the accuracy results). As shown, the best obtained accuracy result is 70.73 % which is achieved by the random forest algorithm; this is 17.6 times better than the baseline ZeroR classification rule.

Table 2. Classification result for the texture problem

Dataset	(1)	(2)	(3)	(4)	(5)	(6)
25cat-40img	4.00	63.16 ∘	58.59 ∘	66.50 ∘	61.92 ∘	70.73 ∘

∘, • statistically significant improvement or degradation

(1) rules.ZeroR " 48055541465867954
(2) lazy.IB1 " -6152184127304895851
(3) trees.J48 '-C 0.25 -M 2' -217733168393644444
(4) functions.MultilayerPerceptron '-L 0.3 -M 0.2 -N 500 -V 0 -S 0 -E 20 -H a' -5990607817048210779
(5) bayes.NaiveBayesMultinomialUpdateable " -7204398796974263186
(6) trees.RandomForest '-I 100 -K 0 -S 1' -2260823972777004705

Considering how little effort and no-expertise is needed in our approach to image feature extraction, we believe that the results are impressive and can serve well in settings where very little domain knowledge is available, or as a starting point from which additional analysis and specialized feature extraction can be made.

5   Conclusions

In this paper we introduce a new parallel processing algorithm for image feature extraction. Given an input corpus of raw RGB images the algorithm computes feature vectors (cases) that represent the images with their associated classification target labels. Using these cases, any standard supervised or unsupervised learning algorithm can learn to classify or cluster the images in the database. A main advantage in our approach is the lack of need for any kind of image or data analysis. Aside of picking once at the start a few small image prototypes, the procedure is automatic and applies to any set of images. It can therefore be very useful in settings with little domain knowledge or as a starting point for a more specialized image data analysis. Our experiments indicate that the algorithm yields relatively high accuracies on image texture classification problems.

Acknowledgement. We acknowledge the support of the nVIDIA corporation for their donation of GPU hardware.

References

1. Fei-Fei, L., Fergus, R., Perona, P.: Learning generative visual models from few training examples: an incremental bayesian approach tested on 101 object categories (2004)
2. Lazebnik, S., Schmid, C., Ponce, J.: A sparse texture representation using local affine regions. IEEE Trans. Pattern Anal. Mach. Intell. **27**(8), 1265–1278 (2005)
3. Chester, U., Ratsaby, J.: Universal distance measure for images. In: Proceedings of the 27th IEEE Convention of Electrical Electronics Engineers in Israel (IEEEI 2012), pp. 1–4. Eilat, Israel, 14–17 November 2012
4. Sayood, K., Otu, H.H.: A new sequence distance measure for phylogenetic tree construction. Bioinformatics **19**(16), 2122–2130 (2003)
5. Ziv, J., Lempel, A.: On the complexity of finite sequences. IEEE Trans. Inf. Theory **22**(3), 75–81 (1976)
6. Chester, U., Ratsaby, J.: Machine learning for image classification and clustering using a universal distance measure. In: Brisaboa, N., Pedreira, O., Zezula, P. (eds.) SISAP 2013. LNCS, vol. 8199, pp. 59–72. Springer, Heidelberg (2013)
7. Belousov, A., Ratsaby, J.: Massively parallel computations of the LZ-complexity of strings. In: Proceedings of the 28th IEEE Convention of Electrical and Electronics Engineers in Israel (IEEEI 2014), pp. 1–5. Eilat, 3–5 December 2014
8. Hall, M., Frank, E., Holmes, G., Pfahringer, B., Reutemann, P., Witten, I.H.: The WEKA data mining software: an update. SIGKDD Explor. **11**(1), 10–18 (2009)

Modeling Concept Drift: A Probabilistic Graphical Model Based Approach

Hanen Borchani[1], Ana M. Martínez[1], Andrés R. Masegosa[2]([✉]),
Helge Langseth[2], Thomas D. Nielsen[1], Antonio Salmerón[3],
Antonio Fernández[4], Anders L. Madsen[1,5], and Ramón Sáez[4]

[1] Department of Computer Science, Aalborg University, Aalborg, Denmark
[2] Department of Computer and Information Science,
The Norwegian University of Science and Technology, Trondheim, Norway
andres.masegosa@idi.ntnu.no
[3] Department of Mathematics, University of Almería, Almería, Spain
[4] Banco de Crédito Cooperativo, Madrid, Spain
[5] Hugin Expert A/S, Aalborg, Denmark

Abstract. An often used approach for detecting and adapting to concept drift when doing classification is to treat the data as *i.i.d.* and use changes in classification accuracy as an indication of concept drift. In this paper, we take a different perspective and propose a framework, based on probabilistic graphical models, that explicitly represents concept drift using latent variables. To ensure efficient inference and learning, we resort to a variational Bayes inference scheme. As a proof of concept, we demonstrate and analyze the proposed framework using synthetic data sets as well as a real financial data set from a Spanish bank.

1 Introduction

Classification, which is the task of predicting the class, Y, of an object based on a set of attributes, $\boldsymbol{X}$, describing that object, has been studied extensively in the machine learning community (see, e.g., [1]). A special instance of this general task is the classification of objects in a streaming context, which amounts to observing objects at different points in time $t = t_1, t_2, \ldots$, and at each time-point t classifying the object based on the information collected up to and including time t, $\bigcup_{j:t_j \leq t} \boldsymbol{x}_{t_j}$.

As pointed out in, e.g., [2], doing classification in the context of data streams raises several issues. Among the challenges is that data in a streaming context should not be assumed to be *i.i.d.* First of all, the objects in the stream may not be independent, and, secondly, concept drift [3–5], where the underlying distribution generating the data changes over time, should be anticipated. The main contribution of this paper is a principled approach based on probabilistic graphical models [6] for modeling concept drift using latent (i.e., unobserved)

H. Borchani, A.M. Martínez, and A.R. Masegosa—These authors are considered as first authors and contributed equally to this work.

© Springer International Publishing Switzerland 2015
E. Fromont et al. (Eds.): IDA 2015, LNCS 9385, pp. 72–83, 2015.
DOI: 10.1007/978-3-319-24465-5_7

variables. This should be contrasted to what is currently the most commonly used technique to accommodate concept drift, namely to learn a classifier as if the data was *i.i.d.*, monitor classification accuracy, and then restart the learning process as soon as accuracy drops significantly (see, e.g., [4]).

We will exemplify the use of our modeling framework by analyzing the economic status of the customers of a Spanish bank over the period from 2007 to 2014. To keep the analysis as simple as possible, we use the *Naïve Bayes* classifier [7] as our base model, even if other classifiers with better dynamic properties (e.g., [8]) could also have been employed. The analysis is thus a proof of concept for the proposed modelling strategy, where we focus on the model's ability to detect and represent concept drift instead of its predictive performance. A related Bayesian approach to concept drift is studied in [9], where focus is on abrupt concept drift with independent drift regimes. This type of concept drift does, however, not fit with the financial domain considered in this paper, where we have a fixed customer base that exhibits a more gradual drift.

Classification in data streams also raises some computational problems [2], as data may arrive with high velocity and is unbounded in size (therefore requiring that old observations are "forgotten" to avoid running out of computer memory). To deal with this issue, our model analysis builds on the AMIDST toolbox[1]. This toolbox provides an efficient implementation of approximate inference and learning methods for streaming data by utilizing the *Bayesian network* modelling framework [6] complemented with variational Bayes inference and learning procedures [10]. Furthermore, the toolbox interfaces to MOA [11], thereby enabling us to directly draw on existing preprocessing and visualization functionality.

The remainder of this paper is organized as follows: In Sect. 2 we describe the real-life data set from the Spanish bank in detail, and discuss its most important dynamic features. Section 3 introduces our approach for explicitly modeling concept drift using latent variables, and in Sect. 4 we briefly sketch the inference machinery employed. In Sect. 5 we discuss the results obtained from synthetic data as well as the financial data set, and we conclude in Sect. 6.

2   The Financial Data Set

2.1   Description of the Data Set

The data set, which was provided by Banco de Crédito Cooperativo (BCC), contains monthly aggregated information for a set of clients of BCC for the period from April 2007 to March 2014. Only "active" clients are considered, meaning that we restrict our attention to individuals between 18 and 65 years of age, who have at least one automatic bill payment or direct debit in the bank. To make the data set as homogeneous as possible, we only retained clients residing in the Almería region (a largely agricultural area in the south-east of Spain), and excluded BCC employees, since they have special conditions. The resulting

---

[1] AMIDST is an open source toolbox available at http://amidst.github.io/toolbox/ under the Apache Software License.

number of clients is close to 50 000. We note that the number of clients who are active varies from month to month: clients with missing values for any of the variables for a given month are removed from the data set for that particular month (this amounts to roughly 25 % of the clients). These missing values mainly occur in relation to the income and expense variables, and represent an absence of movements for the account in that period. Consequently, the customer population may vary across months. These clients are removed to support the subsequent analysis, and not because of limitations of the inference/learning engine.

We extracted 11 quantitative attributes, each of which encodes monthly aggregated information for each of the clients. These attributes include, among others, the income, expenses and account balance, the client's total credit amount in all Spanish financial institutions, outstanding payments in mortgages, credit cards, and other personal loans. Each client has an associated class variable, which indicates if that particular client will default during the following 12 months. Figure 1(a) shows how the fraction of clients who default increases at the beginning of the period, then decreases for a period of almost two years. Next, the fraction increases again, before it eventually stabilizes; the semester/trimester fluctuations are (partly) a consequence of the changes in the customer base over the period, and will be further discussed in Sect. 5. We note here that the values in this and in the following figures have been linearly scaled (e.g., we do not report z_t for a particular variable z but rather $\alpha_z + \beta_z z_t$ where α_z and β_z are not disclosed in the paper). The transformation is performed to withhold business-critical information, while at the same time convey meaningful information about the data.

2.2 Financial Pre-analysis/context

Figure 1(b–f) shows the evolution of 5 of the 11 variables in the domain, namely the total credit amount, income, expenses, account balance, and credit cards. As mentioned above, the values on the y-axis have also been linearly transformed here. The plots reveal that both *seasonal* and *global* trends appear to be present in the data set.

The *seasonal trend* is particularly prominent for the credit reports (Fig. 1(b)), where the values systematically drop after a period, then go up again. The period between drops is six months for the first half of the data set and three months in the second half. Experts at BCC identified this as the effect of fees being charged to accounts of clients that are normally inactive.

It is also possible to observe a *global ascending or descending trend*, which for this set of variables seems to be on-going until the third or fourth trimester of 2012. Other variables, like defaulted payments on credit cards (Fig. 1(f)), also display a global trend, but do not follow the same pattern. This variable seems to drop around the third semester of 2013, something experts at BCC attribute to a sale of debt portfolios.

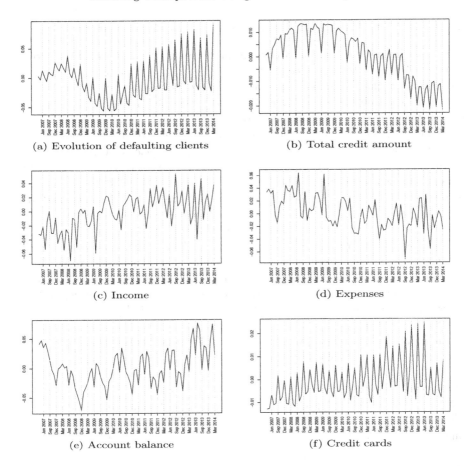

(a) Evolution of defaulting clients

(b) Total credit amount

(c) Income

(d) Expenses

(e) Account balance

(f) Credit cards

Fig. 1. Evolution of (a) defaulting clients and (b–f) 5 of the 11 variables in the financial data set.

2.3 Main Challenges

There are two main factors that should be highlighted and which make concept drift detection in the financial data set more challenging than usual. Firstly, the class variable is highly imbalanced and, as shown in Fig. 1(a), the number of defaulting clients varies across time. Hence, monitoring classification accuracy as a way of detecting concept drift can be misleading. Secondly, the data samples arrive in batches of different sizes, i.e., aggregated information for the active customers in a given month. Monitoring concept drift within the samples of one of these batches will not be meaningful as concept drift can only happen from one month to another.

In order to successfully monitor concept drift in the financial data, both of these factors should be addressed.

3   Modeling Concept Drift Using Latent Variables

In non-stationary domains, the distribution governing the data may change over time. This effect is known as *concept drift* [3–5]. In a classification model, where one wants to classify an instance described by its features $\boldsymbol{x} = (x_1, \ldots, x_n)$ wrt. a class variable y, Gama et al. [5, Eq.(2)] formally define concept drift as the existence of an instance $\boldsymbol{x}$ s.t. $P_{t_0}(\boldsymbol{x}, y) \neq P_{t_1}(\boldsymbol{x}, y)$, where $P_t(\boldsymbol{x}, y)$ denotes the joint distribution over $\boldsymbol{x}$ and y at time t. Concept drift situations can be further classified as either *real concept drift*, when $P_t(y|\boldsymbol{x})$ changes with time, or *virtual concept drift*, when $P_t(\boldsymbol{x})$ drifts while $P_t(y|\boldsymbol{x})$ is constant in t. In this paper the discussions relate to the general notion of concept drift as captured in the expression above, and we do therefore not distinguish between real and virtual concept drift. Concept drift may also appear in many forms, with changes happening abruptly, gradually, incrementally, or with reoccurring behaviour [5].

In what follows we shall consider a new modeling technique for capturing concept drift. The modeling technique will address the general situation, where we, at each time point t, have a collection $(\boldsymbol{x}_i^t, y_i^t)$, for $i = 1 : N_t$, of instances (a.k.a. a window)[2]. We shall assume that concept drift only happens across time steps and not within a collection of instances captured at the same time-point, i.e., the model can only drift every N_t samples.

In a Bayesian paradigm, where the probability distributions are parameterized using latent variables, a simple Bayesian network-based generative model for classification is shown in Fig. 2(a) using plate notation. In this model the parameters are shared for all points in time t and across all instances, and the model does therefore not provide an explicit representation of concept drift. In Fig. 2(b) the model is extended to support a simple form of concept drift by duplicating the parameters over time, and thereby allowing them to change.

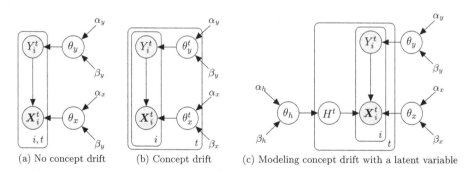

(a) No concept drift   (b) Concept drift   (c) Modeling concept drift with a latent variable

Fig. 2. Modeling concept drift through parameter duplication. In all figures, $\alpha_{(\cdot)}$ and $\beta_{(\cdot)}$ are hyper-parameters for the distributions over the parameters θ_x and θ_y.

Alternatively, concept drift can be modeled explicitly using *latent variables*. For simplicity, assume that only the probability distribution $P(\boldsymbol{x}|y)$ drifts. We

---

[2] For now, we shall assume that the total number of instances N_t does not vary with time t; this assumption is lifted in Sect. 5 when we consider the financial data set.

can model this using a latent variable H^t, which contributes to the conditional distribution for $\boldsymbol{X}_i$ as illustrated in Fig. 2(c). The semantics of the H^t-variable is that it determines the "situation" at time t. For example, if the j'th feature $X_{i,j}^t$ follows a conditional normal distribution, we may use H^t to define a time-dependent component of the mean vector:

$$X_{i,j}^t | \{H^t = h^t, Y_i^t = y\} \sim \mathcal{N}(\delta_{j,y} + \gamma_{j,y} h^t, \sigma_{j,y}^2),$$

where $\delta_{j,y}$, $\gamma_{j,y}$, and $\sigma_{j,y}^2$ are elements of θ_x.

The a priori expected level of concept drift can be expressed through the prior distribution for H^t, i.e., using the hyper-parameters α_h and β_h. All observations inside one point in time share the same instance of the H^t-variable, thus concept drift is modelled as a population-wide effect, as desired. Note also that depending on the nature of the variable H^t, this model allows us to represent both *gradual* (H^t continuous) and *abrupt* (H^t discrete) concept drift [5]. Furthermore, the model can easily be extended to model multiple concepts drifts by introducing multiple latent variables, each representing a different drift regime.

Conditioning on the model parameters the concept drift variables are assumed independent across time with no 'memory effect'. If we, on the other hand, expect a gradual form of concept drift, we may wish to capture the drift across time. The model in Fig. 3 reflects this scenario through the dependence relations among the latent H^t variables.

The latent variable models considered so far provide seamless representations of both gradual and abrupt concept drift relating to continuous features. Similar model types are also applicable when modeling abrupt concept drift for discrete features, but when dealing with gradual concept drift we need to move outside the standard class of conjugate Conditional Linear Gaussian (CLG) models. We shall not consider these types of models further in this paper, however, will instead focus on the case where both the feature variables and the latent variable H^t are continuous, using CLG distributions, and where Y_i^t is discrete with a Dirichlet distribution over its parameters.

We would like to reemphasize that the main element of the proposed framework is the use of latent variables for modeling concept drift. In the models presented in this section, these concept drift variables are used to account for concept drift relative to a simple Naïve Bayes classifier. These types of classifiers could in principle be replaced by other types of more expressive probabilistic classifiers, such as dynamic Naïve Bayes models [12] or general Bayesian networks. However, since the main goal of the present paper is to provide a proof of concept for the proposed modeling framework, we will in the remainder of the paper rely on these simpler models.

4   Bayesian Inference with Streaming Data

In the Bayesian paradigm, model learning can be considered an inference process. Given the data seen so far, denoted by D^t, the learning task reduces to computing the posterior distribution over the quantities of interest, i.e., $P(\theta_x, \theta_y, H^t | D^t)$

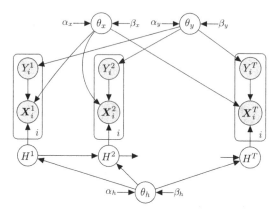

Fig. 3. Concept drift is preserved over time.

for the models described in Sect. 3. This approach can also naturally be applied when dealing with streaming data. A new data sample $(\boldsymbol{x}_{t+1}, y_{t+1})$ in the stream is included by simply updating the above posterior using Bayes' rule, $P(\theta_x, \theta_y, H^{t+1}|D^{t+1})$.

Inference in Bayesian networks is, however, NP-hard in general [13], and given the size of the data sets we are currently considering, exact inference in the underlying models is not feasible. For the models considered in this paper, we will therefore rely on the *variational Bayes* [14] framework for doing approximate inference and learning; a general introduction to the variational Bayes procedure can be found in [10].

In its general form, one considers the random variables $(\boldsymbol{X}, \boldsymbol{Z})$, where $\boldsymbol{X} = \boldsymbol{x}$ is observed and we want to approximate $f(\boldsymbol{z}|\boldsymbol{x})$. We call the approximation $q(\boldsymbol{z})$, where we for simplicity of notation suppress that $q(\boldsymbol{z})$ depends on the observation $\boldsymbol{x}$. We measure the quality of the approximation by the KL distance from q to f. One popular strategy for minimizing this distance is to assume that $q(\boldsymbol{z})$ factorizes into smaller factors, like for instance its separate variables, $q(\boldsymbol{z}) = \prod_i q_i(z_i)$. This approach is commonly known as the *mean-field* approximation.

The calculations can be structured efficiently in conjugate exponential models using a *message passing* scheme [15]. In this scheme, messages are sent along the edges in the graph based on the (expected) natural parameters of the distributions in the model. The message passing scheme outlined above has been implemented for the model classes presented in Sect. 3, and forms the basis for the experimental results presented in the following section.

5   Results

The experimental study is divided into two parts. First, we analyse two synthetic data sets, widely employed as benchmarks in the concept drift literature. Next, we present the results from analysing the financial data set. All the experiments have been performed using MOA [11], where the developed AMIDST model (in Fig. 3) has been integrated as a new Bayesian streaming classifier, named *bayes.amidstModels*. The Java code to reproduce the experiments can be downloaded from http://amidst.github.io/toolbox/.

5.1   Synthetic Data Sets

We first analyse the SEA data set [16] containing 60 000 samples, with 3 attributes (x_1, x_2, x_3) and 2 classes ($y = 0$ and $y = 1$). The attributes are numerical and uniformly distributed between 0 and 10. Only two of the attributes are relevant for the class label, y, which is defined as $y^t = 1$ if $x_1^t + x_2^t \leq \epsilon^t$ and $y^t = 0$ otherwise. Concept drift has been created by changing the threshold ϵ^t as a function of t. The data set covers four "phases", each with a duration of 15 000 samples, and with different ϵ^t (9, 8, 7, and 9.5 for the four phases, respectively). Figure 4 (left) shows the results of this analysis for batches of size N_t equal to 1000. The plot illustrates the progress of the expected value of the latent variable (denoted H^t) as well as the prequential accuracies computed using a sliding windows of size 1000 for a simple Naïve Bayes model (NB) and the adaptive Hoeffding tree model (AHT). As can be observed, the output of our model (i.e., the expected value of H^t) detects the drift points and clearly identifies the occurrences of the four different phases in the data, whereas those phases are less easily detected based on the accuracy results.

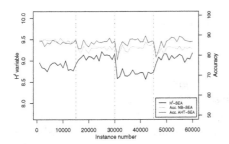 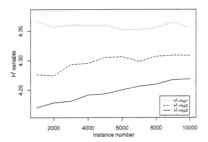

Fig. 4. Left: Results for the SEA data set. Right: Results for the hyperplane data sets

The second data set considered is the rotating hyperplane [17]. This benchmark data set is widely used to simulate "gradual" concept drift problems. We considered three versions of this data set, denoted Hyp1, Hyp2, and Hyp3, each including 10 000 instances. For each data set, 8 out of 9 attributes are drifting but with different magnitudes of change (i.e., 0.1, 0.5, and 1 for the three data sets, respectively), see [17] for details. Figure 4 (right) shows the evolution of the latent variable H^t for each considered data set using a sliding window of size 1000. Here we see that the different drift magnitudes of the three data sets are directly reflected in the development trends of the latent variables. For instance, for the Hyp1 data, the curve of the H^t variable presents a stable behavior which correctly illustrates the very low change magnitude for this data set, i.e., 0.1.

5.2   Financial Data Set

In this section we analyze the financial data described in Sect. 2. Notice that for this data set the batch sizes, N_t, refer to the number of active customer in a given month and can vary from one month to another.

Figure 5(left) shows the evolution of the classification accuracy for the NB model using a latent variable. At first sight, the evolution of the accuracy may reflect some inherent trend in the data; however, a more careful analysis reveals that it simply reflects the evolution of defaulters as shown in Fig. 1(a). This is basically due to the data being imbalanced as pointed out in Sect. 2, and in such settings the use of classification accuracy for detecting concept drift can be misleading. As an alternative performance measure, we may consider the area under the ROC curve as shown in Fig. 5(right). The plot provides a more smooth behaviour with gradual performance improvements over time.

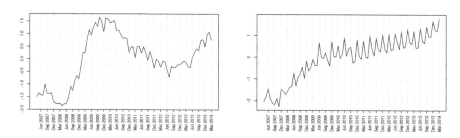

Fig. 5. Evolution of the accuracy (left) and the area under the ROC (right) for the financial data set. For confidentiality reason, the y-axis values have been linearly scaled.

In contrast, in Fig. 6 we plot the evolution of the latent variable H^t over time. Before discussing how this plot may provide insight into the financial data, recall first that in this model (cf. Fig. 3) a single scalar value tries to capture the global trend of 11 variables conditioned on a binary class variable. Moreover, as the vast majority of the clients in the data set are non-defaulters, the latent variable will mostly be influenced by this group of customers. With this basis, at least two observations can now be made about the evolution of the latent variable:

Observation 1: There are regular peaks in the time series. Before 2011, these peaks occur every June and December (6 months period); after 2011 the peaks appear every March, June, September, and December (3 months period). Figure 6 thus seems to represent two time series, one containing the values at the peaks and one containing the remaining observations. The two underlying series evolve in parallel.

Observation 2: Both underlying series increase rapidly until the second or third trimester of 2012 (the highest points in the two series are reached in June/July 2012). Afterwards, the series seem to gradually decrease, and this is particularly evident from the third trimester of 2013.

Our interpretation of these observations relies on the figures presented in Sect. 2, where the temporal evolution of the monthly average of each variable is depicted. To gain some insight into the first observation, we may recall that clients with missing values for *Expenses* or *Income* are discarded when analysing a particular month. We also previously commented that these clients are assumed to be less active than the remainder of the population, and they are consequently not present in the data in the majority of the months; they only appear when fees are deducted from their accounts every semester/trimester (this amounts to approximately 20% of the customers). From the variables in Fig. 1 we can see that these customers have a quite particular profile, which introduces a seasonal effect in the data set. We believe that this is what the latent variable is also capturing. Furthermore, we attribute the fact that the two underlying series are approximately equidistant over time to indicate that they probably represent groups of clients that are similarly affected by the national economical climate.

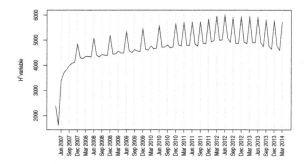

Fig. 6. Evolution of the H^t variable for the financial data set.

Regarding the interpretation of Observation 2, it appears evident that the expected value of the latent variable moves from the very beginning of the period until the second/third trimester of 2012 (the peak is in July 2012), before it remains stable until the second trimester of 2013. Thereafter it moves slightly in the reverse direction. The movements in the latent variable are used to facilitate the evolution of the attributes' distributions, but looking at each variable in Fig. 1 separately, we cannot pinpoint a direct and simple explanation of the above behaviour. For example, both *Expenses* and *Income* continuously move until the first/second trimester of 2012, after which they become more stable. On the other hand, the *Account balance* has a different trend. Thus, when looking at each variable in isolation, it is hard to find a common evolution pattern.

Motivated by the fact that the provided data is expected to reflect the socio-economical status of a significant part of the population in the province of Almería, we now relate the global trend of the latent variable to the history of the financial crisis in Spain during the studied period. In that light, the evolution of the latent variable in Fig. 6 should tell us that the economic climate gets worse from the beginning of the period until the second/third trimester of 2012, then stabilizes until the second trimester of 2013, before it starts recovering slightly. If this interpretation is correct, we should see a correlation between our latent variable and relevant economic factors influencing the socio-economical status of the population during this period of time. Figure 7(left) shows the unemployment rate in the province of Almería, which increases from the beginning of the period. We notice some peaks associated with the seasonality of the tourism and agriculture professions, which are two of the main economic drivers of this region. Taking this seasonality into account, the unemployment rate reaches its maximum value around the turn of year 2012/2013 before it slowly improves. Figure 7(right) shows the relationship between the unemployment rate and the expected value of the latent variable. From the figure we see a close correlation between these two entities.

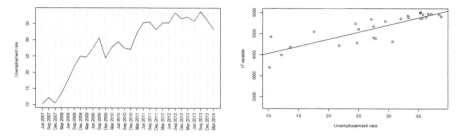

Fig. 7. Economic indicators. Left: Unemployment rate in Almería. Right: Scatter plot of the unemployment rate and the expected value of the latent variable (Spearman's rank correlation coefficient is 0.85).

6   Conclusions

In this paper we have developed a classification model for data streams that is compatible with concept drift scenarios. Our approach distinguishes itself from traditional alternatives by explicitly including the effect of the concept drift in the model using latent variables. We have shown through analysis of both synthetic and real-life data that the model is able to capture and handle both abrupt and gradual concept drift scenarios.

The analysis is a proof of concept for the proposed model class, and the opportunities for future research are manifold: Firstly, we will consider more sophisticated base-classifiers that are better suited for dynamic domains (e.g., the dynamic Naïve Bayes model), which we expect will improve the classification accuracy of the model. Next, we will look at extensions of the concept drift modelling itself, e.g., by using more than one latent variable and thereby being able to represent concept drift that behave differently for different subsets of the variables. Finally, as our development is motivated by the financial dataset, we will look deeper into socio-economical indicators from Spain to understand even better the mechanisms driving the concept drift in this domain.

Acknowledgments. This work was performed as part of the AMIDST project. AMIDST has received funding from the European Union's Seventh Framework Programme for research, technological development and demonstration under grant agreement no 619209. The data set has been provided by Banco de Crédito Cooperativo.

References

1. Hastie, T., Tibshirani, R., Friedman, J.: The Elements of Statistical Learning. Springer New York Inc., New York (2001)
2. Gaber, M.M., Zaslavsky, A.B., Krishnaswamy, S.: A survey of classification methods in data streams. In: Aggarwal, C.C. (ed.) Data Streams - Models and Algorithms. Advances in Database Systems, vol. 31, pp. 39–59. Springer, Berlin (2007)
3. Schlimmer, J.C., Granger, R.H.: Incremental learning from noisy data. Mach. Learn. **1**, 317–354 (1986)
4. Widmer, G., Kubat, M.: Learning in the presence of concept drift and hidden contexts. Mach. Learn. **23**(1), 69–101 (1996)
5. Gama, J., Žliobaitė, I., Bifet, A., Pechenizkiy, M., Bouchachia, A.: A survey on concept drift adaptation. ACM Comput. Surv. **46**, 44:1–44:37 (2014)
6. Jensen, F.V., Nielsen, T.D.: Bayesian Networks and Decision Graphs. Springer, Berlin (2007)
7. Duda, R.O., Hart, P.E.: Pattern Classification and Scene Analysis. Wiley, New York (1973)
8. Zhong, S., Langseth, H., Nielsen, T.D.: A classification-based approach to monitoring the safety of dynamic systems. Reliab. Eng. Syst. Safety **121**, 61–71 (2014)
9. Bach, S., Maloof, M.: A Bayesian approach to concept drift. In: Advances in Neural Information Processing Systems, pp. 127–135 (2010)
10. Jordan, M.I., Ghahramani, Z., Jaakkola, T.S., Saul, L.K.: An introduction to variational methods for graphical models. Mach. Learn. **37**, 183–233 (1999)
11. Bifet, A., Holmes, G., Kirkby, R., Pfahringer, B.: MOA: massive online analysis. J. Mach. Learn. Res. **11**, 1601–1604 (2010)
12. Martínez, M., Sucar, L.E.: Learning dynamic naive Bayesian classifiers. In: Proceedings of the Twenty-First International Florida Artificial Intelligence Research Symposium Conference, 655–659 (2008)
13. Cooper, G.F.: The computational complexity of probabilistic inference using Bayesian belief networks. Artif. Intell. **42**, 393–405 (1990)
14. Beal, M.J.: Variational algorithms for approximate Bayesian inference. Ph.D. thesis, Gatsby Computational Neuroscience Unit, University College London (2003)
15. Winn, J.M., Bishop, C.M.: Variational message passing. J. Mach. Learn. Res. **6**, 661–694 (2005)
16. Street, N., Kim, Y.: A streaming ensemble algorithm (SEA) for large-scale classification. In: 7th ACM SIGKDD International Conference on Knowledge Discovery and Data Mining (KDD), pp. 377–382 (2001)
17. Hulten, G., Spencer, L., Domingos, P.: Mining time changing data streams. In: Proceedings of the Seventh International Conference on Knowledge Discovery and Data Mining, pp. 97–106 (2001)

Diversity-Driven Widening of Hierarchical Agglomerative Clustering

Alexander Fillbrunn[(✉)] and Michael R. Berthold

Chair for Bioinformatics and Information Mining, Department of CIS
and Graduate School Chemical Biology (KoRS-CB), University of Konstanz,
78457 Konstanz, Germany
{Alexander.Fillbrunn,Michael.Berthold}@uni-konstanz.de

Abstract. In this paper we show that diversity-driven widening, the parallel exploration of the model space with focus on developing diverse models, can improve hierarchical agglomerative clustering. Depending on the selected linkage method, the model that is found through the widened search achieves a better silhouette coefficient than its sequentially built counterpart.

1 Introduction

With the rise of multi-processor computer systems and multi-machine clusters, great efforts have been made to adapt machine learning to the changing paradigm of scaling hardware horizontally instead of vertically. Many traditional learning algorithms have been revised to run in a parallelized environment (eg. decision trees [18], neural networks [19] and SVMs [5]). These algorithms mostly focus on making the model building faster, but produce the same models as the non-parallel algorithms. Another approach that focuses on leveraging parallel computing resources to improve models generated by a data mining algorithm, rather than speeding up the computation, has been proposed in [1]. The technique has already been shown to work well for the set covering problem and *KRIMP* [17].

In this paper we describe a widened algorithm for hierarchical agglomerative clustering [6]. Parallel versions of this algorithm have been described in [14], however the focus there is again on acceleration rather than improving the model. Our preliminary results indicate that building multiple, diverse clustering models in parallel can improve the quality of the clustering for different quality metrics.

2 Widening

The widening technique for algorithms has first been described in [1]. It discusses an approach that focuses on leveraging parallel computing resources to improve models generated by a data mining algorithm, rather than speeding up the computation. Instead of greedily traversing the model space in search of a

© Springer International Publishing Switzerland 2015
E. Fromont et al. (Eds.): IDA 2015, LNCS 9385, pp. 84–94, 2015.
DOI: 10.1007/978-3-319-24465-5_8

model that is just good enough, widening seeks to explore the space of all possible models in parallel, focusing on a certain number of best models at a time, iteratively refining them and selecting the best models again. Formalized, the standard way of searching the model space can be written as:

$$m' = s(r(m)) \tag{1}$$

where m is the current model and m' is the next model in the greedy search step. The function $r(\cdot)$ is the refinement of a model and $s(\cdot)$ the selection of the best model. The greedy search of the model space is therefore only a sequence of refinement and selection steps which terminates when a good enough model has been found. Widening, on the other hand, can be described using the following formula:

$$\{m'_1, \ldots, m'_{k'}\} = s(\{r(m_1), \ldots, r(m_k)\}). \tag{2}$$

In a widened algorithm we do not deal with a single model, but with sets of models. The refinement operation produces multiple refinements from a single model and the selection filters them in order to return a set of best k' models. It can therefore be seen as a beam search through the model space. To avoid the selection operation choosing very similar models and not converging to a single solution or multiple very similar solutions, it is beneficial to enforce diversity within the selected models. Techniques for diversity-driven widening are discussed in [7]. One of the proposed methods is *Diverse Top-k Widening*, which makes use of a fixed diversity threshold θ that governs how similar the selected models are allowed to be, given a distance function δ.

3   Related Work

Since this paper focuses on widening a clustering algorithm, we focus here on work related to diversity-focused clustering and refer the reader to [1,7] for research into the general notion of enforcing diversity in model learning.

An approach that concentrates on diversity in clustering models is described in [2]. Here multiple diverse k-means clusterings are created in order to let the user choose the most applicable. Instead of selecting diverse clusterings after overproduction, the paper proposes a method whereby diversity is generated by running the k-means algorithm multiple times with different random initializations and random feature weighting. The large number of clusterings is then clustered at a meta level to present the user with a reasonable number of diverse models. The rationale here is that there are different clusterings for different purposes and the user ultimately knows best which one to choose. This, of course, is only useful for data sets with a low dimensionality.

Another paper that deals with finding better clustering results is [11]. Here the hierarchical clustering problem is solved using a genetic algorithm that tries to optimize the L_2 norm between an ultrametric distance matrix associated with the hierarchical classification and the proximity matrix of the dataset.

4   Widened Hierachical Agglomerative Clustering

In this paper we describe the widening of hierarchical agglomerative clustering. This bottom-up algorithm starts with every data point being a single cluster and subsequently merges the two clusters that are closest to each other. Apart from the distance function used to build the initial distance matrix, there are several possible linkage criteria for calculating the distance between newly formed clusters. Commonly used ones are:

UPGMA. The *Unweighted Pair Group Method with Arithmetic Mean* calculates the distance between two merged clusters A and B and another cluster C as the mean of the distance between A and C and between B and C.

Complete linkage. This method defines the distance of two clusters as the distance between those two data points (one from each cluster) that are farthest away from one another.

Single linkage. Contrary to complete linkage, here the distance of two clusters is the distance between those two data points that are closest to each other.

Centroid linkage. In this linkage method the distance between two clusters is the distance of their respective centroids.

Median linkage. Here the distance between two clusters is the Euclidean distance between their *weighted* centroids.

Centroid and median linkage are notable because they do not lead to a monotone distance measure. The resulting clustering dendrograms can have inversions because the similarity between two clusters increases through a merge of one of them with another cluster. Even though this makes the dendrogram harder to interpret, the linkage criterion is often used because the similarity of two centroids is easy to understand.

The distances calculated with the above linkage methods are used to determine the two clusters to be merged in the next step. The algorithm continues to merge clusters until a predefined number of clusters is reached or until only one cluster is left. Because choosing the closest clusters to be merged is a local decision, what can occur is that the algorithm makes a merge that has a negative influence on future merges, where it may be forced to combine two clusters that do not fit together very well. Due to the greedy nature of the algorithm, widening can help to find better solutions by exploring a larger portion of the model space. While [7] also describes the notion of communication-free widening, we concentrate on the effect diversity has on the model building and allow the direct comparison of models in the selection step. Even though finding better models in the same amount of time is the eventual goal of widening, this paper does not take speed into account and focuses on creating better models than the sequential algorithm.

An efficient implementation of the hierarchical agglomerative clustering algorithm with a time complexity of $\Theta(N^2 \log N)$ can be found in [12]. It is based on priority queues that are used to quickly determine the closest neighbor of a given cluster. To achieve widening, we can make use of these queues by not only merging the closest pair, but also the second, third or hundredth closest and therefore generating many refinements from a single model. The number of refined models k_r in iteration i can be calculated as follows:

$$k_{r,i} = k * (N - i).\qquad(3)$$

Here N is the total number of data points to be clustered. In each iteration two clusters are merged into one, $(N - i)$ therefore denotes the number of clusters present in iteration i.

5   Achieving Diversity

The diversity of the models is enforced in the selection step, where we select k models from k_r refinements. Our goal is to select the most diverse and at the same time also best models to achieve both exploration and exploitation. This multi-objective problem is known as *Maximum-Score Diversity Selection* [13].

In the following chapters we introduce a distance metric for our models, which is based on the Robinson Foulds metric. Furthermore we describe how the quality of our models can be compared with a small extension of the standard heuristic of hierarchical agglomerative clustering.

5.1   Distance Metric for Hierarchical Clustering Models

To have a notion of (dis-)similarity for our models, we first need to define a distance metric. Since the clustering process merges clusters in a bottom-up fashion, the intermediate models are forests, where each tree is either a single data point or a cluster tree on a subset of all data points. Because the leaves of the trees in the forests are the original data points, all models have the same leafset. To calculate a distance between our models, we need a metric that can be applied to the forests. One such metric, even though originally used for calculating the distance between phylogenetic trees, is the Robinson Foulds metric [15]. This metric is based on the number of *bipartitions* shared by two trees. A bipartition is a split of the tree at an edge, so that the leaves are divided into two disjoint sets. Splits at edges that connect a leaf with the rest of the tree are called trivial bipartitions and are ignored for the calculation of the metric since they are present in every tree.

When $B(T)$ denotes the set of nontrivial bipartitions of a tree, the number of bipartitions found in a tree T_1 but not in another tree T_2 can be calculated as

$$|B(T_1) - B(T_2)|.\qquad(4)$$

Using this the Robinson Foulds distance is defined as:

$$d_{RF}(T_1, T_2) = \frac{1}{2}(|B(T_1) - B(T_2)| + |B(T_2) - B(T_1)|).\qquad(5)$$

In order to apply the distance metric to our forests, we define the set of bipartitions for a forest F to be the union of bipartitions of its trees:

$$B(F) = \bigcap_{l=1}^{|F|} B(T_l). \tag{6}$$

While the Robinson Foulds metric is originally devised for unrooted trees, these sets of bipartitions for forests allow us to calculate the distance between our models as well.

An efficient algorithm for computing the metric on trees has been given in [4]. As the first step of the algorithm for unrooted trees is to select one of the leaves as the root node, the fact that the Robinson Foulds distance was meant for unrooted trees is of no regard for our problem. Day's algorithm identifies nontrivial bipartitions by assigning intervals to each inner node of a tree. To obtain the set of intervals for a number of trees $T_1, \ldots, T_n$, we take T_1 and traverse it in a depth first fashion, labeling the leaves according to the order in which they are visited. This will be our reference labeling for the leaf nodes of all trees, which means that if leaf node A has label 1 in the reference labeling, it will have the same label in all of the trees under comparison. The labels are then used to calculate unique intervals for each inner node. An inner node's interval is the tupel of the largest and smallest label of all its descendant leaf nodes. A tree's interval set S_i is the set of tupels from all its inner nodes. Figure 1 shows two trees, where the left has been used to create the reference labeling of the leaves. The Robinson Foulds distance between those trees is 2, since their interval sets differ in two tupels.

In order to use Day's algorithm for our models, the leaf labels have to be assigned across multiple trees in a forest. For one model, its trees are ordered arbitrarily, then iterated and traversed depth first, labeling all the leaf nodes according to the order in which they are visited. Since all models have the same leaf nodes, the labels can be mapped to the nodes of the other forests as well. After obtaining a labeling for the leaves, the interval set for each tree is calculated as described above. To compare two forests F_1 and F_2, we compare the corresponding interval sets $B(F_1)$ and $B(F_2)$ by counting the intervals that occur in one set but not the other. Using this count we can create a $k_r \times k_r$ distance matrix D for all refined models.

5.2   Selecting Diverse Models

In the next step we need to select k models from the k_r refinements, choosing both good and diverse ones to find an even balance between global exploration and local exploitation of the model space. In the original algorithm for hierarchical agglomerative clustering the next model is the one where the two clusters that are closest to each other are merged. In the case of multiple models developed in parallel, we can improve this heuristic by using the aggregated merge distance as criterion. For each refined model m, the score $\phi_{m,i}$ in the current iteration i can be calculated as follows:

$$\phi_{m,i} = \sum_{j=1}^{i} d_{m,j} \tag{7}$$

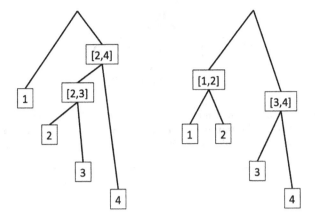

Fig. 1. Example of two trees and the corresponding intervals used by Day's algorithm to compute the Robinson Foulds distance.

where $d_{m,j}$ denotes the distances of the merged clusters in iteration j. The value $d_{m,j}$ depends on the distance metric used to build the initial distance matrix and the linkage criterion that is used to calculate the distance between a merged cluster and all other clusters.

After each model has been assigned an associated score, we need to select models that are not only *good* according to our scoring function but also *diverse* according to our distance metric. While in [7] a Diverse Top-k approach is described, we propose another way of selecting diverse trees that does not rely on a diversity threshold θ. Because the trees get larger with each iteration, the distance between them also increases. A fixed threshold is therefore not suitable for this problem. Instead, diversity can be achieved by clustering the models into k clusters and picking the best model of each cluster for the output of the selection step (see Fig. 2). Given the distance matrix D, we use k-medoid clustering [8] to split the set of models into groups and use $\phi_{m,i}$ to select the best model in each. The effect the model selection method has on diversity is demonstrated in Fig. 3. Here 20 models were built in parallel on the seeds dataset from the UCI repository [10], using k-medoid clustering to enforce diversity. After 200 steps, when 10 clusters were left to be merged, the refinements of the current intermediate models were projected into 2D space using multidimensional scaling [9]. In Fig. 3a the models that are chosen by the k-medoid selector for the next step are marked in red. Figure 3b shows which models would have been selected by a top-k selector. It can be seen that top-k focuses on a small area of the model space while models selected using k-medoid clustering are scattered across the whole space. The top-k approach also selects duplicates that occur in our models. The diversity enforcing clustering approach avoids this naturally as all equal models fall into the same cluster, but only one model is selected from each cluster.

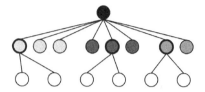

Fig. 2. The first step of widened model building using k-medoid with $k = 3$. Refined models are created from the initial model, then they are clustered into 3 groups and from each group the best model is used for creating the next generation of models.

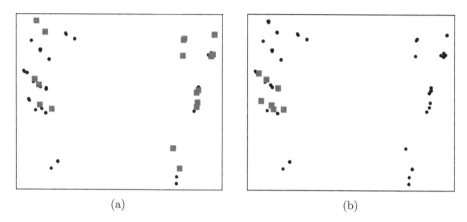

(a)   (b)

Fig. 3. Models projected with multidimensional scaling. In (a) the red squares mark the models selected using the k-medoid approach and in (b) the top-k models (Color figure online).

6   Evaluating Clustering Results

A commonly used quality measure for clustering results is the silhouette coefficient [16]. It is a number between -1 and 1, where values close to the lower bound are a sign of very bad clustering and numbers close to 1 mean that the found clusters are good. For an individual data point o belonging to cluster A the silhouette is defined as

$$s(o) = \frac{\text{dist}(B, o) - \text{dist}(A, o)}{\max\{\text{dist}(A, o), \text{dist}(B, o)\}} \qquad (8)$$

where $\text{dist}(A, o)$ is the average distance between o and all data points in A, and $\text{dist}(B, o)$ is the distance between o and all data points in the next closest cluster B. The silhouette coefficient of a clustering result is the average $s(o)$ over all data points.

The Davies-Bouldin Index (DBI) [3] is another cluster evaluation measure that can be used to compare the quality of multiple clustering results. Like the silhouette coefficient it is an internal evaluation scheme, where only features of the dataset itself are taken into account. The index can be determined with the following formula:

$$DB = \frac{1}{N} \sum_{i=1}^{N} D_i \tag{9}$$

where D_i is defined as:

$$D_i = \max_{j \neq i} \frac{S_i + S_j}{dist(A_i, A_j)} , \tag{10}$$

with A_i being the centroid and S_i the scatter within cluster i:

$$S_i = \frac{1}{T_i} \sum_{d=1}^{T_i} ||X_d - A_i||_p . \tag{11}$$

Here T_i is the size of the cluster and X_d is a data point in the cluster. The Davies-Boulding-Index compares the within-cluster scatter to the between-cluster separation, represented by the distance between the corresponding centroids. A ratio close to zero means that the clusters are dense and well separated.

7   Preliminary Results

As our preliminary tests show, the best of multiple, built-in-parallel, diverse models can have both a better silhouette coefficient and Davies-Bouldin Index in comparison to the model found by the greedy, sequential algorithm. The effectiveness depends on the linkage method and the data set used. Tests have been carried out with the user knowledge modeling data set and the seeds data set from the UCI Machine Learning Repository. The data sets were chosen due to their suitability for clustering and their size. The desired number of clusters to be generated by the algorithms was set to 3 for the seeds data set and to 4 for the user knowledge modeling data set. We used the Euclidean distance as the distance measure for building the initial distance matrix for the data points and to calculate the between-cluster separation for the Davies-Bouldin Index.

In our tests clustering the seeds data set with median linkage shows promising results for the widened version of the algorithm. Figure 4a shows the silhouette coefficient of the best and worst of 10 widened models and the sequential algorithm's silhouette coefficient over the iterations of the algorithm. Here we can see that the widened algorithm generally produces a model with a better silhouette coefficient than the sequential algorithm.

Notable is the steep drop of the traditional algorithm's silhouette coefficient at 5 clusters (iteration 205), clearly visible in Fig. 5a. Here it is forced to make a bad merge due to preceding greedy behavior. The best widened model also had a declining silhouette coefficient in previous iterations but has at that point already recovered with a silhouette coefficient of 0.389. If the data is clustered into 3 groups, the best widened model has a silhouette coefficient of 0.425. The sequential algorithm produces a model that has a silhouette coefficient of 0.264. Similar results can be achieved with centroid clustering. For average, complete and single linkage the silhouette coefficient could not be improved by widening.

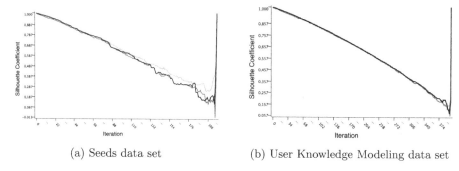

(a) Seeds data set   (b) User Knowledge Modeling data set

Fig. 4. The silhouette coefficient for intermediate models of the sequential algorithm (black) and the best (green) and worst (red) of the widened models for each iteration (Color figure online).

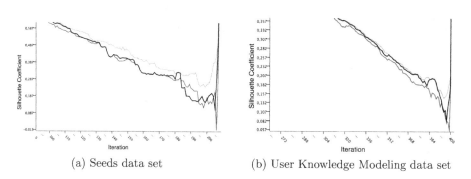

(a) Seeds data set   (b) User Knowledge Modeling data set

Fig. 5. The silhouette coefficients in the last steps of the sequential algorithm (black) and widened algorithm (best model: green, worst model: red) (Color figure online).

The Davies-Bouldin Index, however, can be improved from 0.76 to 0.74 when the UPGMA linkage method is used. The best model obtained through widening the median linkage algorithm also achieves a lower DBI for 3 clusters. The best of the 10 widened models has a score of 0.65, the sequential algorithm achieves a DBI of 1.84.

Similar results can be achieved when clustering the user knowledge modeling data set with complete linkage hierarchical clustering. Figure 4b depicts the silhouette coefficient for the best and worst of 10 widened models and the model generated by the sequential algorithm for each iteration of the algorithm. For 4 clusters the best widened model has a silhouette coefficient of 0.169, for the model generated by the sequential algorithm this value is 0.124. An interesting observation can be made in Fig. 5b, where we see that the greedy algorithm's silhouette coefficient increases in iteration 384 but drops very low subsequently. The best widened model does not exhibit such extreme behavior. There the silhouette coefficient changes only slightly before dropping down to around 0.155.

The Davies-Bouldin Index also shows the improvement that is possible through widening. Clustering the user knowledge modeling data set with 4 desired clusters the widened algorithm produces a result with a DBI of 1.622 while the sequential algorithm achieves an index of 1.699. It is notable that the model with the lowest DBI does not also have the highest silhouette coefficient.

Note that the afore-mentioned widened algorithm's runtime is worse than the sequential algorithm's runtime, despite the possible parallelization of the refinement and selection processes. The reason for this increase in runtime is that calculating the pair-wise distance of many refined models for the matrix D is very time consuming, resulting in overhead for the selection step. This paper focuses on the role diversity plays in the intelligent search of the model space and performance improvements may be achieved by making the widened algorithm communication-less, avoiding the model-by-model comparisons altogether. This, however, is a topic of future research and not in the scope of this work. For an introduction to diverse communication-free widening we refer the reader to [7], where ideas for avoiding communication between parallel workers are described.

8   Conclusions and Future Work

In this paper we have shown the application of widening to the hierarchical agglomerative clustering algorithm. The two main parts of widening are refinement and selection, for both of which we described implementations for hierarchical clustering. Creating refinements of a model utilizes information that is already present in the sequential algorithm, namely the priority queues that are maintained to keep track of the nearest neighbor of each cluster. For the selection of diverse and good models we described a method that groups models using k-medoid clustering and subsequently picks the best model from each group. We visualized how this approach covers the model space better than top-k, which focuses on a small area only. Our results on two public datasets indicate that the models obtained through widening can be better than the results of the sequential algorithm. This is the case for both the Davies-Bouldin Index and the silhouette coefficient, two widely used clustering evaluation metrics.

Future work includes the evaluation of other diversity facilitating methods such as p-dispersion-min-sum as well as making the algorithm communication-free. Removing communication between different branches of refined models would also increase the runtime performance of the algorithm, as less models would have to be compared to each other. This paper shows that spending parallel computing resources on exploring the model space can result in better models and widening the hierarchical agglomerative clustering algorithm is feasible when faster ways of enforcing diversity can be applied.

References

1. Akbar, Z., Ivanova, V.N., Berthold, M.R.: Parallel data mining revisited. better, not faster. In: Proceedings of the 11th International Symposium on Intelligent Data Analysis, pp. 23–34 (2012)
2. Caruana, R., Elhawary, M., Nguyen, N., Smith, C.: Meta clustering. In: 2006 Sixth International Conference on Data Mining, ICDM 2006, pp. 107–118. IEEE (2006)
3. Davies, D.L., Bouldin, D.W.: A cluster separation measure. IEEE Trans. Pattern Anal. Mach. Intell. PAMI **1**(2), 224–227 (1979)
4. Day, W.H.E.: Optimal algorithms for comparing trees with labeled leaves. J. Classif. **2**(1), 7–28 (1985)
5. Graf, H.P., Cosatto, E., Bottou, L., Dourdanovic, I., Vapnik, V.: Parallel support vector machines: the cascade SVM. In: Advances in Neural Information Processing Systems, pp. 521–528 (2004)
6. Hastie, T., Tibshirani, R., Friedman, J., Hastie, T., Friedman, J., Tibshirani, R.: The Elements of Statistical Learning, vol. 2. Springer, New York (2009)
7. Ivanova, V.N., Berthold, M.R.: Diversity-driven widening. In: Tucker, A., Höppner, F., Siebes, A., Swift, S. (eds.) IDA 2013. LNCS, vol. 8207, pp. 223–236. Springer, Heidelberg (2013)
8. Kaufman, L., Rousseeuw, P.: Clustering by means of medoids. Reports of the Faculty of Mathematics and Informatics, Faculty of Mathematics and Informatics (1987)
9. Kruskal, J.B., Wish, M.: Multidimensional Scaling, vol. 11. Sage, Beverly Hills (1978)
10. Lichman, M.: UCI machine learning repository (2013)
11. Lozano, J.A., Larrañaga, P.: Applying genetic algorithms to search for the best hierarchical clustering of a dataset. Pattern Recogn. Lett. **20**(9), 911–918 (1999)
12. Manning, C.D., Raghavan, P., Schütze, H.: Introduction to Information Retrieval, vol. 1. Cambridge university press, Cambridge (2008)
13. Meinl, T.: Maximum-score diversity selection. Ph.D. thesis, University of Konstanz, July 2010
14. Olson, C.F.: Parallel algorithms for hierarchical clustering. Parallel Comput. **21**(8), 1313–1325 (1995)
15. Robinson, D.F., Foulds, L.R.: Comparison of phylogenetic trees. Math. Biosci. **53**(12), 131–147 (1981)
16. Rousseeuw, P.J.: Silhouettes: a graphical aid to the interpretation and validation of cluster analysis. J. Comput. Appl. Math. **20**, 53–65 (1987)
17. Sampson, O., Berthold, M.R.: Widened KRIMP: better performance through diverse parallelism. In: Blockeel, H., van Leeuwen, M., Vinciotti, V. (eds.) IDA 2014. LNCS, vol. 8819, pp. 276–285. Springer, Heidelberg (2014)
18. Srivastava, A., Han, E.-H., Kumar, V., Singh, V.: Parallel formulations of decision-tree classification algorithms. In: Guo, Y., Grossman, R. (eds.) High Performance Data Mining, pp. 237–261. Springer, US (2002)
19. Sundararajan, N., Saratchandran, P.: Parallel Architectures for Artificial Neural Networks: Paradigms and Implementations, 1st edn. IEEE Computer Society Press, Los Alamitos (1998)

Batch Steepest-Descent-Mildest-Ascent for Interactive Maximum Margin Clustering

Fabian Gieseke[1]([✉]), Tapio Pahikkala[2], and Tom Heskes[1]

[1] Institute for Computing and Information Sciences, Faculty of Science,
Radboud University, Nijmegen, The Netherlands
{fgieseke,t.heskes}@science.ru.nl
[2] Department of Information Technology and Turku Centre for Computer Science,
University of Turku, Turku, Finland
aatapa@utu.fi

Abstract. The maximum margin clustering principle extends support vector machines to unsupervised scenarios. We present a variant of this clustering scheme that can be used in the context of interactive clustering scenarios. In particular, our approach permits the class ratios to be manually defined by the user during the fitting process. Our framework can be used at early stages of the data mining process when no or very little information is given about the true clusters and class ratios. One of the key contributions is an adapted steepest-descent-mildest-ascent optimization scheme that can be used to fine-tune maximum margin clustering solutions in an interactive manner. We demonstrate the applicability of our approach in the context of remote sensing and astronomy with training sets consisting of hundreds of thousands of patterns.

1 Introduction

The classification of objects is one of the key tasks in data mining and machine learning. At early stages of the data mining process, no or very few labeled patterns are given. Often, even the goal of the learning process is not clear from the beginning, i.e., the user does not know which clusters might be present in the data. This usually necessitates the use of fully unsupervised techniques. Over the past decades, a large amount of clustering techniques have been proposed. In general, the outcome of such schemes can heavily depend on the specific clustering criterion that is addressed or on the involved model parameters. Since the "true" cluster structure is not known beforehand (and might depend on the user's preferences and goals), one is generally faced with the problem of recurrently applying and fine-tuning the different techniques at hand. Thus, a desirable goal is to "interactively" adapt a given clustering solution by slightly modifying the associated model parameters on the fly.

A recent clustering technique is the so-called *maximum margin clustering* problem [1–7], which extends the concept of *support vector machines* [8–10] to unsupervised learning settings. In a nutshell, this concept aims at detecting two classes in the data such that a subsequent application of a support vector

© Springer International Publishing Switzerland 2015
E. Fromont et al. (Eds.): IDA 2015, LNCS 9385, pp. 95–107, 2015.
DOI: 10.1007/978-3-319-24465-5_9

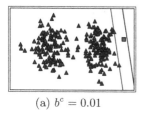
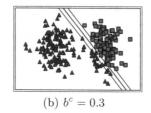
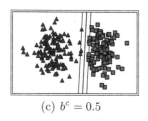

(a) $b^c = 0.01$ (b) $b^c = 0.3$ (c) $b^c = 0.5$

Fig. 1. Influence of the balancing constraint on a two-dimensional artificial data set: Certain clustering outcomes can be "enforced" using corresponding parameter assignment for the balancing constraint b^c (here, $b^c = 0$ corresponds to all points being assigned to the negative class whereas $b^c = 1$ corresponds to positive patterns only).

machine yields the best overall result. The potential of this clustering framework has been evaluated by many authors on various artificial and real-world data sets [1–7]. However, both its combinatorial nature as well its dependency on certain model parameters can render its application difficult in practice. One crucial model parameter is the balancing constraint that determines the amount of patterns being assigned to each of the classes (and which is needed to avoid trivial solutions). In case of no prior knowledge about the class ratios, one usually aims at balanced class assignments with roughly equally-sized clusters. However, this might yield undesired clustering outcomes, especially in case one of the two clusters is considerably smaller. In Fig. 1, the influence of this parameter on a two-dimensional toy example is shown. It can be clearly seen that a "wrong" balancing constraint can lead to (most likely) undesired clustering outcomes.

We propose an optimization framework that is devoted to an interactive version of the maximum margin clustering principle. In particular, the user can adapt the balancing constraint in the course of the overall process to enforce certain new class ratios in case a current clustering partition is inappropriate. As shown in our experimental evaluation, the resulting framework can effectively deal with data sets consisting of hundreds of thousands of training patterns, which renders it a suitable tool for discovering "desired" clustering solutions on the fly. We demonstrate the applicability of our approach in the context of remote sensing and astronomy and consider variants that address constrained clustering tasks with certain patterns being manually fixed to one of the classes.

2   Interactive Maximum Margin Clustering

We start by describing the maximum margin clustering problem including its interactive variant that is addressed in the remainder of this work.

2.1   Maximum Margin Clustering

The original maximum margin clustering problem (MMC) [1] addresses unsupervised learning scenarios with training patterns of the form $T = \{\mathbf{x}_1, \ldots, \mathbf{x}_n\} \subset$

X, where X is an arbitrary input space. From a mathematical point of view, the search for the optimal partition of the unlabeled patterns w.r.t. the general support vector machine objective yields the following optimization task:

$$\underset{\mathbf{y}\in\{-1,+1\}^n, f\in\mathcal{H}_k}{\text{minimize}} \sum_{i=1}^{n} L\big(y_i, f(\mathbf{x}_i)\big) + \lambda\|f\|_{\mathcal{H}_k}^2 \tag{1}$$

Here, $f : X \to \mathbb{R}$ is a *model function*, $\|\cdot\|_{\mathcal{H}_k}$ a norm in a *reproducing kernel Hilbert space* $\mathcal{H}_k$ induced by a *kernel* $k : X \times X \to \mathbb{R}$, $L : \{-1, +1\} \times \mathbb{R} \to [0, \infty)$ a *loss function*, and $\lambda \in \mathbb{R}_+$ a *regularization parameter* [9,10]. Thus, in contrast to standard support vector machines, the labels y_i of the training patterns are part of the optimization task, which renders the problem difficult to solve. To avoid unbalanced solutions (e.g., all patterns being assigned to one class only), some kind of balancing constraint has to be added. A typical candidate is

$$\frac{1}{n}\sum_{i=1}^{n} \max(0, y_i) \approx b^c \tag{2}$$

with user-defined parameter $b^c \in (0, 1)$. As motivated above, this constraint can have a significant influence on the clustering outcome.

The combinatorial nature of this problem renders the task difficult to solve. For this reason, several variants have been proposed in the literature (see below) that are based on other loss function than the standard *hinge loss* $L\big(y, f(\mathbf{x})\big) = \max(0, 1 - yf(\mathbf{x}))$. As pointed out by Zhang *et al.* [6], both the *square loss* $L\big(y, f(\mathbf{x})\big) = \big(y - f(\mathbf{x})\big)^2$ and the ε-insensitive loss $L\big(y, f(\mathbf{x})\big) = \max(0, |y - f(\mathbf{x})| - \varepsilon)$ depict suitable candidates, which often yield practical optimization frameworks that are less susceptible to bad local optima.

2.2 Interactive Clustering

The clustering solutions induced by the maximum margin clustering principle can heavily depend on the particular parameter assignment for the balancing constraint (2). In general, an "optimal" assignment depends on the particular data set at hand as well as on the current application and user preferences. In the remainder of this work, we consider the following "interactive" version of the maximum margin clustering problem: Starting with an user-defined balancing constraint (i.e., a particular assignment for b^c), an initial clustering solution is computed based on the objective (1). This induces a partition of the points into two clusters along with a certain class ratio. Afterwards, the user can manually tune the class ratio by increasing or decreasing the amount of patterns being assigned to one of the classes (i.e., a new balancing constraint is enforced).

The overall workflow is illustrated in Fig. 2 in the context of a remote sensing application: Starting with an initial (inappropriate) clustering solution, the user can interactively fine-tune the outcome via a simple slider operation that determines the class ratio until a satisfying result is achieved. Hence, in each

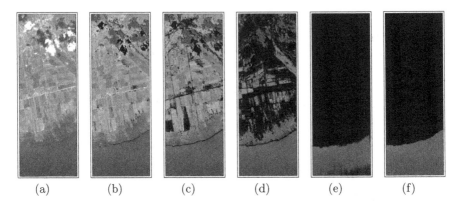

(a)   (b)   (c)   (d)   (e)   (f)

Fig. 2. Interactive exploration of possible clustering outcomes on hyperspectral image data: Eleven grayscale images are composed to a single RGB image, see Figure (a). The clustering takes place in an underlying eleven-dimensional feature space. Starting with an initial clustering solution (Figure (b)), the amount of positive patterns is increased incrementally by the user (Figures (c)–(e)). In the last step, the amount is decreased slightly to achieve a satisfying clustering outcome ('land and cloud' vs. 'water' pixels) insert color figure online.

of the intermediate phases, the algorithm has to decide which patterns should be exchanged between the two current clusters such that the objective is minimized. Further, in case some of the patterns are not automatically moved to one of the "desired" clusters, the user can provide additional input by "fixing" some patterns to one of the clusters (which is related to *constrained clustering* [11]).[1]

2.3 Related Work

Several approaches have been proposed to address the standard maximum margin clustering problem. Among the first approaches is the scheme proposed by Xu *et al.* [1], who reformulate the original task to obtain a semidefinite programming problem. A similar approach with better asymptotical runtimes is given by Valizadegan and Jin [2]. Other techniques are based on, e.g., cutting plane techniques or so-called "label generation" strategies [4,12]. The use of the square loss in the context of maximum margin clustering stems from Zhang *et al.* [6], who pointed out that local search strategies *"can more easily get out of a poor solution"* in case the ε-insensitive or the square loss are used instead of the original hinge loss. This idea is extended by Gieseke *et al.* [3] and Pahikkala *et al.* [5], who make use of matrix-based shortcuts to speed up the involved computations.

While general interactive clustering variants have been addressed in the literature (see, e.g., [13,14]), the process of manually fine-tuning the balancing constraint in the context of the maximum margin clustering problem has not been considered so far. As mentioned above, each phase involves the identification of patterns whose change of clusters yield a valid partition according to

---

[1] Naturally, such schemes are particularly useful if the outcome can be visualized; if this is not possible, one has to resort to other criteria to assess partitions.

Algorithm 1. INTERACTIVE MAXIMUM MARGIN CLUSTERING

Require: Unlabeled patterns $T = \{x_1, \ldots, x_n\}$ and initial balancing constraint b_0^c.
Ensure: Partition $y \in \{-1, +1\}^n$ of unlabeled patterns.
1: Compute initial clustering partition y_0 according to b_0^c
2: $\tau = 1$
3: **while** new user input b_τ^c **do**
4:     Let $K = |n \cdot (b_\tau^c - b_{\tau-1}^c)|$ and $c = \text{sign}(b_\tau^c - b_{\tau-1}^c) \in \{-1, +1\}$
5:     Compute steepest-descent-mildest-ascent values $S(y, 1, c), \ldots, S(y, n, c)$
6:     Rank coordinates j according to $S(y, j, c)$ (ascending order)
7:     $y_\tau \leftarrow y_{\tau-1}$ by flipping the K top-ranked coordinates
8:     $\tau \leftarrow \tau + 1$
9: **end while**
10: **return** $y_{\tau-1}$

---

the new balancing constraint and which are, at the same time, good candidates w.r.t. the objective (1). Thus, in case no additional constraints are enforced by the user, the resulting framework has to compute these partitions in a fully unsupervised manner. Otherwise, in case of additional constraints, the intermediate tasks are related to *constrained clustering* [11] or *semi-supervised learning* [15].

3 Algorithmic Framework

3.1 General Workflow

Different ways exist to address the induced intermediate optimization tasks. A direct one is to retrain an appropriate model from scratch for each new balancing constraint provided by the user. While the current cluster assignments could be used as starting point, one still has to decide which of the patterns have to switch classes such that the new constraint is fulfilled. Further, given large-scale learning problems such as the one shown in Fig. 2 with thousands of patterns, such an approach is, in general, computationally very challenging. Another principled way of addressing the interactive settings is to directly change the cluster assignments of those patterns that would contribute most (or least) to an improvement (or worsening) of the current objective value (1). As we will show in our experimental evaluation, this greedy approach cannot only be implemented much more efficiently but also yields stable and intuitive clustering outcomes.

The general workflow of this approach is shown in Algorithm 1: Starting with an initial clustering solution y_0 (e.g., all patterns being assigned to one class or initialized via a maximum margin clustering solver), one iteratively modifies the partition until no user input is provided anymore. Each user input yields a new assignment b_τ^c for the balancing constraint and for each such input, the algorithm has to select $K = |n \cdot (b_\tau^c - b_{\tau-1}^c)|$ appropriate patterns such that their change of classes leads to a valid partition w.r.t. b_τ^c. These patterns are selected and flipped according to *steepest-descent-mildest-ascent* directions $S(y, j, c)$, where $c = \text{sign}(b_\tau^c - b_{\tau-1}^c) \in \{-1, +1\}$ is the flipping direction (Steps 4–7). As soon as no user input is provided anymore, the final partition is returned.

It remains to define the criterion $S(\mathbf{y}, j, c)$ used in Step 5: Similarly to a standard steepest descent step, we consider those coordinates $j \in \{1, \ldots, n\}$ that yield the best steepest descent or mildest ascent[2] of the objective. More precisely, we suggest the following definition for these coordinate steps:

Definition 1. *Given an objective function* $F : \{-1, +1\}^n \to \mathbb{R}$ *and a binary class label* $c \in \{-1, +1\}$, *we define the steepness for the index* $j \in \{1, \ldots, n\}$ *as*

$$S(\mathbf{y}, j, c) = \begin{cases} F(\mathbf{y} + 2c\mathbf{e}^j) & \text{if } y_j \neq c \\ \infty & \text{otherwise} \end{cases} \tag{3}$$

where $\mathbf{e}^j$ *is the j-th standard basis vector of* $\mathbb{R}^n$.

Note that the second case of the above definition simply assigns ∞ to a coordinate that cannot be flipped since it already belongs to the "correct" class. Thus, given a partition vector $\mathbf{y}$ and a flipping direction $c \in \{-1, +1\}$, the above definition yields n steepness values $S(\mathbf{y}, 1, c), \ldots, S(\mathbf{y}, n, c)$. These values are ranked and the associated K top-ranked coordinates are selected. In general, computing the steepness directions $S(\mathbf{y}, 1, c), \ldots, S(\mathbf{y}, n, c)$ in Step 5 can be computationally very expensive. Below, we describe an efficient implementation for these subtasks that renders the overall approach capable of dealing with large-scale scenarios consisting of hundreds of thousands of training patterns.

3.2 Fast Computation of Ranking Criterion

The above definition is based on an objective function $F : \{-1, +1\}^n \to \mathbb{R}$, which we define next. For a *fixed* partition vector $\mathbf{y}$, it follows from the representer theorem [16] that any optimal solution $f^* \in \mathcal{H}_k$ for the task (1) is of the form

$$f^*(\cdot) = \sum_{i=1}^{n} a_i k(\mathbf{x}_i, \cdot) \tag{4}$$

with coefficients $\mathbf{a} = (a_1, \ldots, a_n)^{\mathrm{T}} \in \mathbb{R}^n$. We follow the related literature [3,5,6] and consider the square loss $L(y, f(\mathbf{x})) = (y - f(\mathbf{x}))^2$. In this case, these coefficients can be determined analytically via $\mathbf{a} = (\mathbf{K} + \lambda \mathbf{I})^{-1} \mathbf{y} =: \mathbf{G}\mathbf{y}$, where $\mathbf{K} \in \mathbb{R}^{n \times n}$ is the kernel matrix consisting of entries $\mathbf{K}_{i,j} = k(\mathbf{x}_i, \mathbf{x}_j)$ and $\mathbf{I}$ the identity matrix. Thus, using $\|f^*\|_{\mathcal{H}_k}^2 = \mathbf{a}^{\mathrm{T}} \mathbf{K} \mathbf{a}$ [10], one obtains [3,5]

$$\underset{\mathbf{y} \in \{-1, +1\}^n}{\text{minimize}} \ F(\mathbf{y}) = (\mathbf{y} - \mathbf{K}\mathbf{G}\mathbf{y})^{\mathrm{T}}(\mathbf{y} - \mathbf{K}\mathbf{G}\mathbf{y}) + \lambda \mathbf{y}^{\mathrm{T}} \mathbf{G}\mathbf{K}\mathbf{G}\mathbf{y}$$

$$= \mathbf{y}^{\mathrm{T}} \left(\mathbf{I} - \mathbf{K}\mathbf{G} - \mathbf{G}\mathbf{K} + \mathbf{G}\mathbf{K}\mathbf{K}\mathbf{G} + \lambda \mathbf{G}\mathbf{K}\mathbf{G} \right) \mathbf{y}, \tag{5}$$

---

[2] Note that enforcing the new balancing constraint b_τ^c might induce a partition vector whose objective is worse than the one for the current partition vector.

Algorithm 2. BATCH STEEPEST-DESCENT-MILDEST-ASCENT OPERATION

Require: A partition $\mathbf{y} \in \{-1, +1\}^n$, the set $\mathcal{S} = \{1, \ldots, n\}$ of possible coordinates, a number $K < |\mathcal{S}|$ of coordinates to be flipped, $c \in \{-1, +1\}$, $\mathbf{p} \in \mathbb{R}^r$, and $\mathbf{Q} \in \mathbb{R}^{r \times n}$.

1: Initialize $\mathbf{d} \in \mathbb{R}^{|\mathcal{S}|}$ with $d_j = \infty$
2: **for** $j \in \mathcal{S}$ **do**
3:     **if** $y_j \neq c$ **then**
4:         $\hat{\mathbf{p}} \leftarrow \mathbf{p} - 2y_j \mathbf{Q}_{:,j}$
5:         $d_j \leftarrow n - \hat{\mathbf{p}}^{\mathrm{T}} \hat{\mathbf{p}}$
6:     **end if**
7: **end for**
8: Sort coordinates $\mathcal{S}$ according to $\mathbf{d}$ (ascending order)
9: **for** $i = 1, \ldots, K$ **do**
10:     $j \leftarrow \mathcal{S}_i$
11:     $y_j \leftarrow -y_j$
12:     $\mathbf{p} \leftarrow \mathbf{p} - 2y_j \mathbf{Q}_{:,j}$
13: **end for**

As shown by Pahikkala *et al.* [5], one can further simplify this objective:

Fact 1. ([5]) *Let* $\mathbf{K} = \mathbf{V}\mathbf{\Lambda}\mathbf{V}^{\mathrm{T}} \in \mathbb{R}^{n \times n}$ *be the eigen decomposition of the kernel matrix* $\mathbf{K}$ *and let the diagonal matrix* $\widetilde{\mathbf{\Lambda}}$ *be defined as* $\widetilde{\mathbf{\Lambda}} = (\mathbf{\Lambda} + \lambda \mathbf{I})^{-1}$. *Then,*

$$F(\mathbf{y}) = n - \mathbf{y}^{\mathrm{T}} \mathbf{V}\mathbf{\Lambda}\widetilde{\mathbf{\Lambda}}\mathbf{V}^{\mathrm{T}} \mathbf{y} \tag{6}$$

holds for the objective function $F(\mathbf{y})$ *defined in (5).*

Computing the full kernel matrix is often computationally infeasible. For this reason, approximation schemes such as the *Nyström method* [17] are usually employed. In particular, assuming one has access to a feature representation $\mathbf{\Phi} \in \mathbb{R}^{n \times r}$ for some $r \ll n$ such that $\mathbf{K} = \mathbf{\Phi}\mathbf{\Phi}^{\mathrm{T}}$, the eigenvectors and eigenvalues can be obtained by computing the economy-sized singular value decomposition of $\mathbf{\Phi}$. That is, one only has to compute the non-zero singular values $\sqrt{\mathbf{\Lambda}} \in \mathbb{R}^{r \times r}$ of $\mathbf{\Phi}$ and their corresponding left singular vectors $\mathbf{V} \in \mathbb{R}^{n \times r}$. This permits the computation of $\mathbf{Q} \in \mathbb{R}^{r \times n}$ with $\mathbf{Q}^{\mathrm{T}}\mathbf{Q} = \mathbf{V}\mathbf{\Lambda}\widetilde{\mathbf{\Lambda}}\mathbf{V}^{\mathrm{T}}$ in $\mathcal{O}(r^2 n)$ time [18], where $1 \leq r \leq n$ determines the degree of approximation.

In Step 3 of Algorithm 1, the values $S(\mathbf{y}, j, c)$ have to be computed. The procedure for computing and ranking these values as well as for updating the partition vector $\mathbf{y}_\tau$ (Steps 5–7) is shown in Algorithm 2: Let $\mathbf{p} := \mathbf{Q}\mathbf{y}$. Then, one can rewrite the objective (6) as $F(\mathbf{y}) = n - \mathbf{p}^{\mathrm{T}}\mathbf{p}$. This closed-form solution of the intermediate objective values is used for computing the steepest-descent-mildest-ascent values (Steps 1–7). Afterwards, the coordinates in $\mathcal{S}$ are sorted according to these values (Step 8) and the K patterns with the lowest values are assigned to class c. Finally, the auxiliary vector $\mathbf{p}$ is updated (Steps 9–13).

Theorem 1. *For each interaction phase, $\mathcal{O}(|\mathcal{S}|r + |\mathcal{S}|\log|\mathcal{S}|)$ time is spent in Algorithm 2. The initialization of $\mathbf{Q} \in \mathbb{R}^{r \times n}$ and $\mathbf{p} \in \mathbb{R}^r$ takes $\mathcal{O}(nr^2)$ time and a total amount of $\mathcal{O}(nr)$ additional space is needed.*

Proof. Each steepest-descent-mildest-ascent value (Steps 3–6) can be obtained in $\mathcal{O}(r)$ time due to $\mathbf{Q}_{:,j} \in \mathbb{R}^r$ and at most $|\mathcal{S}|$ values have to be computed. Similarly, the update of each auxiliary vector $\mathbf{p}$ in Step 12 takes at most $\mathcal{O}(r)$ time, i.e., $\mathcal{O}(Kr) \in \mathcal{O}(|\mathcal{S}|r)$ time in total. Sorting all values takes $|\mathcal{S}|\log|\mathcal{S}|$ time.

Note that a "focus set" $\mathcal{S} \subset \{1, \ldots, n\}$ can be defined by the user to restrict the coordinates that can be flipped. This can be handy in case clustering steps shall only be performed in a certain region of the feature space.

4   Experiments

We demonstrate the applicability of our approach in the context of remote sensing and astronomy. For all use cases, a large amount of patterns can efficiently be processed, which underlines the framework's potential for large-scale scenarios. In principle, other clustering techniques could be adapted in a similar fashion. Due to lack of space, we focus on the interactive maximum margin clustering variant and defer a more extensive experimental comparison to future work.

4.1   Experimental Setup

For all experiments, a standard desktop computer with an `Intel(R) Core(TM)` `i7-4790K` CPU running at 4.00 GHz (4 cores; 8 hardware threads) 32 GB RAM is used. The operation system was `Ubuntu 14.04` (64 Bit) with kernel version `3.13.0-45`. The overall approach is implemented in `Python` (2.7.6) using the `Cython` package for Algorithm 2. Further, the `NumPy` package is used to efficiently compute all matrix decompositions as well as all involved matrix-vector products.[3] For all experiments, we have $X = \mathbb{R}^d$ and make use of an RBF kernel [9,10] with kernel width $\gamma = s^{-1}$, where $s = \sum_{j=0}^{d}\left(\max\{X^j\} - \min\{X^j\}\right)^2$ is an estimate of the average squared distances in the training data (here, $\{X^j\}$ denotes the set of all j attribute values). The regularization parameter λ is fixed to 1.0 and $r = 100$ is the rank of the approximated kernel matrix (see above).

We consider two application domains that involve multi-dimensional image data: The first one is remote sensing, see again Fig. 2. In particular, we make use of satellite data that is obtained from the Hyperion instrument of the EO-1 Earth orbiter [19].[4] While the instrument gathers data at 242 wavelengths via different bands, machine learning models are often applied on a subset of the features only (e.g., due to restricted computational resources onboard of the spacecraft). We follow Castano *et al.* [21] and consider a subset of eleven bands that are used for the onboard SWIL (snow, water, ice, land) classifier resulting to $\mathbb{R}^{11}$ as

---

[3] The code is publicly available under https://github.com/aatapa/RLScore.
[4] Some parts of the data were kindly provided by Wagstaff and Bornstein [20].

feature space. For the interactive clustering process, RGB images that stem from combining different bands are shown to the user. As second application domain, we consider photometric data from the *Sloan Digital Sky Survey* (SDSS) [22]. Here, the raw data stems from five different filters that give rise to five grayscale images for each observed region.

4.2   Applications

The data sets mentioned above give rise to feature spaces *with* an associated image representation. To facilitate the user input, an appropriate interface was developed that can be used to enforce a new balancing constraint ("slider operation") or to select certain regions of interest ("lasso select").

Fore-/Background Separation in Astronomy. The separation of fore- and background is a common problem in many domains. For instance, one of the initial steps given image data in astronomy is to detect objects that are given in a large image or to separate a particular object from the background noise.

Fig. 3. Interactive fore-/background separation for a five-dimensional feature space and $n = 300,000$ pixels: The amount of positive patterns (red) is increased iteratively by the user until a desired separation is achieved. The feature space consists of the RGB pixel values along with x/y coordinates, see, e.g., Lund *et al.* [23] (Color figure online).

In Fig. 3, the application of the interactive maximum margin clustering principle is shown for an RGB image of the SDSS database[5]: Starting with no pixels being assigned to the positive class, the user can incrementally increase the balancing constraint parameter b^c until a desired separation is obtained. Note that for each interaction phase, our framework needs significantly less than a second for this data set instance ($n = 300,000$) to compute and update a new partition vector **y** and, thus, can yield immediate feedback to the user.

---

[5] http://dr12.sdss3.org/.

Clustering Hyperspectral Data. Figure 2 sketches the iterative process of separating 'land' from 'water and cloud' pixels given hyperspectral image data ($n = 179,200$). Again, the approach can handle such data set instances efficiently with intermediate steps taking significantly less than a second. In Fig. 4, the final outcomes of the interactive process (left) and a standard k-means [24] application with $k = 2$ (right) are compared. While both clustering outcomes depict reasonable solutions, the interactive variant permits to fine-tune a certain clustering outcome (e.g., to enforce a smooth transition between 'water' and 'land' pixels).

Fig. 4. Comparison

Interactively Adding More Constraints. The above scenarios are purely unsupervised (except for the balancing constraint inputs). However, if desired, additional constraints can be incorporated into the process. For instance, the user can manually specify some "regions of interest" for the initial clustering partition. Depending on the task at hand, this can give rise to a different clustering process. In Fig. 5, another hyperspectral data set instance is addressed ($n = 228,448$). In case all patterns are initially assigned to the negative class (Figure (a)), the overall process yields 'clouds' vs. 'land and water' as final clustering partition. In Figure (b), some patterns are initially assigned to the 'land' class, which leads to a slightly different partition ('land' vs. 'clouds and water').

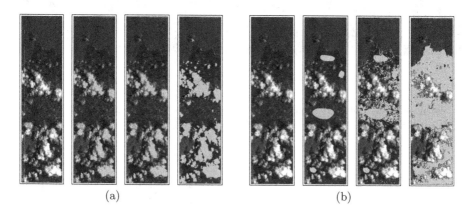

(a)   (b)

Fig. 5. Additional constraints can be incorporated by manually assigning some patterns to one of the clusters. Such an input can be provided as initial partition at the beginning of the interactive process or in each of the following intermediate phases. Further, these patterns can also be "ockedto" one of the clusters (interactive constrained clustering).

5   Conclusion

We addressed the task of "interactively" discovering clustering solutions that are induced by the maximum margin principle. The main contribution of our work is an interactive framework, which can be used to fine-tune clustering solutions by enforcing new class ratios in each interaction phase. The computational efficiency is ensured via a fast implementation of a steepest-descent-mildest-ascent optimization scheme. Our experimental evaluation shows that the framework can successfully be applied on real-world data with hundreds of thousands of patterns. Future work could encompass multi-class extensions of our approach as well as fast implementations for adapting other model parameters on the fly.

Acknowledgements. The authors would like to thank the anonymous reviewers for their careful reading and valuable comments. The work has bee supported in part by the *Radboud Excellence Initiative* of the Radboud University Nijmegen. Funding for the Sloan Digital Sky Survey IV has been provided by the Alfred P. Sloan Foundation, the U.S. Department of Energy Office of Science, and the Participating Institutions. SDSS-IV acknowledges support and resources from the Center for High-Performance Computing at the University of Utah. The SDSS web site is www.sdss.org.

SDSS-IV is managed by the Astrophysical Research Consortium for the Participating Institutions of the SDSS Collaboration including the Brazilian Participation Group, the Carnegie Institution for Science, Carnegie Mellon University, the Chilean Participation Group, the French Participation Group, Harvard-Smithsonian Center for Astrophysics, Instituto de Astrofísica de Canarias, The Johns Hopkins University, Kavli Institute for the Physics and Mathematics of the Universe (IPMU) / University of Tokyo, Lawrence Berkeley National Laboratory, Leibniz Institut für Astrophysik Potsdam (AIP), Max-Planck-Institut für Astronomie (MPIA Heidelberg), Max-Planck-Institut für Astrophysik (MPA Garching), Max-Planck-Institut für Extraterrestrische Physik (MPE), National Astronomical Observatory of China, New Mexico State University, New York University, University of Notre Dame, Observatário Nacional / MCTI, The Ohio State University, Pennsylvania State University, Shanghai Astronomical Observatory, United Kingdom Participation Group, Universidad Nacional Autónoma de México, University of Arizona, University of Colorado Boulder, University of Portsmouth, University of Utah, University of Virginia, University of Washington, University of Wisconsin, Vanderbilt University, and Yale University.

References

1. Xu, L., Neufeld, J., Larson, B., Schuurmans, D.: Maximum margin clustering. In: Advance in Neural Information Proceedings Systems 17, pp. 1537–1544. MIT Press (2005)
2. Valizadegan, H., Jin, R.: Generalized maximum margin clustering and unsupervised kernel learning. In: Advance in Neural Information Proceedings Systems 19, pp. 1417–1424. MIT Press (2007)
3. Gieseke, F., Pahikkala, T., Kramer, O.: Fast evolutionary maximum margin clustering. In: Proceedings of the 26th International Conference on Machine Learning, pp. 361–368. ACM (2009)

4. Li, Y., Tsang, I., Kwok, J., Zhou, Z.: Tighter and convex maximum margin clustering. In: Proceedings of the 12th International Conference on Artificial Intelligence and Statistics, ser. JMLR: Workshop and Conference Proceedings, vol. 5, pp. 344–351. JMLR (2009)

5. Pahikkala, T., Airola, A., Gieseke, F., Kramer, O.: Unsupervised multi-class regularized least-squares classification. In: The 12th IEEE International Conference on Data Mining (ICDM 2012), pp. 585–594. IEEE Computer Society (2012)

6. Zhang, K., Tsang, I., Kwok, J.: Maximum margin clustering made practical. In: Proceedings of the 24th International Conference on Machine Learning, vol. 227, pp. 1119–1126. ACM (2007)

7. Wang, F., Zhao, B., Zhang, C.: Linear time maximum margin clustering. IEEE Trans. Neural Networks $21(2)$, 319–332 (2010)

8. Cortes, C., Vapnik, V.: Support vector networks. Mach. Learn. **20**, 273–297 (1995)

9. Schölkopf, B., Smola, A.: Learning with Kernels: Support Vector Machines, Regularization, Optimization, and Beyond. MIT Press, Cambridge (2001)

10. Steinwart, I., Christmann, A.: Support Vector Machines. Springer-Verlag, New York (2008)

11. Basu, S., Davidson, I., Wagstaff, K.: Constrained Clustering: Advances in Algorithms, Theory, and Applications, 1st edn. Chapman & Hall/CRC, Boca Raton, London, New York (2008)

12. Zhao, B., Wang, F., Zhang, C.: Efficient maximum margin clustering via cutting plane algorithm. In: Proceedings of the SIAM International Conference on Data Mining, pp. 751–762. Society for Industrial and Applied Mathematics (2008)

13. Awasthi, P., Balcan, M., Voevodski, K.: Local algorithms for interactive clustering. In: Proceedings of the 31th International Conference on Machine Learning, pp. 550–558 (2014)

14. Balcan, M.-F., Blum, A.: Clustering with interactive feedback. In: Freund, Y., Györfi, L., Turán, G., Zeugmann, T. (eds.) ALT 2008. LNCS (LNAI), vol. 5254, pp. 316–328. Springer, Heidelberg (2008)

15. Joachims, T.: Transductive inference for text classification using support vector machines. In: Proceedings of the International Conference on Machine Learning, pp. 200–209 (1999)

16. Kimeldorf, G., Wahba, G.: Some results on Tchebycheffian spline functions. J. Math. Anal. Appl. **33**(1), 82–95 (1971)

17. Drineas, P., Mahoney, M.W.: On the nyström method for approximating a gram matrix for improved kernel-based learning. J. Mach. Learn. Res. **6**, 2153–2175 (2005)

18. Golub, G.H., Van Loan, C.: Matrix Computations, 2nd edn. Johns Hopkins University Press, Baltimore (1989)

19. Pearlman, J., Barry, P., Segal, C., Shepanski, J., Beiso, D., Carman, S.: Hyperion, a space-based imaging spectrometer. IEEE Trans. Geosci. Remote Sens. **41**(6), 1160–1173 (2003)

20. Wagstaff, K.L., Bornstein, B.J.: K-means in space: a radiation sensitivity evaluation. In Proceedings of the 26th Annual International Conference on Machine Learning, pp. 1097–1104 (2009)

21. Castano, R., Mazzoni, D., Tang, N., Doggett, T., Chien, S., Greeley, R., Cichy, B., Davies, A.: Learning classifiers for science event detection in remote sensing imagery. In: Symposium on Artificial Intelligence, Robotics and Automation in Space (2005)

22. York, D.G., et al.: The sloan digital sky survey: technical summary. Astron. J. **120**(3), 579–1587 (2000)

23. Lund, M., Handberg, R., Davies, G., Chaplin, W., Jones, C.: K2P^2-A photometry pipeline for the K2 mission. In: CoRR, vol. abs/1504.05199 (2015)
24. MacQueen, J.: Some methods for classification and analysis of multivariate observations. In: Proceedings of the 5th Berkeley Symposium on Mathematical Statistics and Probability, pp. 281–297. University of California Press (1967)

Time Series Classification with Representation Ensembles

Rafael Giusti$^{(\boxtimes)}$, Diego F. Silva, and Gustavo E.A.P.A. Batista

Instituto de Ciências Matemáticas e de Computação, São Carlos, Brazil
{rgiusti,diegofsilva,gbatista}@icmc.usp.br

Abstract. Time series has attracted much attention in recent years, with thousands of methods for diverse tasks such as classification, clustering, prediction, and anomaly detection. Among all these tasks, classification is likely the most prominent task, accounting for most of the applications and attention from the research community. However, in spite of the huge number of methods available, there is a significant body of empirical evidence indicating that the 1-nearest neighbor algorithm (1-NN) in the *time domain* is "extremely difficult to beat". In this paper, we evaluate the use of different data representations in time series classification. Our work is motivated by methods used in related areas such as signal processing and music retrieval. In these areas, a change of representation frequently reveals features that are not apparent in the original data representation. Our approach consists of using different representations such as frequency, wavelets, and autocorrelation to transform the time series into alternative decision spaces. A classifier is then used to provide a classification for each test time series in the alternative domain. We investigate how features provided in different domains can help in time series classification. We also experiment with different ensembles to investigate if the data representations are a good source of diversity for time series classification. Our extensive experimental evaluation approaches the issue of combining sets of representations and ensemble strategies, resulting in over 300 ensemble configurations.

1 Introduction

Undoubtedly, analysis of time series data has attracted an enormous amount of attention in recent years. Time-oriented data are present in several application domains including medicine (*e.g.*, electrocardiography and electroencephalography), engineering (sensor data), entertainment (motion capture data in video games), meteorology (climate data), etc. The research community has answered to such demand with literally thousands of data analysis methods for diverse tasks such as classification, clustering, prediction, and anomaly detection.

This work partially funded by grant #2012/08923-8, #2013/26151-5, and #2015/07628-0, São Paulo Research Foundation (FAPESP); and CNPq #446330/2014-0 and #303083/2013-1.

Classification is likely the most prominent task in time series mining, accounting for most of the applications and attention from the research community. But in spite of the huge number of methods available, there is a significant body of empirical evidence indicating that the 1-nearest neighbor algorithm (1-NN) in the *time domain* is "extremely difficult to beat" for classification tasks [8,18].

In this paper, we evaluate the use of different data representations in time series classification. Our work is motivated by methods used in related areas such as signal processing and music retrieval. In these areas, a change of representation, for instance, from time to frequency or cepstrum, often reveals features that are not apparent in the original data representation. This approach consists of using different representations to transform the time series into alternative decision spaces. A classifier is then used to provide a classification for each test time series in the alternative domain.

Our goal is to investigate how features provided in different domains can help in time series classification. We perform our experiments using the 1-nearest neighbor classifier (1-NN), due to its simplicity and effectiveness in time series classification. The use of a single classification model helps us to rule out the differences in performance due to different classification algorithms. This way, any difference of performance can be attributed on the change of data representation. We also evaluate different ensembles of 1-NN classifiers to investigate if the data representations are good sources of diversity for time series classification.

Although some recent research has addressed the classification of time series using different representations [4,16], our paper is unique in the sense that we evaluate representations irrespectively of classification models. Moreover, we employ a more diverse set of representations and ensemble strategies. Our extensive experimental evaluation approaches the issue of combining sets of representations and ensemble strategies, resulting in over 300 ensemble configurations.

The paper is organized as follows. In Sect. 2 we present an overview of time series classification, time series (dis)similarity and transformation of time series. In Sect. 3 we present notions of ensembles of classifiers and the ensemble configurations used in this work. In Sect. 4 we present our experimental evaluation and discuss our results. Finally, in Sect. 5 we present our conclusions and future work.

2 Time Series Classification and Transformation

Let a time series of length m be an ordered set of values $S = (s_1, s_2, \ldots, s_m)$, $s_t \in \mathbb{R}$ for all $t \in [1, m]$. Each value s_t of S is an observation of the time series at instant t and every pair of consecutive observations (s_t, s_{t+1}) is considered equally spaced in time – *i.e.*, the series is uniformly sampled or the sampling rate can be otherwise disregarded.

Time series classification is an important problem that arises in many practical applications. It consists in assigning a class label $C_{\mathbf{x}}$ to a previously unseen example $\mathbf{x}$ that is somehow related to the process that produced the time series $\mathbf{x}$. The problem of time series classification has attracted great interest from the scientific community. Several approaches are readily available to tackle this problem. One may extract features from the temporal data and use these features to train a classification model, such as the support vector machine [5]. In a different approach, representative segments – shapelets – of temporal data may be extracted from a training data to construct a similarity-based decision tree [19]. However, one of the most popular approaches consists of using the original temporal data as attributes for the k-nearest neighbors classification model.

The k-nearest neighbors classifier – k-NN – is an instance-based classification model. It is built on the nearest-neighbors rule, which roughly translates to the notion that similar instances belong to the same class with high probability. Although simple, the 1-NN classifier with DTW (1-NN-DTW) is repeatedly reported as the best classification model in the average case for time series classification, being considered to be "exceptionally difficult to beat" [8,18].

The concept of (dis)similarity between time series is often estimated with a distance function. The Euclidean distance is a widely used function to estimate the dissimilarity between two time series. A relevant issue of the Euclidean distance is the fact that it is very sensitive to non-linear variations in the time axis known as *warping* [12]. The Dynamic Time Warping (DTW) is a local-warping invariant of the Euclidean distance which minimizes the estimated distance between two time series by finding an optimal alignment between their observations. This alignment promotes the matching of values observed at different relative times under the following constraints: (i) the observations must be monotonically ordered with respect to time; (ii) the alignment should begin in the first and end in the last observations of both time series; and (iii) each value must belong to the optimal alignment – *i.e.*, no value is skipped in any of the time series.

The sampled observations of a time series are a description of how a measurable phenomenon changes with time. Such series is said to be represented in the time domain. "Traditional" classification of time series with the 1-NN classifier is performed in the time domain. However, it is possible to transform a time series to an alternate domain of representation. We define a transformation of time series as a mapping from the time domain to an alternate space of decision. To classify instances with the 1-NN classifier in the transformed space, it suffices to wrap the distance function so that each instance is transformed before being compared. In this work, we transform the time series from the time domain to a different decision space and perform the classification on this new decision space using the 1-NN classifier normally. For certain domains of application, this allows for great classification accuracy. We construct ensembles of the 1-NN classifier for even better results.

There is a huge diversity of time series transformations in the scientific literature [18]. In this work, we attempted to choose transformations that actually provide a distinct decision space that is not a summarization of the original temporal data. Therefore, we have excluded some classical dimensionality reduction techniques, such as Principal Component Analysis [10], SAX [13] and SAX-based transforms [14].

Power Spectrum: The Discrete Fourier Transform – DFT – decomposes a time series as an ordered set of sinusoids of decreasing frequency. Each value of the transformed series is a complex number that encodes both amplitude and phase of a periodic component.

The DFT has been used for a long time as a strategy of dimensionality reduction that allows for efficient indexing of time series [1].

We define the power spectrum representation of a time series as the plot of the complex modulus of its Fourier components. The power spectrum gives the "energy" of the time series in the frequency bands associated with the Fourier components. Periodical trends in the time series may be exposed by the power spectrum, even if the original time series contains noise.

For a detailed and the formal definition of Fourier transform, we refer the reader to [2].

Discrete Wavelet Transform: The DFT concerns only about frequency, not adding any information about when each frequency component is present in a time series. In order to mitigate this problem, wavelet transform creates a time-frequency representation with different resolutions. This is done by calculating the spectrum with sliding windows of different sizes. Discrete wavelet transform (DWT) is a discrete version of the wavelet transform for numerical signals.

Another relevant difference between DWT and DFT is that the latter represents a composition of sinusoidal waves. In the other hand, DWT may work with an infinite number of functions, called mother wavelets.

There is a plethora of works that use DWT in time series classification. A particularly interesting application of this approach was made for matching stock time series [7], in which the authors used the Haar's mother wavelet [6].

Autocorrelation Function: The autocorrelation of a time series measures its predictability at a specific instant from its previous observations. A highly autocorrelated time series is indicative of a very deterministic process while true white noise shows no autocorrelation for pairs of distinct observations. The sample autocorrelation is typically used as an estimate of the autocorrelation of the whole population. In this work, however, we employ the autocorrelation function as a means to transform the time series into a different decision space [4].

3 Representation Ensembles

An ensemble of classifiers is a set of base classifiers whose individual decisions are combined to classify new examples [15]. Each classifier is allowed to independently observe the example and provide a tentative classification output, *i.e.*, a vote. The ensemble then combines the individual votes into a single class label.

The simplest sensible ensemble of classifiers is the majority ensemble. In a majority ensemble, each of the base classifiers votes on a class label. The most voted class label is the ensemble's output.

Well-crafted ensembles tend to be more precise than their base classifiers. When designing ensembles, it is important that component classifiers be individually accurate and collectively diverse. Otherwise, if the classifiers are inaccurate, then the composition of incorrect decisions will lead to incorrect decisions, while base classifiers too similar one to another cause the ensemble to make decisions similar to those of the base classifiers, thus failing to improve on them.

In time series classification, variations of the k-NN have been used to build ensembles of classifiers. Lines and Bagnall [15] employed different distance measures combined into an ensemble of 1-NN classifiers. Previous work by Oates et al. [16] used the SAX representation of time series to compose ensembles where each base classifier was constructed with different parameters. More recently, Lines et al. [4] proposed a "collective of ensembles" that is essentially an "ensemble of ensembles". The base classifiers include complex classification models such as SVM, Rotation Forests, and variations of the k-NN classifier. These include using different distance measures and representation ensembles using the autocorrelation function, the power spectrum, and the shapelet representation.

In this work, we explore how different time series representation may be composed into ensembles of classifiers. Additionally, we are also interested in exploring different strategies of combining base ensembles. We start with the majority ensemble. Then, we explore alternative strategies for weighing base classifiers and composing votes. For clarity sake, we group these strategies into weighted and ranking-based ensembles.

3.1 Weighted-Based Ensemble

One straightforward extension to the simple majority ensemble consists of assigning weights to each base classifier. When deciding on a new example, the weighted sum of the votes for each class C_i is considered, and the class label which receives the highest sum of votes is the ensemble output.

This strategy will be referred to as weighted ensemble. In actuality, the weighted ensemble is a family of ensembles that differ on the strategy adopted to assign weights to base classifiers. The majority ensemble is itself a weighted ensemble that uses equal weight to all base classifiers.

In this work, we have considered the following weighing strategies.

- *Accuracy as weights*: the weight of each base classifier is its estimated accuracy. In our experiments, the accuracy is estimated by means of 10-fold cross-validation on the training data. This is the only ensemble strategy that uses the same set of weights for every new example it is presented. Variations of this ensemble may be easily achieved by imposing a "cut-point" on the weights of the base classifiers. A "hard cut-point" of k implies assigning a weight of 0 (zero) to all but the k most accurate base classifiers. A "soft cut-point" of δ implies assigning a weight of 0 (zero) to all base classifiers that are less accurate than the most accurate base classifier by a value of δ;
- *Distance as weights*: the weight of each base classifier is the normalized distance from the new example $\mathbf{x}$ to its nearest neighbor z_{nn}. Formally, if the

distance function used by the base classifier is f, then the normalized distance is $f'(\mathbf{x}, z_{nn}) = \frac{f(\mathbf{x}, z_{nn})}{f(z_\alpha, z_\beta)}$, where z_α and z_β are instances from the training set such that no other pair of training instances are further apart;

– *Posterior probability as weight*: the weight of each base classifier is the posterior probability of the class given the example. Let C_j be the decision of the j-th classifier. The posterior probability $P(C_j|\mathbf{x})$ is the probability that the true class of the new example $\mathbf{x}$ is, in fact, C_j. The most straightforward approach to estimate the posterior probability is to count the frequency of C_j in the neighborhood of $\mathbf{x}$. This neighborhood is a parameter of the ensemble, and it is usually larger than the neighborhood of the base classifier.

3.2 Ranking-Based Ensembles

While the 1-NN produces a single class label for each new instance $\mathbf{x}$, it may be easily extended to rank classes according to the likelihood that a class C_i is the true class of $\mathbf{x}$. This "extended 1-NN" may be used as the base classifier of an ensemble, provided all other base classifiers also produce rankings as outputs. In this work, this approach is referred to as "ranking ensemble". When a new example is presented to a ranking ensemble, each base classifier is used to produce their own ranking. The ensemble then merges these rankings, much like a single vote is produced from a set of votes in the weighted ensemble. The best-ranked class is chosen as the ensemble decision.

Ranking ensembles differ by the strategy used to construct the rankings. In this work, the merge procedure is the same for all ranking ensembles; namely, it is the mean of ranks. If the classification space has m classes and the ensemble is composed of n base classifiers, then each j-th base classifier votes on a ranking $R_j = \{r_{j1}, r_{j2}, \ldots, r_{jm}\}$, where r_{ji} is the rank assigned to the i-th class label. The final, merged ranking, is given by the partial order of the set $R_f = \{\overline{r_1}, \overline{r_2}, \ldots, \overline{r_m}\}$, where $\overline{r_i} = \frac{\sum_j r_{ji}}{n}$ is the mean of the ranks assigned to the i-th by the base classifiers.

Two different label ranking models were used in this work.

– *Posterior probability*: the posterior class probability of an example $\mathbf{x}$, $P(C_j|\mathbf{x})$, is the probability that the example $\mathbf{x}$ in fact belongs to class C_j. It may be considered a decent estimate of the classifier's "confidence" that its decision is correct. It may also be used in label ranking to score class labels. One method to estimate the posterior class probability of $\mathbf{x}$, proposed by Atiya [3], associates a set of weights, $\{v_1, v_2, \ldots, v_k\}$ such that $v_i \in [0, 1]$ and $\sum v_i = 1$, to the nearest neighbors of $\mathbf{x}$. Each weight v_i reflects how important is the i-th neighbor in estimating the posterior class probability. If $v_1 = 1$ and all other $v_i = 0, i \neq 1$, then only the class of the immediately nearest neighbor should be considered in the estimate. If $v_i = \frac{1}{k}$ for all k-nearest neighbors, then every neighbor is equally important. A linear optimization model is used to to find weights that are optimal according to a training data set. The probability that an example $\mathbf{x}$ belongs to the class C_i is the sum of the weights associated to the neighbors of x that belong to this class. This is better explained with an example. Assume that, for $k = 5$ and a given example x, the classes of its nearest neighbors are C_1, C_2, C_1, C_3, and C_2. The first and the third-nearest neighbors are of class C_1. Therefore, the probability that x belongs to C_1 is given by $P(C_1|x) = v_1 + v_3$. The values of $P(C_j|x)$ are subjected to a partial order, where higher values are better, and a ranking is constructed. The ranks associated with each class label are the base classifier's vote.

– *Simple-ranking based*: the simple-ranking is an instance-ranking strategy used in the anytime classification with the k-nearest neighbors classification model [17]. Basically, the idea of the simple-ranking is to rank the training instances according to their relevance to the classification of a new example. The simple-ranking approach to calculating the importance of each training instance is similar to the leave-one-out validation procedure. Initially, it assigns a score of zero to all training instances. Then, at every round, it removes one training instance from the original data set and use the rest of the training data to predict its class. In the original simple-ranking algorithm, the classification model is the 1-nearest neighbor classifier. The nearest neighbor is then deemed "friendly" or "enemy", depending on whether its classes matches or not the class of the held out instance. If the neighbor is "friendly", then its score is increased by 1. If the neighbor is "enemy", then its score is decreased by $\frac{2}{m-1}$, where m is the number of classes of the decision space. The held out instance is put back into the training data set and the algorithm proceeds to the next round. Finally, a ranking is produced from the scores and the ranks are assigned to the training instances.

Once the training instances have been ranked, the label ranking of a new example x is similar to the procedure of the posterior probability-based method. Each nearest neighbor was previously assigned a simple-rank s_1, s_2, ..., s_k. For each class C_j, a score is computed from the mean of the ranks of neighbors that belong to class C_j. For instance, assume that $k = 5$ and the classes of the nearest neighbors of x are C_1, C_2, C_1, C_3, and C_2. The first and the third-nearest neighbors belong to class C_1. Therefore, the score assigned to this class is $S_1 = \frac{s_1 + s_3}{2}$. Similarly, the score assigned to C_2 is $S_2 = \frac{s_2 + s_5}{2}$ and the score assigned to C_3 is $S_3 = s_4$. The scores S_1, S_2, and S_3 are subjected to a partial order, where lower values are better, and a ranking is constructed. The ranks associated with each class label are the base classifier's vote.

4   Experimental Evaluation

The main goal of this work is to explore different forms of ensemble composition with representation diversity. To achieve that goal, we designed a set of experiments to evaluate all ensemble strategies presented in Sect. 3 using different subsets of base classifiers. Because some ensemble strategies and some transformations have parameters, we also cross-validated the training data.

The base classifiers employed in our experiments were the 1-NN, the 1-NN-DTW, the 1-NN-DTW with Sakoe-Chiba window, and the 1-NN transformed to the representations discussed in Sect. 2. The width of the Sakoe-Chiba window was individually assigned to each data set. Additionally, one base classifier using only the first iteration of the Haar transform was used, alongside with another base classifier using only the approximation coefficients of the first iteration of the Haar transform. This configuration of base classifiers will be referred to as "full set".

For some configurations, we also experimented with limited sets of base classifiers. That is, instead of using the "full set" as base classifiers, we experimented different combinations. These combinations and the difference of accuracy provided by them will be presented and discussed in the next subsection.

The results from these experiments shed light on how the choice of an ensemble configuration and how adding or removing base classifiers affect the classification accuracy. Based on these results, we then devised a set of 6 base classifiers using 4 time series representations, namely 1-NN, 1-NN-DTW, 1-NN-DTW with Sakoe-Chiba window, and 1-NN transformed to Power Spectrum, Haar coefficients, and autocorrelation coefficients. The same ensemble configurations were used. We refer to this set of base classifiers as the "reduced set".

All experiments were conducted in 45 data sets from the UCR time series repository [11]. The UCR repository is arguably the largest source of time series data for classification and clustering, spanning diverse domains of applications such as agronomy, human movements, medicine, and astronomy. One characteristic of the UCR repository is that data sets are shipped with a predefined partitioning of training and test data. As it is commonplace in the scientific community, we keep that partitioning to promote reproducibility.

4.1   Discussion of Results

We evaluated hundreds of ensemble configurations on 45 labeled data sets. This yielded over 17 thousand data points, the totality of which may be found in the accompanying website of this paper [9].

Comparing ensembles with different sets of base classifiers, our results showed that fewer base classifiers tend to provide better results than the "full set". In Table 1, four sets of base classifiers are compared against the "full set". Each column stands for a subset of base classifiers: Time domain, DTW (with Sakoe-Chiba window), Power spectrum, Autocorrelation, and Haar. The values are the frequency of victories and ties assigned to the column ensemble against the respective "full set".

Most configurations produced better results with fewer base classifiers. This led us to repeat the experiments for all configurations with the six base classifiers presented in Sect. 4. In Table 2 we present a summary of ensemble configurations that we deemed representative. The totality of our results may be found in [9].

From Table 2, it is possible to notice that no configuration is better than all other configurations. For instance, though the strategy of weighing base classifiers by their cross-validation accuracy is at least as good as the majority ensemble 86.67 % of the time, it is worse than the strategy of weighing by distance 44.44 % of the time.

Table 1. Comparison of ensembles with reduced sets of base classifiers against the "full set". Letters denote base classifiers: (T)ime-domain with Euclidean distance and (D)TW, (A)utocorrelation domain, (P)ower spectrum domain, and (H)AAR wavelets

	TDPA	TDPH	TDAH	TDPAH
Majority	73.68 %	34.21 %	47.37 %	76.32 %
Posterior (NN)	63.16 %	31.58 %	26.32 %	60.53 %
Accuracy	81.58 %	76.32 %	78.95 %	89.47 %
Distance	94.74 %	94.74 %	97.37 %	97.37 %

Table 2. Comparison of ensemble configurations. Each value is the frequency of victories and ties obtained by the column ensemble against the row ensemble. In the columns, P.P. stands for "posterior probability".

Against	Reference ensemble					
	Majority	Accuracy	Distance	P.P. (rank)	P.P. (weight)	SimpleRank
Majority	—	86.67 %	71.11 %	55.56 %	77.78 %	37.78 %
Accuracy	20.00 %	—	53.33 %	26.67 %	48.89 %	17.78 %
Distance	35.56 %	55.56 %	—	35.56 %	53.33 %	35.56 %
Posterior (rank)	48.89 %	77.78 %	68.89 %	—	75.56 %	37.78 %
Posterior (weight)	28.89 %	60.00 %	51.11 %	28.89 %	—	26.67 %
SimpleRank	62.22 %	82.22 %	64.44 %	64.44 %	75.56 %	—

Surprisingly, more complex strategies based on ranking ensembles, such as the simple-ranking and the posterior probability method, did not yield good results. At first, we suspected this might be caused by overfitting on the training data. However, what we actually observed was an overall superior accuracy of those methods on the test data set, suggesting that these ensembles generalize relatively well from the training data. As an example, Fig. 1 (left) compares the accuracy on the test data against the accuracy on the training set for the posterior ranking ensemble – with neighborhood of size 5. Figure 1 (right) presents a similar analysis for the simple rank ensemble – with neighborhood of size 3.

These results seem to make a good case for composing ensembles of 1-NN on different domains of representation. However, the natural question is: how do these ensembles compare with the state-of-the-art? Considering the overwhelming adoption of the 1-NN-DTW, we did compare our ensemble configurations against it. In Fig. 2 we graphically present two such comparisons. In Fig. 2 (left), the accuracy-weighted ensemble – with "soft cut-point" of 0.1 – is compared against 1-NN-DTW. In Fig. 2 (right), the simple rank ensemble – with neighborhood size 3 – is compared against 1-NN-DTW.

There is a sensible reason for choosing these particular ensembles for comparison against 1-NN-DTW. That particular configuration of the accuracy ensemble was able to beat or tie with 1-NN-DTW in more data sets than most other ensembles. Conversely, that particular configuration of the simple rank ensemble

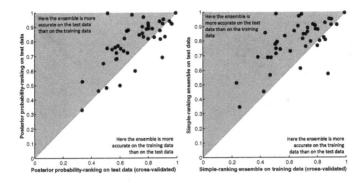

Fig. 1. Comparison of ranking ensembles on the test data against training data, suggesting generalization of the classification models.

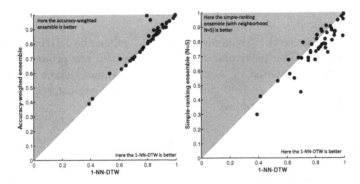

Fig. 2. Comparison of two different ensemble strategies against the 1-NN-DTW.

was defeated by the 1-NN-DTW in more data sets than most other ensembles. Figure 2 therefore gives a glimpse of the range of accuracies of our results when compared with the 1-NN-DTW. The accuracy ensemble won against 1-NN-DTW in 28 data sets, tied in 12, and lost in 5.

Finally, we address the issue of reproducibility. Along this section, we presented several results that we considered representative or interesting. The totality of this analysis is based on evaluations performed with the test data, which is usually not available in "real" situations.

We address this question by performing a data-driven selection of ensembles. Every ensemble configuration was evaluated both on the test data and, with cross-validation, on the training data sets. For each data set, the "dynamic ensemble" chooses the ensemble with the highest accuracy on the training data and evaluates it on the test data. When more than one ensemble configuration yields the highest training accuracy, we apply them all on the test data and give as its accuracy the mean of their test accuracies. This equates to finding the expected value of the "dynamic ensemble" accuracy when equally efficient ensemble configurations are randomly selected with uniform distribution.

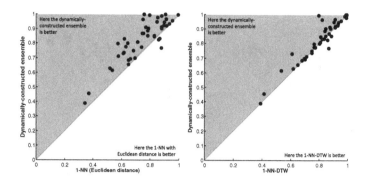

Fig. 3. (left) The best ensemble using the "full set" of base classifiers against 1-NN-DTW; (right) accuracy a data-driven selection of ensemble for each data set comparaed with 1-NN-DTW

In Fig. 3 we present the "dynamic ensemble" against the 1-NN (left) and the 1-NN-DTW (right). This particular "dynamic ensemble" was produced using the six base classifiers presented in Sect. 4. This result shows that it is possible to construct ensembles of classifiers that are competitive against the 1-NN-DTW from a purely data-drive approach.

5   Conclusion and Future Work

In this paper, we have evaluated the use of different data representations in time series classification and ensemble composition. We employed 5 different time series transformations and 6 ensemble strategies. We performed experiments with over 300 ensemble configurations on 45 data sets. Our extensive experimental analysis makes a strong case for the use of representation diversity in ensemble composition. Some ensemble configurations displayed excellent accuracy performance, being competitive with the 1-NN-DTW. Moreover, because we conducted several experiments with cross-validation on the training data, we have strong evidence that data-driven selection of ensemble configuration is possible, and as shown in Sect. 4.1, capable of yielding good results.

As future work, we intend to analyze more time series representations and ensemble strategies. We suspect that some meta-learning techniques would allow for better selection of base classifiers and ensemble configurations.

References

1. Agrawal, R., Faloutsos, C., Swami, A.: Efficient similarity search in sequence databases. In: Lomet, David B. (ed.) FODO 1993. LNCS, vol. 730, pp. 69–84. Springer, Heidelberg (1993)
2. Antoniou, A.: Digital Signal Processing. McGraw-Hill, New York (2006)
3. Atiya, A.F.: Estimating the posterior probabilities using the k-nearest neighbor rule. Neural Comput. **17**(3), 731–740 (2005)

4. Bagnall, A., Lines, J., Hills, J., Bostrom, A.: Time-series classification with COTE: the collective of transformation-based ensembles. IEEE Trans. Knowl. Data Eng. **PP(99)**, 1–14 (2015)

5. Bresolin, A.d.A., Neto, A., Alsina, P.: Digit recognition using wavelet and SVM in Brazilian Portuguese. In: IEEE International Conference on Acoustics, Speech and Signal Processing, pp. 1545–1548 (2008)

6. Burrus, C.S., Gopinath, R.A., Guo, H.: Introduction to Wavelets and Wavelet Transforms, vol. 998. Prentice Hall, New Jersey (1998)

7. Chan, K.P., Fu, A.C.: Efficient time series matching by wavelets. In: International Conference on Data Engineering, pp. 126–133 (1999)

8. Ding, H., Trajcevski, G., Scheuermann, P., Wang, X., Keogh, E.: Querying and mining of time series data: experimental comparison of representations and distance measures. VLDB Endowment **1**(2), 1542–1552 (2008)

9. Giusti, R., Silva, D.F., Batista, G.E.A.P.A.: Time series classification with representation ensembles (2015). http://sites.labic.icmc.usp.br/rgiusti/ida15. (URL verified valid as of July 2015)

10. Jolliffe, I.: Principal Component Analysis. Springer, New York (2002)

11. Keogh, E., Xi, X., Wei, L., Ratanamahatana, C.A.: The UCR time series classification/clustering homepage (2006). http://www.cs.ucr.edu/~eamonn/time_series_data/. (URL verified valid as of July 2015)

12. Keogh, E., Ratanamahatana, C.A.: Exact indexing of dynamic time warping. Knowl. Inf. Syst. **7**(3), 358–386 (2005)

13. Lin, J., Keogh, E., Wei, L., Lonardi, S.: Experiencing SAX: a novel symbolic representation of time series. Data Min. Knowl. Discov. **15**(2), 107–144 (2007)

14. Lin, J., Khade, R., Li, Y.: Rotation-invariant similarity in time series using bag-of-patterns representation. J. Intell. Inf. Syst. **39**(2), 287–315 (2012)

15. Lines, J., Bagnall, A.: Time series classification with ensembles of elastic distance measures. Data Min. Knowl. Discovery **29**, 565–592 (2014)

16. Oates, T., Mackenzie, C., Stein, D., Stansbury, L., Dubose, J., Aarabi, B., Hu, P.: Exploiting representational diversity for time series classification. In: International Conference on Machine Learning and Applications, vol. 2, pp. 538–544 (2012)

17. Ueno, K., Xi, X., Keogh, E.J., Lee, D.J.: Anytime classification using the nearest neighbor algorithm with applications to stream mining. In: IEEE International Conference on Data Mining, pp. 623–632 (2006)

18. Wang, X., Mueen, A., Ding, H., Trajcevski, G., Scheuermann, P., Keogh, E.: Experimental comparison of representation methods and distance measures for time series data. Data Min. Knowl. Discovery **26**, 275–309 (2013)

19. Ye, L., Keogh, E.: Time series shapelets: a new primitive for data mining. In: ACM SIGKDD International Conference on Knowledge Discovery and Data Mining, pp. 947–956. ACM (2009)

Simultaneous Clustering and Model Selection for Multinomial Distribution: A Comparative Study

Md. Abul Hasnat$^{(\boxtimes)}$, Julien Velcin, Stéphane Bonnevay, and Julien Jacques

Laboratoire ERIC, Université Lumière Lyon 2, Lyon, France
{md.hasnat,julien.velcin,julien.jacques}@univ-lyon2.fr,
stephane.bonnevay@univ-lyon1.fr

Abstract. In this paper, we study different discrete data clustering methods, which use the Model-Based Clustering (MBC) framework with the Multinomial distribution. Our study comprises several relevant issues, such as initialization, model estimation and model selection. Additionally, we propose a novel MBC method by efficiently combining the partitional and hierarchical clustering techniques. We conduct experiments on both synthetic and real data and evaluate the methods using accuracy, stability and computation time. Our study identifies appropriate strategies to be used for discrete data analysis with the MBC methods. Moreover, our proposed method is very competitive w.r.t. clustering accuracy and better w.r.t. stability and computation time.

Keywords: Multinomial distribution · Model-Based Clustering

1 Introduction

Model-Based Clustering (MBC) estimates the parameters of a statistical model for the data and produces probabilistic clustering [6,7,15,19]. To use the MBC method for clustering data as well as automatically selecting K (number of clusters), it is necessary to generate a set of candidate models. A simple approach to generate these models is to separately estimate them using an Expectation-Maximization (EM) method [13] with $K = 1, \ldots, K_{max}$. However, it can be computationally inefficient for higher dimensional data and higher K_{max} value.

Figueiredo and Jain [5] proposed a MBC method that integrates both model estimation and selection task within a single EM algorithm. A different strategy, called hybrid MBC [19], generates a hierarchy of models from K_{max} clusters by merging the parameters. Indeed, such an approach naturally saves computation time as it does not explicitly learn $K = K_{max} - 1, \ldots 1$ components models from the data. In this paper, we propose a hybrid MBC method with the Multinomial Mixture (MM) model and then empirically compare it with other MBC methods. Moreover, we explicitly addresses two related issues: (1) initialization [3]: how to set the initial parameters for the EM method and (2) model selection [2]: which criterion to use for selecting the best model. Therefore, based on an empirical

© Springer International Publishing Switzerland 2015
E. Fromont et al. (Eds.): IDA 2015, LNCS 9385, pp. 120–131, 2015.
DOI: 10.1007/978-3-319-24465-5_11

study, we aim to answer the following questions: (a) which method should be used for initialization? (b) how to efficiently generate a set of models? (c) what is the difference among "learning from data" and "estimating from K_{max} model parameters"? and (d) what is the best model selection method?

Our overall contribution is to perform a comparative study among different MBC methods with the MM. Individually, we: (1) propose (Sect. 3.6) a novel MBC method and compare it with the state-of-the-art methods; (2) perform empirical study on different initialization methods (Sect. 3.3) and (3) compare different model selection methods (Sect. 3.5). We conduct experiments with synthetic and real text data (for document clustering [19]) and identify particular methods that should be used for initialization, candidate models estimation and model selection. Therefore, the above contributions and experiments will naturally answer the questions raised at the end of the previous paragraph.

In the remaining part of this paper, we study the background and related work in Sect. 2, discuss different methods in Sect. 3, present the experimental results with discussion in Sect. 4 and finally draw conclusions in Sect. 5.

2   Background and Related Work

Model-Based Clustering (MBC) [6,15] is a well-established method for cluster analysis and unsupervised learning. MBC assumes a probabilistic model (e.g., mixture model) for the data and then estimates the model parameters by optimizing an objective function (e.g., model likelihood). The Expectation Maximization (EM) [13] is mostly used in MBC to estimate the model parameters. EM consists of an Expectation step (E-step) and a Maximization step (M-step) which are iteratively employed to maximize the log likelihood of the data.

MBC methods have been exploited with the Gaussian distribution to analyze continuous data [2,5–7,15]. Besides, they have been proposed to analyze discrete data using the Multinomial distribution [14,17] and directional data using the directional distributions [1,9,10]. In this paper, we only study and compare the MBC methods with the Multinomial distribution.

The Multinomial Mixture (MM) is a statistical model which has been used for cluster analysis with discrete data [14,17,20]. Meilă and Heckerman [14] studied the MBC methods with MM and compared them w.r.t. accuracy, time and number of clusters. They found that the EM method significantly outperforms others, which motivates us to solely focus on the EM related approaches.

Initialization of the EM method has significant impact on the clustering results [3,12,13], because with different initializations it may converge to different values of the likelihood function, some of which can be local maxima, i.e., sub-optimal results. To overcome this, several initialization strategies have been proposed, see [3] for details. Meilă and Heckerman [14] investigated three initialization strategies for the EM with MM. In this paper, we consider their [14] observations as well as empirically evaluate additional initialization methods for the EM method which were discussed by Biernacki et al. [3].

In order to automatically select K (number of components), MBC method can be used by first generating a set of candidate models with different values of K

and then selecting the optimal model using a model selection criterion [6,15]. This strategy needs to address two issues: (a) how to generate the models? and (b) how to select the best model? This paper considers both of these issues. Particularly, we focus on the candidate models generation task and propose a novel solution based on the Hybrid MBC (HMBC) [19] method.

HMBC method is a two-staged model that exploits both partitional and hierarchical clustering. It begins with a partitional clustering with K_{max} clusters and then use the Hierarchical Agglomerative Clustering (HAC) on those cluster parameters to generate a hierarchy of mixture models. It has differences with the Model-Based Hierarchical Clustering (MBHC) which employs the HAC on each data point [6]. In practice, for a large number of samples, such MBHC method is inefficient w.r.t. the required time and memory [19]. Several HMBC methods have been proposed with different probability distributions, see [8,10,18,19]. Among these, [18] proposed a method in the context of Bayesian analysis. However, it requires an explicit analysis of the features, which can be computationally inefficient for higher dimensional data. An efficient mixture model simplification/fusion method is recently proposed in [8] for the Gaussian distribution and in [9,10] for the directional distributions. They use information divergences among the mixture models. In this paper, we follow a similar approach and propose a novel HMBC method with the MM.

Model selection is one of the most prominent issues in cluster analysis [2,5, 7,15]. In general, a statistical model selection criterion is often used with the MBC method, which is also called the parsimony-based approach [15]. See [5] for a list of different criteria. A different approach performs model selection by analyzing an evaluation graph, see [16] for such a method called the L-method. To select model with MM, [14] uses the likelihood value. Recently, [17] proposed the Minimum Message Length (MML) criterion for the MM. In this paper, we aim to present a comparative study among these methods.

This paper has similarity with two previous work [14,17]. However, the key differences are: (1) it proposes a novel method to efficiently generate candidate models; (2) investigate additional initialization methods proposed in [3] and (3) explore a wide range of model selection methods.

3   Methodologies

In the following sub-sections, first we present the model for the data, then discuss the relevant algorithms and finally propose a complete clustering method.

3.1   Multinomial Mixture Model

Let $\mathbf{x}_i = x_{i,1}, x_{i,2}, \ldots, x_{i,D}$ is a D dimensional discrete count vector of order V, i.e. $\sum_{d=1}^{D} x_{i,d} = V$. Moreover, $\mathbf{x}_i$ is assumed to be an independent realization of the random variable $\mathbf{X}$, which follows a V-order Multinomial distribution [4]:

$$\mathcal{M}(\mathbf{x}_i | V, \boldsymbol{\mu}) = \binom{V}{x_{i,1}, x_{i,2}, \ldots, x_{i,D}} \prod_{d=1}^{D} \mu_d^{x_{i,d}} \tag{1}$$

here, $\boldsymbol{\mu}$ is the D dimensional parameter with $0 \leq \mu_d \leq 1$ and $\sum_{d=1}^{D} \mu_d = 1$. The set of samples can be modeled with a Multinomial Mixture (MM) model of K components:

$$f\left(\mathbf{x}_i | \Theta_K\right) = \sum_{k=1}^{K} \pi_k \, \mathcal{M}(\mathbf{x}_i | V, \boldsymbol{\mu}_k) \tag{2}$$

In Eq. (2), $\Theta_K = \{(\pi_1, \boldsymbol{\mu}_1), \ldots, (\pi_K, \boldsymbol{\mu}_K)\}$ is the set of model parameters, π_k is the mixing proportion with $\sum_{k=1}^{K} \pi_k = 1$ and $\mathcal{M}(\mathbf{x}_i | V, \boldsymbol{\mu}_k)$ is the density function (Eq. (1)) associated with the kth cluster.

3.2 Expectation Maximization Method

To cluster data with the model (Eq. (2)), we estimate its parameters using an Expectation Maximization (EM) [13] method that maximizes the log-likelihood:

$$L\left(\Theta\right) = \sum_{i=1}^{N} log \sum_{k=1}^{K} \pi_k \mathcal{M}\left(\mathbf{x}_i | \boldsymbol{\mu}_k\right) \tag{3}$$

where N is the number of samples. In the Expectation step (E-step), we compute posterior probability as:

$$\rho_{i,k} = p\left(z_i = k | \mathbf{x}_i\right) = \frac{\pi_k \prod_{d=1}^{D} \mu_{k,d}^{x_{i,d}}}{\sum_{l=1}^{K} \pi_l \prod_{d=1}^{D} \mu_{l,d}^{x_{i,d}}} \tag{4}$$

where $z_i \in \{0,1\}^K$ denotes the cluster label of the ith sample. In the Maximization step (M-step), we update π_k and $\mu_{k,d}$ as:

$$\pi_k = \frac{1}{N} \sum_{i=1}^{N} \rho_{i,k} \quad \text{and} \quad \mu_{k,d} = \frac{\sum_{i=1}^{N} \rho_{i,k} \, x_{i,d}}{\sum_{i=1}^{N} \sum_{r=1}^{D} \rho_{i,k} \, x_{i,r}} \tag{5}$$

The E and M steps run iteratively until certain convergence criterion (e.g., difference of log-likelihood) is met or until a maximum number of iterations.

3.3 Initialization for the EM Method

The EM method requires the initial values of the parameters as an input. We examine the following five methods to initialize the EM:

- **Random:** set the initial values randomly with $0 \leq \mu_d \leq 1$ and $\sum_{d=1}^{D} \mu_d = 1$.
- **rndEM [12]:** run a large number of random start and select the one which provides maximum likelihood value (Eq. (3)).
- **Small EM (smEM) [3]:** run multiple short runs of randomly initialized EM and choose the one with the maximum likelihood value. Here, short run means we do not wait until convergence and stop the algorithm when limited number of EM iterations is completed.

- **Classification EM (CEM)** [3]: it is similar to the smEM, except a classification stage is inserted between the E and M steps. The classification step involves assigning each point to one of the K components using the conditional probabilities (Eq. (4)) computed in the E step.
- **Stochastic EM (SEM)** [3]: it is similar to the smEM, except a stochastic step is inserted between the E and M steps. The stochastic step assigns $\mathbf{x_i}$ at random to one of the mixture components K according to the Multinomial distribution with the conditional probabilities (Eq. (4)).

3.4 Candidate Models Generation

Multiple EM (Mul-EM): This is the simplest way to generate the candidate models. In this approach, the EM method is run K_{max} times to generate the candidate models with $K = 1, \ldots, K_{max}$ clusters.

Integrated-EM (Int-EM): This approach [5,17] do not explicitly generates the candidate models. Instead, it employs a single EM method that estimates the MM with K clusters and evaluate it at the same time. It begins with $K = K_{max}$ clusters and estimate its parameter. Then it annihilates a cluster with minimum π_k and estimate parameters with $K - 1$ clusters. This process continues within a single EM method until $K = 1$. See the EM-MML algorithm of [17] for details.

EM Followed by Hierarchical Agglomerative Clustering (EM-HAC): This is our proposed model generation method, which aim is to generate a hierarchy of Multinomial Mixture (MM) models. Therefore, we exploit the Hierarchical Agglomerative Clustering (HAC) on the mixture model parameters $\hat{\Theta}_K$. In general, the HAC permits a variety of choices based on three principal issues: (a) the dissimilarity measure between clusters; (b) the criterion to select the clusters to be merged and (c) the representation of the merged cluster.

We use the symmetric Kullback–Leibler Divergence [4] (sKLD) as a measure of the dissimilarity between two Multinomial distributions as:

$$sKLD = \frac{D_{KL}\left(\boldsymbol{\mu}_a, \boldsymbol{\mu}_b\right) + D_{KL}\left(\boldsymbol{\mu}_b, \boldsymbol{\mu}_a\right)}{2} \text{, where, } D_{KL}\left(\boldsymbol{\mu}_a, \boldsymbol{\mu}_b\right) = \sum_{d=1}^{D} \mu_{a,d}\, ln\left(\frac{\mu_{a,d}}{\mu_{b,d}}\right) \tag{6}$$

We choose "minimum sKLD" as the merging criterion (issue (b)). Besides we use the "complete linkage" criteria which is determined empirically.

In this clustering strategy, the set of models is represented by their parameters. After determining the clusters to be merged, similar to [8,10], we compute the merged cluster parameters (issue (c)) as:

$$\pi_{merged} = \sum_{l \in \hat{\Theta}_{sub}} \pi_{l,k} \text{ and } \boldsymbol{\mu}_{merged} = \frac{\sum_{l \in \hat{\Theta}_{sub}} \pi_l \boldsymbol{\mu}_l}{\pi_{merged}} \tag{7}$$

where $\hat{\Theta}_{sub} \subseteq \hat{\Theta}_{K_{max}}$. As an outcome, we obtain a set of MMs with different K, which will be explored further for model selection.

3.5 Model Selection

Consider that, after HAC we have a set of MMs with $K_{max}, \ldots, 1$ components. The task of model selection can be defined as selecting the mixture model with K_o components such that $\hat{\Theta}_{K_o} = \{(\hat{\pi}_1, \hat{\mu}_1), \ldots, (\hat{\pi}_{K_o}, \hat{\mu}_{K_o})\}$. We consider parsimony-based [15] and evaluation graph based [16] methods in this work.

In the parsimony-based method [15], an objective function is employed, which minimizes certain model selection criteria. Such criteria involve the negative log likelihood augmented by a penalizing function in order to take into account the complexity of the model. One of the most widely used criteria is called the Bayesian Information Criterion (BIC) [6]:

$$BIC(K) = -2L(\hat{\Theta}) + \nu log\,(N) \tag{8}$$

where $\nu = KD - 1$ is the number of free parameters of the MM. The Integrated Completed Likelihood (ICL) criterion adds BIC with the mean entropy [2]:

$$ICL(K) = BIC(K) - 2\sum_{i=1}^{N} \log\,(p(z_i|\mathbf{x_i})) \tag{9}$$

where $p(z_i|\mathbf{x_i})$ is the conditional probability of the classified class label $z_i \in \{1, \ldots, K\}$ for the sample $\mathbf{x_i}$. The Minimum Message Length (MML) criterion, which has been recently proposed for MM, has the following form [17]:

$$MML(K) = \frac{D}{2} \sum_{k:\hat{\pi}_k>0} \log\left(\frac{N\,\hat{\pi}_k}{12}\right) + \frac{K_{nz}}{2}\log\frac{N}{12} + \frac{K_{nz}\,(D+1)}{2} - L(\hat{\Theta}) \tag{10}$$

where K_{nz} is the number of clusters with non-zero probabilities. After computing the values of the model selection criteria for different $K \in \{1, ..., K_{max}\}$, we select K_o as the one that provides the minimum value of certain criterion.

For the evaluation graph based method, we consider the L-method (see [16] for details), where the knee point is detected in the plot constructed from the BIC values. The idea is to fit two lines at the left and right side of each point within the range $2,...,K_{max} - 1$. Finally, select the point as K_o that minimizes the total weighted root mean squared error.

3.6 Complete Clustering Method with MM

We propose a complele clustering method with the MM which clusters data and selects the number of clusters automatically. It consists of the following steps:

- **Step 1:** Apply the EM algorithm (Sect. 3.2) to estimate MM parameters with K_{max} clusters, i.e., $\hat{\Theta}_{k_{max}}$.
- **Step 2:** Apply the HAC method (EM-HAC in Sect. 3.4) on $\hat{\Theta}_{k_{max}}$ to generate a set of models $\{\hat{\Theta}_k\}_{k=k_{max}-1,...,2}$.
- **Step 3:** Apply a model selection method (Sect. 3.5) to select $\hat{\Theta}_{K_o}$, i.e., the mixture model with the optimal number of components K_o.

4   Experimental Results and Discussion

We conduct experiments using both simulated and real data. For the evaluation, we compute the Adjusted Rand Index (ARI) [11], which is a pair counting based similarity measure among two clustering. Therefore, high value of ARI indicates highly similar clustering and hence high accuracy. For a dataset, we compute the ARI among the clustering result of a particular method and the true labels.

We evaluate the methods using the clustering accuracy, stability and computation time. We run each experiment 10 times and record the average value of the ARI as the accuracy, standard deviation of the ARI as the stability[1] and the average computation time.

4.1   Experimental Datasets

Simulated Datasets: We draw a finite set of discrete count vectors $\chi = \{\mathbf{x}_i\}_{i,...,N}$ from MMs with different numbers (3, 5 and 10) and types: well-separated (**ws**) and not well-separated (**nws**) of clusters. Similar to [17], the types are verified using the sKLD[2] values. We consider samples of different dimensions: 3, 5, 10, 20 and 40. For each MM, we generate 100 sets of data each having 1000 i.i.d. samples. In the synthetic data generation process, first we contruct a MM model with K clusters. The model parameters ($\boldsymbol{\mu}_k$) for each cluster is sampled from a Dirichlet distribution. The order (V_k) of each cluster is sampled randomly from a certain range between $0.5D$ to $1.5D$. After determining the cluster parameters ($\boldsymbol{\mu}_k$) and orders (V_k) we draw the data samples.

Real Datasets: We consider 8 text datasets used in [20]. They consist of discrete count vectors, extracted from different documents collections. The choice was due to its good representation of different characteristics, such as the number of observations (documents), number of features (terms) and the number of clusters. The chosen datasets are listed in Table 1. We refer the readers to the Sect. 4.2 of [20] for additional details about the construction of these datasets.

4.2   Comparisons

First we compare the initialization strategies listed in Sect. 3.3 and consistently use the best one for the rest of the experiments. Afterward, we evaluate the model generation methods discussed in Sect. 3.4. Finally, we evaluate the model selection strategies discussed in Sect. 3.4.

---

[1] Stability provides a measure of robustness w.r.t. different initializations. A stable method should provide similar results for different runs, irrespective of its initialization. Therefore, a smaller value of the standard deviation indicates similar results for different runs and hence higher stability of the clustering method.

[2] A lower sKLD value among the cluster parameters indicates well-separated clusters, whereas higher value indicates less separation or a certain amount of overlap. Besides computing the sKLD value, we also verified the separation by observing the Bayes error rate among the clusters.

Table 1. Document text datasets for real data experiments. **N** denotes number of samples, **D** denotes number of features and **K** denotes the number of clusters. The source of the datasets are - **NG20**: 20 Newsgroups, **Classic**: ACM/CISI/CRANFIELD/MEDLINE, **Ohscal**: OHSUMED, **K1b**: WebACE, **Hitech**: SJM-TREC, **Reviews**: SJM-TREC, **Sports**: SJM-TREC and **La12**: LAT-TREC.

	NG20	Classic	Ohscal	K1b	Hitech	Reviews	Sports	La12
N	19949	7094	11162	2340	2310	4069	8580	6279
D	43586	41681	11465	21839	10080	18483	14870	31472
K	20	4	10	6	6	5	7	6

Initialization Methods: The experimental settings for the initialization methods (see Sect. 3.3) consist of: 1 trial for *Random*, 100 trials for *rndEM*, 5 trials with 50 maximum EM iterations for *smEM* and *CEM* and 1 trial with 500 maximum EM iterations for *SEM*. The initial parameters obtained from these methods are experimented with the EM method discussed in Sect. 3.2. Figure 1 illustrates the results w.r.t. the clustering accuracy for both simulated[3] and real datasets. From all experimental results we have the following observations:

- For the simulated data, the *smEM* is the best method while the *CEM* is very competitive. However, for the real data *smEM* provides the best accuracy (except the *sport* dataset). The second choice is the *CEM* method.
- In terms of stability, *smEM* is the best for simulated data and *CEM* is best for the real data.
- In terms of computation time, these methods can be ordered as follows: *Random* < *rndEM* < *CEM* < *smEM* < *SEM*.

Similar to [14], we emphasize on the clustering accuracy as the main criteria to evaluate the initialization methods. Therefore, we choose the *SEM* method for further experiments.

Model Generation Methods: In this experiment, we aim to generate a set of candidate models with the methods discusses in Sect. 3.4. Among them, the *Mul-EM* and *EM-HAC* explicitly generate the models and the *Int-EM* generates them implicitly. All methods are initialized with the *smEM* method. Moreover, same initializations are used in *Int-EM* and *EM-HAC*. Settings of these methods consist of: 100 maximum number of EM iterations, 10^{-5} as the convergence threshold for the log-likelihood difference, $K_{min} = 2$ and $K_{max} = 15$, execept for *NG20* $K_{max} = 30$. Figure 2 illustrates a comparison of these methods w.r.t. the accuracy[4] and stability. Table 2 provides a comparison[5] of the computation time for real data. From all experimental results we have the following observations:

---

[3] Due to limited space, we show results only for *nws* simulated samples with $D = 40$.

[4] This computation considers that the true numbers of clusters are known.

[5] Time comparison for the synthetic data provides similar observation as real data. Therefore, to save space we do not present those results.

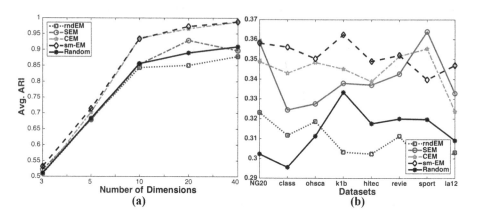

Fig. 1. Illustration of the accuracy of the initialization methods, computed from: (a) simulated *nws* samples with $K = 3$ and (b) real text datasets.

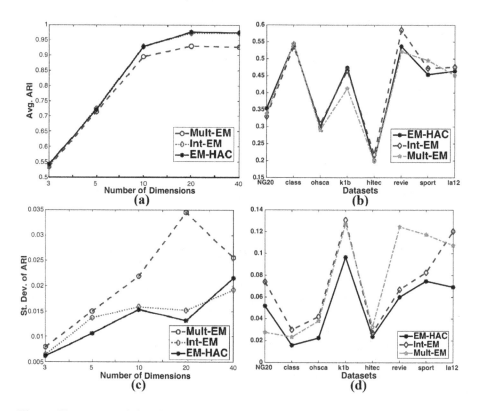

Fig. 2. Illustration of the clustering *accuracy* in (a) and (b), and *stability* in (c) and (d) for the model generation methods. (a) and (c) are computed from the simulated *nws* samples; (b) and (d) are computed from real text datasets.

- For the simulated data: *EM-HAC* and *Int-EM* are very competitive w.r.t. accuracy and time (results not shown). *EM-HAC* is the best on stability. *Mul-EM* was always performing worse except in a very few experiments.
- For the real[6] data, no single method outperforms others w.r.t. the accuracy. *EM-HAC* performs best in 3 datasets, *Int-EM* is best in 4 datasets and *Mul-EM* is best in 1 dataset. *EM-HAC* is best w.r.t. the stability (7 out of 8 datasets). Most interestingly, *EM-HAC* shows significantly better performance in terms of computation time as it is $\sim$ 2.5 times faster than *Int-EM* and $\sim$ 9 times faster than *Mul-EM*.

Based on the above experiments and observations, we can suggest that *Int-EM* is preferred when only accuracy is concerned. However, *EM-HAC* is preferred when stability and time has importantce besides accuracy.

Table 2. Comparison of the computation time (in seconds) among the model generation methods.

	NG20	Classic	ohscal	k1b	hightech	reviews	sports	la12
EM-HAC	**108.5**	**6.9**	**19.2**	**3.8**	**3.6**	**9.9**	**17.7**	**19.9**
Int-EM	353.2	10.8	42.2	9.6	8.2	21.7	46.3	44.2
Mult-EM	2844.0	54.4	95.6	29.1	20.7	59.1	104.1	134.6

Model Selection Methods: We evaluate different model selection criteria (see Sect. 3.5) with the *EM-HAC*. Moreover, we consider the *MML* with *Int-EM*, also called *EM-MML*, as proposed in [17]. Figure 3 illustrates a comparison with both simulated and real data w.r.t. the rate of correct number of components selection. Our observations from these results are as follows:

- For the simulated data: *BIC* provides the best rate (except $K = 3$). *ICL* is equivalent to the *BIC* for higher K. Rate of *MML* decreases with the increase of K. Moreover, *MML* performs better with *EM-HAC* rather than with *Int-EM*. The *LM* provides mediocre accuracy for all clusters. The *LLH* criterion fails significantly.
- For the real data: *LM* provides very good ($\sim$ 90 %) rate for 4 (*classic, hightech, review* and *la12*) datasets. Among the other methods, *MML* shows success in the *review* dataset, *LLH* is successful for the *classic* dataset.

From the above observations we realize that, the L-method (*LM*) is the best choice with the proposed clustering method. However, we want to emphasize that it is yet necessary to conduct further research on the model selection issue as there is no single method which uniquely provides reasonable rate for all data.

---

[6] In this paper we are interested only to compare different MM based MBC methods. We refer readers to [20] for a comparison among different other methods. From [20] we observed that, the *mixmns* (*Mul-EM* in this paper) performs better than the non-MBC methods, such as the *kmns* (k-means) and the *skmns* (spherical k-means).

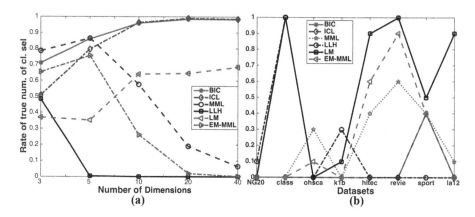

Fig. 3. Illustration of the rate of correct model selection, results in (a) are computed from the simulated samples and results in (b) are computed from real text datasets.

5 Conclusions

In this paper, we present a comparative study among different clustering methods with the Multinomial Mixture models. We experimentally evaluate the related issues, such as initialization, model estimation and generation and model selection. Besides, we propose a novel method for efficiently estimating the candidate models. Experimental results on both simulated and real data show that: (a) small run of EM (smEM) is the best choice for initialization (b) proposed hybrid model-based clustering, called EM-HAC is the best choice for candidate models estimation and (c) L-method is the best choice for model selection. As future work, we foresee the necessity to conduct further research on the model selection issue. Moreover, it is also necessary to evaluate these methods on more real-world discrete datasets obtained from a variety of different contexts.

Acknowledgments. This work is funded by the project ImagiWeb ANR-2012-CORD-002-01.

References

1. Banerjee, A., Dhillon, I.S., Ghosh, J., Sra, S.: Clustering on the unit hypersphere using von mises-fisher distributions. J. Mach. Learn. Res. **6**, 1345–1382 (2005)
2. Biernacki, C., Celeux, G., Govaert, G.: Assessing a mixture model for clustering with the integrated completed likelihood. IEEE TPAMI **22**(7), 719–725 (2000)
3. Biernacki, C., Celeux, G., Govaert, G.: Choosing starting values for the em algorithm for getting the highest likelihood in multivariate gaussian mixture models. Comput. Stat. Data Anal. **41**(3), 561–575 (2003)
4. Bishop, C.M., et al.: Pattern Recognition and Mlearning, vol. 4. Springer, New York (2006)

5. Figueiredo, M.A.T., Jain, A.K.: Unsupervised learning of finite mixture models. IEEE TPAMI **24**(3), 381–396 (2002)
6. Fraley, C., Raftery, A.E.: Model-based clustering, discriminant analysis, and density estimation. J. Am. Stat. Assoc. **97**(458), 611–631 (2002)
7. Fraley, C., Raftery, A.E.: Model-based methods of classification: using the mclust software in chemometrics. J. Stat. Softw. **18**(6), 1–13 (2007)
8. Garcia, V., Nielsen, F.: Simplification and hierarchical representations of mixtures of exponential families. Sig. Process. **90**(12), 3197–3212 (2010)
9. Hasnat, M.A., Alata, O., Trémeau, A.: Unsupervised clustering of depth images using watson mixture model. In: 22nd International Conference on Pattern Recognition (ICPR), pp. 214–219. IEEE (2014)
10. Hasnat, M.A., Alata, O., Treméau, A.: Model-based hierarchical clustering with Bregman divergences and Fishers mixture model: application to depth image analysis. Stat. Comput. 1–20 (2015). doi:10.1007/s11222-015-9576-3, ISSN: 0960-3174
11. Hubert, L., Arabie, P.: Comparing partitions. J. Classif. **2**(1), 193–218 (1985)
12. Maitra, R.: Initializing partition-optimization algorithms. IEEE/ACM Trans. Comput. Biol. Bioinform. **6**(1), 144–157 (2009)
13. McLachlan, G.J., Krishnan, T.: The EM Algorithm and Extensions. Wiley Series in Probability and Statistics, 2nd edn. Wiley, New York (2008)
14. Meilă, M., Heckerman, D.: An experimental comparison of model-based clustering methods. Mach. Learn. **42**(1–2), 9–29 (2001)
15. Melnykov, V., Maitra, R.: Finite mixture models and model-based clustering. Stat. Surv. **4**, 80–116 (2010)
16. Salvador, S., Chan, P.: Determining the number of clusters/segments in hierarchical clustering/segmentation algorithms. In: IEEE Conference on Tools with Artificial Intelligence, pp. 576–584 (2004)
17. Silvestre, C., Cardoso, M.G., Figueiredo, M.A.: Identifying the number of clusters in discrete mixture models. arXiv preprint arXiv:1409.7419 (2014)
18. Vaithyanathan, S., Dom, B.: Model-based hierarchical clustering. In: Proceedings of the Uncertainty in Artificial Intelligence, pp. 599–608 (2000)
19. Zhong, S., Ghosh, J.: A unified framework for model-based clustering. J. Mach. Learn. Res. **4**, 1001–1037 (2003)
20. Zhong, S., Ghosh, J.: Generative model-based document clustering: a comparative study. Knowl. Inf. Syst. **8**(3), 374–384 (2005)

On Binary Reduction of Large-Scale Multiclass Classification Problems

Bikash Joshi[1]([✉]), Massih-Reza Amini[1], Ioannis Partalas[2], Liva Ralaivola[3], Nicolas Usunier[4], and Eric Gaussier[1]

[1] Grenoble Informatics Laboratory, University of Grenoble Alpes, Saint Martin D'heres, France
{bikash.joshi,massih-reza.amini,eric.gaussier}@imag.fr
[2] R.&D. Department, VISEO, Grenoble, France
ioannis.partalas@viseo.com
[3] Fundamental Informatics Laboratory, Université Aix-Marseille, Marseille, France
liva.ralaivola@lif.univ-mrs.fr
[4] Université Technologique de Compiègne, Heudiasyc, Compiègne, France
nicolas.usunier@hds.utc.fr

Abstract. In the context of large-scale problems, traditional multiclass classification approaches have to deal with class imbalancement and complexity issues which make them inoperative in some extreme cases. In this paper we study a transformation that reduces the initial multiclass classification of examples into a binary classification of pairs of examples and classes. We present generalization error bounds that exhibit the interdependency between the pairs of examples and which recover known results on binary classification with i.i.d. data. We show the efficiency of the deduced algorithm compared to state-of-the-art multiclass classification strategies on two large-scale document collections especially in the interesting case where the number of classes becomes very large.

1 Introduction

The overwhelming growth of textual and visual data contents on the Web raises the issue of automatically structuring these collections into large, open-domain taxonomies. These taxonomies contain categories organized in a hierarchical structure such as a tree or a directed acyclic graph. The open directory project, maintained by roughly 90,000 human editors, is an example of such taxonomies: it lists about 4 million websites distributed among more than 1 million classes. In that context, large-scale multiclass classification consists in assigning one class label to each document from the set of leaf nodes of the hierarchy.

In these Web-scale datasets, the classes exhibit a long-tailed distribution [1] in the sense that most of them contain very few examples. As most state-of-the-art multiclass classification approaches learn one scoring function for each class, they do not scale well to large number of classes in terms of training time, and, more importantly, they struggle with under-represented classes that tend to be never predicted. Ultimately, the predictions would be unchanged if most of the least represented classes are ignored.

© Springer International Publishing Switzerland 2015
E. Fromont et al. (Eds.): IDA 2015, LNCS 9385, pp. 132–144, 2015.
DOI: 10.1007/978-3-319-24465-5_12

In this paper, we present a new approach for multiclass classification that can deal with large number of classes with very few representative examples. The approach hinges on a theoretical analysis of algorithms that optimize ranking criteria for multiclass classification, such as those proposed in [17,22]. We provide a generalization error bound based on the Rademacher complexity for interdependent data that provides guarantees for the multiclass classification strategy based on a reduction to binary classification of pairs of couples (instance, class). The analysis suggests that the guarantees in terms of generalization performance degrades linearly with the number of classes for previous approaches that learn one parameter vector per class. To avoid this undesirable scaling of the sample complexity with respect to the number of classes, we present a new approach based on learning a combination of similarity features between instances and classes, where the similarities are computed by identifying a class with the set of its representative examples. Further, the reduction framework described above allows us to learn a single parameter vector with a dimension that does not depend on the number of classes. We empirically demonstrate that our approach is competitive with state-of-the-art multiclass classification approaches, in particular in terms of the macro F-measure, which gives higher emphasis to the correct prediction of rare classes than the classification accuracy. In addition, the number of parameters we learn is of order 10^7 times less than conventional multiclass classification models, which makes the approach appealing for large-scale classification.

In Sect. 2, we position our work with respect to the literature. Section 3 presents our theoretical analysis and our proposed classification strategy. The design of the features and the experimental results are in Sect. 4.

2   Related Work

Several techniques exist to reduce multiclass problems with K classes into binary classification problems. The most popular approaches include the well-known one-versus-one (OVO), one-versus-all (OVA) [10], and Error Correcting Output Codes (ECOC) approaches. In OVO, a binary problem is created for each pair of classes of the initial problem, leading to $K(K-1)/2$ binary problems and, therefore, to as many binary classifiers. The prediction for a new instance is the class which receives the majority of the votes. In OVA, K binary problems are created, each one being associated to a specific class seen as the positive class and the other as forming the negative class. Given real-valued predictors $g_1, \ldots, g_K$, the predicted class for an instance x is given by $\arg\max_y g_y(x)$.

In the ECOC-based approach, a binary code $\mathbf{c}_k$ of length L is assigned to each class k, giving rise to L binary classification problems. One binary predictor is learned for each of the L induced binary problems and, at prediction time, inference is performed by selecting the class that minimizes the Hamming distance between its code and the predicted code. Methods to speed up prediction or training with ECOC have recently been proposed: for example, only a subset of the classifiers may be used at inference time without loss of accuracy [13]; in another direction, a Naive Bayes approach that only requires a single pass over the data for training has proved effective [14].

Methods that achieve logarithmic-time prediction or training have been proposed in [2,3]: they rest on binary tree structures where each leaf corresponds to a class and inference is performed by traversing the tree from top to bottom, a binary classifier being used at each node to determine the child node to develop.

Ranking approaches to multiclass classification [17,22], or the constraint classification framework of [6] can be seen as a reduction using binary classifications of pairs of classes (given an example), similar to ours. The proposed reduction strategy allows to obtain new generalization error bounds, and lead to a different algorithm. While state-of-the-art approaches learn one scoring function per class, and thus have similar computational and sample complexities similar to the OVA approach, we design similarity features between classes and examples allowing to learn a single parameter vector for the whole problem.

A similar approach for learning representations of classes was also proposed in [21]. The latter learns a projection of examples and classes into a low dimensional space, which reduces both training and inference time. In contrast to our approach, the aforementioned learns one parameter vector per class, while we use joint features of classes and examples allowing to reduce the number of vector parameters to one.

3   Multiclass to Binary Reduction

3.1   Framework

We consider monolabel multiclass classification problems defined on a joint space $\mathcal{X} \times \mathcal{Y}$ where $\mathcal{X} \subseteq \mathbb{R}^d$ is the *input space* and $\mathcal{Y} = \{1, \ldots, K\}$ the *output space*, made of K class labels. Elements of $\mathcal{X} \times \mathcal{Y}$ are denoted as $\mathbf{x}^y = (x, y)$. Furthermore, we assume the training set $\mathcal{S} = (\mathbf{x}_i^{y_i})_{i=1}^m$ is made of i.i.d pairs distributed according to a fixed but unknown probability distribution $\mathcal{D}$, and we consider a class of functions $\mathcal{G} = \{g : \mathcal{X} \times \mathcal{Y} \to \mathbb{R}\}$ as our predictors. We define the instantaneous loss of $g \in \mathcal{G}$ on an example $\mathbf{x}^y$ as:

$$e(g, \mathbf{x}^y) = \frac{1}{K-1} \sum_{y' \in \mathcal{Y} \setminus \{y\}} \mathbb{1}_{g(\mathbf{x}^y) \leq g(\mathbf{x}^{y'})}, \tag{1}$$

where $\mathbb{1}_\pi$ is the indicator function that is equal to 1 if the predicate π is true and 0 otherwise. Compared to the classical multiclass error:

$$e'(g, \mathbf{x}^y) = \mathbb{1}_{y \neq \operatorname{argmax}_{y' \in \mathcal{Y}} g(\mathbf{x}^{y'})},$$

the loss of (1) estimates the average number of classes, given any input data, that get a greater scoring by g than the correct class. The loss (1) is hence a *ranking* criterion, and the multiclass SVM of [22] and AdaBoost.MR [17] optimize convex surrogate functions of this loss. This is also used in label ranking [7], where the task is to predict a ranking of all labels instead of predicting a single label y given an instance x. The multiclass classification problem we are going to study is that of finding a function $g \in \mathcal{G}$ using the labeled training set $\mathcal{S}$ with small generalization error $L(g)$:

$$L(g) = \mathbb{E}_{\mathbf{x}^y \sim \mathcal{D}} \left[e(g, \mathbf{x}^y) \right]. \tag{2}$$

Accordingly, the empirical error of $g \in \mathcal{G}$ over $\mathcal{S}$ is

$$\hat{L}_m(g, \mathcal{S}) = \frac{1}{m} \sum_{i=1}^{m} (\underbrace{\frac{1}{K-1} \sum_{y' \in \mathcal{Y} \setminus \{y\}} \mathbb{1}_{g(\mathbf{x}_i^y) \leq g(\mathbf{x}_i^{y'})}}_{e(g, \mathbf{x}_i^{y_i})}) \tag{3}$$

3.2   Reduction Strategy

We further work out the empirical loss of Eq. (3) in order to (i) have it resemble a more usual binary classification loss with, in particular, a single sum running over only one index, (ii) make apparent the need of dealing with non-i.i.d. random variables and (iii) after a theoretical introduction, set the stage for our practical binary reduction approach.

A first step to reshape the empirical loss is to see that the instantaneous loss (1) can be rewritten as

$$e(g, \mathbf{x}^y) = \frac{1}{K-1} \sum_{y' \in \mathcal{Y} \setminus \{y\}} \mathbb{1}_{\tilde{y} h(\mathbf{x}^y, \mathbf{x}^{y'}) \leq 0},$$

where h is defined as $h(\mathbf{x}^y, \mathbf{x}^{y'}) = g(\mathbf{x}^y) - g(\mathbf{x}^{y'})$. This bears strong resemblance with a binary-classification-loss-based risk, a resemblance that can be strengthened by introducing the transformed set $T(\mathcal{S})$ of size $n = m(K-1)$ defined as

$$T(\mathcal{S}) = \{ (\mathbf{Z}_j, \tilde{y}_j) : j = 1, \ldots, n \}, \tag{4}$$

where each $\mathbf{Z}_j$ is one of the pairs $(\mathbf{x}_i^y, \mathbf{x}_i^{y'})$, and $\tilde{y}_j = 1$ if the first observation in $\mathbf{Z}_j$ is constituted by an example $\mathbf{x}_i$ and its true class in $\mathcal{S}$ (i.e. $y = y_i$) and the second observation is constituted by the same example and any other of the $K-1$ classes; and $\tilde{y}_j = -1$ otherwise (i.e. if the order is reverse). This allows us to rewrite the empirical loss of (3) as

$$L_n^T(h, T(\mathcal{S})) = \frac{1}{n} \sum_{j=1}^{n} \mathbb{1}_{\tilde{y}_j h(\mathbf{Z}_j) \leq 0}. \tag{5}$$

With these definitions at hand, it is clear that the selection of a hypothesis in $\mathcal{G}$ minimizing the empirical risk of (3) over the training set $\mathcal{S}$, is equivalent to the search of a hypothesis in $\mathcal{H} = \{ h : h(\mathbf{x}^y, \mathbf{x}^{y'}) = g(\mathbf{x}^y) - g(\mathbf{x}^{y'}), g \in \mathcal{G} \}$ minimizing the empirical risk of (5) over $T(\mathcal{S})$. However, even if the examples in $\mathcal{S}$ are i.i.d., the examples in $T(\mathcal{S})$ are no longer independent since the same observations $\mathbf{x}^y \in \mathcal{S}$ are involved in different pairs of $T(\mathcal{S})$. Thus, in order to obtain generalization error bounds $L_n^T(h, T(\mathcal{S}))$ we need to address the issue of learning with interdependent data.

There exist several ways to tackle this problem among which two settings received particular attention in the literature. The first one deals with learning from mixing processes, where the dependency between random variables decreases over time [12,18]. The second direction, on which the present work is based on, is developed around the idea of graph coloring that divides a graph, representing the relations between random variables, into sets of independent random variables called proper cover of the graph [8].

A proper cover of $T(\mathcal{S})$ is constituted of $K-1$ disjoint sets $(C_k)_{k=1}^{K-1}$ each containing m independent examples. For all $k \in \{1, \ldots, K-1\}$ it is defined as

$$C_k = \{(\mathbf{Z}_{k+j(K-1)}, \tilde{y}_{k+j(K-1)}); j \in \{0, \ldots, m-1\}\}$$

Moreover, $(C_k, \alpha_k)_{k=1}^{K-1}$ is said to be a proper exact fractional cover of $T(\mathcal{S})$, if $(C_k)_{k=1}^{K-1}$ is a proper cover of $T(\mathcal{S})$ and if $\forall k, \alpha_k > 0$ and

$$\forall i \in \{1, \ldots, n\}, \sum_{k=1}^{K-1} \alpha_k \mathbb{1}_{(\mathbf{Z}_i, \tilde{y}_i) \in C_k} = 1.$$

The fractional chromatic number of T, denoted as χ_T^* is then the minimum sum of weights, or the minimum number of sets containing each independent random variables, which for the proposed transformation is equal to $K-1$. Figure 1 depicts the transformation and its associated proper exact fractional on a toy problem.

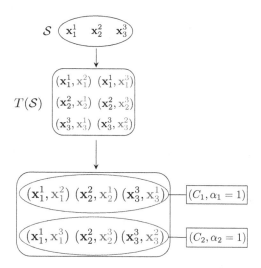

Fig. 1. The proper exact fractional cover of the set $T(\mathcal{S})$ obtained after transformation of the training set $\mathcal{S} = \{\mathbf{x}_1^1, \mathbf{x}_2^2, \mathbf{x}_3^3\}$. For the sake of clarity, the class labels of pairs of examples are omitted. The fractional chromatic number of T is in this case $\chi_T^* = 2$.

Using graph coloring arguments, [8] extended Hoeffding's inequality to sums of interdependent random variables and based on that result, different studies proposed new generalization error bounds for learning with interdependent data, thus proving the consistency of the ERM principle for this case [16,20]. Here we build on [20] who proposed a generalization of [11] concentration inequality to the case of interdependent random variables.

Our theoretical result is the following theorem which provides data-dependent bound on the generalization error of the multiclass classifier (Eq. 2). This result is at the basis of the algorithm for the binary classification of pairs of examples that we expose in the next section. We consider here kernel-based hypotheses with $\kappa : \mathcal{Z} \to \mathbb{R}$ a *positive semidefinite* (PSD) kernel and $\Phi : \mathcal{X} \times \mathcal{Y} \to \mathbb{H}$ its associated feature mapping function, defined as:

$$\mathcal{G}_B = \{\mathbf{x}^y \in \mathcal{X} \times \mathcal{Y} \mapsto \langle \boldsymbol{w}, \Phi(\mathbf{x}^y) \rangle \mid ||\boldsymbol{w}|| \leq B\} \tag{6}$$

where $\boldsymbol{w}$ is the weight vector defining the kernel-based hypotheses and $\langle \cdot, \cdot \rangle$ denotes the dot product. We further define the following associated function class:

$$\mathcal{H}_B = \{(\mathbf{x}^y, \mathbf{x}'^{y'}) \in \mathcal{Z} \mapsto g_w(\mathbf{x}^y) - g_w(\mathbf{x}'^{y'}) \mid g_w \in \mathcal{G}_B\}.$$

Theorem 1. *Let $\mathcal{S} = (\mathbf{x}_i^{y_i})_{i=1}^m \in (\mathcal{X} \times \mathcal{Y})^m$ be a dataset of m examples drawn i.i.d. according to a probability distribution $\mathcal{D}$ over $\mathcal{X} \times \mathcal{Y}$ and $T(\mathcal{S}) = ((\mathbf{Z}_i, \tilde{y}_i))_{i=1}^n \in (\mathcal{Z} \times \{-1, 1\})^n$ the transformed set obtained with the transformation function T defined above. Further let $\kappa : \mathcal{Z} \to \mathbb{R}$ be a PDS kernel, and let $\Phi : \mathcal{X} \times \mathcal{Y} \to \mathbb{H}$ be the associated feature mapping function. Then for all $1 > \delta > 0$ with probability at least $(1 - \delta)$ over $T(\mathcal{S})$ the following generalization bound holds for all $h_w \in \mathcal{H}_B$:*

$$L^T(h_w) \leq \epsilon_n^T(h_w, T(\mathcal{S})) + \frac{2B\mathfrak{G}(T(\mathcal{S}))}{m\sqrt{K-1}} + 3\sqrt{\frac{\ln(\frac{2}{\delta})}{2m}} \tag{7}$$

where $\epsilon_n^T(h, T(\mathcal{S})) = \frac{1}{n}\sum_{i=1}^n \mathcal{L}(\tilde{y}_i h_w(\mathbf{Z}_i))$ with the surrogate Hinge loss $\mathcal{L} : t \mapsto \min(1, \max(1 - t, 0))$, $L^T(h_w) = \mathbb{E}_{T(\mathcal{S})}[L_n^T(h_w, T(\mathcal{S}))]$ and $\mathfrak{G}(T(\mathcal{S})) = \sqrt{\sum_{i=1}^n d_\kappa(\mathbf{Z}_i)}$ with

$$d_\kappa(\mathbf{x}^y, \mathbf{x}^{y'}) = \kappa(\mathbf{x}^y, \mathbf{x}^y) + \kappa(\mathbf{x}^{y'}, \mathbf{x}^{y'}) - 2\kappa(\mathbf{x}^y, \mathbf{x}^{y'})$$

Proof. Exploiting the fact that $\mathcal{L}$ dominates the $0/1$ loss and using the fractional Rademacher data-dependent generalization bound proposed for interdependent data in Theorem 4 of [20] one has

$$L^T(h_w) \leq \epsilon^T(h_w) \leq \hat{\epsilon}_n^T(h_w, T(\mathcal{S})) + \hat{\mathcal{R}}_n^T(\mathcal{L} \circ \mathcal{H}_B, \mathcal{S}) + 3\sqrt{\frac{\chi_T^* \ln(\frac{2}{\delta})}{2n}}$$

Where $\epsilon^T(h_w) = \mathbb{E}_{T(\mathcal{S})}[\hat{\epsilon}_n^T(h_w, T(\mathcal{S}))]$ and $\hat{\mathcal{R}}_n^T(\mathcal{L} \circ \mathcal{H}_B, \mathcal{S})$ is the empirical fractional Rademacher complexity of $\mathcal{L} \circ \mathcal{H}_B$ on $T(\mathcal{S})$. Further, as $\mathcal{L}$ is 1-Lipschitz, so

$$\hat{\mathcal{R}}_n^T(\mathcal{L} \circ \mathcal{H}_B, \mathcal{S}) \leq \hat{\mathcal{R}}_n^T(\mathcal{H}_B, \mathcal{S})$$

where

$$\hat{\mathcal{R}}_n^T(\mathcal{H}_B, \mathcal{S}) = \sum_{k=1}^{K-1} \frac{2\alpha_k}{M} \mathbb{E}_\sigma \sup_{h \in \mathcal{H}_B} \sum_{j=0}^{m-1} \sigma_j h_w(\boldsymbol{Z}_{k+j(K-1)})$$

Now, for all $k \in \{1, .., K-1\}$ and $j \in \{0, .., m-1\}$, let z_{kj} and z_{kj}' be the first and the second pair of $\boldsymbol{Z}_{k+j(K-1)}$, then from the bilinearity of dot product and the Cauchy-Schwartz inequality, $\hat{\mathcal{R}}_n^T(\mathcal{H}_B, \mathcal{S})$ is upper-bounded by

$$\sum_{k=1}^{K-1} \frac{2\alpha_k}{n} \mathbb{E}_\sigma \sup_{h_w \in \mathcal{H}_B} \left\langle \boldsymbol{w}, \sum_{j=0}^{m-1} \sigma_j(\Phi(z_{kj}) - \Phi(z_{kj}')) \right\rangle$$

$$\leq \sum_{k=1}^{K-1} \frac{2B\alpha_k}{n} \mathbb{E}_\sigma \left\| \sum_{j=0}^{m-1} \sigma_j(\Phi(z_{kj}) - \Phi(z_{kj}')) \right\|$$

Further, for all $i, j \in \{0, \ldots, m-1\}^2, i \neq j$, we have $\mathbb{E}_\sigma[\sigma_i \sigma_j] = 0$ so

$$\hat{\mathcal{R}}_n^T(\mathcal{H}_B, \mathcal{S}) \leq \sum_{k=1}^{K-1} \frac{2B\alpha_k}{n} \sqrt{\sum_{j=0}^{m-1} d_\kappa(z_{kj}, z_{kj}')}$$

$$= \frac{2B\chi_T^*}{n} \sum_{k=1}^{K-1} \frac{\alpha_k}{\chi_T^*} \sqrt{\sum_{j=0}^{m-1} d_\kappa(z_{kj}, z_{kj}')}$$

Now as $\sum_{k=1}^{K-1} \frac{\alpha_k}{\chi_T^*} = 1$ and that $t \mapsto \sqrt{t}$ is concave, from Jensen inequality we have

$$\hat{\mathcal{R}}_m^T(\mathcal{H}_B, \mathcal{S}) \leq \frac{2B\chi_T^*}{n} \sqrt{\sum_{k=1}^{K-1} \frac{\alpha_k}{\chi_T^*} \sum_{j=0}^{m-1} d_\kappa(z_{kj}, z_{kj}')}$$

The result follows from rearranging the examples and the equalities $\chi_T^* = K-1$, and $n = (K-1)m$.

3.3   Favoring Low-Dimensional Feature Maps

Our reduction relies on the joint representation $\Phi(\mathbf{x}^y)$ of features and classes. Such feature maps are at the basis of algorithms such as structured SVM (see e.g. [19]), to account for features encoding properties of structures such as sequences or trees. However, in multiclass classification, the output space is unstructured and these algorithms are then applied by taking a "trivial" feature map such that even if a single parameter vector is used, it is in fact the concatenation of one parameter vector per class. In that case, $\Phi(\mathbf{x}^k) \in \mathbb{R}^{dK}$ (with $\mathbf{x} \in \mathbb{R}^d$) is a vector where all entries are zero except those with indices in the range $[1 + (k-1)d; kd]$, which are equal to $\mathbf{x}$. The reduction of multiclass classification to constraint classification of [6] follows the same idea. With this kind of joint (instance, class) representation, the natural regularization is to constrain each

---

Algorithm 1: Multiclass reduced to binary classification (mRb)

Input: Labeled training set $\mathcal{S} = (\mathbf{x}_i^{y_i})_{i=1}^m$;
A binary classifier $\mathcal{A}$;
Initialize
$T(S) \leftarrow \emptyset$;
for $i = 1..m$ **do**
    for $k = 1..K$ **do**
        if $y_i > k$ **then**
          | $T(S) \leftarrow \{(\Phi(\mathbf{x}_i^{y_i}) - \Phi(\mathbf{x}_i^k), +1)\}$;
        end
        if $y_i < k$ **then**
          | $T(S) \leftarrow \{(\Phi(\mathbf{x}_i^k) - \Phi(\mathbf{x}_i^{y_i}), -1)\}$;
        end
    end
end
Learn $\mathcal{A}$ on $T(S)$;

---

parameter vector to have a norm smaller than some B. The whole vector $\boldsymbol{w}$ would then have a norm about KB, leading the capacity term of Theorem 1, $\mathfrak{G}(T(\mathcal{S}))$, to grow linearly with K. To avoid this linear deterioration of the generalization performance guarantees, we might choose to put a stronger regularization on some classes, e.g. the rare classes. But then these heavily regularized classes would be penalized because the magnitude of their predicted scores would be smaller: they would rarely or never be predicted. We propose to give an alternative answer to avoid the dependence of the penalty term on K. We advocate the design of a non-trivial joint feature representation $\Phi(\mathbf{x}^y)$ by using a small number of adequately chosen similarity features between examples and classes, so that this joint feature space is the same for any number of classes. The goal of learning is then to combine these features, using the same parameter vector for all classes. Then, the natural scaling of the penalty term of Theorem 1 should remain constant, and the detrimental effect of having stronger regularization on certain classes disappears. The proposed approach denoted by mRb, for multiclass reduced to binary classification, is hence depicted in Algorithm 1. As the learned classifier from the function class $\mathcal{G}_B$ is linear in the feature space, the output of a function $h \in \mathcal{H}_B$ over an example $(\mathbf{x}^y, \mathbf{x}^{y'})$ can be computed as the dot product between the learned weight vector, $\boldsymbol{w}$, and the difference between the vector representations $\Phi(\mathbf{x}^y) - \Phi(\mathbf{x}^{y'})$. For testing a new example $\mathbf{x}'$, we estimate $\Phi(\mathbf{x}'^y)$ for all $\mathbf{x}'^y$ pairs. Given the learned weight vector $\boldsymbol{w}$, the predicted class is the one which maximizes the dot product $\langle \boldsymbol{w}, \Phi(\mathbf{x}'^y) \rangle$.

4 Experiments

We use non-trivial joint feature representation, which is popularly used in text classification domain. So, we evaluate the proposed method for multi-class classification in a large-scale scenario using DMOZ and Wikipedia datasets of the

Large Scale Hierarchical Text Classification challenge (LSHTC 2011) [15]. These datasets contain 27875 and 36504 categories respectively for DMOZ and Wikipedia and they are provided in a pre-processed format using stop-word removal and stemming. The dimension of the vectorial space (d), the size of the training set (m) and the test set are respectively 594158, 394756 and 104263 for DMOZ and 346299, 456886 and 81262 for Wikipedia. For each of these datasets we randomly draw several samples with increasing number of classes: 100, 500, 1000, 3000, 5000 and 7500 and by keeping the same proportion of examples in the training and the test sets than in the initial collections. For the feature mapping, we used the following features in the vector representation of $\Phi(\mathbf{x}^y)$ (Table 1) by considering a class y as a mega-document, constituted by the concatenation of all of the documents in the training set belonging to it. Almost all the features, except 9 and 10, are classical features employed in learning to rank by assimilating a class and a document to respectively a document and a query. The former two are the distance of the example x to its two nearest neighbours in class y. Since the absolute values of each feature for the documents are different and not comparable, we normalize them such that the feature values are confined within the range of 0 to 1. Following our theoretical result, we used SVM with linear kernel as our binary classification algorithm. The value of the hyperparameter C is chosen from a range of values from 10^{-3} to 10^3 by cross-validation. We compared the proposed approach, mRb (Fig. 1), with the hierarchical reduction approach (LogT) proposed by [3] and the following multiclass classification techniques using the LibLinear package [5] that implements them all: One Vs. All (OVA), One Vs. One (OVO) and Multiclass SVM (M-SVM) proposed by [4]. For all of these methods we adopted the *tfidf* encoding of features as it provided the best performance. Results are evaluated over the test set using the accuracy and the macro F1 measure (MaF$_1$), which is the harmonic average of macro precision and macro recall. The reported performance is averaged over 50 random (train/test) sets of the initial collection for every fixed number of classes we considered. In all of our experiments, we used a server with an intel Xenon 1.8 HGz processor and 16 GB of RAM.

Table 1. Let x_t represent the term frequency of term t in document x, and $\mathcal{V}$ the set of distinct terms within $\mathcal{S}$, then $y_t = \sum_{x \in y} x_t$, $|y| = \sum_{t \in \mathcal{V}} y_t$, $\mathcal{S}_t = \sum_{x \in \mathcal{S}} x_t$, $l_{\mathcal{S}} = \sum_{t \in \mathcal{V}} \mathcal{S}_t$. I_t is the inverse document frequency of term t, and $d_1(\mathbf{x}^y)$ and $d_2(\mathbf{x}^y)$ are the distances of x to its two nearest neighbours in class y.

Features in the vector representation of $\Phi(\mathbf{x}^y)$.			
1. $\displaystyle\sum_{t \in y \cap x} \ln(1 + y_t)$	2. $\displaystyle\sum_{t \in y \cap x} \ln(1 + \frac{l_{\mathcal{S}}}{\mathcal{S}_t})$	3. $\displaystyle\sum_{t \in y \cap x} I_t$	4. $\displaystyle\sum_{t \in y \cap x} \frac{y_t}{|y|}.I_t$
5. $\displaystyle\sum_{t \in y \cap x} \ln(1 + \frac{y_t}{|y|})$	6. $\displaystyle\sum_{t \in y \cap x} \ln(1 + \frac{y_t}{|y|}.I_t)$	7. $\displaystyle\sum_{t \in y \cap x} \ln(1 + \frac{y_t}{|y|}\frac{l_{\mathcal{S}}}{\mathcal{S}_t})$	8. $\displaystyle\sum_{t \in y \cap x} 1$
9. $d_1(\mathbf{x}^y)$	10. $d_2(\mathbf{x}^y)$		

Table 2. Accuracy, MaF1 of methods that could be trained with 7500 classes of DMOZ and Wikipedia collections. N_c is the proportion of classes that are covered. Statistics are given over 50 random samples of training/test sets.

	DMOZ-7500			Wikipedia-7500		
	Accuracy	MaF1	N_c	Accuracy	MaF1	N_c
mRb	$0.499^{\downarrow}{}_{\pm.011}$	$\mathbf{0.352}{}_{\pm.009}$	0.495	$0.467^{\downarrow}{}_{\pm.023}$	$\mathbf{0.378}{}_{\pm.012}$	0.551
OVA	$\mathbf{0.549}{}_{\pm.036}$	$0.282^{\downarrow}{}_{\pm.018}$	0.379	$\mathbf{0.484}{}_{\pm.029}$	$0.348^{\downarrow}{}_{\pm.017}$	0.489
LogT	$0.311^{\downarrow}{}_{\pm.034}$	$0.096^{\downarrow}{}_{\pm.029}$	0.194	$0.231^{\downarrow}{}_{\pm.035}$	$0.151^{\downarrow}{}_{\pm.021}$	0.287

We start our evaluation by analyzing the performance measures of different approaches on the setting with the largest number of classes we considered in our experiments ($K = 7500$). Table 2 summarizes results obtained by mRb, OVA and LogT, as the corresponding training processes of M-SVM and OVO were killed by the system and did not pass the scale. Results are averaged over 50 random splits of tests sets. We use bold face to indicate the highest performance rates, and the symbol ↓ indicates that performance is significantly worse than the

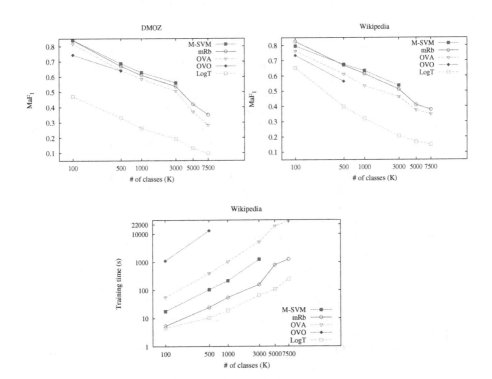

Fig. 2. MaF1 of all methods with respect to the number of classes for DMOZ (top left) and Wikipedia (top right). Training time in seconds of all methods with respect to the number of classes for Wikipedia (bottom).

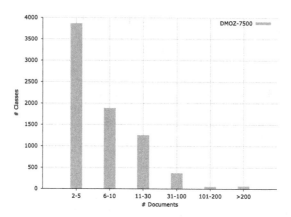

Fig. 3. Distribution of classes with respect to the number of documents they contain for DMOZ-7500.

best result, according to a Wilcoxon rank sum test used at a p-value threshold of 0.01 [9]. The competitive methods are OVA and mRb with a discrepancy over their accuracy and MaF$_1$ measures on both collections. To analyze this divergence we estimated the proportion of classes that have been covered, or for which at least one true positive document was found. It comes out that mRb covers 6 % to 12 % more classes than OVA (that is 465 to 900 more classes on both datasets). The reason here is that OVA is affected by the class imbalance problem especially in the extreme case where classes contain very few documents. For the large scale scenario this problem is accentuated as the class distribution is long-tailed, as for example in DMOZ-7500, more than half of the classes contain less than 5 documents (Fig. 3). We also analyze the behavior of the various algorithms for increasing number of classes. Figure 2 (top) illustrates this by showing the MaF$_1$ measures on DMOZ and Wikipedia with respect to the number of classes. As expected all performance curves decrease monotonically with respect to an increasing number of classes. The breaking points beyond which OVO and M-SVM cannot be trained, happen at the same time on both collections for respectively $K = 500$ and $K = 3000$ classes. The performance of mRb are in between of those of OVA and M-SVM before the breaking point, with a slight advantage for M-SVM, while mRb uniformly outperforms OVA with a larger gap on Wikipedia. We notice that on this collection, mRb achieves for 7500 classes MaF$_1$ score comparable to the OVA's one for 5000 classes. Comparatively, for $K = 3000$, the numbers of parameters of these two models are roughly 5.4×10^8 to 6.5×10^8 on respectively Wikipedia and DMOZ collections which are $O(10^7)$ with respect to the fixed number of parameters of mRb we have. Figure 2 (bottom) summarizes the training time of all methods for an increasing number of classes on Wikipedia. mRb has the second fastest running time after LogT which together with its small number of parameters and its performance makes it appealing for classification in large-scale taxonomies.

5   Conclusion

We presented a new method for large-scale multiclass classification based on a reduction of multiclass classification to binary classification. The theoretical analysis based on the fractional Rademacher complexity shows that learning a single scoring function for all classes, instead of one scoring function per class, avoids the capacity term to grow linearly with the number of classes, contrarily to existing methods. In addition, to have better scalability than existing methods, the features that we designed to jointly represent classes and documents improved the covering of rare classes compared to its counterparts, which is also depicted on MaF_1 score.

Acknowledgments. This work is partially supported by the LabEx PERSYVAL-Lab ANR-11-LABX-0025, and Titan CNRS-Mastodons.

References

1. Babbar, R., Metzig, C., Partalas, I., Gaussier, E., Amini, M.R.: On power law distributions in large-scale taxonomies. SIGKDD Explor. **16**(1), 47–56 (2014)
2. Beygelzimer, A., Langford, J., Ravikumar, P.: Error-correcting tournaments. In: Gavaldà, R., Lugosi, G., Zeugmann, T., Zilles, S. (eds.) ALT 2009. LNCS, vol. 5809, pp. 247–262. Springer, Heidelberg (2009)
3. Choromanska, A., Langford, J.: Logarithmic time online multiclass prediction. CoRR abs/1406.1822 (2014)
4. Crammer, K., Singer, Y.: On the algorithmic implementation of multiclass kernel-based vector machines. J. Mach. Learn. Res. **2**, 265–292 (2002)
5. Fan, R.E., Chang, K.W., Hsieh, C.J., Wang, X.R., Lin, C.J.: Liblinear: a library for large linear classification. J. Mach. Learn. Res. **9**, 1871–1874 (2008)
6. Har-Peled, S., Roth, D., Zimak, D.: Constraint classification: a new approach to multiclass classification and ranking. In: Advances in Neural Information Processing Systems, vol. 15, pp. 365–379 (2002)
7. Hüllermeier, E., Fürnkranz, J.: On minimizing the position error in label ranking. In: Kok, J.N., Koronacki, J., Lopez de Mantaras, R., Matwin, S., Mladenič, D., Skowron, A. (eds.) ECML 2007. LNCS (LNAI), vol. 4701, pp. 583–590. Springer, Heidelberg (2007)
8. Janson, S.: Large deviations for sums of partly dependent random variables. Random Struct. Algorithms **24**(3), 234–248 (2004)
9. Lehmann, E.: Nonparametric Statistical Methods Based on Ranks. McGraw-Hill, New York (1975)
10. Lorena, A.C., Carvalho, A.C., Gama, J.A.M.: A review on the combination of binary classifiers in multiclass problems. Artif. Intell. Rev. **30**(1–4), 19–37 (2008)
11. McDiarmid, C.: On the method of bounded differences. In: Survey in Combinatorics, pp. 148–188 (1989)
12. Mohri, M., Rostamizadeh, A.: Rademacher complexity bounds for non-i.i.d. processes. In: Advances in Neural Information Processing Systems 21, pp. 1097–1104 (2009)
13. Park, S.H., Fürnkranz, J.: Efficient prediction algorithms for binary decomposition techniques. Data Min. Knowl. Disc. **24**(1), 40–77 (2012)

14. Park, S., Fürnkranz, J.: Efficient implementation of class-based decomposition schemes for naïve bayes. Mach. Learn. **96**(3), 295–309 (2014)
15. Partalas, I., Kosmopoulos, A., Baskiotis, N., Artieres, T., Paliouras, G., Gaussier, E., Androutsopoulos, I., Amini, M.R., Galinari, P.: LSHTC: a benchmark for large-scale text classification. ArXiv e-prints, March 2015
16. Ralaivola, L., Szafranski, M., Stempfel, G.: Chromatic PAC-bayes bounds for non-IID data: applications to ranking and stationary β-mixing processes. J. Mach. Learn. Res. **11**, 1927–1956 (2010)
17. Schapire, R.E., Singer, Y.: Improved boosting algorithms using confidence-rated predictions. Mach. Learn. **37**(3), 297–336 (1999)
18. Steinwart, I., Christmann, A.: Fast learning from non-i.i.d. observations. In: Advances in Neural Information Processing Systems 22, pp. 1768–1776 (2010)
19. Tsochantaridis, I., Hofmann, T., Joachims, T., Altun, Y.: Support vector machine learning for interdependent and structured output spaces. In: Proceedings of the Twenty-first International Conference on Machine Learning, p. 104. ACM (2004)
20. Usunier, N., Amini, M.R., Gallinari, P.: Generalization error bounds for classifiers trained with interdependent data. In: Advances in Neural Information Processing Systems 18, pp. 1369–1376 (2006)
21. Weston, J., Bengio, S., Usunier, N.: Wsabie: scaling up to large vocabulary image annotation. In: Proceedings of the International Joint Conference on Artificial Intelligence, IJCAI (2011)
22. Weston, J., Watkins, C.: Multi-class support vector machines. Tech. rep., CSD-TR-98-04, Department of Computer Science, Royal Holloway, University of London (1998)

Probabilistic Active Learning in Datastreams

Daniel Kottke[✉], Georg Krempl, and Myra Spiliopoulou

Knowledge Management and Discovery Lab, Otto-von-Guericke-University,
Universitätsplatz 2, 39106 Magdeburg, Germany
{daniel.kottke,georg.krempl,myra}@iti.cs.uni-magdeburg.de
http://kmd.cs.ovgu.de

Abstract. In recent years, stream-based active learning has become an intensively investigated research topic. In this work, we propose a new algorithm for stream-based active learning that decides immediately whether to acquire a label (selective sampling). To this purpose, we extend our pool-based Probabilistic Active Learning framework into a framework for streams. In particular, we complement the notion of usefulness within a topological space ("spatial usefulness") with the concept of "temporal usefulness". To actively select the instances, for which labels must be acquired, we introduce the Balanced Incremental Quantile Filter (BIQF), an algorithm that assesses the usefulness of instances in a sliding window, ensuring that the predefined budget restrictions will be met within a given tolerance window. We compare our approach to other active learning approaches for streams and show the competitiveness of our method.

1 Introduction

Facing continuously raising amounts of data but limited human supervision capacities, active learning approaches that help in the efficient allocation of these capacities gain in relevance. The task in active learning is to decide for which instances to acquire labels from an oracle. An important active learning scenario is stream-based active learning (also called selective sampling), where data arrives one-by-one on a stream and the algorithm has to decide immediately if the label is acquired [21]. Hence, there is no pool where instances are compared against each other by estimating their usefulness by their position in feature space (spatial usefulness). Instead, the question becomes not only where but also when to query, i.e. the spatial aspect is complemented by a temporal one [14]. Except for [26], the role of the temporal component was just fairly considered in the algorithms as just simple thresholds have been tuned and applied. As it is not possible to tune a parameter without labeled data, we propose a method that ensures that a predefined budget will be definitely met within a desired tolerance window. This also means that labeling resources like experts or money remain constant (within the tolerance window) over time. Application scenarios for those methods can be found in opinion mining of social comment streams or annotation of sensor data like weather data or camera surveillance.

© Springer International Publishing Switzerland 2015
E. Fromont et al. (Eds.): IDA 2015, LNCS 9385, pp. 145–157, 2015.
DOI: 10.1007/978-3-319-24465-5_13

Here, very fast classification systems are required because models might shift very fast (e.g. in twitter or stock exchange data). On the one hand, human experts only have limited (and constant) resources, and on the other hand, collecting a batch means to postpone the model updates.

We propose an active learning framework that explicitly distinguishes between the spatial and temporal component. This allows to study different combinations, and to separate their effects on the classification performance. Furthermore, we contribute an algorithm that chooses the most useful instances over time: the Balanced Incremental Quantile Filter (BIQF). BIQF uses a sliding window over the stream of spatial usefulness values as a representative of the most recent values to estimate an acquisition threshold. An adjustment of this threshold ensures that the aberration of the number of label acquisitions stays within a given tolerance window. We evaluate the performance of our new selective sampling algorithm that combines probabilistic active learning as the spatial and BIQF as the temporal component on multiple datastreams.

We start with a summary of the related work in Sect. 2. We propose our new stream active learning algorithm in Sect. 3 and present our new temporal active learning component BIQF in Sect. 3.2. After a detailed evaluation on several data sets in Sect. 4, we conclude this paper in Sect. 5.

2   Related Work

An active learning system aims to select the most promising instances for labeling, in order to build the best training basis for a given classifier [15]. Thus, in the beginning, no labeled information is available, but the target value (label) can be actively acquired from an oracle. This dynamic learning process develops the performance of the classifier directly over time [20].

In the pool-based setting, active learning has been researched for a long time. One of the simplest and most commonly used approaches, called *uncertainty sampling* [15], aims to request those instances that the classifier is most uncertain about, e.g. by measuring the confidence based on posterior estimates [20]. However, it is fairly easy to construct examples, where uncertainty sampling is not working [21, p.20], due to not doing any exploration [26]. This could also lead to even worse performance than a randomly sampling strategy [22]. Another approach is *Expected Error Reduction* (EER) [18], which aims to directly optimize a performance measure. It simulates each realization of a label for each unlabeled instance and trains a new classifier. On this classifier, it estimates the expected error on a validation set. In [3] it is observed that inaccuracies of the posterior estimates (esp. at the beginning) lead to problems for this algorithm, and the addition of a beta-prior is proposed. Other approaches, like Query by Committee (QbC) [7] minimize the variance between multiple classifiers. More recently, we proposed *Probabilistic Active Learning (PAL)* in [13] which includes the expectation value over the true posterior for a given instance to approximate the influence of an acquired label by the expected effect in its neighborhood. It measures the amount of already acquired labels in a neighborhood and balances exploration and exploitation while directly optimizing a performance measure. Summarizing, EER and PAL optimize a performance measure, which ensures a good trade-off in exploration and exploitation [13,21]. While EER has high complexity, PAL and uncertainty sampling require only constant time per instance [13] which enables their applicability in streams.

For active learning in datastreams, we have to separate those methods that instantly decide whether to acquire a label or not, from those, that collect chunks or batches and apply pool-based methods. Chunk-based approaches use classifier ensembles [24,25] to determine the usefulness of instances or uncertainty-based measures [10,16,24]. A batch incremental stream active learning algorithm that first clusters the chunk and ranks the instances based on an homogeneity and certainty criterion was proposed in [11]. Most recently, we proposed a clustering-based approach in [12] using the probabilistic description to select the cluster to choose instances from. The instantly deciding methods mostly are uncertainty-based: the entropy uncertainty sampling with beta prior is used in [5], an ensemble of radial clusters that evolve over time is proposed in [19], adaptively weighted uncertainty and density scores are suggested in [4]. Zliobaite et al. [26] observes that uncertainty sampling is not sufficient to react to drift and combined it with random sampling. Except for [26], the latter group does not directly consider budget restrictions as they use arbitrary tunable parameters or other implicit descriptions. In [26], an adaptive threshold method is proposed that ensures that the budget is not exceeded. However, this threshold has issues as it is often dominated by the flag that ensures that the budget is not exceeded. This leads to not finding the very best instances but to excluding only the very worse.

In Sect. 3.2, we propose an algorithm based on an incremental quantile filter that handles the budget issue. In literature, quantile filters are primarily researched to address space limitations. A good review of existing methods and their complexity is given in [23]. Quantiles have also been researched under the condition of sliding windows [1], but with estimations for different types of windows and optimizations for approximations to save time and space. Such approximations are not necessary in our setting with relatively short sliding windows.

3   Probabilistic Active Learning in Streams

We propose a probabilistic active learning framework for streams, building upon our original static framework PAL [13]. A core idea of the original, static PAL is to select instances for labeling by its probabilistic gain. Therefore, it considers the observed posterior probabilities $\hat{p}$ (as determined by a classifier) but rather model and exploit the *true* posterior probability p, which we express as a Beta-distributed random variable, as we explain later on. The new stream algorithm uses this probabilistic gain as a measure for the instance's "spatial usefulness". To identify what the spatial usefulness is currently worth in a temporal manner ("temporal usefulness"), we propose the Balanced Incremental Quantile Filter (BIQF). In the last subsection, we summarize all components and show the pseudocode.

3.1 Summary of the Probabilistic Gain Calculation

The probabilistic gain is a measure to determine the spatial usefulness of a labeling candidate x_i for active learning proposed in [13]. We use the term spatial usefulness to describe the usefulness for the instance's location in the feature space (characterized by its feature vector). Using the probabilistic gain, we extend the stream of instances (multi-dimensional feature vectors) by a stream of spatial usefulness values (single values). The core idea is to model the true posterior probability p as a Beta-distributed random variable, instead of using the observed posterior (determined by the classifier) as an estimate for the true posterior. This probability distribution uses the observed posterior probability ($\hat{p}$) and the among of neighbored labeled data (n) as parameters. For $n = 0$, the true posterior distribution is similar to an uniform distribution. The higher the n value, the higher the peak at the observed posterior $\hat{p}$. The final probabilistic gain calculates the expectation value over this true posterior probability p (assumed to be Beta-distributed) and each possible label realization y (assumed to be Bernoulli-distributed) [13].

$$\text{pgain}((n, \hat{p})) = \text{E}_p \left[\text{E}_y \left[\text{gain}_p((n, \hat{p}), y) \right] \right] \tag{1}$$

$$= \int_0^1 \text{Beta}_{n\hat{p}+1, n(1-\hat{p})+1}(p) \cdot \sum_{y \in \{0,1\}} \text{Ber}_p(y) \cdot \text{gain}_p((n, \hat{p}), y) \, dp \tag{2}$$

The values for n and $\hat{p}$ can be determined by any generative classifier [17]. The gain in accuracy is directly derived from the true posterior (p), given the classification decision made from the observed posterior [13].

$$\text{gain}_p((n, \hat{p}), y) = \text{acc}_p(\hat{p}_{new}) - \text{acc}_p(\hat{p}) = \text{acc}_p \left(\frac{n\hat{p} + y}{n + 1} \right) - \text{acc}_p(\hat{p}) \tag{3}$$

$$\text{acc}_p(\hat{p}) = \begin{cases} 1 - p & \hat{p} < 0.5 \\ p & otherwise \end{cases} \tag{4}$$

In the static, pool-based setting, this probabilistic gain is weighted with the candidate's density to incorporate the information about the influence of the accuracy gain for the whole dataset. In a stream environment, any generative classifier gives us information about the label statistics of an incoming instance. As these label statistics are the only input parameters to calculate the probabilistic gain, it is easily applied. In a datastream and especially at the beginning, it is difficult to estimate the influence of a label for the whole dataset reliably. Hence, we here set the density weight to one.

3.2 Balanced Incremental Quantile Filter

Using the probabilistic gain, we extend the stream of feature vectors (from the instances) by a stream of scalars (spatial usefulness values). As higher values mean higher benefit for the classification task, the next step is to select the highest values over time. There exist two related problem formulations in literature: Either to collect a batch and to choose the best within, or to determine immediately which instances are the best. The first strategy is easier but needs additional resources to store the data and delays learning to the end of each batch, thus we decided for the second one. The challenges for this stream of scalars are: (C1) to decide immediately whether to acquire the label or not, (C2) the values are distributed arbitrarily, (C3) acquiring a label changes the classification model, hence the distribution of spatial usefulness values might change (as classification performance should improve over time, the spatial usefulness should decrease), and (C4) the classification model changes due to evolution in the data.

In this section, we propose a new algorithm to determine the most useful instances respecting a predefined budget (b) over time (temporal usefulness), called *Balanced Incremental Quantile Filter (BIQF)*. It is based on an incremental quantile filter to determine a threshold for the spatial usefulness value and a threshold-adjustment-component that ensures that the predefined budget is met. In streams, the relative budget $b \in [0, 1]$ is usually defined as the share of labels that are acquired over time. Additionally, we try to distribute the budget constantly over time such that this enables to detect drift as we always explore the data, and we have constant and predictable annotation cost.

Incremental Quantile Filter. Given a budget $b \in [0, 1]$ and a stream of spatial usefulness values $(u_1, u_2, \dots)$, the incremental quantile filter aims to determine the best values such that a share of b labels is acquired. Thus, it stores the last w (w denotes the window size) values of this input stream in a queue Q as a representation of the most current value distribution. The decision to acquire the label of an instance x_i with its spatial usefulness value u_i is based on its rank (rank_{u_i}) in Q. If Eq. 5 is true, the label is acquired [1]:

$$\text{rank}_{u_i} \leq \lceil \text{len}(Q) \cdot b \rceil \qquad (5)$$

The rank_{u_i} describes the position of the new value u_i in the list Q, e.g. the highest value has a rank of 1, the second highest one has a rank of 2, and so on.

Figure 1 visualizes this process for a window size $w = 6$ and a budget $b = 0.5$. Additionally to the chronologically sorted queue Q (not shown in the figure), the method stores a value-sorted duplicate Q_s. In the first step, the algorithm gets the first usefulness value $u_1 = 1$ from the stream. As Eq. 5 returns true ($\text{rank}_{u_1} = 1 \leq 1 = \lceil 1 \cdot 0.5 \rceil$), the label y_1 of the instance x_1 is acquired. Next, $u_2 = 6$ is added with $\text{rank}_{u_2} = 1$ and Eq. 5 is again true. Hence, the label y_2 is acquired, too. The same happens with value $u_3 = 8$. As value $u_4 = 5$ is added, Eq. 5 results in $\text{rank}_{u_4} = 3 \nleq 2 = \lceil 4 \cdot 0.5 \rceil$, which means that the corresponding label is not acquired. Value $u_5 = 3$ and $u_6 = 4$ are not added, too. Adding value 9 would result in a list length of 7, which is higher than the window size $w = 6$. Thus, the oldest value, determined from the original queue Q, is removed, and the formula is applied again.

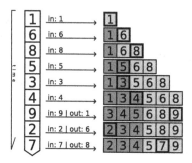

Fig. 1. Scheme of the Incremental Quantile Filter (IQF) for window size $w = 6$ and budget $b = 0.5$. Each usefulness value u_i (left stream) is inserted into the sorted list Q_s. If the incoming value is in the green area, the corresponding label is acquired.

Instead of calculating the rank, it is also possible to determine the usefulness threshold (θ) and check if the current value is higher or equal (Eq. 7). Referring to Fig. 1, the threshold is the most left green value. Depending on the queue's length ($|Q|$) and the predefined budget (b), it is calculated by Eq. 6 (using Eq. 5).

$$\text{thresIdx} = \lfloor |Q| \cdot (1 - b) \rfloor; \qquad \theta = Q_s[\text{thresIdx}] \qquad (6)$$

$$u_i \geq \theta \qquad (7)$$

The implementation of this algorithm was optimized using a B-tree [6] data structure to store and update the sorted list of usefulness values (Q_s). This reduced the computational complexity of sorting a whole list ($\mathcal{O}(w \log(w))$) into inserting (resp. deleting) an element ($\mathcal{O}(\log(w))$). This optimization needs the threshold index description. A complete pseudocode, a Python implementation and a detailed description of this optimization is given at our companion website[1].

Summarizing, this method decides immediately about a label acquisition (C1), works with arbitrary distributions (C2) but is only applicable when the distribution of the incoming usefulness values does not change over time (neither C3, nor C4). The simplest counterexample is a stream of monotonously decreasing values. In this case, no labels will be acquired because the rank is always at the very last position. With no new labels, we are not able to detect changes and the constant budget constraint is violated. This requires a solution which is described in the next subsection.

Balancing. We solve challenges C3 and C4 by a balancing approach that ensures that the predefined budget will be met within a given tolerance window. The tolerance window (w_{tol}) defines the maximal absolute difference between the number of actually acquired labels and the number of labels that should have been acquired so far. This target number of label acquisitions is the result of multiplying the predefined relative budget (b) and the number of processed stream instances. Counting the number of already acquired labels, we determine

---

[1] Companion website: http://kmd.cs.ovgu.de/res/pals.

the number of label acquisitions that should be spent to reach the predefined budget by Eq. 8.

$$acq_{\text{left}} = \#\{\text{processed instances}\} \cdot b - \#\{\text{acquired labels}\} \qquad (8)$$

Using this equation, the number of left labels for acquisition is real-valued and possibly negative (in case that the number of labels is higher than desired). If this value is positive, the acquisition threshold (θ) should be decreased to make the threshold less restrictive and vice versa. The amount of adaptation depends on the predefined tolerance window (w_{tol}) and the range of the most recent usefulness values (denoted as Δ). We use the difference between the first and last element of the sorted queue to calculate the range ($\Delta = Q_s[|Q_s|-1]-Q_s[0]$). Hence, the new threshold is determined by Eq. 9.

$$\theta_{\text{bal}} = \theta - \Delta \cdot \frac{acq_{\text{left}}}{w_{\text{tol}}} \qquad (9)$$

Next, we show that the next label will be acquired if the tolerance window is reached ($w_{\text{tol}} = acq_{\text{left}}$). To calculate the range, we determine the maximal and minimal usefulness values stored in Q_s ($\Delta = u_{\text{max}} - u_{\text{min}}$). Therefore, the threshold is between these values ($\theta \in [u_{min}, u_{max}]$).

$$\theta_{\text{bal}} = \theta - \Delta \cdot \frac{acq_{\text{left}}}{w_{\text{tol}}} = \theta - (u_{\text{max}} - u_{\text{min}}) \cdot \frac{w_{\text{tol}}}{w_{\text{tol}}} \leq u_{\text{min}} \qquad (10)$$

Hence, the new threshold θ_{bal} is below or equal all currently observed usefulness values. As the current usefulness value is already added to Q, we ensured that the corresponding label will be acquired because for all $u \in Q : u \geq u_{\text{min}}$. Analogously, one can show that the next label will not be acquired for the opposite case $w_{\text{tol}} = -acq_{\text{left}}$.

3.3 Pseudocode

Algorithm 1 shows the complete stream active learning procedure using Probabilistic Active Learning (PAL) and the Balanced Incremental Quantile Filter (BIQF). The user defined parameters are the budget (b), the IQF window size (w), and the tolerance window size (w_{tol}). From lines 5–19, the instances are processed one by one. The probabilistic gain is calculated in lines 6–8, followed by the processing of the Incremental Quantile Filter (IQF) (lines 9–12). In line 13, the threshold is adapted by the proposed balancing approach. If the usefulness value (u_i) is greater or equal this balanced threshold (θ_{bal}) in line 14, the label is acquired and this labeled instance is forwarded to the classifier (line 15) and the label acquisition counter (c_{acq}) is increased (line 16).

4 Experiments

The experimental evaluation section consists of two components. First, we show that the BIQF algorithm is able to select the best instances over time and second, we evaluate our algorithm that combines Probabilistic Active Learning (PAL) with BIQF against current baselines on seven datasets.

Algorithm 1. Probabilistic Active Learning in Streams

1: $b \in [0, 1]; w, w_{\text{tol}} \in \mathbb{N}$ {Predefined budget, IQF window size, balancing window size}
2: $C \leftarrow \{\}$ {Generative Classifier}
3: $Q \leftarrow \{\}$ {Queue for IQF algorithm}
4: $i \leftarrow 1, c_{acq} \leftarrow 0$ {Instance counter, counter of acquired labels}

5: **while** Stream delivers new instance x_i **do**
6: {determine spatial usefulness value}
7: $\hat{p} \leftarrow P_C(+|x_i); \quad n \leftarrow \text{KFE}_C(x_i)$
8: $u_i \leftarrow \text{pgain}(\hat{p}, n)$

9: {determine BIQF threshold}
10: $Q.\text{push}(u_i); \quad$ if $|Q| > w$: $Q.\text{pop}()$
11: $Q_s \leftarrow \text{sort}(Q)$
12: $\theta \leftarrow Q_s[\lfloor |Q| \cdot (1 - b) \rfloor]$
13: $\theta_{bal} \leftarrow \theta - \frac{Q_s[|Q_s|-1]-Q_s[0]}{w_{\text{tol}}} \cdot (b \cdot (i - c_{acq}))$

14: **if** $u_i \geq \theta_{bal}$ **then**
15:    $C.\text{retrain}(x_i, \text{getLabel}(x_i))$
16:    $c_{acq} \leftarrow c_{acq} + 1$
17: **end if**
18: $i \leftarrow i + 1$
19: **end while**

4.1 Performance of BIQF

To evaluate the Balanced Incremental Quantile Filter (BIQF), we test BIQF on static, synthetic usefulness streams. Therefore, we generate single-valued streams of different distributions (uniform, normal, gamma and a mixture of two normal distributions). The task of BIQF is to select the highest values as they appear without knowing the future values of that stream. As the distributions of these synthetic streams do not change over time, the optimal solution for a predefined budget b is determined by sorting the values of the whole stream and selecting the highest instances until the budget b is reached. To quantify the performance of BIQF, we calculated the mean of all selected values (resp. to b) and determined the reached percentage compared to the optimal solution. The window size is set to $w = 100$ and the tolerance window to $w_{\text{tol}} = 50$.

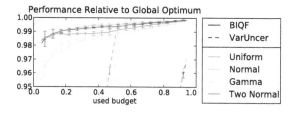

Fig. 2. Comparison of BIQF and the variable threshold method for different distributions.

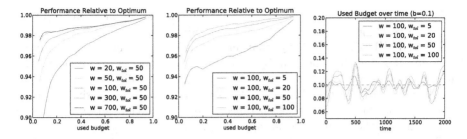

Fig. 3. Performances (left, middle) and visualization of really used budget (right) of the BIQF algorithm for different parameters on a static Gamma-distributed value stream.

In Fig. 2, we show the results in terms of the reached percentage of the optimum as the mean and standard deviation for five streams underlying the same distribution. Additionally, we executed the budget control mechanism from the Variable Uncertainty method (VarUncer), proposed in [26]. The results show that VarUncer does not reach a competing performance as its results mostly are below 95 % compared to the optimal solution. In contrast, the BIQF is always better than 95 % for every budget b which is completely enough for the demands of stream active learning.

For static data, increasing the window size w improves the results especially for low budgets (see Fig. 3 left) but also increases the execution time slightly $(\mathcal{O}(\log(w)))$. Even more relevant, the average age of the queue rises because more old values are considered. Hence, setting the window size to higher values reduces the currency of the model, which impairs the performance in non-static data. Hence, the window size should be set to the highest acceptable delay of recognizing a possibly appearing drift. In our case, the window size $w = 100$ was a good trade-off.

Additionally, Fig. 3 shows the performance of our algorithm for different tolerance window sizes (w_{tol}) on the same value streams. Again, the performance increases for higher tolerance windows as the data is static. Nevertheless, a high variable budget distribution possibly does not recognize drift early enough and does not use the resources of an oracle efficiently as its workload should be constant. The right plot shows the distribution of the really used budget over time. As expected, the variance of $w_{tol} = 5$ is the smallest. Hence, it met the budget restrictions the best in average. We suggest to set the tolerance window to the half of the window size. If the resulting variance is too high for the oracle to process the incoming data, one should reduce it to an acceptable level.

4.2 Stream Active Learning Performance

In this section, we compare our proposed algorithm that combines Probabilistic Active Learning (PAL) with the new Balanced Incremental Quantile Filter (BIQF) against other algorithms in stream active learning: a randomly sampling method (Random), Split and Variable Uncertainty (VarUncer), proposed in [26]. As we noticed some problems with the temporal selection strategy of [26], we further combined their ideas with our method: uncertainty sampling + BIQF (Uncer + BIQF) and Split + BIQF that selects one half of the instances randomly for exploration and the other half by uncertainty sampling for exploitation. The window sizes are the same as above. The generative classifier is a Parzen window classifier with pre-tuned bandwidths. To be able to react to drift, we add a sliding window with a size of 300 instances. All experiments run on a compute cluster running the (Neuro)Debian operating system [8].

The electricity dataset (27 k instances) [9] and the abalone dataset (4 k instances) [2] come from a real-world application. The checker dataset (motivated in [3]) consists of a 4×4 checkerboard (10 k instances) that switches all labels gradually after 50 % of the instances have been processed. The farcluster and movplane (10 k instances) are motivated in [26]. In farcluster an additional cluster appears far the decision boundary. In movplane, the decision boundary rotates slowly after 50 % of the instances have been processed. For the latter three datasets, 10 % of the labels are flipped to add noise. Bars and wave (10 k instances) are synthetic datasets without noise and a well-formed decision boundary. For each datastream, we created 100 random train/test-stream partitions. The results are averaged with respect to the actually used budget. To evaluate the algorithms, we provide learning curves in Fig. 4 for three datasets and an overview of mean accuracies for all datasets in Table 1.[2]

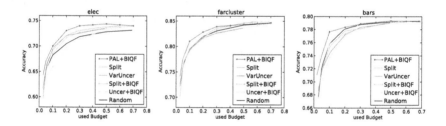

Fig. 4. Accuracy learning curves for datastreams elec, farcluster and bars.

For small budgets, PAL + BIQF is clearly dominating the other algorithms. Except for abalone, this approach always receives higher accuracy values given a budget of $b = 0.1$. For a budget of $b = 0.2$, PAL + BIQF is solely defeated on the wave dataset. This is expected because wave has a very simple and well defined decision boundary with small Bayesian error. Here, it is not necessary to explore the dataset (as PAL does), but to exploit the decision boundary (as uncertainty sampling methods do). Setting the budget to $b = 0.5$, the dominance of PAL + BIQF diminishes. On the one hand, this effect is not surprising in active learning because all sampling techniques should converge to the same level in the end. On the other hand, this might be caused by a problem of PAL with many labels: Especially for high n values, the probabilistic gain can get zero if one single

---

[2] More learning curves are available on http://kmd.cs.ovgu.de/res/pals.

Table 1. Mean accuracy for each algorithm on each dataset for the used budgets $0.1, 0.2, 0.5$ including standard deviation. Higher values are better and the best algorithm is printed in bold.

b = 0.1	PAL+BIQF	Split	VarUncer	Split+BIQF	Uncer+BIQF	Random
abalone	**0.721** ±0.02	0.716 ±0.02	0.721 ±0.02	**0.729** ±0.02	0.689 ±0.02	0.709 ±0.01
bars	**0.776** ±0.02	0.752 ±0.02	0.743 ±0.01	0.758 ±0.01	0.737 ±0.01	0.757 ±0.01
checker	**0.775** ±0.01	0.717 ±0.01	0.706 ±0.02	0.727 ±0.01	0.674 ±0.02	0.742 ±0.01
elec	**0.700** ±0.01	0.692 ±0.01	0.695 ±0.01	0.686 ±0.01	0.659 ±0.01	0.682 ±0.01
farcluster	**0.810** ±0.02	0.795 ±0.01	0.793 ±0.01	0.795 ±0.01	0.792 ±0.01	0.794 ±0.01
movplane	**0.775** ±0.01	0.759 ±0.02	0.756 ±0.01	0.762 ±0.01	0.743 ±0.02	0.760 ±0.01
wave	**0.920** ±0.01	0.912 ±0.01	0.911 ±0.01	0.908 ±0.01	0.904 ±0.01	0.900 ±0.01
b = 0.2	PAL+BIQF	Split	VarUncer	Split+BIQF	Uncer+BIQF	Random
abalone	**0.761** ±0.02	0.738 ±0.02	0.747 ±0.02	0.755 ±0.02	0.728 ±0.02	0.739 ±0.02
bars	**0.783** ±0.02	0.778 ±0.02	0.772 ±0.01	0.773 ±0.01	0.771 ±0.02	0.781 ±0.02
checker	**0.803** ±0.02	0.797 ±0.02	0.790 ±0.02	0.801 ±0.02	0.772 ±0.02	0.798 ±0.02
elec	**0.730** ±0.01	0.720 ±0.01	0.720 ±0.01	0.716 ±0.01	0.697 ±0.01	0.705 ±0.01
farcluster	**0.828** ±0.01	0.820 ±0.01	0.817 ±0.01	0.818 ±0.01	0.814 ±0.01	0.819 ±0.01
movplane	**0.791** ±0.01	0.785 ±0.01	0.786 ±0.01	0.788 ±0.01	0.779 ±0.01	0.778 ±0.01
wave	0.929 ±0.01	0.930 ±0.01	**0.935** ±0.01	0.931 ±0.01	0.934 ±0.01	0.923 ±0.01
b = 0.5	PAL+BIQF	Split	VarUncer	Split+BIQF	Uncer+BIQF	Random
abalone	0.768 ±0.02	0.766 ±0.02	0.761 ±0.02	**0.770** ±0.02	0.757 ±0.02	0.763 ±0.02
bars	**0.794** ±0.01	0.791 ±0.01	nan ±nan	0.793 ±0.01	0.791 ±0.01	0.792 ±0.01
checker	0.839 ±0.01	0.840 ±0.01	nan ±nan	**0.841** ±0.01	0.831 ±0.01	**0.841** ±0.01
elec	**0.744** ±0.01	0.738 ±0.01	nan ±nan	0.736 ±0.01	0.732 ±0.01	0.728 ±0.01
farcluster	0.843 ±0.02	0.846 ±0.01	nan ±nan	**0.847** ±0.01	0.837 ±0.01	0.842 ±0.01
movplane	0.804 ±0.01	0.803 ±0.01	nan ±nan	**0.805** ±0.01	0.804 ±0.01	0.799 ±0.01
wave	0.941 ±0.01	0.941 ±0.01	nan ±nan	0.943 ±0.01	**0.945** ±0.01	0.940 ±0.01

additional label would not change the classifier's decision. Nevertheless, results with small budgets are more important as we aim to save label acquisitions.

Very interesting is the fact that Uncer + BIQF could not improve the uncertainty sampling method with the adaptive threshold (VarUncer) of [26]. Hence, we also could confirm that excluding exploration (the adaptive threshold method solely excludes very certain samples and therefore does exploration) for uncertainty sampling is malicious. Using BIQF for the idea of combining uncertainty and random sampling shows a slight advantage of Split + BIQF against Split. Hence, the idea of random samples for uncertainty sampling is beneficial, although its performance is below the one from PAL. We assume that the superiority of PAL is caused by its direct integration of exploration and exploitation.

5 Conclusion

In this paper, we proposed a new active learning algorithm for datastreams that combines Probabilistic Active Learning to measure the spatial usefulness of each instance, and the new Balanced Incremental Quantile Filter (BIQF) that selects the best over time. Through threshold adaptation, BIQF is able to ensure that the predefined budget is met within a tolerance window. Our experimental evaluation on seven datasets and five competing algorithms showed the superiority of PAL + BIQF, especially for small budgets. We suggest that the reasons are the implicit consideration of exploration and exploitation of the spatial usefulness measure using the probabilistic gain and the selection of the highest spatial values in its temporal context by BIQF. For future work, we will investigate if these effects are also true for the application scenarios mentioned in the introduction, and we will apply our framework in combination with different generative classifiers.

References

1. Arasu, A., Manku, G.S.: Approximate counts and quantiles over sliding windows. In: 23rd ACM SIGMOD-SIGACT-SIGART Symposium on Principles of Database Systems, pp. 286–296. ACM, New York (2004)
2. Asuncion, A., Newman, D.J.: UCI Machine Learning Repository (2007)
3. Chapelle, O.: Active learning for parzen window classifier. In: International Workshop on Artificial Intelligence and Statistics, pp. 49–56 (2005)
4. Cheng, Y., Chen, Z., Liu, L., Wang, J., Agrawal, A., Choudhary, A.: Feedback-driven multiclass active learning for data streams. In: Proceedings of the 22nd ACM International Conference on Information & Knowledge Management, CIKM 2013, San Francisco, California, USA, pp. 1311–1320. ACM, New York (2013). doi:10.1145/2505515.2505528
5. Chu, W., Zinkevich, M., Li, L., Thomas, A., Tseng, B.: Unbiased online active learning in data streams. In: 17th ACM SIGKDD International Conference on Knowledge Discovery and Data Mining, San Diego, California, USA (2011)
6. Comer, D.: Ubiquitous b-tree. ACM Comput. Surv. **11**(2), 121–137 (1979)
7. Freund, Y., Seung, H.S., Shamir, E., Tishby, N.: Selective sampling using the query by committee algorithm. Mach. Learn. **28**(2–3), 133–168 (1997)
8. Halchenko, Y.O., Hanke, M.: Open is not enough. Let's take the next step: an integrated, community-driven computing platform for neuroscience. Front. Neuroinf. **6**, 22 (2012)
9. Harries, M.B., Sammut, C., Horn, K.: Extracting hidden context. Mach. Learn. **32**, 101–126 (1998)
10. Huang, S., Dong, Y.: An active learning system for mining time-changing data streams. Intell. Data Anal. **11**, 401–419 (2007)
11. Ienco, D., Bifet, A., Žliobaitė, I., Pfahringer, B.: Clustering based active learning for evolving data streams. In: Fürnkranz, J., Hüllermeier, E., Higuchi, T. (eds.) DS 2013. LNCS, vol. 8140, pp. 79–93. Springer, Heidelberg (2013)
12. Krempl, G., Ha, C.T., Spiliopoulou, M.: Clustering-based optimised probabilistic active learning (copal). In: 18th International Conference on Discovery Science (DS), Banff (2015)
13. Krempl, G., Kottke, D., Spiliopoulou, M.: Probabilistic active learning: towards combining versatility, optimality and efficiency. In: Džeroski, S., Panov, P., Kocev, D., Todorovski, L. (eds.) DS 2014. LNCS, vol. 8777, pp. 168–179. Springer, Heidelberg (2014)
14. Krempl, G., Zliobaite, I., Brzezinski, D., Hllermeier, E., Last, M., Lemaire, V., Noack, T., Shaker, A., Sievi, S., Spiliopoulou, M., Stefanowski, J.: Open challenges for data stream mining research. SIGKDD Explor. **16**(1), 1–10 (2014)
15. Lewis, D.D., Gale, W.A.: A sequential algorithm for training text classifiers. In: 17th Annual Intenational ACM SIGIR Conference on Research and Development in Information Retrieval, pp. 1–10 (1994)
16. Lindstrom, P., Delany, S.J., Namee, B.M.: Handling concept drift in a text data stream constrained by high labelling cost. In: FLAIRS Conference (2010)

17. Ng, A.Y., Jordan, M.I.: On discriminative vs. generative classifiers: a comparison of logistic regression and naive bayes. In: Advances in Neural Information Processing Systems 14, pp. 841–848. MIT Press (2002)
18. Roy, N., McCallum, A.: Toward optimal active learning through sampling estimation of error reduction. In: International Conference on Machine Learning, ICML 2001, pp. 441–448. Morgan Kaufmann Publishers Inc., San Francisco (2001)
19. Ryu, J.W., Kantardzic, M.M., Kim, M.-W., Ra Khil, A.: An efficient method of building an ensemble of classifiers in streaming data. In: Srinivasa, S., Bhatnagar, V. (eds.) BDA 2012. LNCS, vol. 7678, pp. 122–133. Springer, Heidelberg (2012)
20. Settles, B.: Active Learning Literature Survey. University of Wisconsin, Madison (2010)
21. Settles, B.: Active Learning. Synthesis Lectures on Artificial Intelligence and Machine Learning, vol. 6, no. 1, pp. 1–114 (2012)
22. Tomanek, K., Olsson, F.: A web survey on the use of active learning to support annotation of text data. In: NAACL HLT Workshop on Active Learning for Natural Language Processing, Stroudsburg, PA, USA, pp. 45–48 (2009)
23. Wang, L., Luo, G., Yi, K., Cormode, G.: Quantiles over data streams: an experimental study. In: Proceedings of the 2013 ACM SIGMOD International Conference on Management of Data, SIGMOD 2013, pp. 737–748. ACM, New York (2013)
24. Wang, P., Zhang, P., Guo, L.: Mining multi-label data streams using ensemble-based active learning. In: SIAM Conference on Data Mining, pp. 1131–1140 (2012)
25. Zhu, X., Zhang, P., Lin, X., Shi, Y.: Active learning from stream data using optimal weight classifier ensemble. IEEE Trans. Syst. Man Cybern. Part B Cybern. 40(6), 1607–1621 (2010)
26. Zliobaite, I., Bifet, A., Pfahringer, B., Holmes, G.: Active learning with drifting streaming data. IEEE Trans. Neural Netw. Learn. Syst. 25(1), 27–39 (2014)

Implicitly Constrained Semi-supervised Least Squares Classification

Jesse H. Krijthe[1,2]([⊠]) and Marco Loog[1,3]

[1] Pattern Recognition Laboratory,
Delft University of Technology, Delft, The Netherlands
jkrijthe@gmail.com
[2] Department of Molecular Epidemiology,
Leiden University Medical Center, Leiden, The Netherlands
[3] The Image Group, University of Copenhagen, Copenhagen, Denmark

Abstract. We introduce a novel semi-supervised version of the least squares classifier. This implicitly constrained least squares (ICLS) classifier minimizes the squared loss on the labeled data among the set of parameters implied by all possible labelings of the unlabeled data. Unlike other discriminative semi-supervised methods, our approach does not introduce explicit additional assumptions into the objective function, but leverages implicit assumptions already present in the choice of the supervised least squares classifier. We show this approach can be formulated as a quadratic programming problem and its solution can be found using a simple gradient descent procedure. We prove that, in a certain way, our method never leads to performance worse than the supervised classifier. Experimental results corroborate this theoretical result in the multidimensional case on benchmark datasets, also in terms of the error rate.

1 Introduction

Semi-supervised classification concerns the problem of using additional unlabeled data, aside from only labeled objects considered in supervised learning, to learn a classification function. The challenge of semi-supervised learning is to incorporate this additional information to improve the classification function over the supervised function.

The goal of this work is to build a semi-supervised version of the least squares classifier that has the property that, at least in expectation, its performance is not worse than supervised least squares classification. While it may seem like an obvious requirement for any semi-supervised method, current approaches to semi-supervised learning do not have this property. In fact, performance can significantly degrade as more unlabeled data is added, as has been shown in [6,7], among others. This makes it difficult to apply these methods in practice, especially when there is a small amount of labeled data to identify possible reduction in performance. A useful property of any semi-supervised learning procedure would therefore be that its performance does not degrade as we add more unlabeled data.

© Springer International Publishing Switzerland 2015
E. Fromont et al. (Eds.): IDA 2015, LNCS 9385, pp. 158–169, 2015.
DOI: 10.1007/978-3-319-24465-5_14

We present a novel approach to semi-supervised learning for the least squares classifier that we will refer to as implicitly constrained least squares classification (ICLS). ICLS leverages implicit assumptions present in the supervised least squares classifier to construct a semi-supervised version. This is done by minimizing the supervised loss function subject to the constraint that the solution has to correspond to the solution of the least squares classifier for some labeling of the unlabeled objects. Through this formulation, we exploit constraints inherent in the choice of the supervised classifier whereas current state-of-the-art semi-supervised learning approaches typically rely on imposing additional extraneous, and possibly incorrect, assumptions [19,20].

This work considers a semi-supervised version of the supervised least squares classifier, in which classes are encoded as numerical outputs after which a linear regression model is applied (see Sect. 3.1). By placing a threshold on the output of this model, one can use it to predict class labels. In a different neural network formulation, this classifier is also known as Adaline [22]. There are several reasons why the least squares classifier is a particularly interesting classifier to study: First of all, the least squares classifier is a discriminative classifier. Some have claimed semi-supervised learning without additional assumptions is impossible for discriminative classifiers [19,20]. Our results show this may not strictly hold. Secondly, as we will show in Sect. 3.2, the closed-form solution for the supervised least squares classifier allows us to study its theoretical properties. Moreover, using the closed-form solution we can rewrite our semi-supervised approach as a quadratic programming problem, which can be solved through a simple gradient descent with boundary constraints. Lastly, least squares classification is a useful and adaptable classification technique allowing for straightforward use of, for instance, regularization, sparsity penalties or kernelization [8,16,18,21]. Using these formulations, it has been shown to be competitive with state-of-the-art methods based on loss functions other than the squared loss [18] as well as computationally efficient on large datasets [3].

The main contributions of this paper are

- A novel convex formulation for robust semi-supervised learning using squared loss (Eq. (5))
- A proof that this procedure never reduces performance in terms of the squared loss for the 1-dimensional case (Theorem 1)
- An empirical evaluation of the properties of this classifier (Sect. 5)

We start with a discussion of related work after which we introduce our semi-supervised version of the least squares classifier. In Sects. 4 and 5, we study the non-degradation property of this method both theoretically and by considering the method's behaviour on benchmark datasets. In the final sections we discuss the results and conclude.

2   Related Work

Many diverse semi-supervised learning techniques have been proposed [5,23]. Most of these techniques rely on introducing useful assumptions that link information about the distribution of the features P_X to the posterior of the classes

$P_{Y|X}$. Some have argued unlabeled data can *only* help if P_X and $P_{Y|X}$ are somehow linked through one of these assumptions [20]. While these methods have proven successful in particular applications, such as document classification [14], it has also been observed that these techniques may give performance worse than their supervised counterparts, see [6,7], among others. In these cases, disregarding the unlabeled data would lead to better performance.

The method considered in our work is different from most previous work in semi-supervised learning in that it is inherently robust against this decrease in performance. We show that one does not need extrinsic assumptions for semi-supervised learning to work. In fact, such assumptions may actually be at the root of the problem: clearly if such an additional assumption is correct, the semi-supervised classifier can gain from it, but if the assumption is incorrect, degraded performance may ensue. What we will leverage in our approach are the implicit assumptions that are, in a sense, intrinsic to the supervised least squares classifier. This work is in line with the proposal of [11,12] which set out to improve likelihood based classifiers in a similar way. Our approach, however, does not rely on explicitly formulating the intrinsic constraints on the estimated parameters. Moreover, our approach allows for theoretical analysis of the non-deterioration of the performance of the procedure.

Another attempt to construct a robust semi-supervised version of a supervised classifier has been made in [10], which introduces the safe semi-supervised support vector machine (S4VM). This method is an extension of semi-supervised SVM [2] which constructs a set of low-density decision boundaries with the help of the additional unlabeled data, and chooses the decision boundary, which, even in the worst-case, gives the highest gain in performance over the supervised solution. If the low-density assumption holds, it can be proven this procedure increases classification accuracy over the supervised solution. The main difference with the method considered in this paper, however, is that we make no such additional assumptions. We show that even without such assumptions, robust improvements are possible for the least squares classifier.

3   Method

3.1   Supervised Multivariate Least Squares Classification

Least squares classification [8,18] is the direct application of well-known ordinary least squares regression to a classification problem. A linear model is assumed and the parameters are minimized under squared loss. Let $\mathbf{X}$ be an $L \times (d+1)$ design matrix with L rows containing vectors of length equal to the number of features d plus a constant feature to encode the intercept. Vector $\mathbf{y}$ denotes an $L \times 1$ vector of class labels. We encode one class as 0 and the other as 1. The multivariate version of the empirical risk function for least squares regression is given by

$$\hat{R}(\boldsymbol{\beta}) = \frac{1}{n} \left\| \mathbf{X}\boldsymbol{\beta} - \mathbf{y} \right\|_2^2 \tag{1}$$

The well known closed-form solution for this problem is found by setting the derivative with respect to β equal to $\mathbf{0}$ and solving for β, giving:

$$\hat{\beta} = \left(\mathbf{X}^T\mathbf{X}\right)^{-1}\mathbf{X}^T\mathbf{y} \tag{2}$$

In case $\mathbf{X}^T\mathbf{X}$ is not invertible (for instance when $n < (d+1)$), a pseudo-inverse is applied. As we will see, the closed form solution to this problem will enable us to formulate our semi-supervised learning approach in terms of a standard quadratic programming problem, which is easy to optimize.

3.2 Implicitly Constrained Least Squares Classification

In the semi-supervised setting, apart from a design matrix $\mathbf{X}$ and target vector $\mathbf{y}$, an additional set of measurements $\mathbf{X}_u$ of size $U \times (d+1)$ *without* a corresponding target vector $\mathbf{y}_u$ is given. In what follows, $\mathbf{X}_e = \left[\mathbf{X}^T \ \mathbf{X}_u^T\right]^T$ denotes the extended design matrix which is simply the concatenation of the design matrices of the labeled and unlabeled objects.

In the implicitly constrained approach, we propose that a sensible solution to incorporate the additional information from the unlabeled objects is to search within the set of classifiers that can be obtained by all possible labelings $\mathbf{y}_u$, for the one classifier that minimizes the *supervised* empirical risk function (1). This set, $\mathcal{C}_\beta$, is formed by the β's that would follow from training supervised classifiers on all (labeled and unlabeled) objects going through all possible soft labelings for the unlabeled samples, i.e., using all $\mathbf{y}_u \in [0,1]^U$. Since these supervised solutions have a closed form, this can be written as:

$$\mathcal{C}_\beta := \left\{ \beta = \left(\mathbf{X}_e^\top\mathbf{X}_e\right)^{-1}\mathbf{X}_e^\top \begin{bmatrix} \mathbf{y} \\ \mathbf{y}_u \end{bmatrix} : \mathbf{y}_u \in [0,1]^U \right\} \tag{3}$$

This constrained region $\mathcal{C}_\beta$, combined with the supervised loss that we want to optimize in Eq. (1), gives the following definition for implicitly constrained semi-supervised least squares classification:

$$\begin{aligned} \underset{\beta \in \mathbb{R}^{d+1}}{argmin} \quad &\frac{1}{n}||\mathbf{X}\beta - \mathbf{y}||^2 \\ \text{subject to} \quad &\beta \in \mathcal{C}_\beta \end{aligned} \tag{4}$$

Since β is fixed for a particular choice of $\mathbf{y}_u$ and has a closed form solution, we can rewrite the minimization problem in terms of $\mathbf{y}_u$ instead of β:

$$\begin{aligned} \underset{\mathbf{y}_u}{argmin} \quad &\frac{1}{n}\left\|\mathbf{X}\left(\mathbf{X}_e^\top\mathbf{X}_e\right)^{-1}\mathbf{X}_e^\top \begin{bmatrix} \mathbf{y} \\ \mathbf{y}_u \end{bmatrix} - \mathbf{y}\right\|_2^2 \\ \text{subject to} \quad &\mathbf{y}_u \in [0,1]^U \end{aligned} \tag{5}$$

Solving for $\mathbf{y}_u$ gives a labeling that we can use to construct the semi-supervised classifier using Eq. (2) by considering the imputed labels as the labels for the unlabeled data. The problem defined in Eq. (5), is a standard quadratic programming problem. Due to the simple box constraints on the unknown labels this can be solved efficiently using a quasi-Newton approach that takes into account the simple [0,1] bounds, such as L-BFGS-B [4].

4   Theoretical Results

We will examine this procedure by considering it in a simple, yet illustrative setting. In this case we will, in fact, prove this procedure will *never* give worse performance than the supervised solution. Consider the case where we have just one feature x, a limited set of labeled instances and assume we know the probability density function of this feature $f_X(x)$ exactly. This last assumption is similar to having unlimited unlabeled data. We consider a linear model with no intercept: $y = x\beta$ where y is set as 0 for one class and 1 for the other. For new data points, estimates $\hat{y}$ can be used to determine the predicted label of an object by using a threshold set at, for instance, 0.5.

The expected squared loss, or risk, for this model is given by:

$$R^*(\beta) = \sum_{y \in \{0,1\}} \int_{-\infty}^{\infty} (x\beta - y)^2 f_{X,Y}(x,y)\mathrm{d}x \tag{6}$$

where $f_{X,Y} = P(y|x)f_X(x)$. We will refer to this as the joint density of X and Y. Note, however, that this is not strictly a density, since it deals with the joint distribution over a continuous X and a discrete Y. The optimal solution β^* is given by the β that minimizes this risk:

$$\beta^* = \underset{\beta \in \mathbb{R}}{argmin}\, R^*(\beta) \tag{7}$$

We will show the following result:

Theorem 1. *Given a linear model without intercept, $y = x\beta$, and $f_X(x)$ known, the estimate obtained through implicitly constrained least squares always has an equal or lower risk than the supervised solution:*

$$R^*(\hat{\beta}_{semi}) \leq R^*(\hat{\beta}_{sup})$$

Proof. Setting the derivative of (6) with respect to β to 0 and rearranging we get:

$$\beta = \left(\int_{-\infty}^{\infty} x^2 f_X(x)\mathrm{d}x \right)^{-1} \sum_{y \in \{0,1\}} \int_{-\infty}^{\infty} xy f_{X,Y}(x,y)\mathrm{d}x \tag{8}$$

$$= \left(\int_{-\infty}^{\infty} x^2 f_X(x)\mathrm{d}x \right)^{-1} \int_{-\infty}^{\infty} x f_X(x) \sum_{y \in \{0,1\}} y P(y|x)\mathrm{d}x \tag{9}$$

$$= \left(\int_{-\infty}^{\infty} x^2 f_X(x)\mathrm{d}x \right)^{-1} \int_{-\infty}^{\infty} x f_X(x) \mathbb{E}[y|x]\mathrm{d}x \tag{10}$$

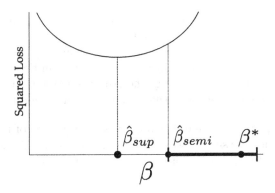

Fig. 1. An example where implicitly constrained optimization improves performance. The supervised solution $\hat{\beta}_{sup}$ which minimizes the supervised loss (the solid curve), is not part of the interval of allowed solutions. The solution that minimizes this supervised loss within the allowed interval is $\hat{\beta}_{semi}$. This solution is closer to the optimal solution β^* than the supervised solution $\hat{\beta}_{sup}$.

In this last equation, since we assume $f_X(x)$ as given, the only unknown is the function $\mathbb{E}[y|x]$, the expectation of the label y, given x. Now suppose we consider every possible labeling of the unlimited number of unlabeled objects including fractional labels, that is, every possible function where $\mathbb{E}[y|x] \in [0, 1]$. Given this restriction on $\mathbb{E}[y|x]$, the second integral in (10) becomes a re-weighted version of the expectation operation $\mathbb{E}[x]$. By changing the choice of $\mathbb{E}[y|x]$ one can vary the value of this integral, but it will always be bounded on an interval on $\mathbb{R}$. It follows that all possible βs also form an interval on $\mathbb{R}$, which we will refer to as the constrained set $\mathcal{C}_\beta$. The optimal solution has to be in this interval, since it corresponds to a particular but unknown labeling $\mathbb{E}[y|x]$. Note from (10) that the boundaries of this interval are typically finite, unless the second moment of X is equal to 0.

Using the set of labeled data, we can construct a supervised solution $\hat{\beta}_{sup}$ that minimizes the loss on the training set of L labeled objects, see Fig. 1:

$$\hat{\beta}_{sup} = \underset{\beta \in \mathbb{R}}{arg\,min} \sum_{i=1}^{L} (x_i \beta - y_i)^2 \qquad (11)$$

Now, either this solution falls within the constrained region, $\hat{\beta}_{sup} \in \mathcal{C}_\beta$ or not, $\hat{\beta}_{sup} \notin \mathcal{C}_\beta$, with different consequences:

1. If $\hat{\beta}_{sup} \in \mathcal{C}_\beta$ there is a labeling of the unlabeled points that gives us the same value for β. Therefore, the solution falls within the allowed region and there is no reason to update our estimate. Therefore $\hat{\beta}_{semi} = \hat{\beta}_{sup}$.
2. Alternatively, if $\hat{\beta}_{sup} \notin \mathcal{C}_\beta$, the solution is outside of the constrained region (as shown in Fig. 1): there is no possible labeling of the unlabeled data that will give the same solution as $\hat{\beta}_{sup}$. We then update the β to be the β within

the constrained region that minimizes the loss on the supervised training set. As can be seen from Fig. 1, this will be a point on the boundary of the interval. Note that $\hat{\beta}_{semi}$ is now closer to β^* than $\hat{\beta}_{sup}$. Since the true loss function $R^*(\beta)$ is convex and achieves its minimum in the optimal solution, corresponding to the true labeling, the risk of our semi-supervised solution will always be equal to or lower than the loss of the supervised solution.

Thus, the proposed update either improves the estimate of the parameter β or it does not change the supervised estimate. In no case will the semi-supervised solution be worse than the supervised solution, in terms of the expected squared loss.

5   Empirical Results

Since we extended the least squares classifier to the semi-supervised setting, we compare how, for different sizes of the unlabeled sample, our semi-supervised least squares approach fares against supervised least squares classification without the constraints. For comparison we included an alternative semi-supervised approach by applying self-learning to the least squares classifier. In self-learning [13], the supervised classifier is updated iteratively by using its class predictions on the unlabeled objects as the labels for the unlabeled objects in the next iteration. This is done until convergence.

A description of the datasets used for our experiments is given in Table 1. We use datasets from both the UCI repository [1] and from the benchmark datasets proposed by [5]. While the benchmark datasets proposed in [5] are useful, in our experience, the results on these datasets are very homogeneous because of the similarity in the dimensionality and their low Bayes errors. The UCI datasets are more diverse both in terms of the number of objects and features as well as the nature of the underlying problems. Taken together, this collection allows us to investigate the properties of our approach for a wide range of problems.

5.1   Comparison of Learning Curves

We study the behavior of the expected classification error of the ICLS procedure for different sizes for the unlabeled set. This statistic has two desired properties. First of all it should never be higher than the expected classification error of the supervised solution, which is based on only the labeled data. Secondly, the expected classification error should not increase as we add more unlabeled data.

Experiments were conducted as follows. For each dataset, L labeled points were randomly chosen, where we make sure it contains at least 1 object from each of the two classes. With fewer than d samples, the *supervised* least squares classifier is known to deteriorate in performance as more data is added, a behavior known as peaking [15,17]. Since this is not the topic of this work, we will only consider the situation in which the labeled design matrix is of full rank, which we ensure by setting $L = d + 5$, the dimensionality and intercept of the

Table 1. Description of the datasets used in the experiments. Features indicates the dimensionality of the design matrix after categorical features are expanded into dummy variables.

Name	# Objects	# Features	Source
Ionosphere	351	33	[1]
Parkinsons	195	22	[1]
Diabetes	768	8	[1]
Sonar	208	60	[1]
SPECT	267	22	[1]
SPECTF	267	44	[1]
WDBC	569	30	[1]
Digit1	1500	241	[5]
USPS	1500	241	[5]
COIL2	1500	241	[5]
BCI	400	118	[5]
g241d	1500	241	[5]

dataset plus five observations. For all datasets we ensure a minimum of $L = 20$ labeled objects.

Next, we create unlabeled subsets of increasing size $U = [2, 4, 8, ..., 1024]$ by randomly selecting points from the original dataset without replacement. The classifiers are trained using these subsets and the classification performance is evaluated on the remaining objects. Since the test set decreases in size as the number of unlabeled objects increases, the standard error slightly increases with the number of unlabeled objects.

This procedure of sampling labeled and unlabeled points is repeated 100 times. The results of these experiments are shown in Fig. 2. We report the mean classification error as well as the standard error of this mean. As can be seen from the tight confidence bands, this offers an accurate estimate of the expected classification error.

We find that, generally, the ICLS procedure has monotonically decreasing error curves as the number of unlabeled samples increases, unlike self-learning. On the Diabetes dataset, the performance of self-learning becomes worse than the supervised solution when more unlabeled data is added, while the ICLS classifier again exhibits a monotonic decrease of the average error rate.

5.2   Benchmark Performance

We now consider the performance of these classifiers in a cross-validation setting. This experiment is set up as follows. For each dataset, the objects are randomly divided into 10 folds. We iteratively go through the folds using 1 fold as validation set, and the other 9 as the training set. From this training set, we then randomly select $L = d + 5$ labeled objects, as in the previous experiment, and use the rest

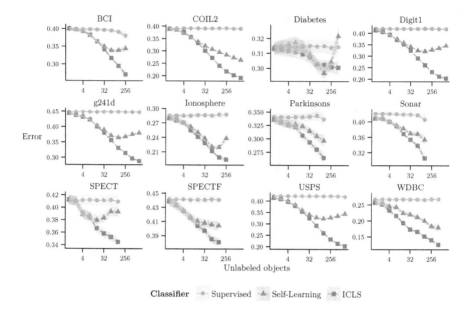

Fig. 2. Mean classification error for $L = \max(d + 5, 20)$ and 100 repeats. The shaded areas indicate $+/-$ the standard error of the mean.

Table 2. Average 10-fold cross-validation error and number of times the error of the semi-supervised classifier is higher than the supervised error for 20 repeats. Oracle refers to the performance of the least squares classifier trained when all labels are known. Indicated in **bold** is when a semi-supervised classifier has significantly lower error than the other, using a Wilcoxon signed rank test at 0.01 significance level. A similar test is done to determine whether a semi-supervised classifier is significantly worse than the supervised classifier, indicated by underlined values.

Dataset	Supervised	Self-Learning	ICLS	Oracle
Ionosphere	0.29	0.24 (1)	**0.19 (0)**	0.13
Parkinsons	0.33	0.29 (3)	0.27 (0)	0.11
Diabetes	0.32	0.33 (16)	**0.31 (2)**	0.23
Sonar	0.42	0.37 (1)	**0.32 (1)**	0.25
SPECT	0.42	0.40 (7)	**0.33 (0)**	0.17
SPECTF	0.44	0.41 (3)	**0.36 (0)**	0.22
WDBC	0.27	0.17 (0)	**0.12 (0)**	0.04
Digit1	0.41	0.34 (0)	**0.20 (0)**	0.06
USPS	0.42	0.35 (0)	**0.20 (0)**	0.09
COIL2	0.40	0.27 (0)	**0.19 (0)**	0.10
BCI	0.40	0.35 (0)	**0.28 (0)**	0.16
g241d	0.45	0.39 (0)	**0.29 (0)**	0.13

as unlabeled data. After predicting labels for the validation set for each fold, the classification error is then determined by comparing the predicted labels to the real labels. This is repeated 20 times, while randomly assigning objects to folds in each iteration.

The results shown in Table 2 tell a similar story to those in the previous experiment. Most importantly for the purposes of this paper, ICLS, in general, offers solutions that give at least no higher expected classification error than the supervised procedure. Moreover, in most of the cross-validation repeats, the error is not higher than the supervised error, although it does occur in some instances.

6 Discussion

The results presented in this paper are encouraging in the light of negative theoretical performance results in the semi-supervised literature [6]. The result in Theorem 1 indicates the proposed procedure is in some way robust against reduction in performance. The empirical results in the previous section indicate a similar result in terms of the expected classification error, at least on this collection of datasets. These empirical observations are interesting because the loss that was evaluated in these experiments is misclassification error and not the squared loss that was considered in Theorem 1. Furthermore the experiments were carried in the multivariate setting with an intercept term using limited unlabeled data, rather than the unlimited unlabeled data setting considered in the theorem. This indicates that minimizing the supervised loss over the subset $\mathcal{C}_\beta$, leads to a semi-supervised learner with desirable behavior, both theoretically in terms of risk and empirically in terms of classification error.

It has been argued that, for discriminative classifiers, semi-supervised learning is impossible without additional assumptions about the link between labeled and unlabeled objects [19,20]. ICLS, however, is both a discriminative classifier and no explicit additional assumptions about this link are made. Any assumptions that are present follow, implicitly, from the choice of squared loss as the loss function and from the chosen hypothesis space. One could argue that constraining the solutions to $\mathcal{C}_\beta$ is an assumption as well. While this is true, it corresponds to a very weak assumption about the supervised classifier: that it will improve when we add additional labeled data. The lack of additional assumptions has another advantage: no additional parameters need to be correctly set for the results in Sects. 4 and 5 to hold. There is, for instance, no parameter to be chosen for the importance of the unlabeled data. Therefore, implicitly constrained semi-supervised learning is a very different approach to semi-supervised learning than current alternatives.

An open question is what other classifiers could benefit from the implicitly constrained approach considered here. Using negative log likelihood as a loss function, for instance, also leads to interesting semi-supervised classifiers, for instance in linear discriminant analysis [9]. For other classifiers, the definition of the constraints used in this work might not lead to any useful constraints at all such that the supervised solution is always recovered. One would have to define additional constraints on the solutions in $\mathcal{C}_\beta$. The minimization of the supervised loss, considered in this paper, could still be relevant in these cases to construct a semi-supervised classifier that has similar robustness against deterioration in performance as ICLS.

7 Conclusion

This contribution introduced a new semi-supervised approach to least squares classification. By implicitly considering all possible labelings of the unlabeled objects and choosing the one that minimizes the loss on the labeled observations, we derived a robust classifier with a simple quadratic programming formulation. For this procedure, in the univariate setting with a linear model without intercept, we can prove it never degrades performance in terms of squared loss (Theorem 1). Experimental results indicate that in expectation this robustness also holds in terms of classification error on real datasets. Hence, semi-supervised learning for least squares classification without additional assumptions can lead to improvements over supervised least squares classification both in theory and in practice.

Acknowledgments. Part of this work was funded by project P23 of the Dutch public-private research community COMMIT.

References

1. Bache, K., Lichman, M.: UCI Machine Learning Repository (2013). http://archive. ics.uci.edu/ml
2. Bennett, K.P., Demiriz, A.: Semi-supervised support vector machines. Adv. Neural Inf. Process. Syst. **11**, 368–374 (1998)
3. Bottou, L.: Large-scale machine learning with stochastic gradient descent. In: Lechevallier, Y., Saporta, G. (eds.) COMPSTAT 2010, pp. 177–186. Springer, Heidelberg (2010)
4. Byrd, R.H., Lu, P., Nocedal, J., Zhu, C.: A limited memory algorithm for bound constrained optimization. SIAM J. Sci. Comput. **16**(5), 1190–1208 (1995)
5. Chapelle, O., Schölkopf, B., Zien, A.: Semi-Supervised Learning. MIT press, Cambridge (2006)
6. Cozman, F., Cohen, I.: Risks of semi-supervised learning. In: Chapelle, O., Schölkopf, B., Zien, A. (eds.) Semi-Supervised Learning, Chap. 4, pp. 56–72. MIT press (2006)
7. Cozman, F.G., Cohen, I., Cirelo, M.C.: Semi-supervised learning of mixture models. In: Proceedings of the Twentieth International Conference on Machine Learning (2003)
8. Hastie, T., Tibshirani, R., Friedman, J.H.: The Elements of Statistical Learning. Spinger, New York (2001)
9. Krijthe, J.H., Loog, M.: Implicitly constrained semi-supervised linear discriminant analysis. In: International Conference on Pattern Recognition, pp. 3762–3767, Stockholm (2014)

10. Li, Y.F., Zhou, Z.H.: Towards making unlabeled data never hurt. IEEE Trans. Pattern Anal. Mach. Intell. **37**(1), 175–188 (2015)
11. Loog, M., Jensen, A.: Semi-supervised nearest mean classification through a constrained log-likelihood. IEEE Trans. Neural Networks Learn. Syst. **26**(5), 995–1006 (2015)
12. Loog, M.: Semi-supervised linear discriminant analysis through moment-constraint parameter estimation. Pattern Recognit. Lett. **37**, 24–31 (2014)
13. McLachlan, G.J.: Iterative reclassification procedure for constructing an asymptotically optimal rule of allocation in discriminant analysis. J. Am. Stat. Assoc. **70**(350), 365–369 (1975)
14. Nigam, K., McCallum, A.K., Thrun, S., Mitchell, T.: Text classification from labeled and unlabeled documents using EM. Mach. Learn. **34**, 1–34 (2000)
15. Opper, M., Kinzel, W.: Statistical mechanics of generalization. In: Domany, E., Hemmen, J.L., Schulten, K. (eds.) Models of Neural Networks III, pp. 151–209. Springer, New York (1996)
16. Poggio, T., Smale, S.: The mathematics of learning: dealing with data. Not. AMS **50**, 537–544 (2003)
17. Raudys, S., Duin, R.P.: Expected classification error of the fisher linear classifier with pseudo-inverse covariance matrix. Pattern Recogn. Lett. **19**(5–6), 385–392 (1998)
18. Rifkin, R., Yeo, G., Poggio, T.: Regularized least-squares classification. Nato Sci. Ser. Sub Ser. III Comput. Syst. Sci. **190**, 131–154 (2003)
19. Seeger, M.: Learning with labeled and unlabeled data. Technical report (2001)
20. Singh, A., Nowak, R.D., Zhu, X.: Unlabeled data: now it helps, now it doesnt. In: Advances in Neural Information Processing Systems, pp. 1513–1520 (2008)
21. Tibshirani, R.: Regression shrinkage and selection via the lasso. J. R. Stat. Soci. Ser. B **58**(1), 267–288 (1996)
22. Widrow, B., Hoff, M.E.: Adaptive switching circuits. IRE WESCON Convention Rec. **4**, 96–104 (1960)
23. Zhu, X., Goldberg, A.B.: Introduction to Semi-Supervised Learning, vol. 3. Morgan & Claypool, San Rafael (2009)

Diagonal Co-clustering Algorithm for Document-Word Partitioning

Charlotte Laclau[(⊠)] and Mohamed Nadif[(⊠)]

LIPADE, Université Paris Descartes, 45 Rue des Saint-Pères, 75006 Paris, France
{charlotte.laclau,mohamed.nadif}@parisdescartes.fr

Abstract. We propose a novel diagonal co-clustering algorithm built upon the double Kmeans to address the problem of document-word co-clustering. At each iteration, the proposed algorithm seeks for a diagonal block structure of the data by minimizing a criterion based on the variance within and the centroid effect. In addition to be easy-to-interpret and efficient on sparse binary and continuous data, Diagonal Double Kmeans (DDKM) is also faster than other state-of-the art clustering algorithms. We illustrate our contribution using real datasets commonly used in document clustering.

1 Introduction

Co-clustering also known as biclustering or block-clustering involves simultaneous clustering of the set of observations and the set of features in a data matrix. By creating permutations of rows and columns, the co-clustering algorithms aim to reorganize the initial data matrix into homogeneous blocks. These blocks also called co-clusters can therefore be defined as subsets of the data matrix characterized by a set of observations and a set of features whose elements are similar. Other types of co-clustering approaches can be found in [11] and [12]. Co-clustering algorithms present several advantages: they reduce the initial matrix into a simpler form with the same basic structure and require far less computation when compared with separate processing of the same two sets; see for instance [8]. As a result, these methods are of interest to data mining.

In this work, we focus on co-clustering methods that seek a block diagonal structure, *i.e.* methods in which the number of clusters of rows is equal to the number of clusters of columns. An illustration is given in Fig. 1 where (a) represents an original binary matrix, (b) represents the same matrix after a proper permutation of rows whilst (c) adds a permutation of columns resulting in a clear block diagonal structure. These methods have proven efficient in dealing with the problem of document-word co-clustering. The objective is to group the documents based on the words within them and to group the words based on the documents in which they appear. The dataset is typically represented by a *document* × *words* matrix. In [10], the author proposed a block diagonal algorithm to deal with binary data. This algorithm alternates the clustering of observations and features minimizing the error between the original

© Springer International Publishing Switzerland 2015
E. Fromont et al. (Eds.): IDA 2015, LNCS 9385, pp. 170–180, 2015.
DOI: 10.1007/978-3-319-24465-5_15

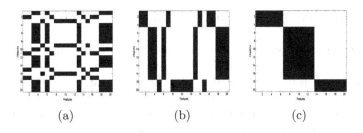

(a)   (b)   (c)

Fig. 1. Original binary data (a), (b) data reorganized according to rows, (c) reorganized according to rows and columns.

data matrix and the reconstructed matrix based on the cluster structure. In [3], the author proposed a spectral based solution. He built a bipartite graph from the *document* × *words* matrix which is partitioned in a way that minimize the cut objective function.

In this paper we propose a new diagonal co-clustering algorithm based on the minimization of an heterogeneity measure of blocks. This measure takes into account both the variance within blocks and a measure named the centroid effect [5] defined as the squared deviation from the mean entry in each block and the maximum entry in the input matrix. The proposed algorithm, in addition to be very efficient in terms of co-clustering on sparse data, are also faster than most of state-of-the art algorithms and therefore can deal with high dimensional data.

The remaining of this paper is organized as follows. Section 2 provides the needed background on the Double Kmeans (DKM) algorithm and presents the challenge of diagonal co-clustering. Section 3 presents the Diagonal Double Kmeans (DDKM) algorithm that we propose. Section 4 is devoted to numerical experiments on real datasets showing the appropriateness of our contribution for binary and continuous data. The final section sums up the study and gives recommendations for further research.

Notation. Let $\mathbf{X} := \{x_{ij}; i \in I; j \in J\}$ be a data matrix of size $n \times p$ where $I = \{1, \ldots, n\}$ and $J = \{1, \ldots, p\}$. The set I corresponds to the set of n objects and the set J to the set of p attributes. In the sequel, our aim consists in obtaining co-clustering of $\mathbf{X}$. Let $\mathbf{Z} = \{z_1, \ldots, z_n\}$ be a label vector, where $z_i \in \{1, \ldots, K\}$, denotes the partition of I into K clusters and $\mathbf{W} = \{w_1, \ldots, w_p\}$ where $w_j \in \{1, \ldots, H\}$ denotes the partition of J into H clusters. The partition of I (respectively J) can be represented by a matrix of elements in $\{0, 1\}^K$ (respectively $\{0, 1\}^H$) satisfying $\sum_{k=1}^{K} z_{ik} = 1$ (respectively $\sum_{h=1}^{H} w_{jh} = 1$). Finally, to simplify the notation, the sums relating to rows, columns, row and column clusters will be subscripted respectively by the letters ($i = 1, \ldots, n, j = 1, \ldots, p$ and, $k = 1, \ldots, K$, without indicating the implicit limits of variation. For example, the sum $\sum_{i,k}$ stands for $\sum_{i=1}^{n} \sum_{k=1}^{K}$.

2   Co-clustering and Diagonal Block Structure

The co-clustering can be formulated as the search for a good matrix approximation of the original data matrix $\mathbf{X}$. The quality is determined by the approximation error which can be measured by a large class of loss functions like the
square Euclidean distances. This approximation is generally achieved through an
alternate least square minimization process (see for instance [1,7]). The Double
Kmeans algorithm [16] is based on this principle.

2.1   Double Kmeans Algorithm

Formally, the aim is to minimize an objective function $J(\mathbf{Z}, \mathbf{W}, \mathbf{G})$ where $\mathbf{Z}$ and
$\mathbf{W}$ are the partitions and $\mathbf{G} := \{g_{kh}; k \in \{1, \dots, K\}, h \in \{1, \dots, H\}$ is a $K \times H$
matrix which can be viewed as a summary of the data matrix X (see Fig. 2).

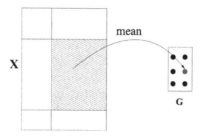

Fig. 2. Original data matrix $\mathbf{X}$ and its summary after co-clustering into 6 co-clusters.

Each element g_{kh} of $\mathbf{G}$ is called a prototype of co-cluster $\mathbf{X}_{kh} :=$
$\{x_{ij}; z_{ik} w_{jh} = 1\}$. Double Kmeans (DK) adopts the squared Euclidean distance
to measure the dissimilarity between the matrix $\mathbf{X}$ and the structure described
in $\mathbf{Z}, \mathbf{W}$ and $\mathbf{G}$. Therefore, $J(\mathbf{Z}, \mathbf{W}, \mathbf{G})$ is given by

$$J(\mathbf{Z}, \mathbf{W}, \mathbf{G}) = \sum_{i,k,j,h} z_{ik} \times w_{jh}(x_{ij} - g_{kh})^2 = ||\mathbf{X} - \mathbf{Z}\mathbf{G}\mathbf{W}^T||^2, \qquad (1)$$

where $||.||$ denotes the Frobenius norm. It is easy to see that for a fixed $(\mathbf{Z}; \mathbf{W})$
the optimal values of $\mathbf{G}$ are the means of $\mathbf{X}_{kh}$'s. The optimal partitions $\mathbf{Z}$ and $\mathbf{W}$
are found using an iterative algorithm. A version of double Kmeans is presented
in Algorithm 1 where $z_{.k}$ (resp. $w_{.h}$) represents the cardinality of the kth cluster
(resp. h^{th} cluster).

2.2   Block Diagonal Structure

The DKM algorithm appears to be not efficient when looking for a one-to-one
correspondence between two partitions $\mathbf{Z}$ and $\mathbf{W}$. In order to deal with this

---

Algorithm 1. Double Kmeans (DKM)

---

input: X, K, H
initialization: Z and **W**
repeat
   (1) Compute $g_{kh} = \sum_{i,j} \frac{z_{ik} w_{jh} x_{ij}}{z_{.k} w_{.h}}$, $\forall k, h$
   (2) Update $z_i = \arg\min_k \sum_{j,h} w_{jh}(x_{ij} - g_{kh})^2$, $\forall i$
   (3) Update $w_j = \arg\min_h \sum_{i,k} z_{ik}(x_{ij} - g_{kh})^2$, $\forall j$
until the J value change is small or there is no change.
output: G, **Z** and **W**

---

specific case, we have to consider w_{jk} instead of a w_{jh}; in other words, we assume that $H = K$. Secondly, the diagonal structure involve to impose some constraints on **G**; for instance by taking $g_{kk} = \delta \ \forall k$. This leads us to consider the following criterion:

$$J(\mathbf{X}, \mathbf{Z}, \mathbf{W}) = \sum_{i,j,k} z_{ik} w_{jk}(x_{ij} - \delta)^2, \qquad (2)$$

where δ is assumed to be known. The choice of this parameter will be discussed in the next section. The couple of partitions $(\mathbf{Z}, \mathbf{W})$ optimizing the criterion given in Eq. 2 are found using the following iterative algorithm

1. Update **Z** the partition of objects, with **W** fixed. This leads to the following formula

$$z_i = \arg\min_k \sum_j w_{jk}(x_{ij} - \delta)^2,$$

2. Update **W**, the partition of features, with **Z** fixed. This leads to the following formula

$$w_j = \arg\min_k \sum_i z_{ik}(x_{ij} - \delta)^2.$$

From these formulae, one observes that seeking the diagonal structure of blocks indirectly introduces a strong dependency between object assignments (respectively features assignments) to a block and the number of features that belong to this block (respectively the number of objects). If we consider object assignments, we have $(x_{ij} - \delta)^2 \geq 0, \forall i, j$; therefore a higher number of features in a block will decrease the chance that an object will be assigned to this particular block. The same phenomenon occurs in the feature assignments. This leads to take into account the size of each co-cluster in order to avoid empty blocks.

3 Diagonal Double Kmeans

3.1 Criterion and Proposed Algorithm

In order to correct the bias introduced by the diagonal structure and to avoid certain blocks from vanishing, we propose a modified criterion that takes into account the number of elements in a block. This criterion takes the following form:

$$J(\mathbf{X}, \mathbf{Z}, \mathbf{W}) = \sum_k \frac{1}{z_{.k} w_{.k}} \sum_{i,j} z_{ik} w_{jk} (x_{ij} - \delta)^2. \tag{3}$$

where $z_{.k}$ and $w_{.k}$ denote respectively the number of objects and the number of features in the k-th block. Furthermore, it is interesting to note that the criterion given in Eq. 3 may be expressed depending on the variance of a given block $(\mathbf{Z}_k, \mathbf{W}_k)$ and the squared deviation of its mean from the maximum input of the data:

$$\begin{aligned}
J(\mathbf{X}, \mathbf{Z}, \mathbf{W}) &= \sum_{i,j,k} \frac{z_{ik} w_{jk}}{z_{.k} w_{.k}} (x_{ij} - \overline{x}_k)^2 + \sum_{i,j,k} \frac{z_{ik} w_{jk}}{z_{.k} w_{.k}} (\overline{x}_k - \delta)^2 \\
&= \sum_k \overline{s}_k^2 + \sum_k (\overline{x}_k - \delta)^2. \tag{4}
\end{aligned}$$

where

$$\overline{x}_k = \frac{1}{z_{.k} w_{.k}} \sum_{i,j} z_{ik} w_{jk} x_{ij} \quad \text{and} \quad \overline{s}_k^2 = \frac{1}{z_{.k} w_{.k}} \sum_{i,j} z_{ik} w_{jk} (x_{ij} - \overline{x}_k)^2$$

denote the mean and the variance within the k-th block respectively. The first term of Eq. 4 ensures the homogeneity of each block while the second one provides the homogeneity between centers of the blocks and δ. This objective function (Eq. 3) is optimized by an alternating optimization of two conditional criteria given $\mathbf{W}$ and $\mathbf{Z}$ respectively.

$$\tilde{J}_1(\mathbf{X}, \mathbf{Z}|\mathbf{W}) = \sum_k \frac{1}{z_{.k}} \sum_i z_{ik} \frac{1}{w_{.k}} \sum_j w_{jk} (x_{ij} - \delta)^2$$

and

$$\tilde{J}_2(\mathbf{X}, \mathbf{W}|\mathbf{Z}) = \sum_k \frac{1}{w_{.k}} \sum_j w_{jk} \frac{1}{z_{.k}} \sum_i z_{ik} (x_{ij} - \delta)^2.$$

The optimization of $\tilde{J}_1$ and $\tilde{J}_2$ lead to the following update rules:

$$z_i = \arg\min_k \frac{1}{w_{.k}} \sum_j w_{jk} (x_{ij} - \delta)^2, \tag{5}$$

$$w_j = \arg\min_k \frac{1}{z_{.k}} \sum_i z_{ik} (x_{ij} - \delta)^2. \tag{6}$$

The proposed algorithm Diagonal Double Kmeans (DDKM) (Algorithm 2) is computationally efficient and its complexity can be shown to be $O(\tau \times npK)$ where τ denotes the number of iterations required to obtain the convergence, n, p and K are the number of objects (i.e. rows), features (i.e. columns) and clusters respectively.

Algorithm 2. Diagonal Double Kmeans (DDKM)

---
input: $\mathbf{X}$ and K
initialization: $\mathbf{Z}$, $\mathbf{W}$ and δ
repeat
   (2) Update $\mathbf{Z}$ according to Eq. 5
   (3) Update $\mathbf{W}$ according to Eq. 6
until the J value change is small or there is no change.
output: $\mathbf{Z}$ and $\mathbf{W}$

3.2   Choice of δ

Herein, we discuss the choice of δ. Specifically, we compare between the optimal value of δ and the maximum entry of the matrix.

1. If we consider δ as an unknown parameter, its optimal value for the criterion minimized is equal to the average of blocks means. Indeed, with $\mathbf{Z}$ and $\mathbf{W}$ fixed and by setting the derivative of J (Eq. 3) to zero we obtain $\delta = \frac{1}{K}\sum_k \bar{x}_k$ where $\bar{x}_k$ denotes the mean of the k-th block. Although this value of δ is the optimal, we can observe that in the context of sparse data *i.e.* when the data matrix contains a high percentage of 0, its value will tend to 0 leading to a diagonal structure of blocks of 0. An illustration of the resulting co-clustering obtained with this value on the CSTR dataset (described in the numerical experiments section) is given in Fig. 3(c).

2. Another way to proceed is to set the value of δ at the initialisation step. DDKM aims at grouping objects and features with the strongest association possible. For instance, in the case of a binary data matrix $\mathbf{X}$, the strongest association between an object i and a feature j is expressed in $x_{ij} = 1$ which is the maximum value of the entry of $\mathbf{X}$. As a matter of fact, choosing the maximum allows to guarantee the homogeneity of diagonal blocks while ensuring blocks of 0 outside. In [5,13], the authors proposed hierarchical algorithms based on this idea. We use the same example as for the optimal value to show the result on Fig. 3(b). It is important to stress that this approach requires for values of a data matrix to be comparable. This is the case for binary data or normalized data as we will see in the next section devoted to the document-word partitioning.

4   Numerical Experiments

4.1   Performance Evaluation

In order to assess and to compare the performance of the proposed algorithm, we use commonly adopted metrics: the Accuracy, the Normalized Mutual Information [15] and the Adjusted Rand Index [9]. We focus only on the quality of

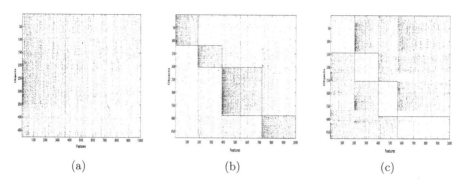

Fig. 3. (a) CSTR the original dataset, (b) CSTR reorganised according to the partitions when $\delta = \max_{i,j} x_{ij}$, (c) CSTR reorganised according to the partitions when δ estimated by $\frac{1}{K} \sum_k \bar{x}_k$.

row clustering. Clustering accuracy noted Acc is one of the most widely used evaluation criterion and is defined as:

$$\text{Acc} = \frac{1}{n} max \left[\sum_{\mathcal{C}_k, \mathcal{L}_\ell} T(\mathcal{C}_k, \mathcal{L}_\ell) \right]$$

where $\mathcal{C}_k$ is the kth cluster in the final results, and $\mathcal{L}_\ell$ is the true ℓ^{th} class. $T(\mathcal{C}_k, \mathcal{L}_\ell)$ is the proportion of objects that were correctly recovered by the clustering algorithm $i.e.$ $T(\mathcal{C}_k, \mathcal{L}_\ell) = \mathcal{C}_k \cap \mathcal{L}_\ell$. Accuracy computes the maximum sum of $T(\mathcal{C}_k, \mathcal{L}_\ell)$ for all pairs of clusters and classes, and these pairs have no overlaps. The second measure employed is the Normalized Mutual Information (NMI) and is calculated as follows:

$$\text{NMI} = \frac{\sum_{k,\ell} \frac{n_{k\ell}}{n} \log \frac{n_{k\ell}}{n_k \hat{n}_\ell}}{\sqrt{(\sum_k \frac{n_k}{n} \log \frac{n_k}{n})(\sum_\ell \frac{\hat{n}_k}{n} \log \frac{\hat{n}_\ell}{n})}}$$

where n_k denotes the number of data contained in the cluster $\mathcal{C}_k (1 \leq k \leq K)$, $\hat{n}_\ell$, the number of data belonging to the class $\mathcal{C}'_k (1 \leq \ell \leq K)$, and $n_{k\ell}$, the number of data that are in the intersection between the cluster $\mathcal{C}_k$ and the class $\mathcal{C}'_k$. The last measure *Adjusted Rand* noted ARI measures the similarity between two clustering partitions. From a mathematical standpoint, the Rand index is related to the accuracy. The adjusted form of the Rand Index is defined as:

$$\text{ARI} = \frac{\sum_{k,\ell} \binom{n_{k\ell}}{2} - \left[\sum_k \binom{n_k}{2} \sum_\ell \binom{\hat{n}_\ell}{2} \right] / \binom{n}{2}}{\frac{1}{2} \left[\sum_k \binom{n_k}{2} + \sum_\ell \binom{\hat{n}_\ell}{2} \right] - \left[\sum_k \binom{n_k}{2} \sum_\ell \binom{\hat{n}_\ell}{2} \right] / \binom{n}{2}}.$$

The value for these three metrics are between 0 and 1, a value close to 1 means a good result in terms of clustering.

4.2 Compared Algorithms

We compare against state-of-the-art (co)-clustering methods including Spherical Kmeans (SpKM)[4], Double Kmeans (DKM) and Spectral Co-Clustering (SpCo) [3]. We also report the clustering results by Kmeans and the Nonnegative Matrix Factorization (NMF) [2] as baseline. The Spherical Kmeans algorithm is basically a Kmeans algorithm that use the cosine dissimilarity instead of the Euclidean distance. It is known to be very efficient on sparse dataset and to converge quickly. We use the matlab implementation for kmeans and NMF. For SpCo algorithm we use the implementation proposed by Assaf Gottlieb[1]. We use the SpKM implementation given in [14]. Finally, we implement CROEUC [6], a fast version of Double Kmeans (DKM); its advantage is due to the use of intermediate matrices of reduced sizes rather than the original data.

4.3 Datasets and Results

We study the effectiveness of our algorithm for some well-known text datasets with different sizes and balances[2]: CSTR, Classic3, WebKB4 and 2 subsets of the 20 Newsgroups dataset. The 20 Newsgroups dataset is organized into 20 topics. Some of the topics are closely related while other are highly unrelated. We describe the topics included in the two subsets in Table 1. The NG2 dataset includes two topics not related (rec.motorcycles and sci.crypt,sci.space) while NG5 includes topics closely related involving a situation with overlapping clusters (rec.sport.baseball, sci.crypt, sci.med, talk.religion.misc, comp.windows.x, soc.religion.christian, talk.politics.mideast). A detailed description of all datasets can be found in Table 1.

Table 1. Description of the datasets in terms of size $(n \times p)$, number of clusters (K), sparsity (%0) and size of the cluster. A partition is assumed balanced if the balance coefficient is close to 1 and unbalanced otherwise.

Dataset	$n \times p$	K	%0	Balance
CSTR	475×1000	4	96.60	0.399
Classic3	3891×4303	3	98.95	0.71
WebKB4	4199×1000	4	91.83	0.307
NG2	500×2000	2	96.90	1
NG5	500×2000	5	97.19	1

Originally each cell of these datasets denotes the number of occurrences of a word in a document. As we are interested in evaluating our algorithm on both binary and continuous data, we use one version of the datasets on which

---

[1] http://adios.tau.ac.il/.

[2] The balance coefficient is defined as the ratio of the number of documents in the smallest class to the number of documents in the largest class.

Table 2. Accuracy, Normalized Mutual Information and Adjusted Rand Index obtained on tf-idf datasets.

Dataset	Metric	Algorithms					
		NMF	Kmeans	SpKM	DKM	SpCo	DDKM
CSTR	Acc	81.47	85.05	88.63	62.95	79.79	**90.95**
	NMI	69.91	64.74	74.07	27.93	66.67	**76.39**
	ARI	70.26	68.14	76.57	46.72	70.20	**82.99**
Classic3	Acc	96.32	90.47	97.33	94.17	70.60	**98.69**
	NMI	84.53	73.81	91.41	80.90	59.64	**96.10**
	ARI	89.04	75.34	94.38	82.82	40.20	**93.32**
WebKB4	Acc	**80.38**	49.46	62.85	38.75	64.32	78.90
	NMI	**52.08**	25.15	37.00	04.65	41.04	51.15
	ARI	**56.48**	18.03	31.55	04.54	38.09	54.93
NG2	Acc	62.60	-	60.92	50.70	88.98	**94.40**
	NMI	4.85	-	11.92	0.15	53.16	**68.88**
	ARI	6.17	-	4.68	0.00	60.69	**78.81**
NG5	Acc	41.48	23.25	56.31	31.06	53.91	**70.54**
	NMI	27.42	6.21	30.69	9.47	45.59	**41.53**
	ARI	13.66	0.34	19.85	4.45	30.03	**41.40**

the data were converted into binary *i.e.* each cell having a value higher to 0 is considered equal to 1 and 0 otherwise, and a second version where a TF-IDF (Term Frequency - Inverse Document Frequency) transformation is applied. The TF-IDF normalization is one of the most used in text mining, and is defined as $x'_{ij} = tf_{ij} \times \log \frac{n}{df_j}$ where tf_{ij} denotes the number of occurrence of the j-th word in the i-th document and df_j denotes the number of documents containing the j-th word.

We set the number of clusters as the true number of classes on all datasets. For each method, given the number of clusters, no parameter selection is needed. We run the algorithms 100 times and report the best result (in percentage), *i.e.* the one that corresponds to a local minimum of the criterion of all trials in Tables 2 and 3. Several observations can be made based on these results: the proposed algorithm outperforms the other method on each dataset whether it is the TF-IDF version or the binary one, except on the TF-IDF version of WebKB4. On NG2 and NG5 whose classes are not well separated, the performance difference is all the more important. We can also note that on the TF-IDF version of NG2, Kmeans is unable to find a partition into two clusters as required.

4.4 Computational Complexity

We study the computational complexity of the compared clustering and co-clustering algorithms. We repeat clustering 100 times for each algorithm on

Table 3. Accuracy, Normalized Mutual Information and Adjusted Rand Index obtained on binary datasets.

Dataset	Metric	Algorithms					
		NMF	Kmeans	SpKM	DKM	SpCo	DDKM
CSTR	Acc	85.68	85.05	88.63	62.95	79.79	**91.37**
	NMI	67.08	64.74	74.07	27.93	66.67	**79.06**
	ARI	70.65	68.14	76.57	46.72	70.20	**83.00**
Classic3	Acc	97.66	90.47	97.33	94.17	70.60	**98.20**
	NMI	88.78	73.81	**91.41**	80.90	59.64	91.31
	ARI	93.06	75.34	94.38	82.82	40.20	**94.61**
WebKB4	Acc	**73.26**	49.46	62.85	38.75	64.32	72.80
	NMI	41.05	25.15	37.00	04.65	41.04	**44.14**
	ARI	43.60	18.03	31.55	04.54	38.09	**44.29**
NG2	Acc	60.60	57.60	60.80	54.60	90.20	**94.60**
	NMI	12.85	12.93	13.09	2.38	55.35	**70.55**
	ARI	4.41	2.26	4.58	0.77	64.57	**79.53**
NG5	Acc	50.10	33.07	52.10	29.66	60.32	**76.75**
	NMI	32.25	16.61	28.31	8.15	50.75	**51.49**
	ARI	20.68	4.08	24.84	2.82	37.31	**51.37**

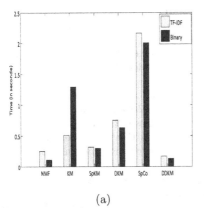
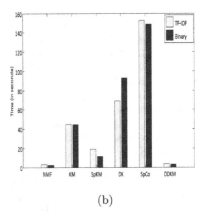

(a)   (b)

Fig. 4. Running time in seconds of the compared algorithms on the binary and the tf-idf versions of CSTR (a) and classic3 (b) datasets.

each dataset. We report the average convergence time in Fig. 4 for the CSTR (a) and Classic 3 (b) datasets. The obtained results show that the proposed algorithm DDKM is only very slightly slower than NMF method while it requires far less time to converge than all other state-of-the-art algorithms. The same observations were made on the other datasets presented in this article.

5 Conclusion

In this paper we presented DDKM, a fast co-clustering algorithm that looks for homogeneous diagonal blocks. Compared with other methods, we demonstrate that our proposed algorithm is more effective for document-word partitioning datasets and especially in presence of classes having a high degree of overlap. In addition, DDKM requires less time to converge; up to 20 times less time than DKM and 40 times less time than SpCo commonly used in the domain of document clustering. In real world application, the knowledge of the number of co-clusters is mostly required. For further research, it will be worthwhile to investigate an efficient way to assess this parameter.

References

1. Baier, D., Gaul, W., Schader, M.: Two-mode overlapping clustering with applications to simultaneous benefit segmentation and market structuring. In: Klar, R., Opitz, O. (eds.) Classification and knowledge organization. Springer, Heidelberg (1997)
2. Berry, M.W., Browne, M., Langville, A.N., Pauca, V.P., Plemmons, R.J.: Algorithms and applications for approximate nonnegative matrix factorization. In: Computational Statistics and Data Analysis, pp. 155–173 (2006)
3. Dhillon, I.S.: Co-clustering documents and words using bipartite spectral graph partitioning. In: KDD 2001, pp. 269–274 (2001)
4. Dhillon, I.S., Modha, D.S.: Concept decompositions for large sparse text data using clustering. Mach. Learn. 42(1–2), 143–175 (2001)
5. Eckes, T., Orlik, P.: An error variance approach to two-mode hierarchical clustering. J. Classif. 10(1), 51–74 (1993)
6. Govaert, G.: Classification croisée. Ph.D. thesis, Université Paris 6, France (1983)
7. Govaert, G., Nadif, M.: Co-Clustering: Models, Algorithms and Applications. Wiley, New York (2013)
8. Govaert, G., Nadif, M.: Block clustering with bernoulli mixture models: comparison of different approaches. Comput. Stat. Data Anal. 52(6), 3233–3245 (2008)
9. Hubert, L., Arabie, P.: Comparing partitions. J. Classif. 2, 193–218 (1985)
10. Li, T.: A general model for clustering binary data. In: Proceedings of the Eleventh ACM SIGKDD International Conference on Knowledge Discovery in Data Mining, KDD 2005, pp. 188–197 (2005)
11. Madeira, S.C., Oliveira, A.L.: Biclustering algorithms for biological data analysis: a survey. IEEE/ACM Trans. Comput. Biol. Bioinf. 1, 24–45 (2004)
12. Mechelen, I.V., Bock, H.H., Boeck, P.D.: Two-mode clustering methods: a structured overview. Stat. Methods Med. Res. 13(5), 363–394 (2004)
13. Mirkin, B., Arabie, P., Hubert, L.: Additive two-mode clustering: the error-variance approach revisited. J. Classif. 12(2), 243–263 (1995)
14. Nguyen, X.V.: Gene clustering on the unit hypersphere with the spherical k-means algorithm: coping with extremely large number of local optima. In: International Conference on Bioinformatics & Computational Biology, BIOCOMP 2008, pp. 226–233 (2008)
15. Strehl, A., Ghosh, J.: Cluster ensembles - a knowledge reuse framework for combining multiple partitions. J. Mach. Learn. Res. 3, 583–617 (2003)
16. Vichi, M.: Double k-means clustering for simultaneous classification of objects and variables. In: Borra, S., Rocci, R., Vichi, M., Schader, M. (eds.) Advances in classification and data analysis, pp. 43–52. Springer, Heidelberg (2001)

I-Louvain: An Attributed Graph Clustering Method

David Combe[1,2,3], Christine Largeron[1,2,3]([⊠]), Mathias Géry[1,2,3],
and Előd Egyed-Zsigmond[4]

[1] Université de Lyon, 42023 Saint-Étienne, France
{david.combe,christine.largeron,mathias.gery}@univ-st-etienne.fr
[2] CNRS, UMR 5516, Laboratoire Hubert Curien, 42000 Saint-Étienne, France
[3] Université de Saint-Étienne, Jean-Monnet, 42000 Saint-Étienne, France
[4] Université de Lyon, UMR 5205 CNRS, LIRIS, 7 Av J. Capelle,
69100 Villeurbanne, France
elod.egyed-zsigmond@insa-lyon.fr

Abstract. Modularity allows to estimate the quality of a partition into communities of a graph composed of highly inter-connected vertices. In this article, we introduce a complementary measure, based on inertia, and specially conceived to evaluate the quality of a partition based on real attributes describing the vertices. We propose also **I-Louvain**, a graph nodes clustering method which uses our criterion, combined with Newman's modularity, in order to detect communities in attributed graph where real attributes are associated with the vertices. Our experiments show that combining the relational information with the attributes allows to detect the communities more efficiently than using only one type of information. In addition, our method is more robust to data degradation.

Keywords: Attributed graph · Graph clustering · Social network · Community detection · Modularity

1 Introduction

Clustering of graph vertices is a task related to community detection within social networks. The goal is to create a partition of the vertices, taking into account the topological structure of the graph, in such a way that the clusters are composed of strongly connected vertices [3,13,20,23,29]. Among the core methods proposed in the literature, we can cite those that optimize a function (modularity, ratio cut or its variants, etc.) in order to evaluate the quality of the partition [10,19,25,30], the hierarchical techniques like divisive algorithms based on the minimum cut [14], the spectral methods [34] or the Markov Clustering algorithm and its extensions [28]. We refer to the survey of Fortunato for a thorough discussion of community detection methods [15].

Graph clustering techniques are very useful for detecting strongly connected groups in a graph but many of them mainly focus on the topological structure,

© Springer International Publishing Switzerland 2015
E. Fromont et al. (Eds.): IDA 2015, LNCS 9385, pp. 181–192, 2015.
DOI: 10.1007/978-3-319-24465-5_16

ignoring the vertices properties. Nowadays, various data sources can be seen as graphs where vertices have attributes and a new challenge in graph clustering consists in combining the relational information corresponding to the network and attributes describing the vertices. Generally, this is not the case in clustering of vertices where only the relationships between the vertices are used, nor in unsupervised classification based only on the attributes. Recently, several methods have been proposed to take into account the relational information as well as the attributes in the aim to detect patterns in attributed graphs [26,31] or to tackle this problem of hybrid clustering [6,11]. In this article, we propose a method, called **I-Louvain**, which allows to partition the vertices of an attributed graph when numerical attributes are associated to the vertices. In social networks, these attributes can correspond to features (age or weight) or *tf-idf* vector representing documents associated to the nodes. This method is based on a local optimization of a global criterion which is a function on the one hand of the modularity [24] and on the other hand of a new measure based on inertia.

After a presentation of related work in Sect. 2, we define this measure, called inertia based modularity, in Sect. 3, and the method **I-Louvain** in Sect. 4. The experimental study of Sect. 5 confirms that clustering, based on the relational information and attributes provides more meaningful clusters than methods taking into account one type of data (attributes or edges) or than ToTeM which exploits attributes and edges [6].

2   Related Work

Recently, methods exploiting both information types were introduced in order to detect communities in social networks or graphs where vertices have attributes.

Steinhaeuser and Chawla propose to measure the similarity between vertices according to their attributes and then to use the result as a weight of the edge linking the two vertices. After this pre-treatment, they use a graph partitioning method in order to cluster the new weighted graph [32]. In the hierarchical clustering of Li *et al.*, after a first phase consisting in detecting community seeds with the relational information, the final communities are built under constraints defined by the attributes [21]. This leads to merging the seeds on the base of their attributes' similarity. So, in these previous methods, the two types of information are not exploited simultaneously.

Zhou *et al.* exploit the attributes in order to extend the original graph [36,37]. They add new vertices representing the attributes and new edges that link original vertices having similar attributes through these new vertices. A graph partitioning is then carried out on this new augmented graph. However, this approach cannot be used when the attributes have continuous values: it works only with categorical attributes.

Ester *et al.* study the "connected k-center problem" and propose a method called **NetScan**, which is an extended version of the **K-means** algorithm with an internal connectivity constraint [12,16]. Under this constraint, two vertices in a same cluster are connected by a path that is internal to the cluster. In NetScan as in many other partitioning methods, the number of clusters has to be known in advance. However, this condition is relaxed in the work of Moser [22].

CESNA was introduced by Yang *et al.* to identify Communities from Edge Structure and Node Attributes [35]. One advantage of this method is its ability to detect overlapping communities by modeling the interaction between the network structure and the node attributes.

There are some other methods, focusing on dense subgraph detection, that integrate the homogeneity of the attributes inside the subgraphs, cf. for instance [17,18].

Finally, we can mention a family of methods which propose to extend the well-known **Louvain** algorithm and for this reason, they are probably the most related works to our concerns. Dang *et al.* suggest to modify the modularity by considering not only the link between two vertices but also the similarity of their attributes. Thus, the two types of information are simultaneously considered in the partitioning process but with this approach, the communities provided can contain non linked vertices [9]. In [7], the optimization phase of the **Louvain** algorithm is based not only on the modularity but also on the entropy of the partition but, again, the two types of information are not exploited simultaneously.

Recently, some of these methods have been compared and these experiments have confirmed that the detection of communities in an attributed graph is not a trivial problem [6,11]. To solve it efficiently, we consider that the attributes and the relational information must be exploited simultaneously and this is not the case for several methods cited. Moreover, the majority of the methods quoted previously exploit categorical attributes but they are not suited for numerical attributes. This is the reason for which, in this article, we propose **I-Louvain**, a method to detect communities in a graph where numerical attributes are associated to the vertices. These attributes can correspond to features (age or weight) or to a *tf-idf* vector representing documents associated to the vertex. **I-Louvain** consists in optimizing on the one hand the modularity introduced by Newman [24] and on the other hand a new measure that is defined in the next section.

3   Inertia Based Modularity

Let V be a set of N elements represented in a real vector space such that each element $v \in V$ is described by a vector of attributes $v = (v_1, \ldots, v_{|T|}) \in \mathbb{R}^{|T|}$. The inertia $I(V)$ of V through its center of gravity g, also called second central moment, is an homogeneity measure defined by $I(V) = \sum_{v \in V} \|v - g\|^2$, where $\|v' - v\|$ denotes the euclidean distance between v and v', $g = (g_1, \ldots, g_{|T|})$, the center of gravity of V is such that $g_j = \frac{1}{N} \sum_{v \in V} v_j$.

The inertia $I(V, v)$ of V through v is equal to the sum of the square euclidean distances between v and the other elements of V: $I(V, v) = \sum_{v' \in V} \|v' - v\|^2$.

Given a partition $\mathscr{P} = \{C_1, \ldots, C_r\}$ of V in r disjoint clusters, we introduce a quality measure $Q_{inertia}(\mathscr{P})$ of $\mathscr{P}$ defined by:

$$Q_{inertia}(\mathscr{P}) = \sum_{(v,v')\in V\cdot V} \left[\left(\frac{I(V,v)\cdot I(V,v')}{(2N\cdot I(V))^2} - \frac{\|v-v'\|^2}{2N\cdot I(V)} \right) \cdot \delta\left(c_v,c_{v'}\right) \right] \quad (1)$$

where c_v denotes the cluster of $v \in V$ and δ is the Kronecker function equal to 1 if c_v and $c_{v'}$ are equal and 0 otherwise.

Thus, while the modularity, introduced by Newman, considers the strength of the link between vertices in order to cluster strongly connected vertices, our measure attempts to cluster elements which are the most similar. This appears in the second term of the Eq. 1, which is a function of the square of the distance between v and v', corresponding to an *observed* distance between v and v'. This *observed* distance between v and v' is compared with an *expected* distance deducted from their respective inertia. This *expected* distance, which appears in the second term of the Eq. 1, is a function of the square distance of each of these elements v and v' to the other elements of V.

Therefore, $Q_{inertia}$ allows to compare, for each pair of elements (v, v') from the same community, the *expected* distance with the *observed* distance. If the former is greater than the latter, then v and v' are good candidates to be affected in a same cluster.

Given the normalization factors in the denominators of the expected and observed distances, the criterion $Q_{inertia}$ ranges between -1 and 1. Indeed, the maximum value of the left term in the subtraction (Eq. 1), containing the product of the inertia for all pairs of elements is 1. Similarly, the right term of the criterion $Q_{inertia}$ (Eq. 1) can not exceed 1. Both terms are strictly positive. Consequently the measure, constrained by the Kronecker function, varies between -1 and 1.

This criterion has several interesting properties. Firstly, it has the same value irrespective of the affine transformation applied to the attribute vectors, in other words the addition of a constant and / or the multiplication by a scalar of the vectors associated to the elements do not affect the value $Q_{inertia}$. Secondly, the order of attributes has no effect on the result.

However, this criterion has also limitations. It is undefined if the vectors are identical, since the total inertia is then zero. This is not really a problem, because in this case, the detection of the communities will be based only on the relational data. Moreover, as the modularity introduced by Newman, this criterion could present a resolution limit. If it is the case, the solution proposed by Arenas *et al.* or Reichardt and *et al.* could be adapted for our criterion [1, 27].

4   I-Louvain

As stated above, a direct application of our measure $Q_{inertia}$ is the community detection in social networks represented by an attributed graph $G = (V, E)$ where V is a set of vertices, E is a set of edges and where each vertex $v \in V$ is described by a real attribute vector $v = (v_1, \ldots, v_j, \ldots, v_T) \in \mathbb{R}^{|T|}$ [36]. In this section, we propose a community detection method for real attributed graphs which exploits the inertia-based modularity $Q_{inertia}$ jointly with the Newman modularity $Q_{NG}(\mathscr{P})$. Our method, called **I-Louvain**, is based on the exploration principle of the **Louvain** method. It consists in the optimization of the global criterion $QQ^+(\mathscr{P})$ defined by:

$$QQ^+(\mathscr{P}) = Q_{NG}(\mathscr{P}) + Q_{inertia}(\mathscr{P}) \tag{2}$$

with:

$$Q_{NG}(\mathscr{P}) = \frac{1}{2m}\Sigma_{vv'}\left[(A_{vv'} - \frac{k_v \cdot k_{v'}}{2m})\delta(c_v, c_{v'})\right] \tag{3}$$

where k_v is the degree of vertex $v \in V$, A is the adjacency matrix associated to G, m is the number of edges and δ the Kronecker function.

It may be noted that another combination of these criteria can be used, for instance to give more importance to one kind of data. However, in the general case where attributes and relational information have the same weight, it is not useful to normalize the criteria $Q_{NG}(\mathscr{P})$ and $Q_{inertia}(\mathscr{P})$ because they have been normalized to take values between -1 and 1, as mentioned in the previous section.

The **I-Louvain** method is presented in Algorithm 1. The process begins with the discrete partition in which each vertex is in its own cluster (line 1). The algorithm is divided in two phases that are repeated.

The first one is an iterative phase which consists in considering each vertex v and its neighbors in the graph and to evaluate the modularity gain induced by a move of v from its community to that of its neighbors. The vertex v is affected to the community for which the gain of the global criterion $QQ^+(\mathscr{P})$, defined in Eq. (2), is maximum. This process is applied repeatedly and sequentially for all vertices until no further improvement can be obtained.

If there is an increase of the modularity during the first phase, the second phase consists in building a new graph G' from the partition $\mathscr{P}'$ obtained at the end of the previous phase. This second phase involves two procedures: *Fusion_Matrix_Adjacency* and *Fusion_Matrix_Inertia*. The procedure *Fusion_Matrix_Adjacency* is identical to the one used in the **Louvain** method [4] and it exploits only the relational information. It consists in building a new graph. The vertices of this new graph G' correspond to the communities obtained at the end of the previous phase. The weights of the edges between these new vertices are given by the sum of the weights of the edges between vertices in the corresponding two communities. The edges between vertices of the same community lead to a self-loop for this community in the new network.

The procedure *Fusion_Matrice_Inertia* exploits the attributes and allows to compute the distances between the vertices of G' from the distances between the vertices of G. If the graph G considered at the beginning of the iterative phase includes $|V|$ vertices then the matrix $\mathcal{D}$ is a symmetric square matrix of size $|V| \times |V|$ in which each term $\mathcal{D}[a, b]$ is the square of the distance between the vertices v_a and v_b of V. At the end of the iterative phase, a partition $\mathscr{P}'$ of V in k communities is obtained, in which each community will correspond to a vertex of V' in the new graph G' built by the procedure *Fusion_Matrix_Adjacency*. The matrix $\mathcal{D}'$ associated to this new graph G' is defined by:

ALGORITHM 1 . I-Louvain

Input : An attributed graph G

Output : A partition $\mathscr{P}_{res}$

1 $\mathscr{P} \leftarrow$ discrete partition of vertices of V;

2 $\mathcal{A} \leftarrow$ adjacency matrix of G;

3 $\mathcal{D} \leftarrow$ matrix of the squares of the euclidean distances between the vertices of V calculated on their attributes;

4 **repeat**

5      $end \leftarrow$ false;

6      $QQ^+_{anterior} \leftarrow QQ^+(\mathscr{P})$;

7   **repeat**

8   **foreach** *vertex u of V* **do**

9              $B \leftarrow$ neighbor community maximizing the gain of QQ^+;

10   **if** *move of u in B induces a strictly positive gain* **then**

11   Affect u to the community B;

12   Update the partition $\mathscr{P}$ after the transfer of u into B;

13   **end**

14   **end**

15   **until** *no vertex can be moved anymore*;

16   **if** $QQ^+(\mathscr{P}) > QQ^+_{anterior}$ **then**

17          $G, \mathcal{A} \leftarrow$ Fusion_Matrix_Adjacency$(\mathcal{A}, \mathscr{P})$;

18          $\mathcal{D} \leftarrow$ Fusion_Matrix_Inertia$(\mathcal{D}, \mathscr{P})$;

19   **else**

20          $end \leftarrow$ true;

21   **end**

22 **until** *end*;

23 $\mathscr{P}_{res} \leftarrow \mathscr{P}$;

$$\mathcal{D}'[x, y] = \sum_{(v_a, v_b) \in V \times V} \mathcal{D}[v_a, v_b] \cdot \delta(\tau(v_a), x) \cdot \delta(\tau(v_b), y) \quad (4)$$

where the function τ gives for each vertex $v \in V$ the vertex $v' \in V'$ corresponding to its cluster in $\mathscr{P}'$.

One advantage of the **Louvain** method is the local optimization of the modularity done during the first phase [2]. In the same way, in **I-Louvain**, the global modularity of a new partition can be quickly updated. There is no need to compute it again from scratch after each move of a vertex. Indeed, the modularity gain can be computed using only local information concerning the move of the vertex from its community to that of its neighbor. Given $\mathscr{P} = (A, B, C_1, .., C_r)$ the original partition and $\mathscr{P}' = (A \backslash \{u\}, B \cup \{u\}, C_1, .., C_r)$ the partition induced by the move of a vertex u from its community A to the community B where $A \backslash \{u\}$ denotes the community A deprived of the vertex u, the modularity gain induced by the transformation of $\mathscr{P}$ in $\mathscr{P}'$ is equal to:

$$\Delta Q_{inertia} = Q_{inertia}(\mathscr{P}') - Q_{inertia}(\mathscr{P}) \quad (5)$$

$$= \frac{1}{N \cdot I(V)} \sum_{v \in B} \left[\frac{I(V, u) \cdot I(V, v)}{2N \cdot I(V)} - D[u, v] \right]$$

$$-\frac{1}{N \cdot I(V)} \sum_{v \in A \setminus \{u\}} \left[\frac{I(V,u) \cdot I(V,v)}{2N \cdot I(V)} - D\left[v, v'\right] \right] \quad (6)$$

The proof of this proposition is not given due to the limited size of the article but it is detailed in [5]. One can notice that the variation of modularity resulting from the move of the vertex u from its community to an other one is the same whatever its new community. It follows that the modularity gain can be computed in taking only into account the increase (or decrease) induced by its affectation in its new community corresponding to the first term in Eq. 6. This confirms that the optimization of $Q_{inertia}$ can be done using a local computation based on the information related to the affectation of the vertex u in its new community.

5   Evaluation of I-Louvain method

Our first experiments aim at evaluating on a real dataset the performances of **I-Louvain**, which exploits attributes and relational data, compared with methods based only on one type of data, K-means for the attributes and Louvain for the relations and with ToTeM, an other community detection method designed for attributed graphs which exploits the two types of information, notably numerical attributes [6]. In the following experiments, we study the robustness of our method to various degradations of an artificial network and we compare its performances, according to the accuracy as well as the normalized mutual information, with K-means, Louvain and ToTeM. Among the methods exploiting the both kinds of data (relationships and attributes), Totem has been retained because it has been showned experimentally that it provides better results than simpler methods [5,6] Finally, the last experiments aim at studying the impact of increasing the number of vertices and edges on the run-time evolution.

The **I-Louvain** source code and the dataset used for the experiments in the paper are available for download[1]. The **Louvain** source code is one proposed by Thomas Aynaud in 2009[2].

5.1   Evaluation of I-Louvain method on a real network

Firstly, we present results obtained on a real dataset built using the databases DBLP (06/18/2014) and Microsoft Academic Search (02/03/2014). DBLP allows to generate a graph $G = (V, E)$ with $|V| = 2515$ and $|E| = 5313$ that reflects the coauthor relationship: a vertex represents an author and two authors are linked if they have copublished at least one article in a conference in computer science also refereed in Microsoft Academic Search. The 23 keywords (data mining, Computer vision, etc.) associated to the conferences in the Microsoft Academic Search database are used to define 23 attributes on the vertices: the number

---

[1] I-Louvain source code and dataset: http://bit.ly/ILouvain.
[2] http://perso.crans.org/aynaud/communities/.

of publications of an author in conferences associated to a given keyword corresponds to a component of his attribute vector. These keywords allow also to define a partition corresponding to the ground truth for this dataset: the true community of an author corresponds to the research field, identified by the corresponding key word, in which he has mainly published.

The results are evaluated using the Normalized Mutual Information (NMI) derived from the mutual information (MI) and entropy (H), and defined by: [33]

$$NMI(\mathscr{P}_1, \mathscr{P}_2) = \frac{MI(\mathscr{P}_1, \mathscr{P}_2)}{\sqrt{H(\mathscr{P}_1)H(\mathscr{P}_2)}} \tag{7}$$

Table 1 presents the results provided by I-Louvain and those obtained by Louvain, K-means with $K = 22$ and ToTem. In this experiment, where we have a ground truth, the results confirm the interest of using the two kinds of information. Indeed the NMI of K-means is equal to 0.58 whereas the number of clusters that must be identified is given as parameter for this algorithm, when it is equal to 0.69 for Louvain. Moreover, with a NMI equals to 0.72, the proposed method outperforms ToTeM which obtains only 0.69. These results confirm the interest of I-Louvain to improve the detection of the communities.

Table 1. Evaluation according to the normalized mutual information (NMI)

	Louvain	K-means	ToTeM	I-Louvain
NMI	0.69	0.58	0.69	**0.72**

5.2 Evaluation of I-Louvain method on artificial data

In this second set of experiments, we evaluate the robustness of our method on artificial networks after different transformations of a reference network R, composed of 168 edges and 99 vertices uniformly distributed into 3 classes. This reference network has also been generated with the model proposed by Dang [8]. Moreover, each vertex is described by an attribute following a normal distribution with a standard deviation σ equal to 7 and a mean equal to $m_1 = 10$ for the first class, $m_2 = 40$ for the second class and $m_3 = 70$ for the third class. The class of the vertex in R is used as a ground truth for the evaluation. From this reference network R we built four families of networks:

- R.1.x in which the relational information is weakened in R, by the substitution of a percentage p of edges within class by edges between classes with $p = 0.25$ for R.1.1 and $p = 0.5$ for R.1.2;
- R.2.x in which the values of the attributes are less representative of each class, with a standard deviation $\sigma = 10$ for R.2.1 and $\sigma = 12$ for R.2.2;
- R.3.x which contain more vertices than R, 999 vertices for R.3.1 and 5,001 for R.3.2;
- R.4.x which contain more edges than R by introducing respectively 5 edges per new vertex in R.4.1 and 10 in R.4.2.

Table 2. Evaluation according to the accuracy (AC) and the number of clusters (#cl) (* means that the transformation has no influence on the results for this method)

	Louvain		K-means	ToTeM		I-Louvain	
	AC	#cl	AC	AC	#cl	AC	#cl
Reference network							
R	84 %	4	96 %	97 %	3	**98 %**	3
Degradation of the relational information							
R.1.1	33 %	8	96 %*	18 %	30	**78 %**	5
R.1.2	23 %	9	96 %*	14 %	36	**63 %**	6
Degradation of the attributes							
R.2.1	84 %*		90 %	95 %	3	**96 %**	3
R.2.2	84 %*		87 %	20 %	26	**98 %**	3
Number of vertices							
R.3.1	50 %	11	**97 %**	**97 %**	3	84 %	4
R.3.2	40 %	12	**98 %**	0,5 %	1,518	85 %	4
Number of edges							
R.4.1	**96 %**	3	96 %*	95 %	3	94 %	3
R.4.2	97 %	3	96 %*	**98 %**	3	**98 %**	3

Table 3. Evaluation according to the NMI (* means that the transformation has no influence on the results for this method)

NMI	Louvain	K-means	ToTeM	I-Louvain
Reference network				
R	0.78	0.88	0.86	**0.93**
Degradation of the relational information				
R.1.1	0.22	0.88*	0.48	**0.60**
R.1.2	0.11	0.88*	**0.37**	0.35
Degradation of the attributes				
R.2.1	0.78*	0.72	0.81	**0.88**
R.2.2	0.78*	0.63	0.56	**0.93**
Number of vertices				
R.3.1	0.59	**0.88**	0.85	0.80
R.3.2	0.58	**0.89**	0.37	0.77
Number of edges				
R.4.1	**0.84**	0.88*	0.80	0.81
R.4.2	0.87	0.88*	**0.91**	**0.91**

The results of **I-Louvain** are compared to those of the **Louvain** method, **K-means** with k = 3 and **ToTeM**. Tables 2 and 3 present respectively the accuracy (AC) and normalized mutual information (NMI). In exploiting the attributes and the relational information, the **I-Louvain** method is more robust than the **Louvain** method in the case of a degradation of the relational information. The **K-means** gives good results when the size of the network increases, but it requires the number of clusters as parameter. Despite this advantage, it obtains less good results than **I-Louvain** in front of a degradation of the attributes, notably for the NMI. Finally, compared to **ToTeM**, **I-Louvain** produces better or similar results. It is notably better for a larger number of vertices.

5.3   Run-Time of I-Louvain

In the last set of experiments, we evaluate the run-time of **I-Louvain** on different networks. Figure 1 presents the run-time evolution against the number of vertices $|V|$. In our experiments, we consider attributed networks with two attributes and where the number of edges $|E| = 3 \times |V|$. These results indicate that **I-Louvain** is able to handle large graphs.

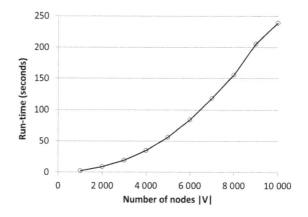

Fig. 1. Run-time of **I-Louvain** on different networks $G = (V, E)$ with $|E| = 3 \times |V|$

6   Conclusion

In this article, we studied the problem of attributed graph clustering when the vertices are described by real attributes. Inspired by the Newman modularity, we introduce a modularity measure, based on inertia. This measure is suited for assessing the quality of a partition of elements represented in a real vector space. We also introduced **I-Louvain**, an algorithm which combines our criterion with Newman's modularity in order to detect communities in attributed graphs. We demonstrated formally that this new algorithm can be optimized in its iterative phase. As we show in the experiments, using jointly the relational information and the attributes, **I-Louvain** detects more efficiently the communities than ToTeM or methods using only one type of data. Moreover, the method is resistant toward a degradation of the relations or the attributes, an increase in the density of the relations or the size of the network. Finally, the experiments confirm the scalability of the method.

Acknowledgments. The authors would like to thank P.N. Mougel for his help in building the bibliographic dataset.

References

1. Arenas, A., Fernández, A., Gómez, S.: Analysis of the structure of complex networks at different resolution levels. New J. Phys. **10**(5), 053039 (2008)
2. Aynaud, T., Blondel, V., Guillaume, J.L., Lambiotte, R.: Multilevel local optimization of modularity. In: Graph Partitioning, pp. 315–345. Wiley (2013)
3. Bichot, C., Siarry, P.: Graph Partitioning. Wiley, New York (2013)
4. Blondel, V.D., Guillaume, J.L., Lambiotte, R., Lefebvre, E.: Fast unfolding of community hierarchies in large networks. CoRR abs/0803.0476 (2008)
5. Combe, D.: Detection de communautes dans les reseaux d'information utilisant liens et attributs. In: Ph.D. Thesis, Jean Monnet University, Lyon (2013)
6. Combe, D., Largeron, C., Egyed-Zsigmond, E., Géry, M.: Combining relations and text in scientific network clustering. In: International Conference on Advances in Social Networks Analysis and Mining (ASONAM), pp. 1280–1285 (2012)
7. Cruz, J.D., Bothorel, C., Poulet, F.: Entropy based community detection in augmented social networks. In: Computational Aspects of Social Networks (CASoN 2011), pp. 163–168 (2011)
8. Dang, T.A.: Analysis of community in social networks. In: Ph.D. Thesis, Paris 13 (2013)
9. Dang, T.A., Viennet, E.: Community detection based on structural and attribute similarities. In: International Conference on Digital Society (ICDS), pp. 7–12 (2012)
10. Ding, C., He, X., Zha, H., Gu, M.: A min-max cut algorithm for graph partitioning and data clustering. In: ICDM, pp. 107–114 (2001)
11. Elhadi, H., Agam, G.: Structure and attributes community detection: comparative analysis of composite, ensemble and selection methods. In: 7th Workshop on Social Network Mining and Analysis, SNAKDD 2013, pp. 10:1–10:7. ACM, New York (2013)
12. Ester, M., Ge, R., Gao, B., Hu, Z., Ben-Moshe, B.: Joint cluster analysis of attribute data and relationship data: the connected k-center problem. In: SIAM International Conference on Data Mining, pp. 25–46. ACM Press (2006)
13. Fjällström, P.O.: Algorithms for graph partitioning: a survey. Science **3**(10), 1–36 (1998)
14. Flake, G., Tarjan, R., Tsioutsiouliklis, K.: Graph clustering and minimum cut trees. Internet Math. **1**(4), 385–408 (2003)
15. Fortunato, S.: Community detection in graphs. Phys. Rep. **486**(3–5), 75–174 (2010)
16. Ge, R., Ester, M., Gao, B.J., Hu, Z., Bhattacharya, B., Ben-Moshe, B.: Joint cluster analysis of attribute data and relationship data. ACM Trans. Knowl. Disc. Data **2**(2), 1–35 (2008)

17. Günnemann, S., Farber, I., Boden, B., Seidl, T.: Subspace clustering meets dense subgraph mining: a synthesis of two paradigms. In: ICDM, pp. 845–850 (2010)
18. Günnemann, S., Boden, B., Seidl, T.: DB-CSC: a density-based approach for subspace clustering in graphs with feature vectors. In: Machine Learning and Knowledge Discovery in Databases, pp. 565–580 (2011)
19. Kernighan, B.W., Lin, S.: An efficient heuristic procedure for partitioning graphs. Bell Syst. Tech. J. **49**(2), 291–307 (1970)
20. Lancichinetti, A., Fortunato, S.: Community detection algorithms: a comparative analysis. Phys. Rev. E **80**(5), 056117 (2009)
21. Li, H., Nie, Z., Lee, W.C.W., Giles, C.L., Wen, J.R.: Scalable community discovery on textual data with relations. In: 17th ACM Conference on Information and Knowledge Management, pp. 1203–1212 (2008)
22. Moser, F., Ge, R., Ester, M.: Joint cluster analysis of attribute and relationship data without a-priori specification of the number of clusters. In: 13th ACM SIGKDD Conference on Knowledge Discovery and Data Mining, pp. 510–519 (2007)
23. Newman, M.: Detecting community structure in networks. Eur. Phys. J. B-Condensed Matter and Complex Systems **38**(2), 321–330 (2004)
24. Newman, M.: Modularity and community structure in networks. Proc. Nat. Acad. Sci. U.S.A. **103**(23), 8577–8696 (2006)
25. Newman, M., Girvan, M.: Finding and evaluating community structure in networks. Phys. Rev. E **69**(2), 1–16 (2004)
26. Prado, A., Plantevit, M., Robardet, C., Boulicaut, J.F.: Mining graph topological patterns: finding covariations among vertex descriptors. IEEE Trans. Knowl. Data Eng. **25**(9), 2090–2104 (2013)
27. Reichardt, J., Bornholdt, S.: Statistical mechanics of community detection. Phys. Rev. E **74**(1), 016110 (2006)
28. Satuluri, V., Parthasarathy, S.: Scalable graph clustering using stochastic flows: applications to community discovery. In: 15th SIGKDD Conference on Knowledge Discovery and Data Mining, pp. 737–746 (2009)
29. Schaeffer, S.: Graph clustering. Comput. Sci. Rev. **1**(1), 27–64 (2007)
30. Shi, J., Malik, J.: Normalized cuts and image segmentation. IEEE Trans. Pattern Anal. Mach. Intell. **22**(8), 888–905 (2000)
31. Stattner, E., Collard, M.: From frequent features to frequent social links. Int. J. Inf. Sys. Model. Des. (IJISMD) **4**(3), 76–98 (2013)
32. Steinhaeuser, K., Chawla, N.: Community detection in a large real-world social network. In: Social Computing, Behavioral Modeling, and Prediction, pp. 168–175 (2008)
33. Strehl, A., Ghosh, J.: Cluster ensembles - a knowledge reuse framework for combining multiple partitions. J. Mach. Learn. Res. **3**, 583–617 (2003)
34. Von Luxburg, U.: A tutorial on spectral clustering. Stat. Comput. **17**(4), 395–416 (2007)
35. Yang, J., McAuley, J.J., Leskovec, J.: Community detection in networks with node attributes. In: ICDM, pp. 1151–1156 (2013)
36. Zhou, Y., Cheng, H., Yu, J.: Graph clustering based on structural/attribute similarities. VLDB Endowment **2**(1), 718–729 (2009)
37. Zhou, Y., Cheng, H., Yu, J.X.: Clustering large attributed graphs: an efficient incremental approach. In: ICDM 2010, pp. 689–698 (2010)

Class-Based Outlier Detection: Staying Zombies or Awaiting for Resurrection?

Leona Nezvalová[1,2], Luboš Popelínský[1,2]([✉]), Luis Torgo[1,2],
and Karel Vaculík[1,2]

[1] KD Lab, FI MU Brno, Brno, Czech Republic
{popel,xvaculi4}@fi.muni.cz
[2] Faculty of Science, University of Porto, Porto, Portugal
xnezva36@mail.muni.cz, ltorgo@dcc.fc.up.pt

Abstract. This paper addresses the task of finding outliers within each class in the context of supervised classification problems. Class-based outliers are cases that deviate too much with respect to the cases of the same class. We introduce a novel method for outlier detection in labelled data based on Random Forests and compare it with existing methods both on artificial and real-world data. We show that it is competitive with the existing methods and sometimes gives more intuitive results. We also provide an overview for outlier detection in labelled data. The main contribution are two methods for class-based outlier description and interpretation.

1 Introduction

Outlier detection [2] is an area of data analysis that aims at finding anomalies in data. Data cleansing to improve statistical model fraud detection or computer network intrusion detection are examples of some successful application areas of outlier analysis. Main stream of outlier detection defines, for a given statistical distribution, an outlier (or a series of outliers in the case of contextual outliers) as a case that differs from normal cases. This is typically taken as an unsupervised task in the sense that there are no labels indicating to the models which are the normal and the outlier cases. Nevertheless, there are also approaches that assume the existence of a supervised training set with examples of outlier cases and normal cases where the goal is to obtain a model that is able to accurately discriminate these two situations. Moreover, semi-supervised approaches have also been used in these application areas, where only a part of the available data is labelled.

In this paper we address another type of use of the concept of outliers. The context of the problem we are tackling is that of standard supervised classification tasks. Cases are labelled into a set of pre-defined classes in these problems and the goal is to learn a classification model from a provided training set. Outlier detection in labelled data, as a specific task, was initiated in [9,16] and further elaborated in [8]. Class-based outliers are those cases that look anomalous when the class labels are taken into account, but they do not have to be

© Springer International Publishing Switzerland 2015
E. Fromont et al. (Eds.): IDA 2015, LNCS 9385, pp. 193–204, 2015.
DOI: 10.1007/978-3-319-24465-5_17

anomalous when the class labels are ignored. In [8] two class outlier detection methods have been introduced as adaptations of methods for classical outlier detection setting, one based on frequent pattern mining, the other on clustering, and their use for Custom Relation Management was demonstrated. A distance and density-based approach has been published in [10] and its slightly improved version is now available in RapidMiner. Usability of these methods in Custom Relation Management and also in educational data was demonstrated [8,18].

In [3] a novel unsupervised way of detecting outliers for two-class problems by Inductive Logic Programming is presented. In the following text we will call it CB-ILP. The essential idea is that the outliers somehow disrupt the model of the data. The detection is done by creating a model, then for each possible outlier (or a set of outliers) excluding this outlier(s), learning a new model and comparing it with the original model. The same is done for a dual problem where positive and negative examples have been swapped. If coverages of two learned rule sets (with and without an example) differ more than a threshold, the example is an outlier. This approach then allows, by comparison of coverages of those four learned models, us to characterize the anomalies more finely, and to divide outliers into three groups according to the way they disrupt models learned with the whole data set - Irregularities, Anomalies and Outliers. The main drawback is its computational complexity.

Class-based outlier detection can be seen similar to label noise detection in classification tasks [7], more precisely to its sub-part of noise elimination. The first work that exploited class-based outliers, although not explicitly named, was C45Robust [11], where detected misclassified cases were removed before learning a new model. A similar idea has been recently elaborated for SVM [17]. The most important difference from our approach lies in a different measure of interestingness (rank). For noise elimination it seems to correspond only to the influence of a potential outlier to learning the correct hypothesis. In class-based outlier detection, the detection of an outlier is the goal and its interestingness may not depend only on classification accuracy but also on its novelty. Class-based outlier detection is also close to works on Exceptional model mining [13].

In this paper, we present RF–OEX, a new approach to class-based outlier detection based on Random Forests (RF) implemented in Weka [6]. It consists of two parts, an outlier detection module and an outlier interpretation module. We compare outliers obtained with RF–OEX with results of eCODB [10] and CB–LOF, an adaptation of LOF to labelled data. We show that RF–OEX is comparable with them, both on artificial data and real-world data, or gives even more intuitive results. Two new methods for class-based outlier interpretation, one based on tree reduction, the other on finding frequent branches in those trees, have been implemented. We describe these methods and compare the results with CB-ILP, an ILP approach to outlier detection [3].

In the following section we give an overview of the class-based outlier detection problem. In Sect. 3 we describe class outlier detection with RF–OEX, experimental evaluation of RF–OEX and comparison with the other methods. Two novel methods for outlier interpretation are described in Sect. 4. There we also bring a review of existing methods for class-based outlier interpretation and compare the results of RF–OEX with their interpretation. We conclude with discussion of results and directions for future work. Supplementary information can be found at http://www.fi.muni.cz/~popel/685269.

2   Class-Based Outlier Detection

Class-based outliers are cases that are *different* from the rest of the members of their own class. There are two main types of ways of being different from the members of the same class:

1. Cases that are too far (in terms of distance) from the bulk of cases of the same class.
2. Cases that, although not too far from the same class, are nearer to cases of another class.

Figure 1 illustrates both situations. (a) shows the first situation, where the case in red is too far from the members of the same class (x), while (b) illustrates the second situation, where the red case is nearer to members of the other class (y), even though it is not too far from the members of the same class (x), and thus regarded by us as a class-based outlier.

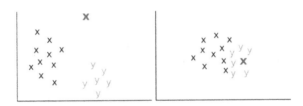

Fig. 1. The first (a) and the second (b) type of class-based outliers.

While the case (a) could be easily detected by standard distance-based outlier detection algorithms, the case (b) would not be captured by these methods as they are class-agnostic. This means that detecting this second type of class-based outliers is the key issue / innovation on this research line.

The concept of class outliers – outliers in labelled data – was introduced in [8] as a generalisation of two concepts: *semantic outliers*, i.e. data points that differ from other members of the same class while looking normal (similar) to data points in another class [8], and *cross-outliers* that deviate from data points in another class [16]. In [8] the authors define the problem of **Class Outlier Detection** as finding observations (data points) with class labels that arouse suspicions when those class labels are taken into account. Let

- C_i be a set of observations with the same class label cl_i,
- $DB = \{C_1, C_2, ..., C_m\}, C_i \cap C_j = \emptyset$ for $i \neq j$, be a data set,
- $Sp(DB)$ be the set of all unions of subsets of DB,
- T be an element of DB (i.e. $T = C_j$ for $j \in \{1, 2, ..., m\}$),
- $p \in T$ where p is an observation and T a target set.

The **Class Outlier Detection** problem is to find for two classes $C_i, C_j, i \neq j$, those observations $p \in C_i$ that differ from members of C_i and C_j. Let $COF(p, C_i)$ be the class outlier factor for $p \in T$. If $C_i = T$, i.e. the problem is to find those observations $p \in T$ that differ from other members of the same class T, then we call it **Local Class Outlier Detection** and use $LCOF(p)$ as the local class outlier factor. If $C_i \neq T$, i.e. the problem is to find those observations $p \in T$ that differ from members of the other class C_i, then we call it **Reference Class Outlier Detection** and use $RCOF(p, C_i)$ as the reference class outlier factor. If $DB = T$ then the class outlier detection problem is reduced to the common outlier detection problem.

For example, assume a two-class problem, where C_1 are positive and C_2 negative examples, $p \in C_1$, then p may be a local outlier, i.e. a reference class outlier w.r.t class C_1 with class outlier factor $LCOF(p) = RCOF(p, C_1)$ (or a semantic outlier in terms of [9]). It may be a reference class outlier w.r.t class C_2 with class outlier factor $RCOF(p, C_2)$ (or a cross-outlier by [16]).

The main idea presented in [8] lies in the computation of class-based outlier factor as an aggregation of the local factor and reference factors.

3   RF–OEX: Outlier Detection

3.1   Method

Random Forests [4] is an ensemble method that combines bagging (each tree is constructed by a different bootstrap sample from the original data) with the idea of random selection of features. More specifically, each split of a tree is chosen from a random subset of the data set features. Only these features are then used for selecting the best split at each node and this random process is repeated for all splits and all trees.

Random Forests can be used as an outlier detection method[1] in the following way. After each tree is built, all of the data are run down the tree, and proximity values are computed for each pair of cases. If two cases occupy the same terminal node, their proximity is increased by one. At the end of the run, the proximity values are normalized by dividing by the number of trees and the average proximity is computed for each instance.

The main idea of RF–OEX lies in a different way of exploitation of the proximity matrix. The main difference then lies in the fact how RF–OEX exploits the information about the class label. The outlier factor for an instance p is computed as a sum of three different measures of proximity or outlierness – proximity to the members of the same class OF_1, misclassification measure (proximity to the members of other classes) OF_2 and ambiguity measure OF_3. A similar idea, but only for the first two addends, has been elaborated in [8]. In the following, p stands for an element for which we compute the outlier factor. The value of the outlier factor is given by:

$$OF(p) = OF_1(p)_{same-class} + OF_2(p)_{misclassification} + OF_3(p)_{ambiguity}$$

---

[1] https://www.stat.berkeley.edu/~breiman/RandomForests/cc_home.htm#outliers.

$OF_1(p)_{same-class}$. In this case, only proximities to points from the same class are taken into account. Proximity of point p from class C_p is computed as an aggregation of proximities to all points from the same class. Four aggregation functions have been implemented: *sum, sum of squared proximity values, product, and cube root of sum of cubic values*. For simplicity, we will use *sum* function in the resulting formula. In principle, the higher the proximity is, the lower its outlierness is, so we use the inverse value of the proximity: $OF_1(p) = \frac{1}{\sum_{cl(p)=cl(q)} Prox(p,q)}$. where $cl(p)$ is the class label of element p. Finally, we normalize the result because of different sizes of different classes.

$OF_2(p)_{misclassification}$. We already stated that the similarity with members of a different class should increase the class outlier factor of p. We define $Top_{|C_p|}(p)$ as $|C_p|$ poins that are closest to point p. Then we compute how many of those points are labelled by different class than point p belongs to. To be comparable with OF_1 and OF_3, the value is multiplied by constant c, which is computed as the maximum from all values OF_1 divided by 4: $c = \frac{max_{q \in DB} OF_1(q)}{4}$. The resulting formula is then defined as $OF_2(p) = c \cdot \frac{|\{q \mid cl(q) \neq cl(p) \ \& \ q \in Top_{|C_p|}(p)\}|}{|C_p|}$.

$OF_3(p)_{ambiguity}$. To increase the importance of outliers that are far from all points, we add the third addend OF_3. We compare the sum of proximites of points $Top_{|C_p|}(p)$ to point p with the ideal situation when proximity to all examples is 1 and the sum is equal to $|C_p|$. At the end, we multiply it with the same constant as in the case of OF_2: $OF_3(p) = c \cdot \frac{|C_p| - \sum_{q \in Top_{|C_p|}(p)} Prox(p,q)}{|C_p|}$.

3.2   Parameter Settings

The RF–OEX method has a few parameters but in most cases the user does not need to change the default values of these parameters. At most the user may need to try a few alternatives for the parameter that controls how many random features are used for split selection at each tree node. Below we describe the values used for the parameters of our method. More information on parameter settings and work with RF–OEX can be found on the supplementary web page.

Number of Trees was set to 1000. We also checked smaller values, between 100 and 1000, and for a lot of situations 100 was sufficient. *Number of Random Features* for each split selection step was set to half of the number of input attributes. *Minimum cases per node* is equivalent to -m parameter of C45. It does not allow to grow the tree when few examples reached the node. We set this parameter to 10 for real-world data sets and 0 for artificial data because they contained very few instances. *Maximum depth of Trees* was set to 0, i.e. depth of trees was not limited. *Attribute distribution of multiset for Random tree* was set to *Normal*, so each tree starts with the same original set of attributes. The information gain of attributes is then taken into account before building each node of tree. *Variant of summing point's proximities* denotes the method of summing sample proximities and was set to *Addition squared values*. *Normalize according to* affects the normalization of outlier factor within the bounds of experiment. The *Average* option was chosen for this parameter. We checked both *Count with mistaken class penalty* and *Count with ambiguous classification penalty* parameters to consider similarity of given instance with the rest of samples ($OF_2(p)_{misclassification}$ and $OF_3(p)_{ambiguity}$) when calculating the outlier factor. The *Use data bootstrapping* parameter was checked to generate trees of different quality.

3.3   Data Sets Used for Experiments

For experiments we used the following data sets.

Artificial Data. We created several artificial data sets – two-class problems, with two numeric attributes – to check the behaviour of the systems on controlled situations. An example of such a dataset with two classes is in Fig. 2, all the data sets can be found at http://www.fi.muni.cz/~popel/685269/Results/OutlierDetection/top_5_artificial.pdf.

Votes. The Votes (or House Votes 84 – Republicans vs. Democrats) data set contains 16 key congress votes for each U.S. House of Representatives Congressman, 267 democrats and 168 republicans and was also used in [8,10]. It has been observed that several congressmen have opinions almost exactly opposite to what is common in their political party (meaning they vote similarly to their political opponents).

Student Solutions Data. The data [18] (a total of 873 student solutions) was obtained in a bachelor course on Introduction to Logic at FI MU. It contains the resolution tree together with dynamics of the solutions, i.e. all the actions performed together with temporal information. Here we use only the resolution trees. First all subgraphs that correspond to an application of the resolution rule were found and generalized. Then each resolution tree has been transformed to 0/1 matrix where those graphs served as boolean attributes (1=the subgraph appeared in the tree, 0=otherwise). Among these 873 different students' solutions of resolution proofs in propositional calculus, 101 of them were classified as incorrect and 772 as correct [18].

As calculation of proximity matrix is quadratic to the number of instances, the method becomes time-consuming for big data sets. Therefore, we have restricted our selection of data sets to those having less than 1000 instances. For example, runtime of Votes data set, which has 423 instances, is less than one minute. Running the student solutions data set, which has 873 instances, takes 10 min. Optimization of our method to be applicable to bigger data sets is part of future extensions.

3.4   Experiments and Results

We compared results of RF–OEX with eCODB [10] and a variant of LOF that follows the model described in Sect. 2. eCODB [10] combines distance-based and

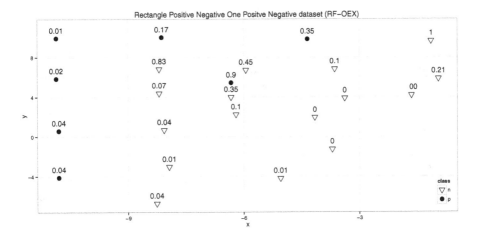

Fig. 2. Results of RF–OEX on an artificial data set; outlier factors are above the datapoints and they are normalized to $[0,1]$ interval, where 1 means the most outlying.

density-based approach w.r.t class attribute. The Class Outlier Factor $COF(T)$ for an instance T and parameter K (K nearest neighbors of the instance T) is computed as

$$COF(T, K) = PCL(T, K) - norm(Deviation(T)) + norm(Kdist(T, K))$$

where $PCL(T, K)$ is the probability of the class label of T w.r.t. the K nearest neighbors (i.e. the frequency of the class label among those K neighbors), $Deviation(T)$ is the sum of distances from all elements from the same class, and $Kdist(T, K)$ is the distance between T and its K nearest neighbors. $norm()$ means normalization. eCODB is now a part of RapidMiner[2]. Following the model from [8], we implemented CB–LOF, a variant of LOF that is capable to manage class labels. We compute CB–LOF (class-based local outlier factor) as an aggregation of two factors, dissimilarity of the case to members of the same class and similarity to members of other classes. As aggregation functions we tested maximum and average. For comparison we use the latter, which performs better in general than maximum.

When compared with RF–OEX, eCODB returned much worse results on the Student solution data. The reason is mainly because of the use of too rough metrics – density and distances – to nearest neighbours and to all members of the class, which does not work well for this 0/1 multidimensional data (number of attributes = 20). Moreover, it is much more difficult to obtain a comprehensive explanation why a particular instance is an outlier. The situation was similar for CB–LOF, although the results were slightly better than with eCODB. For one of the artificial data sets, results of RF–OEX and eCODB can be found in Figs. 2 and 3. More results can be found on www.fi.muni.cz/~popel/685269.

---

[2] http://docs.rapidminer.com/studio/operators/data_transformation/data_cleansing/outlier_detection/detect_outlier_cof.html.

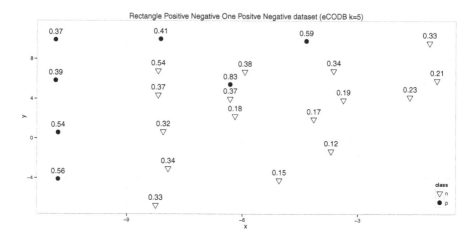

Fig. 3. Results of eCODB (k=5) on an artificial data set; outlier factors are above the datapoints and they are normalized to [0, 1] interval, where 1 means the most outlying.

4 Outlier Interpretation

As argued elsewhere [1], the outlier factor alone, i.e. the rank of an example, is insufficient for adequate outlier interpretation and explanation. Thus, finding the reason, or reasons, for being an outlier is highly relevant on several application domains. Several methods for constructing an interpretation of outliers have been recently published [1,5,14,15] but only two for class-based outliers.

The first one is CB-ILP [3] briefly described in Sect. 1. The explanation that CB-ILP offers actually consists of two rule sets - the starting theory (i.e. the rules that have been learned from the full data set) and the ending theory (rules learned after removing an outlier(s)).

The method in [8] analyses frequent patterns that cover an instance/example and takes supports of those patterns for finding the most significant attribute-value couples as an explanation. They define the contradict-ness of an itemset X with respect to a transaction t (in terms of association rule mining) in the following way:

$$Contradict - ness(X, t) = (card(X) - card(t \cap X)) * support(X)$$

The motivation is as follows. The more the itemset X deviates from t, the more contradictory it is. Moreover, the greater the support of X is, the more t deviates from other instances.

We observed that this method gives counter-intuitive results even in very simple situations. The problem is that itemsets containing more items from t can have the same contradict-ness score as itemsets which do not have these items. It is enough if these items occur at least in those transactions in which the other items occur. For example, assume a transaction $t = \{A_1, A_2, ..., A_n\}$, itemsets $X_0 = \{B\}, X_1 = \{B, A_1\}, X_2 = \{B, A_1, A_2\}, ..., X_n = \{B, A_1, A_2, ..., A_n\}$, and $support\{A_1, A_2, ..., A_n\} = 1$. It is clear that support of all these itemsets is the same, i.e. it is equal to $support(X_0)$. Furthermore, it holds for all these itemsets that $card(X) - card(t \cap X) = 1$. Thus, the contradict-ness of all these itemsets is equal to $support(X_0)$. In such a case the contradict-ness score is not appropriate for outlier explanation because items $A_1, A_2, ..., A_n$ do not distinguish t from other instances at all and therefore they are superfluous. Another example, for the ZOO data set, can be found on the supplementary web page. For that drawback we did not use this method.

For class outlier explanation we developed two new methods. Both use already learned random trees and return interpretation of outliers as a set of conjunctions of attributes or attribute-value couples with weights, where a weight is proportional to the expressive power of the conjunction.

4.1   Reduction of Random Trees

For an outlier, we take all trees that classified this instance into an incorrect class. Actually, we now work with two classes – O as outlier and N as normal – like in the classical outlier detection settings, which allows us to prune the trees, see Fig. 4. Specifically, all subbranches that classify into N can be removed. In the next step, we remove internal nodes in the branch that do not influence classification by checking all values the nodes can have. After this pruning is done, sets of attributes are collected by running outlying instance down each tree. Each of those attribute sets interprets outlierness of the examined point with a weight that is given by the occurrence frequency in the pruned trees. Let us inspect the interpretation of three instances belonging to the most outlying instances in the *iris* data set. The full list of interpretations can be found on the web page.

```
Instance number: 71, Class: Iris-versicolor petalwidth>=1.6, 0.6
Instance number: 84, Class: Iris-versicolor petallength>=4.9, 0.63
Instance number: 37, Class: Iris-setosa sepallength>=5.4 &&
sepalwidth<3.7, 1
```

This method is much more efficient when compared with the ILP approach. However, it prefers short interpretations and sometimes oversees more complex interpretations. The following method is able to find also longer conjunctions.

4.2   Analysis of Frequent Branches

The second method looks for a frequent combination of attributes, i.e. a combination with support higher than min_supp, again on the trees that classify the instance incorrectly. For each frequent combination we express the whole data set only by attributes that appeared in that frequent combination and observe how much the outlier factor changed. To compare these two values of the outlier factor, we first have to normalize each one of them. The results are as follows.

```
Instance number: 71, Class: Iris-versicolor petalwidth=1.8, 0.88
```

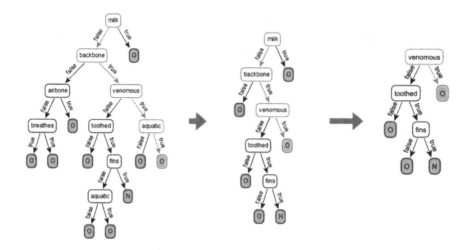

Fig. 4. Tree pruning.

It means that the outlierness of instance no. 71 is caused from 88 % by value 1.8 of attribute *petalwidth*. Now let us have a look at the third most outlying instance number 84:

```
Instance number: 84, Class: Iris-versicolor
petallength=5.1, 0.74
sepallength=6 && petallength=5.1, 0.26
```

Instance outlierness is caused from 74 % by the value of *petallength*. There is also a significant increase in outlierness if we combine attribute *petallength* with attribute *sepallength*. This combination participates in outlierness with 26 %. Thus, frequent attribute set allows to find more complex interpretation more frequently than the first method. As previously mentioned, supplementary material and results for other data sets can be found on www.fi.muni.cz/~popel/685269.

4.3   Comparison with CB-ILP

For comparison we used Votes data set. The runtime of CB-ILP was 30 min, compare to less than a minute of RF–OEX, and it detected 3 negative (republican) and 2 positive (democrat) outliers with gains varying from 0.15 to 0.67. 16 negative examples were labelled as irregularity for being a fact in direct theory as well as 3 positive. There were 7 other positive irregularities, with gain just a little over 0.05. We also detected 6 negative anomalies with gain up to 0.53 and 6 positive anomalies with gain up to 0.68. Detected cases with the highest gain are in Fig. 5 together with results of RF–OEX and eCODB. CB-ILP detected Example 389 (democrat) as anomaly with gain 0.68, because he voted for freezing physician fee, against Synfuels corporation cutback and against duty free exports. Negative example 268 (republican) was identified as outlier with positive gain 1.00

Instance	Class	RF-OEX	Score	eCODB	Score	ILP	Gain
408	Dem.	1.	36.97	1.	1.31	3. (O.)	1/0.32
7	Dem.	2.	33.21	-	-	2. (O.)	1/0.55
243	Rep.	3.	32.68	-	-	7. (A.)	0.38
268	Rep.	4.	29.32	4.	1.44	1. (O.)	1/0.67
389	Dem.	5.	26.80	-	-	1. (A.)	0.68
394	Rep.	6.	22.69	-	-	-	-
169	Dem.	7.	21.93	-	-	5. (A.)	0.29
108	Rep.	8.	20.50	-	-	-	-

Fig. 5. Comparison-Votes-RF-CODB-ILP.

5 Conclusion

In this contribution we argue that outlier detection in labelled data is challenging area both for research and for applications. We brought a review of existing approaches to that problem and introduced a novel method based on Random Forests that is competitive or overcome existing method. Two new methods for class-based outlier description and interpretation were presented and their results were compared with the ILP-based approach.

The open question is evaluation of class-based outlier detection. We performed only a small step in this direction and built several artificial data sets. Building benchmark data for this task more systematically will be the next step. To improve efficiency of RF–OEX, especially its interpretation part, ensemble-based noise elimination and also local models [7] look as good starting points.

Besides the applications mentioned earlier, there are many others that can exploit information about class-based outliers or employ similar techniques, e.g. in the field of subgroup discover [12]. A challenging one is fake text recognition, e.g. an email that pretends to be written by a woman (or a member of a particular group in general), or a similar kind of fake chat contribution.

Now it is up to the reader to answer the question that is in the title of this contribution.

Acknowledgments. We thanks to IDA reviewers for valuable comments and suggestions and to Vaclav Blahut for implementation and experiments with CB-ILP. We would like to thank also to the members of KDLab FI MU for their help. This work has been partially supported by Faculty of Informatics, Masaryk University, Brno.

References

1. ODD2 Ws on Outlier Detection & Description under Data Diversity, KDD (2014)
2. Aggarwal, C.C.: Outlier Analysis. Springer, New York (2013)
3. Angiulli, F., Fassetti, F.: Exploiting domain knowledge to detect outliers. Data Min. Knowl. Discov. **28**(2), 519–568 (2014)

4. Breiman, L.: Random forests. Mach. Learn. **45**(1), 5–32 (2001)
5. Dang, X.H., Micenková, B., Assent, I., Ng, R.T.: Local outlier detection with interpretation. In: Blockeel, H., Kersting, K., Nijssen, S., Železný, F. (eds.) ECML PKDD 2013, Part III. LNCS, vol. 8190, pp. 304–320. Springer, Heidelberg (2013)
6. Hall, M., et al.: The weka data mining software: an update. SIGKDD Explor. Newsl. **11**(1), 10–18 (2009)
7. Frenay, B., Verleysen, M.: Classification in the presence of label noise: a survey. IEEE Trans. Neural Netw. Learn. Syst. **25**(5), 845–869 (2014)
8. He, Z., Xu, X., Huang, J.Z., Deng, S.: Mining class outliers: concepts, algorithms and applications in CRM. Expert Syst. Appl. **27**(4), 681–697 (2004)
9. He, Z., Deng, S., Xu, X.: Outlier detection integrating semantic knowledge. In: Meng, X., Su, J., Wang, Y. (eds.) WAIM 2002. LNCS, vol. 2419, p. 126. Springer, Heidelberg (2002)
10. Hewahi, N., Saad, M.: Class outliers mining: distance-based approach. Int. J. Intell. Technol. **2**(1), 5568 (2007)
11. John, G.H.: Robust decision trees: removing outliers from databases. In: Knowledge Discovery and Data Mining, pp. 174–179. AAAI Press (1995)
12. Konijn, R.M., Duivesteijn,W., Kowalczyk, W., Knobbe, A.J.: Discovering local subgroups, with an application to fraud detection. In: Proceedings of PAKDD 2013, pp. 1–12 (2013)
13. Leman, D., Feelders, A., Knobbe, A.J.: Exceptional model mining. In: Daelemans, W., Goethals, B., Morik, K. (eds.) ECML PKDD 2008, Part II. LNCS (LNAI), vol. 5212, pp. 1–16. Springer, Heidelberg (2008)
14. Micenková, B., Ng, R.T., Dang, X.H., Assent, I.: Explaining outliers by subspace separability. In: IEEE ICDM 2013, pp. 518–527 (2013)
15. Müller, E., Keller, F., Blanc, S., Böhm, K.: *OutRules*: A framework for outlier descriptions in multiple context spaces. In: Flach, P.A., De Bie, T., Cristianini, N. (eds.) ECML PKDD 2012, Part II. LNCS, vol. 7524, pp. 828–832. Springer, Heidelberg (2012)
16. Papadimitriou, S., Faloutsos, C.: Cross-outlier detection. In: Hadzilacos, T., Manolopoulos, Y., Roddick, J., Theodoridis, Y. (eds.) SSTD 2003. LNCS, vol. 2750. Springer, Heidelberg (2003)
17. Smith, M.R., Martinez, T.R.: Improving classification accuracy by identifying and removing instances that should be misclassified. In: IJCNN, pp. 2690–2697. IEEE (2011)
18. Vaculík, K., Nezvalová, L., Popelínský, L.: Educational data mining for analysis of students' solutions. In: Agre, G., Hitzler, P., Krisnadhi, A.A., Kuznetsov, S.O. (eds.) AIMSA 2014. LNCS, vol. 8722, pp. 150–161. Springer, Heidelberg (2014)

Using Metalearning for Prediction of Taxi Trip Duration Using Different Granularity Levels

Mohammad Nozari Zarmehri[(⊠)] and Carlos Soares

INESC TEC, Faculdade de Engenharia, Universidade do Porto,
Rua Dr. Roberto Frias, 378, Porto, Portugal
{mohammad.nozari,csoares}@fe.up.pt

Abstract. Trip duration is an important metric for the management of taxi companies, as it affects operational efficiency, driver satisfaction and, above all, customer satisfaction. In particular, the ability to predict trip duration in advance can be very useful for allocating taxis to stands and finding the best route for trips. A data mining approach can be used to generate models for trip time prediction. In fact, given the amount of data available, different models can be generated for different taxis. Given the difference between the data collected by different taxis, the best model for each one can be obtained with different algorithms and/or parameter settings. However, finding the configuration that generates the best model for each taxi is computationally very expensive. In this paper, we propose the use of metalearning to address the problem of selecting the algorithm that generates the model with the most accurate predictions for each taxi. The approach is tested on data collected in the Drive-In project. Our results show that metalearning can help to select the algorithm with the best accuracy.

Keywords: Metalearning · Data mining · Machine learning · Trip duration prediction

1 Introduction

With fast-growing of Intelligent Transportation Systems (ITS) and Advanced Travelers Information Systems (ATIS), data collected by those systems can be useful to understand and improve processes in taxi companies and other organizations dealing with transportation, i.e. public transportation companies, logistics companies, and local government.

An example of a problem that can benefit from the analysis of data is trip duration in taxi companies; Especially knowing the estimated trip time duration beforehand can be very informative for taxi companies, drivers, and passengers to make the right decision for the scheduling and route planning. Data concerning the taxi trips (essentially GPS data) collected by taxis can be used for that purpose.

© Springer International Publishing Switzerland 2015
E. Fromont et al. (Eds.): IDA 2015, LNCS 9385, pp. 205–216, 2015.
DOI: 10.1007/978-3-319-24465-5_18

Data mining approaches can be used for the prediction of the trip duration. Using the data collected by taxis, these approaches relate trip duration with several variables describing the trip like origin, destination, time of day, day of week, and the weather.

Several algorithms have been introduced and can be used for the prediction of trip duration. But their predictive performance varies and causes several challenges. An important challenge for using data mining is to find out which algorithm has the best performance for a specific problem. But it has already been shown that there is no commonly best algorithm for a broad problem domain [1]. Algorithm selection for a specific problem is either based on a trial-and-error approach or expert advice. Neither way is thoroughly acceptable for the end user who wishes to access the technology cost-effectively [2]. An approach to deal with this problem is metalearning [3]. Metalearning uses a machine learning approach to relate the performance of machine learning algorithms with the characteristics of the data.

The problem of algorithm selection is more complex in applications with multiple sources of data (e.g., multiple taxis). In this case, it may be expected that the best algorithm varies for different sources. For instance, the best algorithm to predict trip duration may vary for different taxis, due to differences in the brand of the vehicle, its usage, and driving habits. Therefore, algorithm selection should be made not at the global level but at a lower one, such as taxi itself.

On the other hand, in applications with multiple sources of data in which the data schema is the same, it is possible that the quality of the model for a given source can be improved by training it with data from other sources. Therefore, the problem of algorithm selection is also extended to the dataset granularity selection. For the purpose of trip duration prediction, each taxi can use its data, data from its neighbors, data collected at the nearest road-side unit, or whole dataset which is collected centrally throughout the city.

In this paper, we investigate the use of a metalearning approach to the problem of algorithm selection in a case study of predicting trip duration for a taxi company. The taxi dataset is obtained from the Carnegie Mellon Portugal project, DRIVE-IN (Distributed Routing and Infotainment through Vehicular Inter-Networking) [4]. Selection is made between four different machine learning algorithms and two levels of granularity; Two levels of granularity are taxi itself and the collected data in whole month. Four machine learning algorithms used at the base-level are: random forest, support vector machines (SVMs), linear regression and decision tree. The experiment is done on the data from five months in 2013, from February to June. In each month, the data is collected by 440 taxis.

The approach is evaluated at the meta-level (i.e. the ability of choosing the most accurate base-level algorithm) and at the base-level (i.e. the base-level performance of the algorithm selected by the metalearning approach). The results obtained are positive at both levels.

2   Background

We start by discussing approaches to predict trip duration (Sect. 2.1) and then metalearning (Sect. 2.2).

2.1   Trip Duration

There has been a significant amount of research on trip duration prediction. Kwon et al. [5] use the flow and occupancy data from single loop detectors and historical trip duration information to forecast trip duration on a freeway. Using real traffic data, they found out that simple prediction methods can provide a good estimation of trip duration for trips starting in the near future (up to 20 min). On the other hand, for the trips starting more than 20 min away, better predictions can be obtained with historical data. The same approach is used by Chien et al. [6]. Zhang et al. [7] propose using a linear model to predict the short-term freeway trip duration. Trip duration is a function of departure time. Their results show that for a small dataset, the error varies from 5 % to 10 % while for a bigger dataset, the variation is between 8 % and 13 %.

Support Vector Regression (SVR) is used for prediction of trip duration by Wu et al. [8]. They utilize real highway traffic data for their experiments. They suggest a set of SVR parameter values by trial-and-error which lead to a model that is able to outperform a baseline model. Balan et al. [9] propose a real-time information system that provides the expected fare and trip duration for passengers. They use historical data consisting of approximately 250 million paid taxi trips for the experiment.

Considering the rapid change of behavior of vehicular networks, using the same algorithm for forecasting the travel time over a long period and for different vehicles, will eventually end in unreliable predictions. Therefore, it is important to find the best algorithm for each context. One possibility is to use a trial and error approach. This means finding out the algorithm that fits best to the specific dataset (i.e. for a specific vehicle and for a specific period) by evaluating multiple algorithms and choosing the best one [10]. This approach would be very time consuming, given the amount of alternatives available. One alternative approach is metalearning which is still missing.

2.2   Metalearning

The algorithm selection problem was formally defined by Rice in 1976 [11]. The main question was to predict which algorithm has the best performance for a specific problem.

The first formal project in this area was MLT project [12]. The MLT project creates a system called *Consultant-2* which can help to select the best algorithm for a specific problem.

Over the years, metalearning research has addressed several issues [13]. It may be important to select the best base-level algorithm not for the whole dataset, but rather for a subset of the examples [14] or even for individual examples [15].

Tuning the parameters of base-level algorithms is another task that metalearning can be helpful to (e.g. the kernel width of SVM with Gaussian kernel [13,16]). Rijn et al. [17] have investigated the use of metalearning for algorithm selection on data streams. The metafeatures are calculated on a small data window at the start of the data stream. Metalearning uses this metafeatures to predict which algorithm is the best in the next data windows.

3   Methodology

In this section, the data used in this work (Sect. 3.1), the metalearning approach (Sect. 3.3) and the evaluation methodology (Sect. 3.4) are presented.

3.1   Taxi Dataset

The dataset is obtained from a large-scale scenario [4], one of the taxi companies in the city of Porto. Porto is the second largest city in Portugal, with an area of $41.3 \, km^2$, and comprises 965 km of roads. It is the central city in a metropolitan area with more than one million inhabitants. There are 63 taxi stands in the city and the main taxi union has 441 vehicles. Each taxi has an on-board unit with a GPS receiver and collects the travel log. The provided dataset by the project [4] consists of five months in 2013 for all the vehicles. The dataset contains 13 variables characterizing events in the data:

id (ID): Event identifier.
driver (D): Taxi driver identifier.
ts (T): Timestamp of the event. It is a UNIX timestamp, in seconds.
st   (ST): Taxi state (Offline $= 0$, Pause $= 1$, InStand $= 2$, Free $= 3$, OnPickup $= 4$, OnPickupAfterACall $= 5$, Busy $= 6$, Login $= 7$).
Taxi ID (TID): Taxi identifier.
pst (PST): Previous state identifier. This is the same as 'st', but it refers to the state of the previous event.
track (TR): GPS track, encoded with polyline algorithm.
src (S): GPS coordinates of the source position.
dst (DST): GPS coordinates of the destination position.
dd (DD): Distance between src and dst (meters).
n (N): Name of the taxi stand, only if the state is 2 (i.e. if it is stopped in a stand).
pos (P): Location of the taxi stand, only if the state is 2 (i.e. if it is stopped in a stand).
dt (DT): Duration of the trip (seconds).

3.2   Base-level Approach

In this section the methodology which is used at the base-level is presented. In the traditional data mining, each entity E_i is described by a set of features,

X_i, and there is a target variable, Y_i. So the dataset used for the traditional data mining is like $DB = \{E_i, X_i, Y_i\}, \forall i \in \{1, ..., n\}$, while n is the number of entities.

At the base-level, the same scheme is used. The features used at the base-level are described in Sect. 3.1. Each taxi is represented by an entity in the scheme, $E_i = T_i$. The target variable is the trip duration ($Y_i = DT$). So the base-level scheme is like $DB = \{T_i, X_i, DT_i\}, \forall i \in \{1, ..., n\}$. Four algorithms are applied on the dataset (DB) at the base-level to predict the target variable: Decision Tree (DT), Random Forest (RF), Support Vector Machine (SVM), and Linear Regression (LM).

3.3   Metalearning at Different Granularity Levels

In this section the metalearning methodology is presented. The taxi application introduces an interesting challenge for metalearning. Each taxi generates enough data to learn its own model. However, it can be expected that, in some cases, the quality of the model generated from the full set of data, i.e. concerning all taxis, can be better than the model generated solely with "local" data. Therefore, besides selecting an algorithm to learn the best model for a taxi, a decision can be made also concerning whether only data from the taxi or global data.

In terms of the metalearning approach, the possibility of generating meta-examples at different levels of granularity of the data, adds another dimension to the meta-dataset. So for each entity, instead of having just one set of X_i, other feature sets can be generated for different levels or categories of the data, $C_i^1, C_i^2, C_i^3, ..., C_i^k$, where k is the number of levels or categories. Therefore the meta-dataset for using in the metalearning process is $DB = \{T_i, C_i^j, Y_i\}, \forall i \in \{1, ..., n\}, \forall j \in \{1, ..., k\}$.

The proposed model used in this article is shown in Fig. 1.

In the proposed model, there are two different levels: taxi itself and the data for whole month. At the level one, each taxi (T_i) creates a unique category, $C_i^1, \forall i \in \{1, ..., n_1\}$ where n_1 is the number of taxis. The level two has only one category joining all the data from 440 taxis.

So after organizing the dataset in customized format, $DB = \{T_i, C_i^j, Y_i\}, \forall i \in \{1, ..., 440\}, \forall j \in \{1, 2\}$, it is delivered to the performance evaluation process. In this stage, each taxi is evaluated by different algorithms, applying in different levels. As result, for each taxi, there are different performance indicators: P_{ig}^k which means the performance of the algorithm g at level k for taxi i.

$$P_{iw}^j : \quad \forall w \in \{1, ..., 4\}, \forall j \in \{1, 2\}, \forall i \in \{1, ..., 440\} \tag{1}$$

Where w stands for the algorithms, i indicates taxis, and j shows levels.

On the other hand, the metafeatures are calculated for each taxi and at different levels. In general mf_i^j is the calculated metafeatures for taxi i at the level j. For each taxi, the best performance obtained from the performance evaluation part is selected according to the Eq. 2:

$$P_{best i} = \max_{w,j}(P_{iw}^j), \quad \forall w \in \{1, ..., 4\}, \forall j \in \{1, 2\} \tag{2}$$

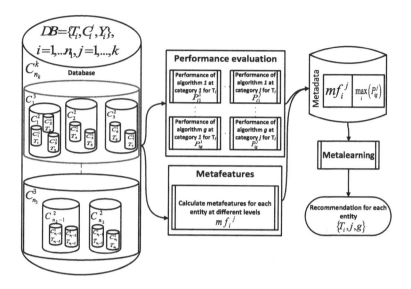

Fig. 1. Proposed methodology used for metalearning

Finally the metadata structure for each taxi consists of the taxi identification, metafeatures for the first and the second level and the best performance obtained from Eq. 2.

$$T_i, \; mf_i^1, \; mf_i^2, \; P_{best_i} \qquad (3)$$

The main idea in metalearning is to find out the best algorithm and the best level to apply the algorithm depending on the metafeatures obtained at different levels. Consequently, the metalearning maps the extracted features from the original datasets to the best performance obtained at different levels by applying different algorithms on the original dataset.

Our model recommends a level and an algorithms for each taxi in which, applying the recommended algorithm on the recommended level produces the best performance with high probability (see Eq. 4).

$$Model\,Output \; : \; \{ \; \underbrace{T_i}_{taxi}, \; \underbrace{j}_{recommended\,level}, \; \underbrace{g}_{recommended\,algorithm} \; \} \qquad (4)$$

3.4   Evaluation

Base-level Evaluation. At the base-level, the problem of prediction of the trip duration is a regression problem. Each algorithm is applied on the dataset and tried to predict the trip duration. This prediction is evaluated by the Normalized Root-Mean-Square Error (NRMSE). RMSE is a frequently used measure which shows the differences between the predicted value by a model and the actual observed value. In results, the NRMSE is the RMSE divided by the standard deviation of the variable being predicted (See Formulas 5 and 6). Using R [18], the package hydroGOF [19] is used for calculation of NRMSE. The standard deviation is used for the normalizing the RMSE.

$$RMSE = \sqrt{\frac{\sum (\hat{Dt_i} - Dt_i)^2}{n_1}} \qquad (5)$$

$$NRMSE = 100 * \frac{RMSE}{\sigma} \qquad (6)$$

Where n_1 is the length of the predicted values, σ is the standard deviation of the predicted variable, Dt_i is the actual trip duration, and $\hat{Dt_i}$ is the predicted trip duration. Having the NRMSE for all the possible runs, the algorithm with the best NRMSE (the lowest one) is selected as the best algorithm for each taxi to be used at the meta-level.

Meta-level Evaluation. At the meta-level, the proposed model predicts a base-level algorithms along the level of granularity which will have the best performance (lowest NRMSE) for a given taxi and month. Therefore, the problem in this level is a classification problem. This decision is taken based on metafeatures describing the dataset characteristics.

The performance of the proposed model is evaluated by the accuracy of the prediction. In addition, we also evaluate the performance of the proposed model relative to the possible range of base-level performance. $Scaled_{error}$ shows the relative NRMSE of the metalearning model with respect to the best and the worst NRMSE of the base-level. It is shown in the following equation:

$$Scaled_{error} = \frac{NRMSE_{ML} - NRMSE_B}{NRMSE_W - NRMSE_B} \qquad (7)$$

Where $NRMSE_{ML}$ is the NRMSE of the proposed metalearning model, $NRMSE_B$ is the best NRMSE obtained by the base-level algorithms, and $NRMSE_W$ is the worst NRMSE obtained by the base-level algorithms. The range of $Scaled_{error}$ is between 0 and 1. In addition, the lower the $Scaled_{error}$ the better performance is expected for the meta-level experiment.

Metafeatures. The extracted metafeatures noted above, are described briefly in this section. A comprehensive study was done by Peng et al. [20] for feature selection. Totally 31 metafeatures were proposed to describe the structure of the dataset. These metafeatures are selected based on the regression problem. Their effectiveness through extensive experiments were evaluated. A list of all metafeatures that we used for this study with a brief description is provided in Table 1. The detail description of each metafeature is explained in [20].

Table 1. Extracted metafeatures used in metalearning

No.	Feature description
1	Number of examples
2	$log(10)$ of the number of examples
3	Number of attributes
4	Ratio of number of examples by number of attributes
5	$log(10)$ of the ratio of number of examples by number of attributes
6	Number of continuous attributes
7	Number of symbolic attributes
8	Number of binary attributes
9	Proportion of continuous attributes
10	Proportion of symbolic attributes
11	Proportion of binary attributes
12	Correlation between continuous attributes
13	Average absolute correlation between continuous attributes
14	Minimum absolute correlation between continuous attributes
15	Maximum absolute correlation between continuous attributes
16	The ratio between the standard deviation and the standard deviation of alpha trimmed mean
17	Number of continuous attributes with outliers
18	Proportion of continuous attributes with outliers
19	Correlation matrix between attributes and target
20	Average correlation continuous attribute/target
21	Minimum correlation continuous attribute/target
22	Maximum correlation continuous attribute/target
23	Check if standard deviation is larger than mean
24	Ratio of the standard deviation and the mean of the target attribute
25	Sparsity based on the coefficient of variation
26	Sparsity based on the absolute coefficient of variation
27	Standard deviation of the proportions of a histogram with 100 bins of target values
28	textith.outlier value, as calculated for the continuous attributes
29	Outlier detection based on the notion of outliers used for continuous attributes
30	Mean distance between each target value and its two neighbors (sorted by value)
31	Average mean distance between each target value and its two neighbors (sorted by value)

4   Results

4.1   Meta-level Results

The overall results of the calculated $Scaled_{error}$ for each month are shown in Fig. 2. The results seem interesting while the $Scaled_{error}$ is very low and near zero. It shows that the performance of the meta-level is close to the best performance obtained by the base-level.

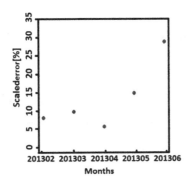

Fig. 2. The average $Scaled_{error}$ [%] over all taxis for each month

This result also illustrates the usefulness of using metalearning. By using the dataset characteristics, the metalearning can guess the algorithm with the best performance at the base-level that should be used. It reduces the cost of running several algorithms on probably large datasets to find the one with the best performance at the base-level.

The distribution of calculated $Scaled_{error}$ for each taxi is shown in Fig. 3. As we expected, the density concentrated around zero. This results show that the metalearning is useful because the results of metalearning are almost near the best performance obtained at the base-level. The normal distribution for RF and DT algorithms (black lines) show that on average the $Scaled_{error}$ is less than 0.2 in both cases. Although the density of $Scaled_{error}$ for RF algorithm has high concentration near the origin.

4.2   Base-level Results

To know the performance of the base-level, Fig. 4 shows the box-plot of calculated NRMSE for different taxis and in the different levels of granularity in each month. It can be seen that the NRMSE for all months is less than 5 %. The average NRMSE for each month is around 1 %. So the base-level error on average is 1 % which sounds considerably good. This means that the base-level algorithms can predict the trip duration very precisely.

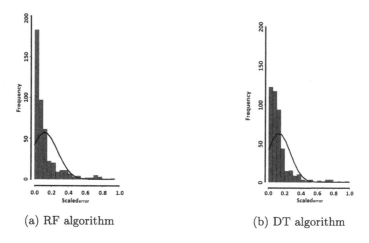

(a) RF algorithm   (b) DT algorithm

Fig. 3. Distribution of $Scaled_{error}$ over each taxi

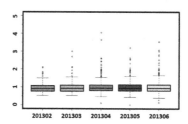

Fig. 4. NRMSE[%] for different months

4.3   Base-level vs. Meta-level Results

In metalearning one of the most important metric for evaluation is the accuracy. The comparison of accuracy between the base-level and the meta-level is presented in Fig. 5a. According to this result, the performance of the meta-level outperforms the base-level for most of the months. In April 2013, due to the lack of enough observations for calculating the metafeatures, the performance of metalearning is dropped.

The accuracy of the base-level is calculated based on the majority algorithm with the best performance at the base-level. Although, the accuracy of the metalearning is calculated by considering the algorithm with the best performance at the base-level. On average, the meta-level accuracy is 17 % higher than the base-level accuracy that can be converted to 39 % improvement on the base-level.

To obtain the algorithm with the best performance at the base-level, performing a lots of algorithms is required. Therefore, the computational cost is considerably high. But by using metalearning, the algorithm with the best performance is found by high probability and lower computational cost.

In addition, the prediction of the best algorithm by metalearning is almost followed the best algorithm obtained by the base-level (Fig. 5b).

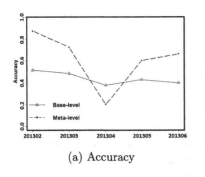

(a) Accuracy

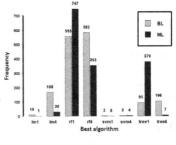

(b) The best performance algorithm

Fig. 5. Base-level (BL) vs. meta-level (ML)

5   Conclusion

We proposed the use of metalearning for prediction of trip duration. The experiments are performed on the taxi dataset from Drive-In project. The machine learning and data mining algorithms are performed at two different levels of granularity: taxi and month levels. The results show that the metalearning can help predicting the algorithm with the best performance at the base-level with high accuracy. Furthermore the performance of the base-level itself is also considerably applicable. Therefore, the overall results show that the metalearning predicts the trip duration with the error rate less than 5 %.

Acknowledgment. This work is financed by the ERDF - European Regional Development Fund through the COMPETE programme (operational programme for competitiveness) within project GNOSIS, cf. "FCOMP-01-0202-FEDER-038987". It is also funded by the North Portugal Regional Operational Programme (ON.2 – O Novo Norte), under the National Strategic Reference Framework (NSRF), through the European Regional Development Fund (ERDF), and by national funds, through the Portuguese funding agency, Fundação para a Ciência e a Tecnologia (FCT) through projects "NORTE-07-0124-FEDER-000057" and "NORTE-07-0124-FEDER-000059". The work is also financed by the ERDF – European Regional Development Fund through the COMPETE Programme (operational programme for competitiveness) and by National Funds through the FCT – Fundação para a Ciência e a Tecnologia (Portuguese Foundation for Science and Technology) within projects "FCOMP-01-0124-FEDER-037281" and "SFRH/BD/71438/2010". The research leading to these results has also received funding from the ECSEL Joint Undertaking, the framework programme for research and innovation horizon 2020 (2014–2020) under grant agreement n° 662189-MANTIS-2014-1.

References

1. Wolpert, D., Macready, W.: No free lunch theorems for optimization. IEEE Trans. Evol. Comput. **1**(1), 67–82 (1997)

2. Giraud-Carrier, C., Vilalta, R., Brazdil, P.: Introduction to the special issue on meta-learning. Mach. Learn. **54**(3), 187–193 (2004)
3. Brazdil, P., Giraud-carrier, C., Soares, C., Vilalta, R.: Metalearning: applications to data mining. In: Cognitive Technologies. Springer, Heidelberg (2009)
4. Cmuportugal.org: Drive-in: Distributed routing and infotainment through vehicular inter-networking (2014)
5. Kwon, J., Coifman, B., Bickel, P.: Day-to-day travel-time trends and travel-time prediction from loop-detector data. Transp. Res. Rec.: J. Transp. Res. Board **1717**(1), 120–129 (2000)
6. Chien, S.I.J., Kuchipudi, C.M.: Dynamic travel time prediction with real-time and historic data. J. Transp. Eng. **129**(6), 608–616 (2003)
7. Zhang, X., Rice, J.A.: Short-term travel time prediction. Transp. Res. Part C: Emerg. Technol. **11**(3), 187–210 (2003)
8. Wu, C.H., Ho, J.M., Lee, D.T.: Travel-time prediction with support vector regression. IEEE Trans. Intell. Transp. Syst. **5**(4), 276–281 (2004)
9. Balan, R.K., Nguyen, K.X., Jiang, L.: Real-time trip information service for a large taxi fleet. In: Proceedings of the 9th International Conference on Mobile Systems, Applications, and Services, MobiSys 2011, pp. 99–112. ACM, New York (2011)
10. Brazdil, P., Soares, C., Costa, J.D.: Ranking learning algorithms: using IBL and meta-learning on accuracy and time results. Mach. Learn. **50**, 251–277 (2003)
11. Rice, J.R.: The algorithm selection problem. In: Rubinoff, M., Yovits, M.C. (eds) Advances in Computers, vol. 15, pp. 65–118. Elsevier (1976)
12. Kodratoff, Y., Sleeman, D., Uszynski, M., Causse, K., Craw, S.: Building a machine learning toolbox (1992)
13. Rossi, A.L.D., de Leon Ferreira de Carvalho, A.C.P., Soares, C., de Souza, B.F.: MetaStream: a meta-learning based method for periodic algorithm selection in time-changing data. Neurocomputing **127**, 52–64 (2014)
14. Brodley, C.: Recursive automatic bias selection for classifier construction. Mach. Learn. **20**(1–2), 63–94 (1995)
15. Todorovski, L., Džeroski, S.: Combining classifiers with meta decision trees. Mach. Learn. **50**(3), 223–249 (2003)
16. Soares, C., Brazdil, P.B., Kuba, P.: A meta-learning method to select the kernel width in support vector regression. Mach. Learn. **54**(3), 195–209 (2004)
17. van Rijn, J.N., Holmes, G., Pfahringer, B., Vanschoren, J.: Algorithm selection on data streams. In: Džeroski, S., Panov, P., Kocev, D., Todorovski, L. (eds.) DS 2014. LNCS, vol. 8777, pp. 325–336. Springer, Heidelberg (2014)
18. R Core Team: R: A Language and Environment for Statistical Computing. R Foundation for Statistical Computing, Vienna, Austria (2014)
19. Zambrano-Bigiarini, M.: hydroGOF: Goodness-of-fit functions for comparison of simulated and observed hydrological time series (2014) R package version 0.3-8
20. Peng, Y.H., Flach, P.A., Soares, C., Brazdil, P.B.: Improved dataset characterisation for meta-learning. In: Lange, S., Satoh, K., Smith, C.H. (eds.) DS 2002. LNCS, vol. 2534, pp. 141–152. Springer, Heidelberg (2002)

Using Entropy as a Measure of Acceptance for Multi-label Classification

Laurence A.F. Park[✉] and Simeon Simoff

School of Computing, Engineering and Mathematics,
University of Western Sydney, New South Wales, Australia
{lapark,s.simoff}@uws.edu.au
http://www.scem.uws.edu.au/~lapark

Abstract. Multi-label classifiers allow us to predict the state of a set of responses using a single model. A multi-label model is able to make use of the correlation between the labels to potentially increase the accuracy of its prediction. Critical applications of multi-label classifiers (such as medical diagnoses) require that the system's confidence in prediction also be provided with the multi-label prediction. The specialist then uses the measure of confidence to assess whether to accept the system's prediction. Probabilistic multi-label classification provides a categorical distribution over the set of responses, allowing us to observe the distribution, select the most probable response, and obtain an indication of confidence by the shape of the distribution. In this article, we examine if normalised entropy, a parameter of the probabilistic multi-label response distribution, correlates with the accuracy of the prediction and therefore can be used to gauge confidence in the system's prediction. We found that for all three methods examined on each data set, the accuracy increases for the majority of the observations where the normalised entropy threshold decreases, showing that we can use normalised entropy to gauge a systems confidence, and hence use it as a measure of acceptance.

1 Introduction

Multi-label learning is the process of learning the association of L binary labels y of the response space, to a given point in a explanatory space x. A multi-label classifier may have a high dimensional explanatory space $\mathbb{R}^M$, and a high dimensional response space $\mathbb{B}^L$ (where $\mathbb{B}$ is $\{0, 1\}$), depending on the data. Therefore there may be many suitable responses for a given x, but only the most likely is provided as the predicted response. A review of multi-label learning is found in [5].

Critical applications of multi-label learning, such as medical diagnoses, military support or political decisions, require that multi-label predictions are accurate. Therefore it is essential that all predictions are paired with a measure of the multi-label system's confidence in its prediction. If the confidence is high, the specialist can accept the systems prediction. If the confidence is low, the specialist will not accept the prediction, but may also examine the cause of the low confidence.

© Springer International Publishing Switzerland 2015
E. Fromont et al. (Eds.): IDA 2015, LNCS 9385, pp. 217–228, 2015.
DOI: 10.1007/978-3-319-24465-5_19

Probabilistic multi-label learning is the process of assigning a categorical distribution over the $\mathbb{B}^L$ space for a given $\boldsymbol{x}$. Each of the 2^L elements $\boldsymbol{y}$ in the space $\mathbb{B}^L$ are assigned a probability. By examining the distribution, we can determine the most likely response to the input $\boldsymbol{x}$, and also examine if other response label sets have high probability, giving us confidence in the response and an indication of the relationship between the labels.

When many labels exist, it is difficult to examine and compare the distribution over the 2^L label combinations. It is also not always simple to determine a system's confidence by observing the response distribution. Therefore it would be useful to summarise the distribution with a parameter that can be used to measure a system's confidence of its prediction.

In this article, we examine if the accuracy of a probabilistic multi-label system's response is correlated to a parameter of the response distribution. We hypothesise that the normalised entropy of the response distribution will provide us with a measure of confidence. The contributions of this article are:

- a discussion on the use of normalised entropy of the response distribution to assess prediction accuracy (Sect. 3),
- an analysis of the relationship between accuracy and normalised entropy for probabilistic multi-label classification (Sect. 4), and
- a probabilistic version of the label powerset multi-label classifier (Sect. 2.3)

The article will proceed as follows: In Sect. 2 we examine the concept of probabilistic multi-label learning and examine three models for computing the joint distribution over the powerset of labels. Section 3 discusses the use of the response distribution to assess the accuracy of the predicted response label set. Finally, Sect. 4 empirically examines the relationship between normalised entropy and accuracy of a response.

2   Probabilistic Multi-label Learning

For a given input space $\mathbb{R}^M$ and a set of L labels l_i, a probabilistic multi-label classifier learns the probability distribution over the powerset of labels $\mathbb{B}^L$. A probabilistic multi-label classifier maps an input vector $\boldsymbol{x} \in \mathbb{R}^M$ to a categorical probability distribution $\theta \in \mathbb{S}^{2^L}$, where $\mathbb{S}^{2^L}$ is the 2^L dimensional simplex. Using the categorical distribution, we can identify the probability of each label set being the correct response to $\boldsymbol{x}$

$$\theta_i = P(\boldsymbol{y}_i | \boldsymbol{x}) \tag{1}$$

where $\boldsymbol{x}$ is the input vector to be classified, $\boldsymbol{y}_i$ is the ith element in the powerset of labels $\mathbb{B}^L$, and θ_i is the probability that $\boldsymbol{y}_i$ is the correct label set of $\boldsymbol{x}$. For example, given the three labels, l_1, l_2 and l_3 and an input vector $\boldsymbol{x}$, a probabilistic multi-label classifier will provide a distribution over the eight elements of the powerset shown in Table 1, where $\sum_{i=1}^{2^L} \theta_i = 1$.

Table 1. The powerset elements y_i of the labels l_1, l_2 and l_3, and the associated probability θ_i of each label set computed by the probabilistic multi-label learner.

y_i	{}	$\{l_1\}$	$\{l_2\}$	$\{l_3\}$	$\{l_1,l_2\}$	$\{l_1,l_3\}$	$\{l_2,l_3\}$	$\{l_1,l_2,l_3\}$
$P(y_i\|x_j)$	θ_1	θ_2	θ_3	θ_4	θ_5	θ_6	θ_7	θ_8

Constructing a probabilistic multi-label classifier is equivalent to modelling the joint distribution of labels, conditioned on the input x:

$$P(l_1, l_2, \ldots, l_L | x) = P(y_i | x) \tag{2}$$

We will now examine probabilistic forms of three common multi-label classifiers.

2.1 Probabilistic Binary Relevance

The simplest form of probabilistic multi-label classifier, called Probabilistic Binary Relevance (PBR), treats each of the labels as independent of each other, giving us:

$$P(l_1, l_2, \ldots, l_L | x) = \prod_{i=1}^{L} P(l_i | x) \tag{3}$$

The task is then simplified to learning the probabilities $P(l_i|x)$ for each label i. This independence assumption ignores any correlation between labels and so is equivalent to constructing L independent probabilistic binary classifiers.

2.2 Ensemble of Probabilistic Classifier Chains

Rather than assuming independence, the joint probability can be expressed in terms of a product of conditional probabilities:

$$P(l_1, l_2, \ldots, l_L | x) = P(l_1 | x) \prod_{i=2}^{L} P(l_i | l_{i-1}, \ldots, l_1 x) \tag{4}$$

This form of joint probability decomposition is known as a probabilistic classifier chain [2]. When learning the conditional probabilities from data, the joint probability becomes dependent on the label order. To remove this dependence, it was suggested that an ensemble of probabilistic classifier chains (EPCC) be used, where each of the classifier chains is constructed using a randomised ordering of labels.

2.3 Probabilistic Label Powerset Using Pairwise Coupling

The Label Powerset multi-label classifier has one binary classifier for each label combination, meaning if there are L labels, then at most 2^L binary classifiers

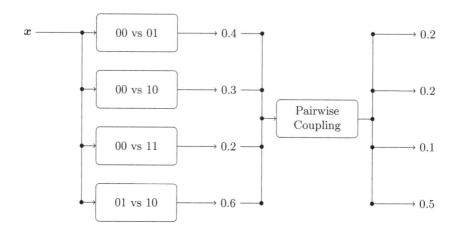

Fig. 1. A Label Powerset multi-label classifier using a set of probabilistic binary classifiers computes the Bernoulli distribution for each label. Pairwise coupling must be used to obtain the categorical distribution over the label set.

are required. If we replace the binary classifiers with probabilistic binary classifiers (as done with the previous two methods), we would compute the probability of the given response, independent of all other responses. This means that Label Powerset using probabilistic binary classifiers will provide us with a set of Bernoulli responses rather than a categorical distribution, and hence not provide us with the joint probability. The Bernoulli responses show the probability that the given label set is true and the probability that the given label set false, meaning that the probability of the other label sets are not taken into account. To obtain the joint probability over all label sets, we must compute the probability of a given response, with respect to the probability of all other responses.

To compute the categorical distribution over the powerset of labels, we use multi-class Pairwise Coupling [3] of the powerset of labels. Note that, we can compute the multi-label joint distribution using any probabilistic multi-class method over the 2^L label combinations; we chose Pairwise Coupling because it allows us to construct the probabilistic multi-label classifier using a collection of probabilistic binary classifiers.

The Pairwise Coupling model (Fig. 1) requires that we train a binary classifier for all *pairs* of label combinations. Each binary classifier allows us to fit a Bernoulli random variable, therefore, for each probabilistic binary classifier, we obtain $p_{i,j}$, the probability of state i being correct and $\bar{p}_{i,j} = 1 - p_{i,j}$, the probability of state j being correct. The set of all pairwise probabilities are then coupled to obtain the complete joint distribution using the following method.

Given each element of a categorical distribution θ_k with $k \in \{1, 2, \ldots, 2^L\}$ states, the probability of being in one state, relative to another is given by:

$$p_{i,j} = \frac{\theta_i}{\theta_i + \theta_j} \tag{5}$$

This gives us at most $\sum_{i=1}^{2^L-1} i = 2^{L-1}(2^L - 1)$ pairwise probabilities to compute the 2^L probabilities of the categorical distribution θ. We find the set of 2^L categorical probabilities θ_k as the categorical distribution that provides the best fit of Eq. 5 for all k and j using the algorithm from [3]. If the training data contains u unique label combinations, then the joint model will compute only $u(u-1)/2$ pairwise probabilities. Therefore the computation required for the joint model is dependent on the number of unique label combinations available at training time.

Note that each pairwise binary classifier is trained at training time, but the categorical distribution is dependent on the given observations x, therefore the coupling is performed during the prediction stage. The pairwise coupling method requires a large number of binary classifiers to perform prediction, but we must remember that each classifier is trained using a subset of the data (only those objects that are associated to the selected pair of label sets for each pairwise classifier), speeding up the training process.

3   Examining the Label Set Distribution

When performing binary classification, it is enough to present the results of the classification as the probability of the class with greatest probability. Once this probability is known, we are able to deduce the probability of the other class. If the probability is close to 0.5, then the classification system has low confidence in its decision. If the probability is close to 1.0, then the classification system has high confidence in its decision.

Multi-label classification consists of many combinations of labels which are all assigned a probability. By reporting only the probability of the label set of greatest probability, we are providing little information to the user. A label set with probability close to 1.0 implies that the system is confident in its prediction, but unlike binary classification, a lower probability has little meaning unless we have the rest of the distribution to compare it to.

The shape of the class distribution gives us a measure of confidence in the predicted results, which is very useful information to any practitioner. For example, let's consider a multi-label problem with only two labels, where the distribution over the four combinations of labels is $\{0.31, 0.3, 0.29, 0.1\}$ for a given value of x. If our system predicted the most likely label combination, without providing us with the class distribution, we would accept the result without second thought, which is likely to lead to incorrect predictions. We can see from the distribution that the second and third most probable label sets have similar probability to the label set with the largest probability. This means that there is high uncertainty in the class of x. The label set distribution provided by our system for each sample, allows us to compare the probability of each possible response. This in turn allows us to make a judgement on whether we accept the most likely response as the prediction.

We would expect that a system, very confident in its decision, would provide a label set distribution containing one label set with probability 1 and the remaining label sets with probability 0. A system with no confidence would provide equal probability for all label sets. All other probability combinations would provide varying levels of confidence between these two bounds. If we need to quantitatively measure the confidence level provided by a label set distribution, we can measure the entropy of the distribution:

$$H = - \sum_{\boldsymbol{y}_i \in \mathbb{B}^L} P(\boldsymbol{y}_i) \log \left(P(\boldsymbol{y}_i) \right) \qquad (6)$$

which measures the uncertainty provided by the label set distribution [4] ($H = 0$ means no uncertainty), where $0 \times \log(0) = 0$. The range of H depends on the number of label sets in our multi-label problem. To adjust the range to $[0, 1]$, we can use normalised entropy:

$$H^\star = - \sum_{\boldsymbol{y}_i \in \mathbb{B}^L} P(\boldsymbol{y}_i) \frac{\log \left(P(\boldsymbol{y}_i) \right)}{\log \left(2^L \right)} \qquad (7)$$

where $H^\star = 1$ is provided when the probability of all class combinations are equal.

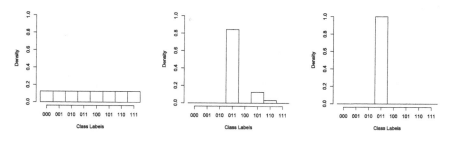

Fig. 2. Multi-label distributions with normalised entropy ($H^\star$) of 1 (left), 0.5 (centre) and 0 (right). In this case there are three labels and hence eight label combinations.

Figure 2 shows us examples of distributions and their entropy (using base e). Note that the only distribution to provide a normalised entropy of 1 assigns all elements with equal probability (as shown in the left plot of Fig. 2). A normalised entropy of 0.5 implies that one item has a much greater probability than the others (as in the centre plot of Fig. 2). Also, an entropy of 0 implies that one element has probability 1, with the remaining elements having probability 0 (shown in the right plot of Fig. 2).

Note that the measure of entropy is used to identify a systems confidence in its response, but it should not be used to measure the quality of a set of systems without regard to the systems' accuracy. For example a system that provides high levels of entropy for all responses is not worse than a system that provides low levels of entropy. If both systems happen to have a low accuracy, then the former may be preferred over the latter.

4   Using Entropy as a Measure of Acceptance

We introduced the topic of measuring uncertainty using the normalised entropy of the multi-label distribution in Sect. 3. In this section, we will examine if entropy is correlated to accuracy. Our reasoning is:

- If a portion of the sample space can easily be classified, there is little uncertainty in the results and hence the entropy of the multi-label distribution will be low. Low uncertainty also implies that any future predictions should be accurate, meaning that low entropy corresponds to high accuracy.
- If a portion of the sample space is difficult to classify, there will be high uncertainty in the results and hence the entropy of the multi-label distribution will be high. This high uncertainty implies that future predictions are not likely to be correct, meaning that high entropy corresponds to low accuracy.

In this section, we will first describe the data and multi-label models used. We will then examine the relationship of probabilistic multi-label entropy to accuracy.

4.1   Experimental Environment

To perform our investigation, we will use the set of probabilistic multi-label classifiers presented in Sect. 2: Probabilistic Label Powerset (PLP), Probabilistic Binary Relevance (PBR), and Ensemble of Probabilistic Classifier Chains (EPCC). Each of the methods require the use of a set of binary classifiers that provide a probability measure of its associated label set prediction. In each of our experiments, we use Support Vector Machines with a Radial Basis kernel, where the probabilities were estimated using a Laplace prior [1]. The kernel parameter was kept at the default value of $1/m$, where m is the number of explanatory variables for each observation. The SVM cost parameter for each binary classifier was tuned using 2 shuffle, 5 fold cross-validation on the training data.

The number of probabilistic binary classifiers required for each method is shown in Table 2. We find that the Probabilistic Binary Relevance classifier uses the least number of binary classifiers, while Probabilistic Label Powerset is expected to use the most.

We chose the three data sets shown in Table 3 to perform our analysis; two that are commonly used in multi-label research (Emotions and Scene) and the third from the STARE project[1] (the set of diagnoses from a set of retinal images).

---

[1] http://www.ces.clemson.edu/~ahoover/stare/.

Table 2. The number of binary classifiers used by each probabilistic multi-label classifier, where n is the number of binary response variables, u is the number of unique label combinations of response variables within the training data, and e is ensemble size.

Method	Binary classifiers
PBR	n
PLP	$u(u-1)/2$
EPCC	en

Table 3. The data sets used to examine the probabilistic multi-label methods in this article.

Name	Items	Train	Test	Features	Labels	Avg label card	Uniq label comb
Emotions	593	250	343	72	6	1.8685	27
Scene	2407	1211	1196	294	6	1.0740	15
Stare	373	200	173	44	15	1.3217	42

The Stare data contains medical diagnoses, where the confidence of prediction is essential and so is a perfect candidate for this research. Note that these data sets are relatively small, but to perform our analysis, we require results for each of the three probabilistic multi-label methods. The Probabilistic Label Powerset method requires $42 \times 41/2 = 861$ binary classifiers for the Stare data set, which consumes most of the CPU time and memory on a modern computer. Therefore it would be difficult to obtain results for larger data sets.

To give perspective on each method, we have presented the training and testing times for each on each data set in Table 4.

Table 4. The time taken in seconds, for training the model and predicting the state of one object for each method on the Emotions, Stare and Scene data sets.

Methods	Emotions		Stare		Scene	
	Train	Test	Train	Test	Train	Test
PBR	25.51	0.01	21.85	0.96	1147.03	0.02
PLP	101.06	0.66	275.38	3.01	724.75	2.24
EPCC	76.96	0.30	198.38	19.68	3443.75	1.61

To evaluate the classification accuracy of the models, we report results using the 0/1 loss function (if the system returns the correct label set as the most likely label set, it is correct, otherwise it is incorrect). We also examined the use of Hamming and Jaccard similarity for partial matching of labels and found the results to be similar to those reported using the 0/1 loss function.

4.2   Experiment

We computed the normalised entropy for each test sample in each of our three data sets for all three methods. We then examined the accuracy when only considering the k observations from the test set with the lowest response distribution entropy. We expected that when considering the mean accuracy of the chosen k observations, the score should decrease as k increases (since increasing k introduces observations with greater response entropy into the mean calculation). The results of this experiment are shown in Figs. 3, 4 and 5 for data sets Emotion, Scene and Stare respectively. Note that k is labelled "Decisions made" in the set of plots, since k can be likened to an entropy threshold in which a practitioner accepts the prediction of the system (makes a decision) when the response distribution is lower than the threshold, while the remainder are discarded as untrustworthy.

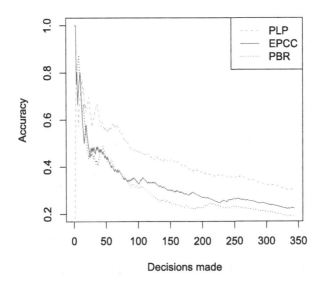

Fig. 3. Using normalised entropy as a measure of prediction acceptance for the Emotion data.

The lines in these plots were computed by ordering all of the test observations in order of their normalised entropy. The Accuracy is then computed as the mean of the accuracies of the observation with lowest entropy, the lowest and second lowest, the lowest to third lowest, and so on, until the final value is the mean of all accuracies. Computing the mean in this way causes the first portion of the plot to be jittery since the mean is computed using a small number of samples. As the sample size increases the plot smooths out. The varying number of decisions made in each of the plots is due to the number of observations available in the associated data test sets.

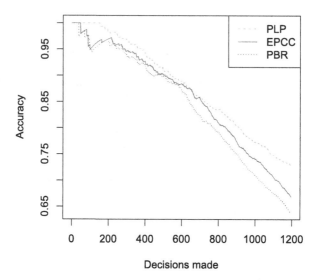

Fig. 4. Using normalised entropy as a measure of prediction acceptance for the Scene data.

4.3   Analysis of Results

The plots show the accuracy, ordered by normalised entropy of the response distribution. An increase in the plot line towards an accuracy of 1 means that an accurate prediction was made, a decrease in the line towards an accuracy of 0 means an inaccurate prediction was made. An optimal measure of system confidence would have a plot where the line stays at 1 (placing all of the accurate predictions first), followed by a decrease (placing all of the inaccurate predictions last).

We find that PLP and EPCC have some inaccurate predictions with low normalised entropy (shown by the initial zig-zagging), but then smoothly decrease just after the 50 mark. PBR has the initial zig-zagging but then dips at about the 170 mark, showing a poor ordering of accuracy. The Scene data shows a desired curve from PLP (flat then decreasing), where EPCC and PBR have some initial zig-zagging, but then a decreasing slope. We also find that each of the three methods begin with an initial zig-zag and then gradually decrease for the Stare data.

The general shape of the curves for each plot (flat and then decreasing) show that normalised entropy is a good candidate for measuring confidence of a systems prediction. The variance between methods and plots is due to the different methods used to compute the joint distribution and their behaviour on each data set. We also see from the plots that by accepting only those predictions that had low normalised entropy, the mean accuracy of accepted predictions is increased by a significant margin for all methods on all data sets. Therefore normalised entropy can be used as a measure of acceptance for probabilistic multi-label classification.

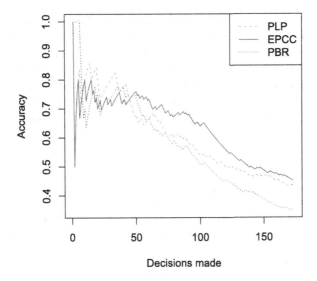

Fig. 5. Using normalised entropy as a measure of prediction acceptance for the Stare data.

Note that the usefulness of normalised entropy as a measure of acceptance is dependent on the accuracy of the system. If we generated random response distributions, some may have low normalised entropy, but also be inaccurate. Therefore a specialist needs to first choose an appropriate probabilistic multi-label classifier for their data before normalised entropy can be used.

For most of the data sets, there is little difference in accuracy between methods at the low "Decisions made" end of the plots. This is likely to be due to a small sample of points that are simple to classify and hence an independent multi-label classifier is good enough to accurately classify these. The simplicity of their classification would also imply that their multi-label distributions would have low entropy.

5 Conclusion

Multi-label classification allows us to predict the response of many labels at once, using the correlation between the labels to hopefully improve the prediction accuracy. Critical applications of multi-label learning (such as those used in health, military and government) require that predictions are paired with a measure of confidence in the prediction. Probabilistic multi-label classification provides us with a conditional categorical distribution over the powerset of labels, providing us with an indication of confidence. Unfortunately, it is not always obvious what confidence the system has by observing this distribution. Therefore a single measure of confidence would be useful for specialists using this system.

In this article, we presented a method of determining a probabilistic multi-label system's confidence in its prediction using normalised entropy. We examined correlation of three popular probabilistic multi-label classification method's accuracy with normalised entropy, and found that all three provided a general increase accuracy as the normalised entropy decision threshold reduced. This result shows that we can gauge a systems confidence in its prediction by examining the normalised entropy of the predicted label set distribution.

References

1. Chang, C.C., Lin, C.J.: Libsvm: a library for support vector machines. ACM Trans. Intell. Syst. Technol. (TIST) **2**(3), 27 (2011)
2. Dembczyński, K., Waegeman, W., Cheng, W., Hüllermeier, E.: On label dependence and loss minimization in multi-label classification. Mach. Learn. **88**(1–2), 5–45 (2012)
3. Hastie, T., Tibshirani, R.: Classification by pairwise coupling. In: Proceedings of the 1997 Conference on Advances in Neural Information Processing Systems 10, NIPS 1997, pp. 507–513. MIT Press, Cambridge (1998)
4. Shannon, C.E.: A mathematical theory of communication. Bell Syst. Tech. J. **27**, 379–423 (1948)
5. Zhang, M., Zhou, Z.: A review on multi-label learning algorithms. IEEE Trans. Knowl. Data Eng. **26**(8), 1819–1837 (2013)

Investigation of Node Deletion Techniques for Clustering Applications of Growing Self Organizing Maps

Thilina Rathnayake[1]([✉]), Maheshakya Wijewardena[1], Thimal Kempitiya[1],
Kevin Rathnasekara[1], Thushan Ganegedara[1], Amal S. Perera[1],
and Damminda Alahakoon[2]

[1] Department of Computer Science and Engineering, University of Moratuwa,
Moratuwa, Sri Lanka
thilinarmtb.10@cse.mrt.ac.lk
[2] La Trobe Business School, College of Arts, Social Sciences and Commerce,
La Trobe University, Bundoora, VIC, Australia

Abstract. Self Organizing Maps (SOM) are widely used in data mining and high-dimensional data visualization due to its unsupervised nature and robustness. Growing Self Organizing Maps (GSOM) is a variant of SOM algorithm which allows nodes to be grown so that it can represent the input space better. Without using a fixed 2D grid like SOM, GSOM starts with four nodes and keeps track of the quantization error in each node. New nodes are grown from an existing node if its error value exceeds a pre-defined threshold. Ability of the GSOM algorithm to represent input space accurately is vital to extend its applicability to a wider spectrum of problems. This ability can be improved by identifying nodes that represent low probability regions in the input space and removing them periodically from the map. This will improve the homogeneity and completeness of the final clustering result. A new extension to GSOM algorithm based on node deletion is proposed in this paper as a solution to this problem. Furthermore, two new algorithms inspired by cache replacement policies are presented. First algorithm is based on Adaptive Replacement Cache (ARC) and maintains two separate Least Recently Used (LRU) lists of the nodes. Second algorithm is built on Frequency Based Replacement policy (FBR) and maintains a single LRU list. These algorithms consider both recent and frequent trends in the GSOM grid before deciding on the nodes to be deleted. The experiments conducted suggest that the FBR based method for node deletion outperforms the standard algorithm and other existing node deletion methods.

1 Introduction

SOM algorithm invented by Kohonen [7] is a popular technique in unsupervised learning due to its wide applicability. SOM is a dimensionality reduction technique that maps high dimensional data into a 2D grid of nodes. Each node i in the 2D grid has an associated weight vector W_i (with the same dimension as the

© Springer International Publishing Switzerland 2015
E. Fromont et al. (Eds.): IDA 2015, LNCS 9385, pp. 229–240, 2015.
DOI: 10.1007/978-3-319-24465-5_20

input data) and represents a region V_i in the input space where all the points in V_i are closer to W_i than any other weight vector in the 2D grid [7]. Before training the SOM algorithm, size of the 2D neuron grid has to be specified. User needs to have knowledge of the structure of the training data in advance to make a reasonable estimate of the size of the grid to be used. Several tests might be required to identify a suitable grid size that best represents the given input data. Main drawback handled by GSOM algorithm is overcoming such constrained learning requirements found in SOM algorithm.

Growing Self Organizing Map (GSOM) introduced by Alahakoon et al. [1] is an unsupervised learning algorithm which has been successfully employed in knowledge discovery problems and can be considered as one of the successful structure adapting models based on SOM. GSOM is a dynamic variant of SOM that has the ability to adapt to the distribution and structure of training data and provides a set of parameters to control the granularity of the clusters to be formed. GSOM can be successfully used for hierarchical clustering by starting with coarse grain clusters and generating fine grain clusters out of them. Apart from extending SOM algorithm to eliminate time-consuming testing required for parameter estimation, GSOM has a number of advantages compared to other dynamic SOMs [1].

GSOM starts with a grid of four initial nodes and grows additional nodes to adjust the grid according to the input data distribution. This is done by keeping track of quantization error for each node and then growing new nodes from existing nodes that accumulate a high quantization error (See Fig. 1). High quantization error in a node i is an indicator that the associated region V_i in input space is underrepresented by that node. So the new nodes are grown from node i to produce a more detailed representation of the region V_i. This approach avoids the necessity to specify the grid size in advance and also removes the restriction for the final arrangement of nodes to be rectangular, thus allowing the nodes to adapt to a shape that best reflects the input data space. Normally, during the node growth, maximum possible number of new nodes are grown from a node depending on the degree of freedom of the node (degree of freedom of a node can be any value between 0 and 3 inclusive) as it is computationally expensive to identify the best new node to be grown out of a given node [1].

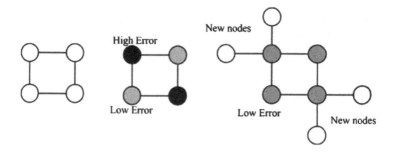

Fig. 1. Node growth in GSOM

Applicability of GSOM for a particular task depends on how accurately it maps the input space into the output space (2D grid of nodes). In general, input space can be non-convex, discontinuous and can contain high dimensional clusters [3]. However, the final outcome of GSOM algorithm is a fully connected structure and thus it is incapable of identifying discontinuities in the input space. Also, some of the newly created nodes that represent low probability regions in the input space can affect homogeneity in the final clustering outcome of GSOM. Hence, deleting these *poorly-formed* nodes is essential for attaining more accurate clustering of input data with GSOM.

The graph in Fig. 2 was obtained by running GSOM algorithm on iris dataset from UCI machine learning library [2]. The graph shows the number of nodes having a particular hit count (hit count is the number of times a node in the 2D grid becoming the closest node to an input vector while training. Training procedure of the GSOM algorithm is described in detail under the section *GSOM*). It can be seen that most of the nodes have never become a winner.

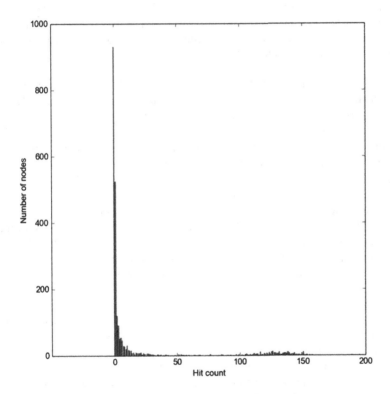

Fig. 2. Hit count frequency

An appropriate technique should be introduced to identify the *poorly-formed* nodes. Fritzke [4] has invented a method for deleting nodes by estimating the probability of the input space represented by a node. Nodes representing an input space with estimated probability approximately equal to zero are deleted. Also Blackmore and Miikkulainen [3] have come up with a deletion mechanism for the connections between nodes based on a threshold value. In this paper, two variations of node deletion mechanisms inspired by cache replacement algorithms are presented.

The rest of the paper is organized as follows. First, the related work is discussed and then the new methodologies for node deletion are explained. Next, experimental results are presented and finally the paper concludes with the conclusion.

2   Related Work

2.1   GSOM

GSOM algorithm mainly operates in three phases, namely *initialization phase*, *growing phase* and *smoothing phase*. These phases are run sequentially. The parameters of the GSOM algorithm are discussed below. These parameters are used in the growing phase and smoothing phase of the algorithm and can be adjusted separately for each of the two phases.

- **N_ITER:** Number of iterations the algorithm make through the input data set. During each iteration, complete input data set is fed to the algorithm. Ordering of the input presentation is irrelevant.
- **SF:** The spread factor. This parameter controls the growth of nodes in the 2D map. Thus, this can be used to control the spread of the 2D grid of nodes. A high spread factor creates a large number of nodes where as a low spread factor creates a small number of nodes. Value of spread factor should be a non zero number between 0 and 1.
- **NS:** Initial neighbourhood size or neighbourhood radius. For each input vector, weight values of some of the vectors in 2D map will be adjusted and this parameter controls the number of nodes to be included in weight adjustment.
- **LR:** Initial learning rate. This controls the amount of weight value adaptation of the vectors in a neighbourhood for a particular input vector.

1. Initialization phase
   (a) Initialize the 2D map with a set of nodes (usually 4) with their weights set to random numbers (See Fig. 1) (Other methods instead of random initialization exist as well. e.g. PCA).
   (b) Calculate the Growth threshold (GT) for the given data set depending on user requirements. Growth threshold $(GT) = -D \times \ln SF$. Here the value of spread factor is set by the user.
2. Growing phase
   (a) Feed an input vector to the grid.
   (b) Determine the weight vector that is closest to the current input. That is, find the closest quantized vector in the current grid to the presented input vector. Any distance metric defined on both the input space and

mapped space (grid) can be used to find the distance between the input and quantized vectors. Most commonly used metric is the Euclidean distance. The quantized vector which minimizes the metric is selected as the winner for that particular input vector.

(c) Increase the error value of the winner by the difference between input vector and winner. Difference (distance) is calculated by a distance metric like Euclidean distance.

(d) Then the weight vector adaptation takes place in the winner and neighbourhood of the winner determined by neighbourhood size, **NS**. Neighbourhood size is reduced exponentially (or linearly) during the process of presenting input to the grid. Even within a neighbourhood, vectors that are closer to winner are affected more by weight adjustment than those at further.

(e) If $TE_i \geq GT$, then grow nodes if i is a boundary node, else distribute error to neighbours of i. Here TE_i is the total accumulated error of the current winner node i (See Fig. 1).

(f) New node weights are initialized based on the topology of the map, i.e., based on the number of immediate neighbours of the new node and their position.

(g) Repeat steps **a–f** for all input vectors.

(h) Repeat steps **a–g N_ITER** times.

3. Smoothing phase

(a) Reduce learning rate and fix a small starting neighbourhood size.

(b) Find winner and adapt the weights of the winner and neighbours in the same way as in growing phase.

2.2   Fritzke's Method

A probabilistic method for node deletion has been invented by Bernd Fritzke based on the probability estimation $P(V_i)$ of the input space V_i represented by a node i [4]. If the probability $P(V_i)$ is approximately zero, the associated node i can be deleted since it does not hold adequate information about the input space and does not contribute to the quality of the output of the algorithm. If node i represents such a zero probability region, then chances of node i becoming the winner will be very low. Hence it can be concluded that the longer a node i was not a winner, it is more likely to represent a zero probability region in the input space. A single metric derived from this observation has been used by Fritzke to decide on the nodes that should be deleted.

In Fritzke's method, number of input vectors presented to the SOM grid is counted and in each node in the grid, the number of the last input for which the node became the winner is stored. Then a metric called k_{remove} is calculated periodically and used to decide which nodes to be deleted. If the difference between the current input vector count and the number stored in a node exceeds k_{remove}, the node is deleted. The value of k_{remove} is calculated using a probabilistic approach depending on the number of nodes in the SOM grid, average number of input vectors need to be presented to trigger the generation of one new node and a user specified confidence (probability) value (p_{sure}).

Frequency of a node becoming a winner is not considered in this approach and can be considered as a drawback of the method. A particular node in the grid can become a winner frequently at the early stages of training and not so often in the latter stages due to the order of input data presented to the algorithm. Although this node may be a candidate for deletion under Fritzkes algorithm, it is not a good idea to delete a node which had a relatively high frequency of becoming a winner as it may represent a region in the input space which was encountered in an earlier period during the presentation of the input dataset. It is not uncommon for similar data items to appear together in real world datasets.

2.3   Blackmore and Miikkulainen's Method

Blackmore and Miikkulainen [3] have proposed an incremental algorithm based on feature maps for unsupervised learning. A method based on a threshold value to delete connections between the nodes has also been suggested to enhance the capability of feature maps to represent more diverse and complex input spaces. Algorithm starts with four initial nodes as in GSOM and adds nodes in the perimeter area of the grid where the corresponding input area is not adequately represented. Connection between a pair of nodes is deleted when the Euclidean distance between the two nodes grow beyond a predetermined threshold.

It is important to notice that in this method, nodes themselves are not deleted but only the connection between the nodes are deleted. But in GSOM, the notion of connection is bound to the position of a node in the 2D grid and there are no separate connections between the nodes. Two nodes are automatically connected if they are an unit distance apart from each another i.e., if they are horizontally or vertically adjacent. So a method based on deleting connections rather than the nodes themselves cannot be used in GSOM.

3   Methodology

Two node deletion algorithms based on cache algorithms which take both the frequency and recency of a node becoming a winner into consideration are proposed to overcome the drawbacks of Fritzke's method. This is the main improvement introduced in this paper. By considering both frequency and recency, the new algorithms are capable of identifying both the frequent and recent changes in the 2D grid of nodes and delete *poorly-formed* nodes considering this new information. The proposed algorithms are based on two different caching algorithms.

Caching is used in computing for speeding up the response time for information (or data) requests. Normally, results from previous calculations that may be used in future or duplicate copies of data are stored in a cache. If a requested item is found in cache (i.e., a cache hit), it can be served quickly. If the requested item is not found (i.e., a cache miss), data needs to be brought in from their original location or certain calculations will have to be carried out before the request is served. In case of a cache miss, it will be more efficient to store these new (calculated or brought) items in the cache due to locality of reference.

Since caches have limited capacity, it is not possible to store items related to all the past requests. A suitable cache item replacing policy should be implemented to decide which items in the cache should be replaced in order to find space for the new items. These policies are known as cache algorithms (cache replacing policies) and there are a considerable number of algorithms developed for different types of applications [6,8,10]. These algorithms use certain metrics (reference counts, last access time, etc.) to find the most suitable item currently residing in the cache for replacement.

Although there is no restriction in GSOM for the number of nodes in the grid, identifying the *poorly-formed* nodes is essential for node deletion. If these *poorly-formed* nodes can be identified, they can be removed periodically during the training period of the algorithm. So the same policies used by the cache algorithms to identify least *important* items can be used in GSOM to identify the *poorly-formed* nodes.

As mentioned above, removal of an item in the cache is triggered when the cache size is too small to accommodate the new items brought into the cache during the cache misses. One of the basic ideas behind GSOM is to automatically find a suitable grid size for input data distribution rather than user having to specify it manually. So in the case of GSOM, the decision of when the *poorly-formed* nodes should be removed must be taken without adding restrictions on the size of the nodes in the grid. Hence the algorithms presented in this paper periodically checks for the nodes which rank poorly according to the used cache policy and remove them from the grid. This removal is not triggered by a size limit but done periodically (for example, after completing one training epoch). Cache policy is used to decide which nodes to be deleted. Two algorithms were implemented based on the cache policies used by Adaptive Replacement Cache (ARC) [8] and Frequency Based Replacement (FBR) [10] cache.

3.1   Node Deletion Based on ARC

The ARC is a self-tuning, low-overhead algorithm that responds on-line to changing access patterns [8]. ARC adapts itself between frequency and recency of an element becoming a cache hit. ARC detects the most important access pattern out of frequency and recency and remove elements to support current access pattern. ARC can be implemented using two lists.

Two Least Recently Used (LRU) lists, L_1 and L_2 are used by ARC [8]. Items that have been seen only once (recent items) are held in L_1 and items that have been seen at least twice (frequent items) are held in L_2. These lists do not have fixed capacities (number of items that can be kept in the list) and are adaptive subject to two conditions, $|L_1| < c$ and $|L_1| + |L_2| < 2c$ where c is the maximum capacity of L_1.

A very simplified version of the algorithm used in ARC can be stated as follows. In case of a cache miss, brought in (or calculated) new items are inserted at the start of L_1 and then gradually pushed to the back of L_1 when more and more new items enter L_1. In case of a cache hit, any item in L_1 or L_2 that is referenced once again is moved to the front of L_2 and gradually pushed back in when more and more re-referenced items enter L_2. Cache replacement policy of ARC is based on the total capacity of the cache (combined capacity of L_1 and L_2) and the capacity of L_1. If L_1 is at its maximum capacity, LRU element in L_1 is replaced, otherwise if the total capacity of the cache is at its maximum, LRU element of L_2 is replaced.

During the experiments, two LRU lists were maintained with references (position of the node in the 2D grid) for nodes in the current GSOM grid. A node was inserted to L_1 when it became the winner for the first time. Cache hits and misses were handled similar to the above technique. No size restrictions were imposed on the two lists L_1 and L_2 to ensure that the natural growth of the grid was not hindered; instead the *poorly-formed* nodes identified based on the cache policy were removed periodically (after each full training iteration).

3.2   Node Deletion Based on FBR

Another approach for node deletion using a cache based on FBR was experimented. Unlike ARC, there is only one list. Information about frequency of a node becoming a winner is maintained using a counter called reference counter. Recency of an item becoming a cache hit is maintained by partitioning cache list into three separate sections called new, middle and old (See Fig. 3). These sections are maintained by using references for new boundary and old boundary. Reference count and the section of an item in the cache can be used to decide which item should be replaced when the cache is full.

Length of each section is a parameter of the algorithm and it is up to the user to decide the length of each section. In our adaptation, the lengths were stated as fractions of the total length, thus avoiding the need to specify a cache size. One obvious selection for the lengths is to use equal sizes for the three lists i.e., first 1/3 of the cache is allocated for the new section, second 1/3 for the middle section and the rest for the old section.

FBR algorithm works as follows. In case of a cache miss, the missing item is brought into the cache and placed in the beginning of the new section with the reference count initialized to one. FBR uses a concept called "factoring out locality" for reference counts [10]. Unlike most of the cache algorithms which use a reference count, in FBR count is not incremented when an item in the

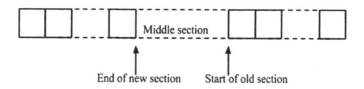

Fig. 3. FBR cache

new section becomes a hit. Reference count is incremented only if the referenced item is in middle or old section. This is done to detect the items that are only referenced frequently during a very short period of time and never referenced again. So, in case of a cache hit, the re-referenced item is brought to the beginning of the new section and the reference count is incremented only if the re-referenced node was in either middle section or old section. In FBR, cache replacement choices are confined to the old section of the cache. A Typical method is to remove the element with least reference count in the old section.

In the implementation of FBR based node deletion for GSOM, a node was inserted into the cache whenever it was created and the cache was updated each time the node became a winner (This is different from ARC based method. In ARC a node was inserted into the cache only when it became a winner). After each main input iteration of the GSOM algorithm, a node was removed based on the above-mentioned replacement policy. After the first few iterations (approx. after 20–30 input iterations, this number depends on several things), the new node generation in the GSOM grid becomes almost zero. Node deletion is not performed after the algorithm reaches this saturation stage.

4   Experimental Results

Experiments were conducted to compare the two new algorithms with Fritzke's algorithm and the standard GSOM algorithm. They were conducted using the datasets from UCI [2] machine learning repository. Three datasets were used (zoo, ecoli, wine) and 80 % of each dataset was used for training and the rest was used for evaluation. In all the test runs, GSOM was trained using 150 input iterations using a learning rate of 0.3 and a neighbourhood size of 4. Spread factor was increased from 0.2 to 0.7 with a step size of 0.05. After training GSOM at each spread factor value, generated nodes in the 2D grid were clustered using the K-means clustering algorithm [5]. Clusters to which the data points in test data sets belong were identified by feeding them into trained GSOMs and the corresponding clusters were assigned to them. These assignments of clusters were evaluated using five metrics. This process was repeated 50 times for a single spread factor value and average of each metric (average of its 50 values) was then calculated and used as the value of the metric for that particular spread factor value. Also, when evaluating the Fritzke's algorithm, p_{sure} parameter was set to 0.98.

Since algorithms were tested on clustering data in the experiments, evaluations of the results were done using cluster quality metrics. Evaluating goodness of a clustering often lacks rigour and has been identified as a critical and difficult empirical problem. However, some measurements are there which perform a passable evaluation of cluster quality [11]:

- Homogeneity Score (HS): Each cluster needs to contain only data points that are members of a single class.
- Completeness Score (CS): All of the data points that are members of a given class should be elements of the same cluster.

As the measurement of these two criteria are roughly the opposite of each other [11], V-measure was also used. V-measure is an entropy-based measure that explicitly evaluates how successfully the criteria of homogeneity and completeness have been sufficed. V-measure is computed as the harmonic mean of distinct homogeneity and completeness scores [11]. Apart from these empirical measurements, two metrics based on information theory have been used to evaluate the cluster quality: Adjusted Mutual Index (AMI) and Adjusted Rand Score (ARS) [9]. All of these metrics have a value between 0 and 1 and a higher value indicates a better clustering.

Table 1. Experimental Results using zoo dataset

	ARS	AMI	HS	CS	V-measure
GSOM	0.72	0.68	0.94	0.81	0.84
FBR	0.74	0.70	0.95	0.82	0.84
ARC	0.70	0.67	0.94	0.81	0.83
Fritzke	0.69	0.66	0.94	0.81	0.83

Table 1 summarizes the best results for zoo dataset (rounded to two decimal places) across all the spread factor values of each algorithm.

In all the metrics, FBR based method was able to score the best values. All the algorithms achieved their best results when the spread factor is around 0.3–0.4. Results drops drastically when the spread factor exceeds this range. When the spread factor increases, the rate of the new node generation increases (the GSOM grid spreads wide) and this has a degrading affect on the final results due to the generation of *poorly-formed* nodes. Two algorithms proposed in the paper are not designed to work under such a large generation of new nodes as these methods only remove a single node after each input iteration.

A separate experiment was carried out using the ecoli dataset. Following table summarizes the best results of each algorithm (rounded to two decimal places) (Table 2).

Table 2. Experimental Results using ecoli dataset

	ARS	AMI	HS	CS	V-measure
GSOM	0.72	0.68	0.94	0.81	0.84
FBR	0.74	0.70	0.95	0.82	0.85
ARC	0.70	0.67	0.94	0.81	0.83
Fritzke	0.69	0.67	0.94	0.81	0.83

The graph below (Fig. 4) represents the maximum value of ARS (for ecoli dataset) for each spread factor value and algorithm which produced it.

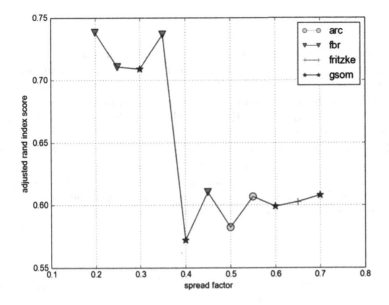

Fig. 4. Variation of adjusted rand score with spread factor - ecoli

Another experiment was carried out using the wine dataset. Following table summarizes the best results of each algorithm (rounded to two decimal places) (Table 3).

Table 3. Experimental Results using wine dataset

	ARS	AMI	HS	CS	V-measure
GSOM	0.61	0.58	0.93	0.65	0.70
FBR	0.64	0.59	0.93	0.66	0.71
ARC	0.60	0.57	0.93	0.64	0.69
Fritzke	0.58	0.55	0.92	0.64	0.68

Although FBR based method performs better, ARC based method does not show any significant improvement. This is due to the fact that ARC based method is not good at responding to the effects of the frequency as the FBR based method. According to the implementation of ARC, it can only distinguish between the nodes which were accessed once and the nodes which were accessed more than once. But FBR based method keeps track of the number of times each node accessed.

5 Conclusion

Some of the new nodes created by GSOM accumulate only a very small number of hits (number of times the node became the winner) and effect the quality of the final result. For example, identifying these nodes and removing them from the GSOM grid can increase the homogeneity and completeness of clusters generated by an algorithm like K-means which can be run using the nodes of the generated grid as input.

Existing approaches for node deletion in dynamic SOMs were investigated and the possibility of their adaptation to GSOM was examined. In addition, two novel approaches for node deletion based on two cache replacement policies were presented. The experiments conducted suggests that the algorithm based on FBR produces the best results in all the five metrics used.

References

1. Alahakoon, D., Halgamuge, S.K., Srinivasan, B.: Dynamic self-organizing maps with controlled growth for knowledge discovery. IEEE Trans. Neural Netw. **11**(3), 601–614 (2000)
2. Bache, K., Lichman, M.: UCI machine learning repository (2013). http://archive.ics.uci.edu/ml
3. Blackmore, J., Miikkulainen, R.: Incremental grid growing: encoding high-dimensional structure into a two-dimensional feature map, vol. 1, pp. 450–455 (1993)
4. Fritzke, B.: Let it grow - self-organizing feature maps with problem dependent cell structure. In: Kohonen, T., Simula, O., Kangas, J. (eds.) Artificial Neural Networks, pp. 403–408. North-Holland, Amsterdam (1991)
5. Hartigan, J.A., Wong, M.A.: Algorithm as 136: a k-means clustering algorithm. Appl. Stat. **28**, 100–108 (1979)
6. Johnson, T., Shasha, D.: 2q: a low overhead high performance buffer management replacement algorithm. In: Proceedings of the 20th International Conference on Very Large Data Bases, VLDB 1994, pp. 439–450. Morgan Kaufmann Publishers Inc., San Francisco (1994). http://dl.acm.org/citation.cfm?id=645920.672996
7. Kohonen, T., Schroeder, M.R., Huang, T.S. (eds.): Self-Organizing Maps, 3rd edn. Springer-Verlag New York Inc., Secaucus (2001)
8. Megiddo, N., Modha, D.: Arc: a self-tuning, low overhead replacement cache. In: Proceedings of the 2003 Conference on File and Storage Technologies FAST, pp. 115–130 (2003)
9. Rand, W.: Objective criteria for the evaluation of clustering methods. J. Am. Stat. Assoc. **66**(336), 846–850 (1971)
10. Robinson, J.T., Devarakonda, M.V.: Data cache management using frequency-based replacement. In: Proceedings of the 1990 ACM SIGMETRICS Conference on Measurement and Modeling of Computer Systems, SIGMETRICS 1990, pp. 134–142. ACM, New York (1990). http://doi.acm.org/10.1145/98457.98523
11. Rosenberg, A., Hirschberg, J.: V-measure: a conditional entropy-based external cluster evaluation measure. In: Eisner, J. (ed.) EMNLP-CoNLL, pp. 410–420. ACL (2007). http://www.aclweb.org/anthology/K/K07/

Exploratory Topic Modeling
with Distributional Semantics

Samuel Rönnqvist$^{(\boxtimes)}$

Turku Centre for Computer Science – TUCS,
Department of Information Technologies, Åbo Akademi University, Turku, Finland
sronnqvi@abo.fi

Abstract. As we continue to collect and store textual data in a multitude of domains, we are regularly confronted with material whose largely unknown thematic structure we want to uncover. With unsupervised, exploratory analysis, no prior knowledge about the content is required and highly open-ended tasks can be supported. In the past few years, probabilistic topic modeling has emerged as a popular approach to this problem. Nevertheless, the representation of the latent topics as aggregations of semi-coherent terms limits their interpretability and level of detail.

This paper presents an alternative approach to topic modeling that maps topics as a network for exploration, based on distributional semantics using learned word vectors. From the granular level of terms and their semantic similarity relations global topic structures emerge as clustered regions and gradients of concepts. Moreover, the paper discusses the visual interactive representation of the topic map, which plays an important role in supporting its exploration.

(Topic mapping code and demo available at http://samuel.ronnqvist.fi/topicMap/)

Keywords: Topic modeling · Distributional semantics · Visual analytics

1 Introduction

Following the increase in digitally stored and streamed text, the interest for computational tools that aid in organizing and understanding written content at a large scale has soared. Natural language processing and machine learning techniques demonstrate strength in their feats of handling the challenging intricacies of human language to extract information and in their aptitude for scanning big data sets. However, while we can model what information is likely to be interesting, humans alone are capable of a deeper understanding that involves evaluating information against a wide and diverse body of knowledge in nuanced ways, which motivates a focus on human-computer interaction and visual analytics in text mining [17].

This paper concerns analysis of text by means of *exploratory topic modeling*, by which I emphasize the exploratory use of models that convey topic structure.

© Springer International Publishing Switzerland 2015
E. Fromont et al. (Eds.): IDA 2015, LNCS 9385, pp. 241–252, 2015.
DOI: 10.1007/978-3-319-24465-5_21

To this end, I put forward a new method for topic modeling based on distributional semantics using continuous word vector representations, for the construction of models called *topic maps*. On the one hand, the focus is set explicitly on unsupervised learning to allow maximum coverage in terms of domain and language without need for adaption, while taking advantage of recent advances in word vector training by neural networks. On the other hand, the role of the human user is acknowledged as an important part of the analysis process as the one who understands and explores the modeling results; therefore, visual interactive presentation is discussed as part of the contribution alongside map construction and perceived as equally important to exploratory topic modeling.

Probabilistic topic modeling [4] is a family of machine learning algorithms for uncovering thematic structure in text documents that are widely used, and applicable both for exploratory analysis of topics and as a discrete dimensionality reduction method in support of other learning tasks. Based on co-occurrence of terms in documents, probabilistic topic modeling extracts a number of latent topics. In the seminal algorithm, Latent Dirichlet Allocation (LDA), the number of topics to infer is given as a parameter. Assuming that each document may discuss a mixture of topics, it attempts to isolate coherent topics. Each topic is defined as a probability distribution over terms, where the terms collectively carry the meaning of the latent topic. While LDA and many of its variations are theoretically solid and rest on an interpretation-friendly probabilistic basis, issues of interpretability are nevertheless commonplace and well recognized [6]. First, the unsupervised modeling offers no guarantees that the topic division is semantically meaningful; some topics may seem similar and hard to distinguish, whereas others turn out very specific. These issues may be mitigated by selecting appropriate parameters, including the number of topics in the case of LDA. Second, the terms within topics may appear semantically incoherent and confusing to a human. Various efforts have been made to improve coherence (e.g., [14,15]), yet for humans to form an understanding of what a topic signifies based on a set of weighted terms, interpretation inevitably involves a certain cognitive load, only increased by the iterative task of contrasting topics against each other to grasp the broader picture.

Thoughtful visual representation of the topic structure and terms can ease the task (see, e.g., [7,18]), but I argue that in many cases it is more meaningful to choose to operate from the level of individual terms that represent concrete concepts and their bilateral semantic similarity relations. A discrete division of topics is practical in many use cases, but is somewhat unnatural for exploratory purposes, and mere aggregation of terms inevitably leads toward less interpretable abstractions. Instead, it is more fitting to allow for a topic structure to emerge as a global property from the local semantic similarity relations among terms. Such a semantic network allows the human user to flexibly identify topics as regions through proper visualization, while the network also supports quantitative analysis such as community detection [9] (overlapping clustering, which handles ambiguous terms) to identify discrete topics.

The following section introduces the method for building the semantic network model, the topic map, whereas Sect. 3 discusses its visualization, and Sect. 4 reports on experiments conducted to demonstrate the mapping method, followed by some concluding remarks.

2 Building the Topic Map

Distributional semantics models the meanings of words based on their contexts, namely the surrounding words in a sentence, according to the aphorism "you shall know a word by the company it keeps" [8]. While modeling has traditionally been based on counting of context words, recent approaches that work by learning to predict words instead have been highly successful [1]. A popular way of representing the semantics is by vectors, e.g., through projection [19] or later through neural network training [3]. Lately, Mikolov et al. [13] have shown how neural networks can be efficiently used to train semantic models based on corpora at the scale of billions of words, in order to achieve very high semantic accuracy. Their continuous skip-gram model is a neural network trained to predict context words based on the center word, using a single hidden layer. Through supervised training, the network optimizes its hidden layer weights, which results in the learned array of hidden nodes providing fixed-length vector representations of word semantics, i.e., word vectors. The word vectors embed words into a semantic space that supports measuring similarities among words by their vectors (e.g., by cosine similarity), as well as other vector arithmetic operations (e.g., addition and subtraction for regularities prediction).

For the purpose of modeling the general topic composition of corpora, I use the neural network skip-gram method to model word-level semantic similarity, and from pairwise relations let the broader topic structure emerge. Whereas the focus in word vector training generally is to approximate the semantics of language in general, which can be achieved by training on large and diverse enough text, the idea is here to explicitly model the semantics of the language in one's corpus alone. The model then reflects how words relate in the discourse of the corpus rather than elsewhere. Thereby, the discrepancies between the word similarities presented by the model and the observers own, more general understanding and less data-informed expectation of how the words relate, constitute telltales of the thematic nature of the underlying text. (Kulkarni et al. use word vectors accordingly to study linguistic change in English over time [11].) For topic modeling to be meaningful, it naturally needs to work for corpora far smaller than billions of words. As will be demonstrated in Sect. 4, skip-gram models can learn usefully accurate word vectors on much smaller data sets, too.

Apart from semantic similarity, the topic map incorporates term frequencies, used to represent the prevalence of terms in the corpus, and in combination with their semantic neighborhood provide a sense of the overall importance of sections of the map, reflecting the prevalence of specific concepts or topics. Probabilistic topic modeling similarly uses topic-wise probability distributions over terms to represent their degree of importance within the topic.

Algorithm 1. Topic map construction (in: tokens, V, C, E, N, P, L; out: net)

\# WORD VECTOR TRAINING
model = Word2Vec(*tokens*, vector_size=*V*, context_size=*C*, epochs=*E*)
\# NETWORK CONSTRUCTION
for i1 **in** range(0, *N-1*):
  for i2 **in** range(i1+1, *N*):
    t1, t2 = top_N_terms[i1], top_N_terms[i2]
    net.add_link(t1, t2, weight=model.similarity(t1, t2))
\# NETWORK PRUNING
threshold = percentile([link.weight **for** link **in** net.links], *P*)
for node **in** net.nodes:
  cap = sorted(net.links[node], key=lambda link: link.weight)[-1*L].weight
  for link **in** net.links[node]:
    if link.weight < max(cap, threshold):
      net.remove_link(link)
ws = [link.weight **for** link **in** net.links]
for link **in** net.links:
  net.links[link].weight = (link.weight-min(ws)) / (max(ws)-min(ws))

Using the word vector model and term counts, a semantic network that constitutes the topic map can be constructed according to Algorithm 1 as described in the following. First, the text of a corpus is processed and tokenized into meaningful and well normalized terms. Then, the map is constructed through the following two main steps.

Word Vector Training. Given the main parameters, vector size (V) and context size (C), word vectors are trained on term sequences by the method of Mikolov et al. (word2vec). Vector size determines the dimensionality of the semantic space and is customarily in the range of 50 to 1000, where higher dimensionality allows for a finer model given enough data. The size of the word context to consider is typically about 5–10 words, but for the current task even contexts up to 25 words have proved satisfactory. Training in multiple epochs (E) (e.g., 3–10) tends to improve the quality of the model noticeably, especially with little data available.

Network Construction. Once the vectors have been trained, we can use the model to measure similarity of pairs of terms. The most frequent terms in the corpus are picked for comparison, preferably excluding stopwords. Typically in the range 100–1000, the number of unique terms to include (N) defines the maximum level of detail in the topic map and limits the computational complexity of building it. For each pair, the cosine similarity between their vectors ($sim(t_1, t_2) = \boldsymbol{v}(t_1) \cdot \boldsymbol{v}(t_2)$, with unit vectors) is computed and stored.

Network Pruning. As only similar terms are meaningful to relate and as we seek to build a network that is neither too dense and cluttered nor too sparse and disconnected, the pairs with highest similarity scores are retained as links between the term nodes. With varying sizes of the vector and corpora, the similarity scores vary considerably as well. Thus, filtering of pairs is performed by a threshold defined as a percentile of all scores stored (P), typically at the 97–99th percentile, which makes the parameter's effect more stable. Moreover, an upper bound on number of links per term (L) helps reduce cluttering density due to general terms that may measure as very similar to many terms. Typical cap values are 8–15 links per term. All links are finally weighted according to its normalized similarity score, as a standard measure of link strength ($w' \in [0,1]$).

In order to optimize parameter selection the quality of the topic maps must be evaluated. While the exploratory task ultimately calls for qualitative evaluation, semantic prediction accuracy will be used for initial guidance in word vector training, which is the more computationally demanding step. The evaluation method and data, borrowed from Mikolov et al., measures syntactic and semantic regularities such as "man is to woman as king is to *queen*", "Athens is to Greece as Baghdad is to *Iraq*" and "code is to coding as dance is to *dancing*", where accuracy in predicting the last word is evaluated. Measuring how well the model approximates general English, the relative performance on this task can help to rule out models that are too simple and produce suboptimal maps because they lack ability to appropriately model the semantics. The highest accuracy, however, does not necessarily provide the best topic map, as its quality relies on a balance between specificity and generality of its relations. The experiments in Sect. 4 illustrate this further.

Apart from local link accuracy, the network should ideally show good structure in terms of how broader clusters emerge, too. This is highly dependent on both calibration of the network parameters and how the network is analyzed. The experiments in this paper focus on visual analysis based on force-directed layouting, in which case desirable network structures contain some degree of clustering into coherent and meaningful regions, without excessive cross-linking between terms in different clusters to avoid overlaps. The network construction parameters (P, L, N) may be adjusted to optimize the readability of the map, which in practice can be done instantaneously while visualizing the network. Hence, optimization of the word vector parameters is the more cumbersome groundwork that begets good maps, and evaluation of accuracy helps by reducing the search space.

3   Visualizing the Topic Map

Exploration of complex models such as topic models calls for presentations that provide as much detail as meaningfully possible. The most information-dense mode of communication is visualization, whereas interactivity helps expand the space of information that can be presented intelligibly on a finite screen. The visual analytics paradigm [10] embraces visual interactive interfaces as they offer a means of communication that is both rich and reactive, thus, helping users in making sense of models and data. Visualization of the topic map incorporates Shneiderman's visual information-seeking mantra, "overview first, zoom and filter, then details-on-demand" [20], by providing both overview of a corpus and a scaffold for exploration of its details. Visualization of the two main aspects of the map, term frequencies and word vectors, is discussed in the following, as well as their combination into a visual topic map.

Among the most popular forms of text visualization are word clouds, which are simple yet useful. Their main property, representing word importance by size, is powerful because it utilizes a preattentively recognized visual variable, i.e., relative word importance is recognized effortlessly and without requiring focused attention, in parallel across the field of vision at the early stage of the human visual system [21]. While word clouds have received some criticism relating to other properties such as the (dis)organization of words, studies have sought improvement and in terms of readability evaluated various approaches such as clustered [12] and semantic word clouds [2] that impose some semantically meaningful organization of words. However, so far none of the approaches have used distributional semantics, which offers advantages by being arguably more specific than tried clustering approaches, and unsupervised as opposed to database approaches.

By contrast, a common approach to visualizing word vectors is to plot words according to their two-dimensional projections by PCA (or other multidimensional scaling methods), which achieves a basic form of semantic organization, albeit easily cluttered at the center. While word clouds commonly place words as closely as possible, regarding order or not, projection uses planar distance to communicate the degree of semantic similarity (a spatial visual metaphor) as well as ordering. Nevertheless, projection into two dimensions is bound to produce overlap between semantically unrelated sets of words, which motivates the visualization of semantic relations by drawn line connections that is more explicit [16]. For visualization of the topic map network, I propose to use a force-directed layout (a projection method) that optimizes word positions explicitly based on semantic relations present in the network model, rather than the whole word vector model. In particular, the D3 force algorithm [5] is suitable as it can counter overlap of terms (by node charge) to preserve readability, even when they are densely connected. It can also run in real time to allow for interactive adjustment of positions which lets the user explore multiple local optima of positioning.

The visual topic map lends from word clouds the word sizing relative to their corpus frequency, and uses force-directed layouting to organize the map semantically. Drawing the network of words, the strength of each link is encoded by opacity, which makes more explicit the relative importance of individual links, and together with the emergent density of links it provides an aggregate impression of the varying density of the map.

Interactive exploration of the map is enabled foremost by zoom/pan capabilities, which in a very direct way allows more terms to be displayed, and highlighting of links of specific terms. The filtering of terms by frequency can be responsive to the level of zoom to seamlessly provide more detail on demand. The percentile filter used to construct the network can be relaxed if the visual interface can counter the added complexity, and the number of terms can be increased accordingly. Hence, the scalability of the topic map visualization depends largely on interaction design. The semantic network of frequent terms also functions as a canvas for other types of information, such as mapping of local term neighborhoods and relational information, touched upon in Sect. 5.

4 Experiments

The topic map will be demonstrated and tested using two different corpora. The first corpus is a sample of news articles from Reuters (U.S. online edition) containing 23 k articles and 9.2 M words (167 k unique) and the other is a collection of financial patent application abstracts from the U.S. Patent and Trademark Office comprising 14 k abstracts and 1.7 M words (20 k unique). In accordance with the exploratory aim of this article, a topic map is trained and visualized for each corpus as discussed above, in hope of gaining insight into the thematic composition of each (see Figs. 1 and 2). The most prevalent terms representing concrete concepts are displayed and their semantic similarity relations provide organization that portray topics implicitly as regions and gradients between them.

The experiment starts by selecting the parameters for word vector training, guided by quantitative accuracy and qualitative assessment of the map (as discussed in Sect. 2). Having exhaustively tested various settings, their relationship

Fig. 1. Topic map of financial news articles, interactive version available at: http://samuel.ronnqvist.fi/topicMap/

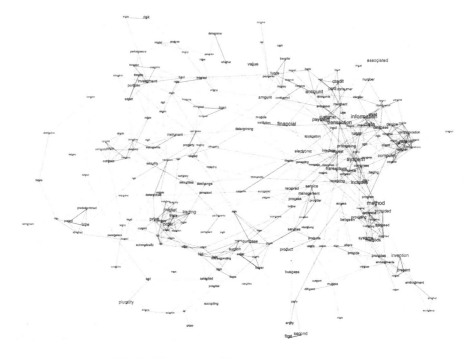

Fig. 2. Topic map of financial patent abstracts

can be described as follows. With a fixed context size of 15 for the Reuters corpus, accuracy reaches a plateau from vector sizes 200 to 500 (on average at 17 %, with $E = 3$), decreasing afterwards. Meanwhile, at a given vector size, accuracy tends to asymptotically approach a limit with increased context size. Qualitatively, the best network structure appears to result from settings where accuracy is close to the limit but context size is kept moderate.

The experiments show that the map is surprisingly robust with respect to the training parameters, producing largely comprehensible results even at vector sizes of 25 or 600 and context sizes of 5 and 50 respectively. Nevertheless, the quality of the Reuters map is noticeably best at vector sizes 200–400 and context sizes 10–20, where larger contexts benefit from larger vectors. Simpler models produce networks with smaller regions that are tightly clustered, but result in either few or arbitrary connections between regions, depending on the threshold (P). Networks from complex models have similar problems, although the strong connections tend to be very specific and semantically accurate, which explains their good testing performance.

The qualitatively optimal models in between strike a balance between, on the one hand, semantic accuracy that provides a map of meaningful connections and, on the other hand, generality by connecting parts of the map through more abstract but still helpfull term relations. Hence, measured accuracy provides fundamental guidance in learning a model that handles the language well, but the map then benefits from a slight regularizing or smoothing effect achieved by using a simpler model than the quantitatively optimal. While large vectors and contexts combined can achieve maximum accuracy (about 22 % for the Reuters corpus), it does not seem productive to surpass contexts of about 25 words, and given a limited context size, it is motivated to choose a vector size towards the beginning of the accuracy plateau. The number of training epochs has a strong effect on accuracy, e.g., the settings $V = 400$, $C = 15$ and $E = \{1, 3, 5\}$ give accuracies 7.3, 16.7 and 19.1, but the two latter cases do not show any notable qualitative difference for the Reuters data.

The topic map in Fig. 1 was produced with the settings $V = 250$, $C = 12$, $E = 5$, $N = 500$, $P = .985$ and $L = 12$ (accuracy 17.6 %, training time 14.5 min on 4 cores). It depicts the topic landscape of the Reuters financial news corpus by its most frequent terms excluding stop words (including automatically detected bi-gram phrases). The similarity threshold set at the 98.5th percentile provides an appropriate degree of connectivity. The cap on links per term helps improve readability especially in the dense region surrounding the terms *business* and *technology*. The map uncovers an uneven distribution of terms, where smaller concentrations highlight cliques of terms (e.g., president, ceo, etc. down left) that represent a rather distinct general concept. Larger concentrated regions form to highlight a broader topic division of the corpus, the three main regions broadly reflecting discourse on business-related activities, realized performance and expected performance.

The map in Fig. 2 similarly illustrates the lay of specific concepts and more general topics as they occur in the set of patent abstracts. A few themes can be identified, such as payment systems, telecommunications, trading, portfolio management and patent-specific language. The map includes 350 terms and links for the top 2 % most similar pairs. As the patent corpus is much smaller the vector size was reduced according to vocabulary size heuristically by $\frac{V_1^2}{|vocab_1|} \approx \frac{V_2^2}{|vocab_2|}$ to $V = 85$, context size was kept at 12 not to reduce the already scarce data and training was run in 10 epochs (training time 3.2 min on 4 cores).

To conclude the evaluation of the generated topic maps, I compare the news corpus against a benchmark obtained by LDA (results for the patent corpus are similar but omitted due to space constraints). The same preprocessing of the text is used as above, and the topics are modeled with standard parameter settings into 8 topics. Each topic is presented by their top-10 terms according to the topic-term probability distributions, as the most direct way of presenting the model. Stop words are excluded to make the results more informative. While several methods have been proposed that rerank terms to better support interpretation of the topics (cf. [7, 18, 22]), no such method seems to have been unanimously or widely adopted. The obtained topics are:

Topic 0: million, net, quarter, year, financial, income, company, share, operating, total
Topic 1: securities, class, relevant, number, options, option, price, form, code, relevant security
Topic 2: company, shares, fitch, fund, rating, share, ratings, information, financial, available
Topic 3: u.s, bank, new, company, financial, government, state, group, year, years
Topic 4: first, people, world, new, patients, home, years, health, year, games
Topic 5: company, information, new, services, business, market, products, forward-looking
        statements, technology, solutions
Topic 6: q2 2014, jul amc, call, company, 29 jul, corp, earnings conf, jul bmo, trust, share
Topic 7: percent, year, million, billion, market, u.s, sales, shares, growth, down

For some topics it is possible to discern a latent meaning, while others prove hard to interpret. For instance, Topics 0 and 7 appear to relate to realized financial performance, but it is difficult both to form a more detailed explanation of them and to distinguish logically between them. As mentioned in Sect. 1, recognizing a distinct topic from an aggregate of terms is challenging, as is the task of understanding how multiple topics relate. While the topic map includes many of the same frequent terms, its natural, semantic organization makes it easier to view and grasp the overall topic composition and scope. Local neighborhoods of the map tend to be more coherent than LDA topics, and the relation between different sections of the map is made more explicit. While exploration of LDA topic models can be supported by meaningful presentation (e.g., [7, 18]), the topic map's alternative way of approaching topic modeling remains well motivated for exploration.

5 Discussion

My aim has been to introduce a new approach of using distributional semantics, specifically word vectors trained by neural networks, to explore topics in bodies of text. A problem commonly addressed by probabilistic topic modeling, this approach sets out to tackle it with finer granularity, by building a topic map bottom-up from concrete terms towards general topics, rather than forcing interpretation of implicit meaning among an explicit, but not necessarily coherent, set of topic terms. Distributional-semantic modeling provides meaningful word-to-word similarity relations and organization that is easy to navigate. In addition, I put forward a visualization design for the map that provides overview and means for linking to further details, thus supporting interactive exploration. As a network model, the map also supports quantitative network analysis, in particular community detection as a form of second-level clustering to provide explicit topics, which are useful in some cases. The topic map opens up to a range of possible extensions to be explored.

As the map provides a projection of the semantic space of a corpus, another interesting type of information is the relational, i.e., how different concepts are referenced together in text. Mapping such relations onto the topic map may lead to still more informative ways of summarizing the contents of texts. Document-level co-occurrence of terms used in probabilistic topic modeling represents a crude way of harnessing relational information to extract topic information, but it is likely beneficial to treat distributional word context similarity and word-to-word co-occurrence as separate aspects that both contribute toward summarizing the discourse of a corpus. Thus, the approach of constructing a topic map outlined in this paper should be seen as elementary to future extensions that among other things include sophisticated analysis of relations in text and powerful visual interactive interfaces to make the semantic space and its linked information readily browsable. The semantic network is the basic data structure, which can be meaningfully presented in many other ways as well, e.g., using more structured network layouts or non-graphical representation, possibly emphasizing search with a completely local focus rather than overview.

Studying immediate neighborhoods of specific terms may in fact be a desirable mode of exploration, which can be supported in other ways than described above. Rather than starting from the frequent term set, terms with the closest vectors can be searched. By recursively traversing the nearest neighbors of a term, a close-up view of its semantic context in the corpus is obtainable.

Vector similarity comparisons can also be performed with compound vectors that average two or a few word vectors, for instance, as a way to disambiguate a term (e.g.: *financial* by *financial+group*, *financial+results*) or merge closely related terms (e.g., *customer+customers*). The latter could be applied to enhance the map by reducing term redundancy and thereby visual clutter, while joining their term counts. Another way to generalize across terms would be to smooth term counts to some extent among direct neighbors, in order to make the representation of prevalence of regions more congruent.

In this paper, word vectors and term frequencies were obtained from the same set of text, which may lead to problems of accuracy for the study of smaller sets of text (e.g., in the order of 10–100 k rather than 1 M words). It is possible to separate these, letting the word vectors be trained on a larger background corpus while counting terms on a smaller foreground set, as long as they are related in nature. For instance, the background corpus may consist of text from a single source over a certain period of time, while texts from smaller intervals during that period would be used as foreground corpora to allow for more specific study of varying term prevalence over time, still benefiting from a more robust semantic model.

As efficient word vector training with neural networks has opened up many new possibilities in natural language processing, I hope to introduce it for the purpose of exploring topics in masses of text by proposing a methodology for building and visualizing topic maps. Unsupervised word-level modeling of semantics offers very flexible and detailed means for analysis that deserve further study. The concluding discussion has outlined a few interesting future directions, and ultimately the utility of topic maps and their visual representations should be tested by how they support users' understanding in a variety of real-world settings.

References

1. Baroni, M., Dinu, G., Kruszewski, G.: Don't count, predict! a systematic comparison of context-counting vs. context-predicting semantic vectors. In: Proceedings of the 52nd Annual Meeting of the Association for Computational Linguistics, vol. 1, pp. 238–247 (2014)
2. Barth, L., Kobourov, S.G., Pupyrev, S.: Experimental comparison of semantic word clouds. In: Gudmundsson, J., Katajainen, J. (eds.) SEA 2014. LNCS, vol. 8504, pp. 247–258. Springer, Heidelberg (2014)
3. Bengio, Y., Ducharme, R., Vincent, P., Janvin, C.: A neural probabilistic language model. J. Mach. Learn. Res. **3**, 1137–1155 (2003)
4. Blei, D.M.: Probabilistic topic models. Commun. ACM **55**(4), 77–84 (2012)
5. Bostock, M., Ogievetsky, V., Heer, J.: D3: data-driven documents. IEEE Trans. Vis. Comp. Graph. **17**(12), 2301–2309 (2011). (Proc. InfoVis)

6. Chang, J., Gerrish, S., Wang, C., Boyd-graber, J.L., Blei, D.M.: Reading tea leaves: how humans interpret topic models. In: Advances in Neural Information Processing Systems, pp. 288–296 (2009)
7. Chuang, J., Manning, C.D., Heer, J.: Termite: visualization techniques for assessing textual topic models. In: Advanced Visual Interfaces (2012)
8. Firth, J.: A synopsis of linguistic theory 1930–1955. In: Studies in Linguistic Analysis, pp. 1–32. Philological Society, Oxford (1968)
9. Fortunato, S.: Community detection in graphs. Phys. Rep. **486**(3–5), 75–174 (2010)
10. Keim, D.A., Mansmann, F., Schneidewind, J., Thomas, J., Ziegler, H.: Visual analytics: scope and challenges. In: Simoff, S.J., Böhlen, M.H., Mazeika, A. (eds.) Visual Data Mining. LNCS, vol. 4404, pp. 76–90. Springer, Heidelberg (2008)
11. Kulkarni, V., Al-Rfou, R., Perozzi, B., Skiena, S.: Statistically significant detection of linguistic change. arXiv preprint arXiv:1411.3315 (2014)
12. Lohmann, S., Ziegler, J., Tetzlaff, L.: Comparison of tag cloud layouts: task-related performance and visual exploration. In: Gross, T., Gulliksen, J., Kotzé, P., Oestreicher, L., Palanque, P., Prates, R.O., Winckler, M. (eds.) INTERACT 2009. LNCS, vol. 5726, pp. 392–404. Springer, Heidelberg (2009)
13. Mikolov, T., Chen, K., Corrado, G., Dean, J.: Efficient estimation of word representations in vector space. In: Proceedings of Workshop at International Conference on Learning Representations (2013)
14. Mimno, D., Wallach, H.M., Talley, E., Leenders, M., McCallum, A.: Optimizing semantic coherence in topic models. In: Proceedings of the Conference on Empirical Methods in Natural Language Processing, EMNLP 2011, pp. 262–272 (2011)
15. Newman, D., Bonilla, E.V., Buntine, W.: Improving topic coherence with regularized topic models. In: Advances in Neural Information Processing Systems 24, pp. 496–504 (2011)
16. Palmer, S., Rock, I.: Rethinking perceptual organization: the role of uniform connectedness. Psychon. Bull. Rev. **1**(1), 29–55 (1994)
17. Risch, J., Kao, A., Poteet, S.R., Wu, Y.-J.J.: Text visualization for visual text analytics. In: Simoff, S.J., Böhlen, M.H., Mazeika, A. (eds.) Visual Data Mining. LNCS, vol. 4404, pp. 154–171. Springer, Heidelberg (2008)
18. Rönnqvist, S., Wang, X., Sarlin, P.: Interactive visual exploration of topic models using graphs. In: Eurographics Conference on Visualization (EuroVis) (2014)
19. Schütze, H.: Dimensions of meaning. In: Proceedings of the 1992 ACM/IEEE Conference on Supercomputing, Supercomputing 1992, pp. 787–796 (1992)
20. Shneiderman, B.: The eyes have it: a task by data type taxonomy for information visualizations. In: Proceedings of the IEEE Symposium on Visual Languages, pp. 336–343 (1996)
21. Treisman, A.: Features and objects in visual processing. Sci. Am. **255**(5), 114–125 (1986)
22. Wilson, A.T., Chew, P.A.: Term weighting schemes for latent dirichlet allocation. In: Human Language Technologies: The 11th Annual Conference of the North American Chapter of the Association for Computational Linguistics, pp. 465–473 (2010)

Assigning Geo-relevance of Sentiments Mined from Location-Based Social Media Posts

Randall Sanborn$^{(\boxtimes)}$, Michael Farmer, and Syagnik Banerjee

University of Michigan-Flint, Flint, MI, USA
{rasanbor, farmerme, syban}@umflint.edu

Abstract. Broad adoption of smartphones has increased the number of posts generated while people are going about their daily lives. Many of these posts are related to the location where that post is generated. Being able to infer a person's sentiment toward a given location would be a boon to market researchers. The large percentage of system-generated content in these posts posed difficulties for calculating sentiment and assigning that sentiment to the location associated with the post. Consequently our proposed system implements a sequence of text cleaning functions which was completed with a naive Bayes classifier to determine if a post was more or less likely to be associated with an individual's present location. The system was tested on set of nearly 30,000 posts from Foursquare that had been cross-posted to Twitter which resulted in reasonable precision but with a large number of posts discarded.

1 Introduction

The short text format exemplified by Twitter and extended by Foursquare (microblogs) presents a unique data processing problem. This short format has forced researchers to adjust methods previously used for natural language processing on long-form text. The posts are valuable as they contain opinions of individuals at specific times and specific locations, which can shed light on more general sentiment relating to these locations. Sentiments expressed on such social media platforms are known to correlate with customer satisfaction indices like the American Consumer Satisfaction Index (ASCI) developed at University of Michigan - which gives businesses reasons to mine sentiments [1]. This sentiment could be leveraged to increase service at a business, open new business opportunities where consumers are unhappy, or encourage governments to improve services and facilities.

Taking advantage of these features of social media entries, Banerjee et al. explored the volume of check-ins according to business type, user gender, and check-in time to infer food and entertainment preferences by gender and time of users in New York City. This gave insights into meal rush times, and both day of the week and time preferences based on business type [2]. This did not, however, explore the content of those posts to infer additional information about the sentiment of the user posting the content, but simply counted every user who made a comment. Other studies have extracted social media data by searching for words, phrases, and metadata that directly links the social media post with the location. e.g. Diakopoulos and Shamma search for hashtags that directly reference the elections and the debates to find tweets relating to

E. Fromont et al. (Eds.): IDA 2015, LNCS 9385, pp. 253–263, 2015.
DOI: 10.1007/978-3-319-24465-5_22

the 2008 presidential elections, which they then processed to find time and sentiment of the tweet [3].

The dataset we have extracted is based purely on location of the user when the post was made. Unfortunately, this does not necessarily mean the content is directly related to the location. For example a student may be in a coffee shop complaining about the research paper she is writing. The content of that post doesn't directly correspond to the coffee shop. As an additional complication, many services have default check-in text if the user chooses not the enter anything. Other times the post simply may not be related to the location [4].

This research will explore we will explore the unique issues posed by data mining content posted on location-based social media services. Specifically we will explore the association between entries made at a location and implied sentiment about that location. Further, if not all sentiment is related to the location or positive about the location, then we will seek to differentiate those entries and assign them to appropriate categories.

2   Background in Social Media Content Analysis and Related Work

Social media is a subject of active research, finding new ways to extract meaningful information about the state of the world from unstructured data. Sentiment analysis in particular has enjoyed a surge of interest since 2001 primarily with the rise of the Internet and subsequent increases in user generated content, with 73 % of Internet-using adults using some social networking site [5, 6]. For general-purpose sentiment analysis, content is generally queried using keywords and topic indicators like hashtags. Items are grouped by topic and then sentiment is analyzed and compared. This method has been used to evaluate brand sentiment [7], and movie preferences [8]. It has also been expanded to determine user television viewing profiles and then make recommendations based on other people with similar profiles [9]. Bhayani, et al. developed a system for Twitter sentiment analysis which yielded an accuracy ranging from 78.8–83.0 % [10].

Searching social media based on keyword searches yields data sets that are very likely to be related to the keyword of a brand, for instance. Searching based on location, however, implies only that the user was at a location when they created a particular post. This requires a necessary caution in arbitrary application of traditional sentiment analysis methods to data acquired using location criteria.

Users were found to share their location for three primary reasons: (1) To coordinate and connect with friends during social events, (2) to "project an interesting image of oneself" [11] or, in other words, to associate the location with themselves for others to see, and (3) to participate in gamification elements in services like badges, or to receive incentives, coupons, and rewards [11, 12].

In this research we will attempt to determine location and post content association. We have found no instances where other researchers have attempted this. This is a subtly difficult problem because entries may not all be directly related to the location from which they were made. For example, in a set of posts related to travel locations (hotels, airports, subway stations), all of the following posts were present:

"Missed my train because my professor went over time. I hate Mondays (@ MBTA North Station w/3 others) http://t.co/lWSdnkys"

"I'm at Raped by the MBTA Fare Hikes (Boston, MA) http://t.co/ZvvOffOs"

"I'm at Onyx Hotel (Boston, MA) w/2 others http://t.co/262TuS7v"

The first post has a distinctly negative sentiment, but the sentiment is not related to the Massachusetts Bay Transportation Authority, it's related to the user's general feelings about the day. The second post is specifically targeted at the MBTA and sentiment contained within that post is related to the MBTA. The third post is the default text created by Foursquare in the instances when a user chooses to simply check-in and not enter any user generated content.

A somewhat related problem to sentiment analysis is subjectivity analysis where a message is analyzed to determine if it is an objective, or a subjective statement. A sentence such as, "I'm out star gazing." is an objective statement and contains little or no sentiment but does contain information on my current activities whereas a similar sentence like, "I met Tom Cruise and I'm star struck." is more subjective and contains an element that may indicate sentiment (star). The words in both sentences are similar and information extraction and sentiment analysis system could be easily fooled if evaluated by a simple lexicon based analysis.

A high precision, low-supervision subjectivity analysis algorithm was described by Wiebe and Riloff called HP-Obj and HP-Subj, respectively. The algorithm takes a pre-defined list of words associated with subjectivity to classify sentences. These sentences are parsed for "syntactic patterns" that are likely to correspond to subjective sentences. These classifiers are high precision but low recall. The HP-Subj classifier has just over 90 % precision, but only 40 % recall [13].

Many researchers use features representing the presence of a specific word (gram/unigram) or group of words (grams/bigrams/trigrams/etc.). Pang et al. found simple unigrams to be very effective in classifying movie reviews, and noted that selecting the top 2633 unigrams was nearly as effective as selecting all available unigrams (16165) [14]. This is relevant in resource-constrained applications. Agarwal et al. was able to get a 4 % gain in accuracy by adding 100 "Senti-features" which contain items like percentage of capitalized text, number of URLs, number of negation words, and number of positive adverbs [15]. This combines elements of lexicon based sentiment analysis, machine learning, and language parsing to improve accuracy.

3 Proposed Approach

The overall approach of the proposed system is to import the data to be processed, perform any preprocessing steps, tokenize the text into the constituent words, use the optional naive Bayes classifier, and then assign sentiment for evaluation as shown in Fig. 1. In Sect. 4 we will define a collection of processing scenarios that employ

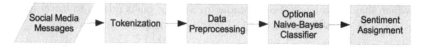

Fig. 1. Overview of processing flow

increasing collections of processing scenarios based on the processing steps defined in the following subsections. We will run a series of experiments to determine which set of these methods are most effective for location-based sentiment analysis.

3.1 Tokenization

In order to find words on sentiment lists, calculate sentiment, or do naive Bayes analysis, we need a unit of text smaller than the entire post. Breaking up the post into these smaller units is called tokenization. Tokens were selected to be the size of one word, also known as a unigram. A simple regular expression was used to break the larger posts into unigrams. For example, "Here! It's a sample message." would turn into the following array: ["Here", "it", "s", "a", "sample", "message"]. Spaces and non-alphanumeric characters are removed, and the array can be iterated through to evaluate each token. The sample post points out two concerns with using this method to tokenize the string. First, it removes potentially interesting characters like exclamation points that may give insight into sentiment. Second, it splits words with apostrophes into two distinct tokens. To overcome this, apostrophes were removed from sentiment and slang databases, and apostrophes are removed from posts before being tokenized.

3.2 Preprocessing

Social media entries in general, and Twitter entries in particular contain elements which contain no explicit sentiment information. URLs and mentions of other Twitter usernames don't increase knowledge about the sentiment. Similarly, special characters used for Twitter specific purposes like the hash symbol (#) also do not contribute additional information themselves. Preprocessing cleans the text by removing ostensibly superfluous punctuation and extra whitespace, and generally make the posts easier to evaluate. We applied three optional data scrubbing steps to clean the data prior to evaluating sentiment: (i) Default Foursquare text removal, (ii) slang translation, and (iii) stop word removal.

Additionally, apostrophes were removed from all posts, and from all lookup lists, to accommodate poor punctuation in messages. Words like "won't" and "wont" would be treated the same. This has potential advantages and drawbacks that aren't explored in-depth here, namely it increases the hit rate of stop-word removal, but it can also cause some confusion between words like "I'll" and "ill".

Foursquare check-in text contains text not explicitly entered by the user like the location they're posting from and the URL appended to the post. These can unintentionally trigger other sentiment analysis rules. The colon and forward slash characters in a URL can be confused for an emoticon representing confusion or annoyance. Words like "street", "palace", and "union" can all trip sentiment rules on the ANEW database. Locations like "Union Station" or "The Palace" would receive artificially inflated sentiment scores. Regular expressions are a well-established method for finding patterns in text. Five regular expressions are used to find and eliminate default text (Table 1).

Table 1. Regular expressions used to remove default text

Goal	Regular Expression
URL Removal	http:VVt\.co(V[A-Za-z0-9\._V~%\-\+&\#\?!=\()@]*)
Attached Image Note	\[pic\]\:
Default Check-In Text	I"m at .*(\s\(.*,\s[A-Z]+\))?
Location Meta-Data	\(@.*\)
Addition Guests	wV [0-9]* others

Many posts in the data set contain acronyms and slang, which often contain or refer to words that have an associated sentiment. Rather than attempt to modify the ANEW database with slang manually, we found a slang translation database which would translate the words for sentiment analysis. Slang words and acronyms are translated in the remaining text using the NoSlang.com slang translation database, which contains 5261 slang word/phrase entries. Each word is compared to the slang database and replaced with its corrected or expanded form if found. Translation only happens with exact matches. Slang translation allows common acronyms ('lol' becomes laughing out loud) and intentional misspellings ('h8' becomes hate) to be considered in both the naive Bayes classifier and sentiment analysis.

Finally, stop words are removed using the stop word list provided with MySQL. Stop word removal has been used in other text analyses and was included in here simply to see if it had an effect. Stop word removal was implemented similarly to slang

Table 2. Data scrubbing examples

Data Scrub Method	Message
Baseline	I'm working and standing by at the same time!! Lol (@ The Fake Hotel) http://t.co/h4Xe9JHd
Removing Foursquare	I'm working and standing by at the same time!! Lol
Slang Translation	I'm working and standing by at the same time!! laughing out loud (@ The Fake Hotel) http://t.co/h4Xe9JHd
Stop Word Removal	working standing time!! Lol (@ Fake Hotel) http://t.co/h4Xe9JHd
Apostrophe Removal	Im working and standing by at the same time!! Lol (@ The Fake Hotel) http://t.co/h4Xe9JHd
Combined	working standing time!! laughing loud

translation and was a simple, exact string compare. If the word was found in the database, it was removed. This removes words contained on a 571-item list of common words. Examples of each data-scrubbing step are shown in Table 2.

3.3   Naive Bayes Classifier

The naive Bayes classifier was created to identify which posts were related to the location at which the post was created. A phrase like, "The pizza is great here. (@ Famous Pizza)" is likely related to the location. A post such as, "I had the worst day at work ever! (@ The Bus Stop)" probably isn't related to the location. Naive Bayes was selected, as its accuracy in text sentiment classification was extremely similar to other machine learning methods, including support vector machines and maximum entropy [10]. Meanwhile, naive Bayes is much easier to implement to quickly test the proposed approach.

Feature selection was inspired by sentiment analysis classifiers. It includes unigrams, emoticon presence, and exclamation point presence. The classifier used here is a Boolean naive Bayes classifier and tests simply for the a presence of a feature, and not it's relative frequency.

3.4   Sentiment Assignment

Sentiment is assigned using the Affective Norms for English Words (ANEW) database. This database contains words and three values: valence, arousal, and dominance that correspond to the particular sentiment of a given word. Valence is the pleasantness of a word, arousal is how exciting a word is, and less strongly related is dominance, which relates to control [16]. The total sentiment of a post is computed as the sum of the sentiment of all the words in the post divided by the total number of words. This accounts for the relative sentiment of an entry as a function of the number of words. A short post with many sentiment-containing words would be rated with a higher overall sentiment than a long post with relatively few sentiment-containing entries. In this implementation, removing words skews the computed valence. The post, "I hate this place" has one sentiment containing word - hate - and four words total so the sentiment included in hate would be divided by four words. If we apply stop word removal the post might become "hate place" and the sentiment included in hate would only be divided by two words.

4   Experimental Evaluation

4.1   Methodology

The data set used was a collection of 28,344 Foursquare check-ins that were cross posted to Twitter originating in 6 major cities: New York, Boston, Chicago, Washington D.C., Seattle, and San Francisco. Both the sentiment analysis method and the naive Bayes classifier are deterministic and yield the same results every time, so only one run of each method was required. The goal is to determine the effectiveness of the naïve Bayes geo-relevance classifier while also evaluating the effects of the required cleaning functions on the data set to be processed by the classifier.

The data set was run through each of the following processing scenarios:

- Baseline - No Data Scrubbing (Base)
- Removing Default Foursquare Text (4S)
- Translating Slang (ST)
- Removing Default Foursquare Text, and Translating Slang (4S, and ST)
- Removing Default Foursquare Text, Translating Slang, and Removing Stop Words (4S, ST, and SW)
- Removing Default Foursquare Text, Translating Slang, and using a naive Bayes Classifier (4S, ST, and NB)
- Removing Default Foursquare Text, Translating Slang, Removing Stop Words, and using a naive Bayes Classifier (4S, ST, SW, and NB).

A post was only included in the result if it contained a valence greater than zero. This eliminated any posts with no associated sentiment. Likewise, an individual location was only included if it contained a minimum number of posts that had a non-zero sentiment. Each model was run ten times with the minimum required posts from 1 to 10. This was to determine the minimum number of required posts at which the sentiment variations of a single-post would no longer cause fluctuations in overall mean sentiment. The goal was to determine the floor at which locations with low post count are no longer misrepresented by outliers.

In the models using the naive Bayes classifier, the classifier was trained on a data set of 3,000 Foursquare posts which were cross posted to Twitter. The training set was hand-coded by the author as either "related" or "unrelated" where the post appeared to be related to the location at which the post was generated, or unrelated. The classifier was then used to determine which posts in the larger data set were related. Any unrelated sentiments were ignored.

4.2 Results

The original data set had a total of 2967 unique locations. As seen in Table 3, adding the constraint that a location has at least one post that contains a sentiment reduced the number of represented locations to 2083. As the number of sentiment posts per location is increased Table 3 shows the resultant reduction in locations that can be processed. Likewise, the number of posts in the dataset also is reduced as the number of required valid sentiment posts per location is increased as also seen in Table 3 where the original set of 28,344 posts is reduced to just 15,063 with one post required, and reduces down to roughly 11,000 available posts to process when ten sentiment posts are required.

With the exception of the model containing the naive Bayes classifier, as the minimum number of sentiment containing posts increases, the number of total posts represented generally decreases by between 3 % and 8 %, while the number of represented locations generally decreases between 10 % and 20 %. Without this step, more than half the data would be inappropriately used.

Table 3. Number of unique posts and locations remaining in dataset versus increasing number of valid sentiment posts per location after each processing stage.

Minimum Posts	Unique Posts					Unique Locations				
	Base	4S	4S, ST	4S, ST, NB	4S, ST, SW, NB	Base	4S	4S, ST	4S, ST, NB	4S, ST, SW, NB
1	15063	5493	5840	1002	959	2083	1300	1342	523	503
2	14108	4842	5171	472	626	1128	649	673	143	170
3	13538	4454	4769	328	454	843	455	472	71	84
4	13073	4148	4448	190	358	688	353	365	25	52
5	12689	3852	4164	166	286	592	279	294	19	34
6	12284	3602	3909	141	221	511	229	243	14	21
7	11954	3416	3681	123	179	456	198	205	11	14
8	11590	3185	3457	102	165	404	165	173	8	12
9	11262	3033	3265	94	149	363	146	149	7	10
10	10965	2898	3130	67	131	330	131	134	4	8

One issue with location-based sentiment analysis is that there may be only a few posts with exceptionally high or low sentiment which can skew the sentiment calculation. As more posts are required, any given sentiment containing post is less likely to strongly skew the sentiment. Thus we expect the standard deviation of the mean sentiment scores for all locations in a given run to approach a stable value once a sufficient number of posts are required to infer a mean sentiment of a location. We infer that when the standard deviation stops changing significantly, the models are stable, and inferences can be made about the general minimum required post count at a location.

Sentiment itself isn't used to compare one processing scenario to another scenario and total computed valence may appear higher or lower in a given scenario. For example, a scenario that includes stop word removal will have a higher average valence as the same number of sentiment containing words will generally be divided by fewer words. This is acceptable as the sentiment is plotted to determine when the standard deviation approaches an asymptote, at which point it stops changing significantly.

The two other processing scenarios, slang translation, and stop word removal impact the overall data set less, and are supplementary. Stop word removal does very little except in the case of the naive Bayes classifier. This is expected, as these words are so common that they carry little interesting information, including sentiment. Slang translation does increase the number of represented locations and posts, and also increases the mean sentiment. This, too, is intuitive. Slang translation expands acronyms and short-hand allowing words contained within to be counted in sentiment analysis where they wouldn't have been previously. Shorthand like "h8" (hate) or "lol" (laughing out loud) aren't included in the ANEW database, but have strong sentiment values.

Shown in Table 4, the naive Bayes classifier had relatively high precision but the lower recall eliminated a large number of posts. As a result, so many posts are removed that a similarly high number of locations are eliminated and aren't considered for sentiment analysis. The small size of our data set was sensitive to the removal of posts and left too few locations for evaluation. However, the classifier does show promise. For a first effort, our recall (29–38 %) compares favorably to HP-Subj with Patterns (40 %), and our precision was acceptable (68–72 %) compared to HP-Subj with Patterns (90 %) [15]. interestingly, stop word removal did increase the recall of the naive Bayes classifier while not drastically reducing precision. This resulted in an increase in number of locations represented in the final data as shown in the final column of Table 3.

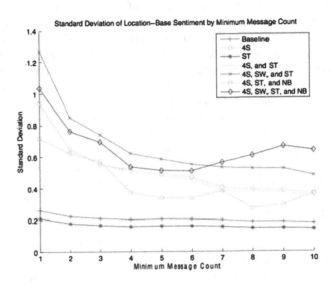

Fig. 2. Standard deviation of computed valence after each scrubbing step is applied and as minimum post count is incremented.

Reviewing individual naive Bayes results revealed some interesting trends. With short posts, individual features can have a very strong influence. Several short posts ("Yaaaay!", "Waiting :/") were strongly influenced by a small number of features like exclamation point presence or emoticon presence. One-word posts in particular will be judged by a single feature in this model, the relative frequency of that word in one class or another. Other posts were long and clear and still misclassified ("Settling into my home for the week. How I love #jetsetting!", "Riding a trolley to work lol how fun"). These may present opportunities for improvements with larger training sets.

Table 4. F1 score for naive Bayes classifier

	Base	4S	4S, ST	4S, SW, ST
Precision	0.800	0.681	0.718	0.697
Recall	0.019	0.290	0.327	0.376
F1 Score (Accuracy)	0.365	0.407	0.449	0.489

5 Conclusions and Future Work

The results indicate that simple application of off-the-shelf sentiment tools and methods to Foursquare data can lead to inaccurate results. The Foursquare data had significant amounts of additional data that confused traditional sentiment analysis methods. Inferring sentiment about a given location without at least a minimum number posts to represent said location leads to a large standard deviation of mean sentiments which means that a location's sentiment fluctuates significantly with the change of a single post. Additionally, a simple review of the data itself shows that many posts are system-generated text. Simply removing the text automatically added by the Foursquare service removed over 60 % of the posts even with a one post minimum per location (Table 3). These posts contained no user-generated content, but would contribute to a location's sentiment, if not accounted for. Accurate results rely on a deep understanding of the data, and require preprocessing prior to applying tools like ANEW. Our results indicate a minimum of seven representative posts before aggregating sentiment to make assumptions about a location (Fig. 2). After removing default data, and observing this floor, the number of represented locations is less than 10 % of those in the original data (Table 3). Application of up-front data review and scrubbing yields results more strongly related to the true aggregate sentiment of a location, instead of a skewed sentiment based on few comments. It also ensures that posts that are completely unrelated to a given establishment are appropriately removed prior to analysis.

The high precision found in this case is compelling (Table 4), and the recall is high enough to warrant attempts to improve the classifier.

In all cases, we demonstrated that a deeper understanding of the structure and content of the data is necessary to extract accurate information and draw correct conclusions. The preprocessing steps outlined here significantly increase the correctness and applicability of the results, even if they reduce the number of entries from the original data set. Those entries were red herrings anyway.

References

1. Bricker, E.: Can social media measure customer satisfaction? NetBase report, August 2011. (http://info.netbase.com/CanSocialMediaMeasureCustomerSatisfaction.html)
2. Banerjee, S., Viswanathan, V., Raman, K., Ying, H.: Assessing prime-time for geotargeting with mobile big data. J. Mark. Analytics 1(3), 174–183 (2013)
3. Diakopoulos, N., Shamma, D.: Characterizing debate performance via aggregated twitter sentiment. In: Proceedings of the SIGCHI Conference on Human Factors in Computing Systems, p. 1195 (2010)
4. Cheng, Z., Caverlee, J., Lee, K., Sui, D.: Exploring millions of footprints in location sharing services. In: Proceedings of the Fifth International AAAI Conference on Weblogs and Social Media, pp. 81–88 (2011)
5. Pang, B., Lee, L.: Opinion mining and sentiment analysis. Found. Trends Inf. Retrieval 2 (1-2), 1–135 (2008)

6. Social Networking Fact Sheet. Internet: http://www.pewinternet.org/fact-sheets/social-networking-fact-sheet/ (27 December 2013)
7. Mostafa, M.: More than words: social networks' text mining for consumer brand sentiments. Expert Syst. Appl. **40**(10), 4241–4251 (2013)
8. Hodeghatta, U.: Sentiment analysis of Hollywood movies on Twitter. In: Proceedings of the 2013 IEEE/ACM International Conference on Advances in Social Networks Analysis and Mining, pp. 1401–1404 (2013)
9. Zhang, Y., Chen, W., Yin, Z.: Collaborative filtering with social regularization for TV program recommendation. Knowl.-Based Syst. **54**, 310–317 (2013)
10. Go, A., Bhayani, R., Huang, L.: Twitter sentiment classification using distant supervision. CS224N Project report, pp. 1–12 (2009)
11. Patil, S., Norcie, G., Kapadia, A., Lee, A.: Check out where I am! In: CHI 2012 Extended Abstracts on Human Factors in Computing Systems, pp. 1997–2002 (2012)
12. Cramer, H., Rost, M., Holmquist, L.: Performing a check-in: emerging practices, norms and "conflicts" in location-sharing using foursquare. In: Proceedings of the 13th International Conference on Human Computer Interaction with Mobile Devices and Services, pp. 57–66 (2011)
13. Riloff, E., Wiebe, J.: Learning extraction patterns for subjective expressions. In: Proceedings of the 2003 Conference on Empirical Methods in Natural Language Processing, pp. 105–112 (2003)
14. Pang, B., Lee, L., Vaithyanathan, S.: Thumbs up? Sentiment classification using machine learning techniques. In: Proceedings of the ACL 2002 Conference on Empirical Methods in Natural Language Processing, pp. 79–86 (2002)
15. Agarwal, A., Xie, B., Vovsha, I., Rambow, O., Passonneau, R.: Sentiment analysis of Twitter data. In: Proceedings of the Workshop on Languages in Social Media, pp. 30–38 (2011)
16. Bradley, M., Lang, P.: Affective norms for English words (ANEW): instruction manual and affective ratings (1999). http://a.parsons.edu/~spani621/thesis/context/ANEW.pdf (4 January 2014)

Continuous and Discrete Deep Classifiers for Data Integration

Nataliya Sokolovska[1,2,3]([✉]), Salwa Rizkalla[1,2,3], Karine Clément[1,2,3], and Jean-Daniel Zucker[1,2,4]

[1] Institute of Cardiometabolism and Nutrition, ICAN, Assistance Publique Hôpitaux de Paris, Pitié-Salpêtrière Hospital, Paris, France
nataliya.sokolovska@upmc.fr
[2] Sorbonne Universités, UPMC University Paris 6, UMR_S 1166, ICAN, NutriOmics Team, Paris, France
[3] INSERM, UMR S U1166, NutriOmics Team, Paris, France
[4] Research Institute for Development, UMI 209, UMMISCO, Bondy, France

Abstract. Data representation in a lower dimension is needed in applications, where information comes from multiple high dimensional sources. A final compact model has to be interpreted by human experts, and interpretation of a classifier whose weights are discrete is much more straightforward. In this contribution, we propose a novel approach, called Deep Kernel Dimensionality Reduction which is designed for learning layers of new compact data representations simultaneously. We show by experiments on standard and on real large-scale biomedical data sets that the proposed method embeds data in a new compact meaningful representation, and leads to a lower classification error compared to the state-of-the-art methods. We also consider some state-of-the art deep learners and their corresponding discrete classifiers. We illustrate by our experiments that although purely discrete models do not always perform better than real-valued classifiers, the trade-off between the model accuracy and the interpretability is quite reasonable.

Keywords: Dimensionality reduction · Heterogeneous data integration · Bioinformatics

1 Introduction

Data integration is a challenging task with an ambitious goal to increase performance of supervised learning by introducing into a model data residing in different sources, since data of different nature tend to contain different parts of information about a problem. Multi-modal learning, heterogeneous data fusion, or data integration, involves relating information of different nature. In biological and medical applications, data coming from one source are already high-dimensional. Hence, data integration increases the dimensionality of a problem even more, and some feature selection or dimensionality reduction procedure

© Springer International Publishing Switzerland 2015
E. Fromont et al. (Eds.): IDA 2015, LNCS 9385, pp. 264–274, 2015.
DOI: 10.1007/978-3-319-24465-5_23

is absolutely needed both to make the computations tractable and to obtain a model which is compact.

Medical and biological knowledge can be naturally organised into hierarchies or deep structures: symptoms of diseases are observed and pathological states on all levels of "omics" (e.g., lipidomics, metagemomics) data are hidden. Therefore, there is a hope that hierarchical structures, which also involve data integration, reveal dependencies in data, including dependencies between data of different nature.

A hierarchical model that combines pieces of data issued from various sources, has to be interpreted by experts, e.g., by clinicians or biologists. It is not always obvious how to interpret a model whose parameters are continuous. However, it is much easier to interpret a classifier whose weights are discrete $\{-1, 0, 1\}$ [2]. It is, e.g., a situation where biologists would like to estimate gene richness (gene abundance), and stratify patients according to the number of genes in two – ill or healthy – groups. Another example would be the case of data integration in a classification task where we would like to measure the impact of each heterogeneous data source.

Our contribution is multi-fold:

- We introduce a novel kernel-based deep dimensionality reduction method which constructs layers of a deep structure simultaneously.
- We illustrate that the proposed framework is efficient on standard data sets and on a real original rich heterogeneous MicrObese data set [3].
- We consider corresponding discrete deep learners. Since the problem of discrete classification is NP-hard, we apply a simple randomised rounding to discretize the fractional solution.

The paper is organized as follows. We introduce our approach in Sect. 2. We show the results of our experiments in Sects. 3 and 4. Concluding remarks and perspectives close the paper.

2 Deep Continuous and Discrete Dimensionality Reduction

In this section, we consider a state-of-the-art deep learner, the deep restricted Boltzmann machines (stacked RBM) [7,9] and its discrete version. We also introduce a deep data integration framework which performs dimensionality reduction by constructing a multi-level hierarchy of new, more compact, data representations. We discuss a corresponding discrete classifier, i.e. classifier whose parameters are discrete $\{-1, 0, 1\}$.

To learn a hierarchical model, a training algorithm has access to n i.i.d. labeled pairs $(X_i, Y_i)_{1 \leq i \leq n}$. The input variable or covariate is $X \in \mathcal{X}$, and the class variable is $Y \in \mathcal{Y}$. The covariate variables are high-dimensional, and $X_i = (X_{i,1}, \ldots, X_{i,d})$, where d is the dimensionality of the problem. We are interested, in particular, to perform a dimensionality reduction so that the dimensionality of our problem becomes $r \ll d$, and so that we can carry out a classification task on a much more compact, and probably less noisy, feature space.

2.1 Randomized Rounding

To get discrete classifiers, we use randomized rounding in our experiments. Randomized rounding is a natural idea for rounding fractional solutions [11]. The algorithm starts from a real-valued solution, and for each parameter j of a model it draws a discrete solution from $\{-1, 0, 1\}$ according to $p(\theta_j)$, where θ_j is a value of parameter j after some bound constrained optimization.

2.2 Deep Restricted Boltzmann Machines

The restricted Boltzmann machines (RBM) [7,9] is undirected graphical model with observed ($\mathbf{v}$) and hidden ($\mathbf{h}$) variables, and it defines a probability distribution over $\mathbf{v}$ and $\mathbf{h}$:

$$\log P(\mathbf{v}, \mathbf{h}) \propto - \mathrm{E}(\mathbf{v}, \mathbf{h}) =$$
$$-\frac{1}{2\sigma^2}\mathbf{v}^T\mathbf{v} + \frac{1}{\sigma^2}(\mathbf{c}^T\mathbf{v} + \mathbf{b}^T\mathbf{h} + \mathbf{h}^T W \mathbf{v}), \tag{1}$$

and the conditional probability of hidden layers is given by

$$p(h_j|\mathbf{v}) = \mathrm{sigmoid}\Big(\frac{1}{\sigma^2}(b_j + \mathbf{w}_j^T\mathbf{v})\Big). \tag{2}$$

The graph has connections between $\mathbf{v}$ and $\mathbf{h}$ but no edges within hidden variables or within observed variables.

We use greedy layer-wise training followed by fine-tuning. In our experiments, we train a multimodal model, i.e., we train a deep RBM over concatenated heterogeneous data. To perform the fine-tuning, we use a standard resilient backpropagation (rprop).

2.3 Supervised Deep Kernel Dimensionality Reduction

Here we introduce our approach which is based on a kernel dimensionality reduction technique, and which constructs the layers of the deep framework simultaneously.

The semiparametric method known as Kernel Dimensionality Reduction (KDR) [4,5], is based on the estimation and optimization of a particular class of operators on reproducing kernel Hilbert spaces (RKHS). The idea is to relate dimensionality reduction to the problem of conditional independence, and to construct an objective function for optimization.

The KDR method assumes that it is possible to find a projection of initial covariate variables into a lower dimension space. The approach is based on an assumption that there is a r-dimensional subspace ($r \ll d$) which is referred to as the effective subspace. The dimensionality reduction can be viewed as a procedure testing conditional independence of variables such that

$$p(y|x) = \hat{p}(y|\theta^T x). \tag{3}$$

The covariance operator on RKHS is responsible for capturing conditional independence between variables. The new representation in a more compact feature space is a linear combination of observations.

The KDR method aims to minimize the following objective function

$$\det \hat{\Sigma}_{YY|U} = \frac{\det \hat{\Sigma}_{[YU][YU]}}{\det \hat{\Sigma}_{YY} \det \hat{\Sigma}_{UU}}, \tag{4}$$

where

$$U = \theta^T X, \tag{5}$$

and

$$\hat{\Sigma}_{[YU][YU]} = \begin{pmatrix} \hat{\Sigma}_{YY} & \hat{\Sigma}_{YU} \\ \hat{\Sigma}_{UY} & \hat{\Sigma}_{UU} \end{pmatrix} = \tag{6}$$

$$\begin{pmatrix} (\hat{K}_Y + \epsilon I_n)^2 & \hat{K}_Y \hat{K}_U \\ \hat{K}_U \hat{K}_Y & (\hat{K}_U + \epsilon I_n)^2 \end{pmatrix}. \tag{7}$$

$\hat{K}_Y$ and $\hat{K}_U$ are the centralized Gram matrices defined as follows:

$$\hat{K}_Y = \left(I_n - \frac{1}{n}1_n 1_n^T\right) G_Y \left(I_n - \frac{1}{n}1_n 1_n^T\right), \tag{8}$$

$$(G_Y)_{ij} = k(Y_i, Y_j), \tag{9}$$

$$\hat{K}_U = \left(I_n - \frac{1}{n}1_n 1_n^T\right) G_U \left(I_n - \frac{1}{n}1_n 1_n^T\right), \tag{10}$$

$$(G_U)_{ij} = k(U_i, U_j). \tag{11}$$

The Gaussian kernel

$$k(a,b) = \exp\left(\frac{-\|a-b\|^2}{\sigma^2}\right) \tag{12}$$

is used throughout the paper and in our experiments.

To optimize the criterion, a gradient descent with line search can be used. The matrix of parameters is updated on iteration t according to

$$\theta^{t+1} = \theta^t - \gamma \frac{\partial \log \det \hat{\Sigma}_{YY|U}}{\partial \theta} = \tag{13}$$

$$\theta^t - \gamma 2\epsilon Tr[\hat{\Sigma}_{YY|U}^{-1} \hat{K}_Y (\hat{K}_U + \epsilon I_n)^{-1} \frac{\partial \hat{K}_U}{\partial \theta} (\hat{K}_U + \epsilon I_n)^{-2} \hat{K}_U \hat{K}_Y], \tag{14}$$

where

$$\hat{\Sigma}_{YY|U} = (\hat{K}_Y + \epsilon I_n)^2 - \hat{K}_Y \hat{K}_U (\hat{K}_U + \epsilon I_n)^{-2} \hat{K}_U \hat{K}_Y. \tag{15}$$

Therefore, the KDR approach produces a new reduced representation of the data X which is $\theta^T X$.

It was reported that the KDR is an efficient state-of-the art method of dimensionality reduction on real data [4,5]. In general, if we want to combine the advantages of the KDR with a hierarchical "smoothing" structure, we could construct a cascade of KDRs, where an output of one run of the KDR would be an input for another run. However, in this situation we would obtain a solution which is approximated, and not exact.

The proposed deep dimensionality reduction technique is as follows. Each layer of the hierarchical structure is a new data representation $X'' = \theta_i^T X'$ of the layer underneath X', and where X', in its turn, is a reduced representation of some lower layer. An iterative process such as a convex optimization algorithm which updates parameters of a model, makes an update for parameters of all levels of the hierarchy on each iteration, i.e. simultaneously.

We introduce a deep semiparametric model with D layers

$$p(y|x) = \hat{p}\Big(y|\theta_D^T(\theta_{D-1}^T \ldots (\underbrace{\theta_1^T(\underbrace{\theta_0^T x}_{x'})))}_{x''})\Big), \tag{16}$$

$$\underbrace{}_{\ldots}$$

where x', x'', $\ldots$, are new representations in the deep structure that are learned simultaneously in one optimization procedure.

We clearly see that θ_{j+1} depends on θ_j for all $j \in \{1, \ldots D\}$, and optimization can not be done separately for each layer. By the implicit function theorem, applying the chain rule, for each θ_j, except for θ_0, we have

$$\frac{\partial \ell(\theta)}{\partial \theta_j} = \frac{\partial \ell(\theta)}{\partial \theta_{j'}}\Big(\frac{\partial \ell^2(\theta)}{\partial \theta_{j'}^2}\Big)^{-1}\frac{\partial \ell^2(\theta)}{\partial \theta_j \partial \theta_{j'}}, \tag{17}$$

where $\ell = \det \hat{\Sigma}_{YY|U}$.

To optimize parameters associated with a layer, and to compute the first derivative with respect to parameters of this layer, we also need the second derivative of the layer underneath. Using Eq. (17) we update simultaneously all θ in one iteration of a gradient descent, and new compact representations associated with different levels of generalization are estimated simultaneously according to

$$\theta_j^{t+1} = \theta_j^t - \gamma\frac{\partial \ell(\theta)}{\partial \theta_j}. \tag{18}$$

2.4   KDR Versus DKDR: Discussion

A natural question which arises is why the deep KDR is better than the KDR. Although it is currently impossible to provide a theoretical foundation for it, there is an intuition why the deep method is expected to perform and performs better in practice. Note that real data are always noisy, and a "good" clustering or dimensionality reduction can significantly reduce the noise. The principal idea is that if features are tied into clusters of "high quality", then it is easier to detect a signal from data, and therefore the generalizing classification accuracy is higher. The hierarchical dimensionality reduction plays here a role of a filter, and a filter with multiple layers seems to perform better than a one-layer filter.

Also note that the DKDR criterion is convex, and we can apply any gradient-based method to optimize the model parameters.

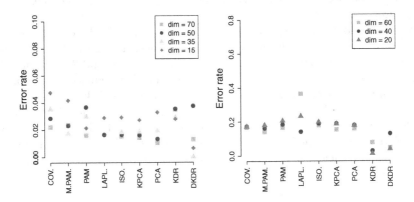

Fig. 1. Experiments on Golub Data Set (on the left) and Alon Data (on the right). Error rate as a function of dimensionality reduction method and dimension in reduced models.

3   Experiments on Standard Data Sets

In this section we show our results on two standard biological data sets, the Golub et al. (1999) data and Alon et al. (1999) set.

We compare the performance of the Deep Kernel Dimensionality Reduction method to some standard unsupervised dimensionality reduction approaches such as: (1) Principal Component Analysis (PCA), (2) Kernel Principal Component Analysis (KPCA), (3) Isomap (ISO), (4) Laplacian Eigenmaps (LAPL), (5) robust clustering methods, such as the Partitioning Around Medoids (PAM) which is a robust version of the k-means, where medoids are representatives of clusters, (6) PAM clustering, where the representatives of clusters are median values of instances in clusters (M.PAM). We also compare our results to the following supervised approaches: (1) the full model, i.e. the model with the original high-dimensional feature space, (2) the supervised dimensionality reduction learning procedure KDR. We apply an SVM with an RBF kernel to learn reduced models. The cross validation method (5-folds cross validation) is used to adjust hyper-parameters of all approaches being tested.

In Golub [6] data we dispose of 72 patients and about 7000 gene expressions (Affymetrix probes). Among these patients, 47 subjects have acute lymphoblastic leukemia, and 25 are diagnosed with acute myeloid leukemia, therefore, we have a classification problem with 2 classes. Figure 1 on the left illustrates the results in terms of 5-folds cross validation error rate. We consider reduced models with 70, 50, 35, and 15 parameters. The choice of the reduced dimensions is due to the number of observations: for several dimensionality reduction methods (PCA, KPCA, Isomap) the reduced dimension of parameters has not to be bigger than one of observations. So, in the DKDR case this leads to a hierarchy with 4 layers (with the numbers of features equal to 70, 50, 35, 15). We see quite clearly that the proposed DKDR approach outperforms all other methods, and the best accuracy is reached by models with the least number of parameters, i.e., 15 and 35 features.

The Alon data set [1] contains 62 patients and 2000 gene expressions (Affymerix origonucleaotide array) of colon tissues. The patients are coming from two classes: 40 patients are diagnosed with a tumor, and 22 patients have normal colon tissues. The results on the dimensionality reduction experiments are shown on Fig. 1 on the right (5-folds cross validation). Taking into consideration that the number of patients is 62, we reduce the dimensionality to 60, 40, and 20 parameters. The results are similar to ones we obtained on the Golub data. Here, however, the KDR slightly outperforms the DKDR. As in the Golub data, the most efficient models are the most compact ones among tested models.

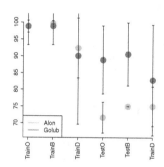

Fig. 2. Accuracy on Golub and Alon data sets: experiments with continuous (standard) deep restricted Boltzmann machines and discrete deep restricted Boltzmann machines.

Figure 2 provides some insights into performance of discrete classifiers. We show accuracy on training and test sets for Golub and Alon data as a function of learning method with the deep restricted Boltzmann machines. "TrainO" and "TestO" stand for performance with the original method; "B" stands for the optimisation with bound constraints as described in Sect. 2.2, and "D" is the performance of the discrete classifier (obtained with the randomized rounding). In these experiments we used a deep RBM with three hidden layers (100, 10, and 1 hidden variables respectively). We observe that the resilient backpropagation with bound constraints achieves a very reasonable performance. Note, however, that the deep RBM has a strong tendency to overfit [10], and the gap between accuracy on training and testing data is quite significant.

4 Experiments on Real Biomedical MicrObese Data

In this section, we show that the framework introduced above in Sect. 2, can be efficiently applied to a real high-dimensional heterogeneous data integration problem.

We describe our results on the MicrObese data [3], and we compare the performance of the deep kernel dimensionality reduction to some state-of-the-art dimensionality reduction methods.

The MicroObese cohort [3] combines heterogeneous data, including clinical data of patients, abundance of gut flora genes, and gene expressions of adipose tissue. In our experiments, we consider models which integrate these heterogeneous sources pairwise and altogether. Our primary goal is to illustrate that the DKDR is an efficient dimensionality reduction method. Another question is what data source or a combination of data sources is more informative for the patients classification.

The problem is a perfect illustration of $n << p$ problem, i.e., where the number of observations is much smaller than the number of parameters. The number of patients in the cohort is 35. We dispose of 20 clinical and alimentary parameters, 24,000 genes of gut flora, and 350 genes of adipose tissue.

4.1 Deep Dimensionality Reduction on MicrObese Data

We compare the results of the DKDR on the MicrObese data set to the state-of-the-art dimensionality reduction methods mentioned above, in Sect. 3. Note that "ALL" method stands for the result with all original features. To train models with and without reduced dimensionality, we use an SVM with an RBF kernel [8], since a non-linear separator reaches a higher accuracy on our data than a linear classifier. We show the results in terms of the 5-folds cross validation error rate. As mentioned before, we have three types of data, and we test various combinations of them to find the best one. We run our experiments on the following combinations:

- Gut Flora metagenomics (GF abbreviation on Fig. 3)
- gene expressions of Adipose Tissue (AT)
- Clinical parameters, Gut Flora abundance, and gene expressions of Adipose Tissue (C/GF/AT)
- Clinical parameters and Gut Flora metagenomics (C/GF)
- Clinical parameters and gene expressions of Adipose Tissue (C/AT)
- Gut Flora metagenomics and gene expressions of Adipose Tissue (GF/AT)

We construct the deep framework DKDR as follows. Although the choice of the number of layers in the hierarchy is a delicate matter, here, without loss of generality, we fix dimensionality of each level to be 2 times smaller than the dimensionality of its lower level. The number of genes of gut flora is about 24,000, and all models including this data source contain more than 24,000 parameters. So, for all models with gut flora, we construct a hierarchy with 6 levels. The models without the gut flora have 3 levels only.

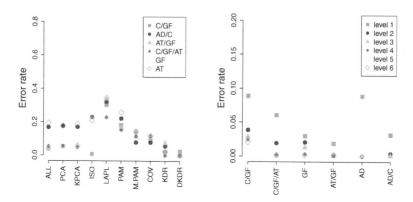

Fig. 3. MicrObese Cohort. On the left: error rate as a function of dimensionality reduction method and data integrated into the model. On the right: error rate as a function of data integrated and level in the hierarchy.

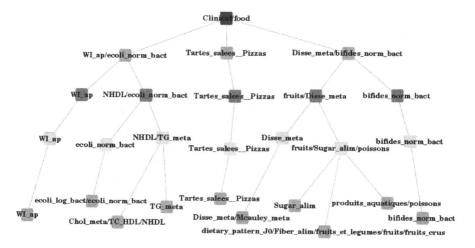

Fig. 4. A hierarchy of clinical parameters of MicrObese data constructed by a discrete approach.

Figure 3 on the left shows the error rate as a function of a dimensionality reduction method for data involved into the classification task. We have observed that data integration has a positive effect: integrating all data sources leads to a lower error on a testing set (5-folds cross validation error rate). It is also easy to see that the proposed DKDR approach reaches a higher accuracy than other methods.

We notice that the most compact models achieve quite a high accuracy. It also happens for some data sources that performance of several levels is similar, and that further dimensionality reduction does not ameliorate the accuracy anymore.

Figure 4 illustrates a hierarchy of clinical parameters and alimentary patterns of MicrObese data set, and Table 1 provides a brief description of the parameters.

Table 1. Description of clinical parameters of MicrObese data.

WI_ap	Walking index based on physical activity
ecoli_log (norm)_bact	Escherichia coli in log scale and normalized
Chol_meta	Total cholesterol
TC_HDL, NHDL	Ratio of cholesterol, non-HDL cholesterol
TG_meta	Triglycerides
Tartes_salees_Pizzas	Savory pies and pizza
Disse_meta, Mccauley_meta	Insuline sensitivity
Sugar_alim	Sugar intake
produits_aquatiques_poissons	Fish and fish products
dietary_pattern, Fiber_alim	Diatary quality clusters
fruits_et_legumes, fruits, fruits_crus	Fruit and vegetables intake

In the deep structure on Fig. 4, each level is a generalization of its lower level. E.g., if we look at the leftmost branch of the tree, we will see that for a reasonable patients classification it is sufficient to measure walking index and particular bacteria (the yellow node), and spending efforts on measuring total cholesterol, ratio of total cholesterol to HDL cholesterol, non-HDL cholesterol, and triglycerides does not bring any additional information. Note that the predictive power of the upper level (the yellow one, with a quite small number of parameters) is not worse than of the lowest level of the tree.

5   Conclusion

Data integration is a delicate problem, especially in applications where data are high-dimensional and the number of observations is small. We have proposed to reduce dimensionality by a deep kernel-based approach which learns new representations of data simultaneously in a hierarchical way, and which do not waste any effort on modeling data distributions, as most state-of-the-art methods do. We have considered continuous and discrete deep classifiers, and although the discrete classifiers do not always reach the best performance, the corresponding models are easily interpretable. We show that the novel deep kernel dimensionality reduction is efficient on standard data sets and on a real medical complex cohort. The proposed deep SVM-based classifier significantly outperforms modern state-of-the-art approaches. Moreover, the multi-level hierarchy, especially one based on a discrete classifier, can provide new scientific hypotheses for biologists doing pre-clinical research, and help to develop methods of personalized medicine.

Acknowledgments. The clinical work was supported by Agence Nationale de la Recherche (ANR MICRO-Obes), KOT-Ceprodi and the association Fondation Coeur et Arteres. All ethical agreement are obtained. This work is also part of the European Unions Seventh Framework Program under grant agreement HEALTH-F4-2012-305312 (Metacardis project).

References

1. Alon, U., Barkai, N., Notterman, D.A., Gish, K., Ybarra, S., Mack, D., Levine, A.J.: Broad patterns of gene expression revealed by clustering analysis of tumor and normal colon tissues probed by oligonucleotide arrays. Proc. Nat. Acad. Sci. **96**(12), 6745–6750 (1999)
2. Chevaleyre, Y., Koriche, F., Zucker, J.-D.: Rounding methods for discrete linear classification. In: ICML (2013)
3. Cotillard, A., et al.: Dietary intervention impact on gut microbial gene richness. Nature **500**, 585–588 (2013)
4. Fukumizu, K., Bach, F., Jordan, M.: Dimensionality reduction for supervised learning with reproducing kernel hilbert spaces. J. Mach. Learn. Res. **5**, 73–99 (2004)
5. Fukumizu, K., Bach, F., Jordan, M.I.: Kernel dimensionality reduction for supervised learning. In: NIPS (2003)
6. Golub, T.R., Slonim, D.K., Tamayo, P., Huard, C., Gaasenbeek, M., Mesirov, J.P., Coller, H., Loh, M.L., Downing, J.R., Caligiuri, M.A., Bloomfield, C.D., Lander, E.S.: Molecular classification of cancer: class discovery and class prediction by gene expression monitoring. Science **286**(5439), 531–537 (1999)
7. Hinton, G.E., Salakhutdinov, R.R.: Reducing the dimensionality of data with neural networks. Science **313**, 504–507 (2006)
8. Karatzoglou, A., Smola, A., Hornik, K., Zeileis, A.: Kernlab - an S4 package for kernel methods in R. J. Stat. Softw. **11**(9), 1–20 (2004)
9. Ngiam, J., Khosla, A., Kim, M., Lee, H., Ng, A.Y., Nam, J.: Multimodal deep learning. In: ICML (2011)
10. Srivastava, N., Hinton, G., Krizhevsky, A., Sutskever, I., Salakhudinov, R.: Dropout: a simple way to prevent neural networks from overfitting. J. Mach. Learn. Res. **15**, 1929–1958 (2014)
11. Williamson, D.P., Shmoys, D.B.: The design of approximation algorithms. Cambridge University Press, Cambridge (2011)

A Bayesian Approach for Identifying Multivariate Differences Between Groups

Yuriy Sverchkov[1]([⊠]) and Gregory F. Cooper[2]

[1] University of Wisconsin—Madison, Madison, WI, USA
yuriy@biostat.wisc.edu
[2] University of Pittsburgh, Pittsburgh, PA, USA
gfc@pitt.edu

Abstract. We present a novel approach to the problem of detecting multivariate statistical differences across groups of data. The need to compare data in a multivariate manner arises naturally in observational studies, randomized trials, comparative effectiveness research, abnormality and anomaly detection scenarios, and other application areas. In such comparisons, it is of interest to identify statistical differences across the groups being compared. The approach we present in this paper addresses this issue by constructing statistical models that describe the groups being compared and using a decomposable Bayesian Dirichlet score of the models to identify variables that behave statistically differently between the groups. In our evaluation, the new method performed significantly better than logistic lasso regression in indentifying differences in a variety of datasets under a variety of conditions.

1 Introduction

There are many circumstances in which data collected from different sources are similar in some respects, but nonetheless differ in ways that are interesting to report. Such circumstances arise naturally in observational studies, where, for example, a clinical researcher may observe a difference in the prevalence of a condition between two groups of patients and would like to explore the reasons behind the difference; in randomized trials, where we might be interested not only in the effectiveness of a treatment but also whether its effects are particular to subgroups of the subjects and if so, what the relevant contextual relationships are; in comparative effectiveness research, where an observed difference between two clinical treatment approaches is to be explained; and other application areas. Identifying patterns of differences is also useful in abnormality and anomaly detection scenarios, where data on a potentially anomalous population of samples are compared to a "normal" baseline population.

We approach the problem of identifying interesting patterns of differences from a statistical standpoint, where given a pair of data groups over a vector of discrete random variables we would like to identify variables that exhibit statistical differences. A variable might have a different marginal distribution in the two groups and/or a different conditional distribution when conditioning on

© Springer International Publishing Switzerland 2015
E. Fromont et al. (Eds.): IDA 2015, LNCS 9385, pp. 275–285, 2015.
DOI: 10.1007/978-3-319-24465-5_24

the values of some of the other variables. We present and evaluate a method for identifying differences in both of those categories.

The method accomplishes this task by building models for each of the groups and for both groups, scoring local differences in distribution by comparing how well these alternative parameterizations fit the data locally, and using these local scores to obtain a score of how different the two groups are as a whole. In this paper, the performance of our method for identifying differences between groups at the variable-level is evaluated using data based on four UCI Machine Learning Repository data sets [1].

2   Background

We review some general background literature about distribution comparison followed by background relevant to Bayesian networks, which is the model that our method uses, with a particular focus on learning models from data and the Bayesian Dirichlet score which we use.

2.1   Comparing Distributions

There are various statistical methods that are applicable to the problem of identifying differences across a pair of groups. The statistical approach that most closely relates is that of *contrast set mining*. Bay and Pazzani [2] present contrast-set mining as the discovery of joint variable-value assignments that have different levels of support in different groups. The approach taken parallels association-rule mining in that the space of possible joint variable-value assignments is searched to maximize a score (in association-rule mining, this score is the lift of a rule, while in contrast-set mining a chi-square test is used). The main challenge in contrast-set mining is the search of the exponentially large space of possible sets (joint variable-value assignments), and much of the literature is dedicated to discussing heuristics and pruning rules to make the search feasible. The output of contrast-set mining is the list of joint variable-value assignments (the sets) which have differing support across groups, ranked by the extent of that difference and tested for significance. Novak et al. [11] summarize further literature on contrast-set mining and its relation to association-rule mining, emerging pattern mining, and subgroup mining. While these approaches address a similar task to that of our method, these are all value-based approaches. Their task is to identify specific value ranges in which the differences between the groups are most pronounced. In contrast, our approach is variable-based, meaning that we identify variables the distributions of which are different across the groups.

The variable-based nature of our approach bears some similarity to traditional statistical methods. There are multiple traditional statistical tests that are designed to compare distributions. For categorical variables, the Chi-Square test is applicable, it tests whether two groups are independent. This can be used to determine if a variable has different distributions across two groups by testing whether it is dependent on the group variable. For continuous variables, the

Kolmogorov-Smirnov test is often used to determine equality of distributions. Note that these tests are univariate, and cannot therefore be used to compare two multivariate groups of data directly. There are other measures of distribution differences that are multivariate in nature, such as Hotelling's T-squared test, mutual information, or Kullback-Leibler divergence. These measures are multivariate, but they do not allow for examining the contributions of differences in individual variables to the overall measure of difference across the groups. The approach we present bridges this gap by providing both a measure of overall difference, as well as a breakdown into contributions in the differences of distributions of individual variables.

2.2 Bayesian Networks

As mentioned above, the approach we present relies on building statistical models for the data groups to be compared. In particular, the model we construct is a Bayesian Network (BN). A BN over the variables $\mathbf{X} = (X_1, \ldots, X_n)$, where each variable X_i is discrete and takes K_i values, consists of a directed acyclic graph (DAG) where each node represents a variable X_i and each node is associated with a conditional probability table (CPT) defined by a set of parameters

$$\theta_{ijk} = P(X_i = x_{ik} | \Pi_i = \pi_{ij}) \tag{1}$$

where x_{ik} represents the k-th value X_i takes and π_{ij} represents the j-th configuration of X_i's set of parents Π_i [8].

In order to obtain a BN from data, the DAG structure is needed. In some cases the structure or elements of the structure for a given domain may be known, but often the structure must be learned from data. Daly et al. [5] provide an extensive review of BN structure learning and divide existing methods into constraint-based methods, where conditional independencies (CI) in the data are used to constrain the structure; and score search, where the space of BN structures is searched for a structure that has the best score according to some scoring criterion. Constraint-based methods use CIs obtained from statistical tests on the data to eliminate possible arcs in the network structure, such as the the PC algorithm by Spirtes and Glymour [13], for example. Score-based techniques seek to optimize some score function of the graph based on the data. The space over which many methods in this category search is that of possible DAGs, which is combinatorial in the number of variables, and the task of optimizing the score is NP-hard in general [3]. Algorithms that feasibly search the entire space of DAGs in the case of up to approximately 30 variables include dynamic programming approaches [10, 12] and an application of A* search to the space of DAGs [14]. For data with more variables, many search methods apply various heuristics and do not perform an exhaustive search of the space; most commonly these methods employ some sort of greedy search strategy [5].

In our implementation we used greedy-thick-thinning, an algorithm described but not named in [8], which maximizes the K2 score [4] in a greedy fashion by starting with an empty graph, adding arcs that most increase the score until no more arc additions can increase the score, and then performs arc removals that increase the score most until no more removals increase the score. Any score search strategy can be used with our method.

2.3   Bayesian Dirichlet Scores for Bayesian Networks

In this work we use Bayesian Dirichlet (BD) scoring in order to leverage both the mathematical properties of the score and its statistical interpretation. The BD score is motivated by the search for a maximum *a posteriori* (MAP) model, a graph structure $\mathcal{M}$ that is most probable given the data $\mathcal{D}$ and prior belief. Directly computing a posterior $P(\mathcal{M}|\mathcal{D})$ for the structure is an intractable task; however, we can show that it is proportional to an easily computable quantity. From Bayes' rule we have that $P(\mathcal{M}|\mathcal{D}) \propto P(\mathcal{M})P(\mathcal{D}|\mathcal{M})$, where $P(\mathcal{M})$ is a prior for the graph structure. Often the graph structure prior is assumed to be uniform, an assumption that we make in this paper, but one that can be easily relaxed, and the goal becomes to maximize $P(\mathcal{D}|\mathcal{M})$, which is a marginal likelihood. Under the assumptions of global and local parameter independence, and parameter modularity [9], the marginal likelihood for the full model $P(\mathcal{D}|\mathcal{M})$ is the product of local marginal likelihoods:

$$P(\mathcal{D}|\mathcal{M}) = E_{\boldsymbol{\Theta}|\mathcal{M}} \prod_{i=1}^{n} \prod_{j=1}^{J_i} P(\mathcal{D}|\boldsymbol{\Theta}_{ij}, \mathcal{M}) = \prod_{i=1}^{n} \prod_{j=1}^{J_i} E_{\boldsymbol{\Theta}_{ij}|\mathcal{M}} P(\mathcal{D}|\boldsymbol{\Theta}_{ij}, \mathcal{M}). \quad (2)$$

Here we treat BN parameters as random variables with a prior distribution rather than as point values; that is, the particular value for a network parameter θ_{ijk} is just a point in the continuum of possible values that a random variable Θ_{ijk} takes. In the context of a BD score such as K2 [4] or the BDeu score [9], the prior distribution of $\boldsymbol{\Theta}_{ij} = (\Theta_{ij1}, \dots, \Theta_{ijK_i})$ is Dirichlet with parameters $\boldsymbol{\alpha}_{ij} = (\alpha_{ij1}, \dots, \alpha_{ijK_i})$. For a given structure, the distribution of a variable X_i given a parent configuration π_{ij} is Dirichlet-multinomial, with a closed-form marginal likelihood

$$E_{\boldsymbol{\Theta}_{ij}|\mathcal{M}} P(\mathcal{D}|\boldsymbol{\Theta}_{ij}, \mathcal{M}) = \frac{\Gamma(\alpha_{ij\cdot})}{\Gamma(\alpha_{ij\cdot} + N_{ij\cdot})} \prod_{k=1}^{K_i} \frac{\Gamma(\alpha_{ijk} + N_{ijk})}{\Gamma(\alpha_{ijk})} \quad (3)$$

where J_i is the number of configurations of the parent set Π_i, $\alpha_{ij\cdot} := \sum_{k=1}^{K_i} \alpha_{ijk}$, N_{ijk} is the number of samples in the data for which $X_i = x_{ik}$ and $\Pi_i = \pi_{ij}$, and $N_{ij\cdot} := \sum_{k=1}^{K_i} N_{ijk}$. Different choices of the Dirichlet parameter priors lead to different BD scores: for example, the K2 score is obtained from using uniform priors (all $\alpha_{ijk} = 1$), and the BDeu score is obtained from using priors with $\alpha_{ijk} = \frac{\alpha^*}{J_i K_i}$ where α^* is the Equivalent Sample Size (ESS) hyperparameter.

Having outlined the differences of the proposed method with common approaches to the statistical comparison of data and reviewed the relevant background regarding about BNs and the BD score, we next describe our method.

3   Method

Consider two groups of data $\mathcal{D}_1$ and $\mathcal{D}_2$ over the same set of variables $\mathbf{X} = (X_1, \ldots, X_n)$, and denote the concatenation of $\mathcal{D}_1$ and $\mathcal{D}_2$ by $\mathcal{D}_\cup$. If $\mathcal{D}_1$ and $\mathcal{D}_2$ are not different in a statistical sense, they follow the same distribution, which is therefore the distribution of $\mathcal{D}_\cup$. Let $\mathcal{M}_1$, $\mathcal{M}_2$, $\mathcal{M}_\cup$ denote maximum a posteriori (MAP) models within some space of models for the data in $\mathcal{D}_1$, $\mathcal{D}_2$, and $\mathcal{D}_\cup$ respectively. In the case where $\mathcal{D}_1$ and $\mathcal{D}_2$ are the same, we expect that $P(\mathcal{D}_1|\mathcal{M}_1) \times P(\mathcal{D}_2|\mathcal{M}_2) \leq P(\mathcal{D}_\cup|\mathcal{M}_\cup)$ in the large sample limit, since modeling the two groups as governed by independent distributions does not yield a better fitting model than when the groups are modeled as coming from the same distribution. In the case where $\mathcal{D}_1$ and $\mathcal{D}_2$ are statistically different, we expect $P(\mathcal{D}_1|\mathcal{M}_1) \times P(\mathcal{D}_2|\mathcal{M}_2) > P(\mathcal{D}_\cup|\mathcal{M}_\cup)$ in the large sample limit.

Let us extend this idea from the model level to the parameters of the models, an extension that can be applied when the models have the following properties: the distribution of a variable X_i is defined by a vector of parameters $\boldsymbol{\theta}_i$, parameters $\boldsymbol{\theta}_i$ are drawn from a distribution $\boldsymbol{\Theta}_i$, and parameter independence holds, such that, $\boldsymbol{\Theta}_i \perp \boldsymbol{\Theta}_{i'}$ for $i \neq i'$. BNs with Dirichlet parameter priors have these two properties. In order to compare parameters across models, the parameters compared must match in meaning. First we will consider the case where $\mathcal{M}_1$, $\mathcal{M}_2$, and $\mathcal{M}_\cup$ have the same structure, and therefore, have parameters that can be perfectly matched across models; next we will extend the approach to the more general case of structures that have consistent ordering, where matching happens between sets of parameters.

In the case where $\mathcal{M}_1$, $\mathcal{M}_2$, and $\mathcal{M}_\cup$ have the same structure, we can consider each Dirichlet-multinomial component of the full model in isolation. Consider comparing the marginal likelihood of modeling $\boldsymbol{\theta}_{ij} = P(X_i|\pi_{ij})$ independently across the two groups of data

$$T_{ij} = P(\mathcal{D}_1, \mathcal{D}_2|\boldsymbol{\Theta}_{ij}^{(1)} \perp \boldsymbol{\Theta}_{ij}^{(2)}) = $$
$$\left(E_{\boldsymbol{\Theta}_{ij}|\mathcal{M}_1} P(\mathcal{D}_1|\boldsymbol{\Theta}_{ij}, \mathcal{M}_1)\right) \left(E_{\boldsymbol{\Theta}_{ij}|\mathcal{M}_2} P(\mathcal{D}_2|\boldsymbol{\Theta}_{ij}, \mathcal{M}_2)\right) \quad (4)$$

to the marginal likelihood of modeling $\boldsymbol{\theta}_{ij}$ as being the same for both groups

$$S_{ij} = P(\mathcal{D}_1, \mathcal{D}_2|\boldsymbol{\Theta}_{ij}^{(1)} = \boldsymbol{\Theta}_{ij}^{(2)}) = E_{\boldsymbol{\Theta}_{ij}|\mathcal{M}_\cup} P(\mathcal{D}_\cup|\boldsymbol{\Theta}_{ij}, \mathcal{M}_\cup). \quad (5)$$

The ratio T_{ij}/S_{ij} of these quantities is a Bayes factor that we can use to quantify the difference in the distribution $X_i|\pi_{ij}$ across the two groups of data.

Next, let us consider the more general case where the structures of $\mathcal{M}_1$, $\mathcal{M}_2$, and $\mathcal{M}_\cup$ differ, but have consistent ordering, meaning that if X_i is an ancestor of X_j in any one of the networks, X_j cannot be an ancestor of X_i in any other network. Note that constraining the ordering of the variables in a BN does not constrain the space of joint probability distributions that can be represented. In our evaluation we enforce that constraint by learning $\mathcal{M}_\cup$ without order constraints and use the topological order of the learned network to constrain $\mathcal{M}_1$ and $\mathcal{M}_2$. There are many other possible approaches to enforcing these constraints, ranging from obtaining an order *a priori* to minimizing the number of explicit constraints using an iterative process. Exploring these alternative approaches is outside of the scope of this paper.

In this more general setting, the parent sets of a variable X_i can turn out to be different in the three models, and may have some partial overlap. To handle such overlap, we introduce a new index η as follows: Denote the parent sets of X_i in $\mathcal{M}_1$, $\mathcal{M}_2$, and $\mathcal{M}_\cup$ by $\Pi_i^{(1)}$, $\Pi_i^{(2)}$, $\Pi_i^{(\cup)}$ respectively. Let $J_i^{(\cdot)}$ be the number of possible configurations of $\Pi_i^{(\cdot)}$, and enumerate those configurations by $j = 1, \ldots, J_i^{(\cdot)}$. Let $\Pi_i^\cap$ denote $\Pi_i^{(1)} \cap \Pi_i^{(2)} \cap \Pi_i^{(\cup)}$. Let H_i be the number of possible configurations of $\Pi_i^\cap$ and enumerate those configurations by $\eta = 1, \ldots, H_i$. For example, suppose that in data where all variables are binary, for a variable X_1 we have $\Pi_1^{(\cup)} = \{X_2, X_3, X_4\}$, $\Pi_1^{(1)} = \{X_2, X_3, X_5\}$, and $\Pi_1^{(2)} = \{X_2, X_4, X_5\}$. Then we have that $\Pi_1^\cap = \{X_2\}$, and there are two possible configurations $\eta = 1$ and $\eta = 2$ for this set, corresponding to x_{21} and x_{22}. Let $J_i(\eta)$ indicate the subset of parent configurations $j \in \{1, \ldots, J_i\}$ that are consistent with configuration η. That is, for example, if $\eta = 1$ represents x_{21} in our example, then $J_1^\cup(1)$ is the set of j-values that correspond to the set of parent assignments $\{(x_{21}, x_{31}, x_{41}), (x_{21}, x_{31}, x_{42}), (x_{21}, x_{32}, x_{41}), (x_{21}, x_{32}, x_{42})\}$.

We can then then compare the marginal likelihood of modeling the entire parameter set indexed by η as independent

$$S_{i\eta} = P(\mathcal{D}_1, \mathcal{D}_2 | \boldsymbol{\Theta}_{i\eta}^{(1)} \perp \boldsymbol{\Theta}_{i\eta}^{(2)}) =$$

$$= \left(\prod_{j \in J_i^1(\eta)} E_{\boldsymbol{\Theta}_{ij} | \mathcal{M}_1} P(\mathcal{D}_1 | \boldsymbol{\Theta}_{ij}, \mathcal{M}_1) \right) \left(\prod_{j \in J_i^2(\eta)} E_{\boldsymbol{\Theta}_{ij} | \mathcal{M}_2} P(\mathcal{D}_2 | \boldsymbol{\Theta}_{ij}, \mathcal{M}_2) \right) \quad (6)$$

to the marginal likelihood of modeling the parameter set indexed by η as identical

$$T_{i\eta} = P(\mathcal{D}_1, \mathcal{D}_2 | \boldsymbol{\Theta}_{i\eta}^{(1)} = \boldsymbol{\Theta}_{i\eta}^{(2)}) = \prod_{j \in J_i^\cup(\eta)} E_{\boldsymbol{\Theta}_{ij} | \mathcal{M}_\cup} P(\mathcal{D}_\cup | \boldsymbol{\Theta}_{ij}, \mathcal{M}_\cup). \quad (7)$$

In the case of identical structures, $S_{i\eta}$ and $T_{i\eta}$ are equivalent to S_{ij} and T_{ij}.

One interesting and useful task is the detection of differences in the distributions when only a few parameters (out of many) differ between the two groups. We can use the marginal likelihoods derived above to obtain a measure that is sensitive to the presence of changes in only some conditional distributions of a variable X_i, while other conditional distributions may indeed be identical across groups. Particularly, we can compute the posterior odds of seeing a difference in X_i as follows:

$$O_i = \frac{1 - P(\boldsymbol{\Theta}_i^{(1)} = \boldsymbol{\Theta}_i^{(2)} | \mathcal{D}_1, \mathcal{D}_2)}{P(\boldsymbol{\Theta}_i^{(1)} = \boldsymbol{\Theta}_i^{(2)} | \mathcal{D}_1, \mathcal{D}_2)} = \left(\prod_{\eta=1}^{H_i} \frac{1}{P(\boldsymbol{\Theta}_{i\eta}^{(1)} = \boldsymbol{\Theta}_{i\eta}^{(2)} | \mathcal{D}_1, \mathcal{D}_2)} \right) - 1. \quad (8)$$

Since the η-level is defined to be the finest level at which parameters can be compared across the two groups, we consider only the two cases of $\boldsymbol{\Theta}_{ij}$ either being independent for the two groups or being identical for the two groups. By introducing priors for these two cases we are able to compute Eq. (8). Let $p_{i\eta} = P(\Theta_{i\eta}^{(1)} = \Theta_{i\eta}^{(2)})$ denote the prior probability that the distribution of $X_i | \pi_{i\eta}$ is the same across the two groups. Then we have that

$$\frac{1}{P(\Theta_{i\eta}^{(1)} = \Theta_{i\eta}^{(2)} | \mathcal{D}_1, \mathcal{D}_2)} = \frac{S_{i\eta}(1 - p_{i\eta}) + T_{i\eta} p_{i\eta}}{T_{i\eta} p_{i\eta}}. \tag{9}$$

Plugging Eq. (9) into Eq. (8) gives

$$O_i = \left(\prod_{\eta=1}^{H_i} \left(\frac{S_{i\eta}(1 - p_{i\eta})}{T_{i\eta} p_{i\eta}} + 1 \right) \right) - 1. \tag{10}$$

In the absence of information that would lead one to expect differences in some parameters more than in others, the priors $p_{i\eta}$ can be related to the prior probability p_i of seeing no difference in the conditional distribution of variable X_i by the relation $p_{i\eta} = p_i^{1/H_i}$.

The same approach can be extended to obtain posterior odds of observing a difference in any parameter of the model, expressed as

$$O = \frac{1 - P(\Theta^{(1)} = \Theta^{(2)} | \mathcal{D}_1, \mathcal{D}_2)}{P(\Theta^{(1)} = \Theta^{(2)} | \mathcal{D}_1, \mathcal{D}_2)} = \left(\prod_{i=1}^{n} \prod_{\eta=1}^{H_i} \left(\frac{S_{i\eta}(1 - p_{i\eta})}{T_{i\eta} p_{i\eta}} + 1 \right) \right) - 1. \tag{11}$$

Using (11) entails that the prior for seeing no difference between the two groups is $p = \prod_{i=1}^{n} \prod_{\eta=1}^{H_i} p_{i\eta}$. Given such an overall prior p, a natural choice for non-informative priors is $p_{i\eta} = p^{1/(nH_i)}$: this choice of priors assumes that we are equally and independently likely to see a difference in each variable, and equally and independently likely to see a difference in each conditional probability distribution of each variable.

4   Evaluation

We evaluated the performance of the odds ratio O_i in Eq. 10 as a score for detecting variable-level differences. Next we describe the baseline method against which we compared our method and the experimental setup, followed by the experimental results.

4.1   Baseline Method

As mentioned in the introduction, to our knowledge there is no prior work that addresses the difference detection problem in the same manner as our approach: a variable-based analysis, accounting for multivariate relationships, identifying variable-level differences, and requiring no informative prior knowledge. As a result, we chose to simulate a process often followed by analysts and researchers, where logistic regression models with interactions are constructed to predict a variable X_i using candidate predictors, and the researcher would judge a predictor's relevance based on the strength of its corresponding weight.

For this purpose, we use lasso-regularized logistic regression [7], which maximizes an $\mathcal{L}_1$-regularized log-likelihood of a logistic model, where the strength of the regularization is modulated by a parameter λ. The effect of regularization is that as λ decreases from $+\infty$, predictors enter the model (their coefficients in the logistic model become nonzero). To detect variable-wise differences across two pre-defined groups using lasso-regularized logistic regression, we take the data from the two groups and add a group-indicator variable Z to the data. The group indicator Z is a binary variable that takes the value 1 for cases coming from one of the groups, and the value 0 for cases coming from the other group. A regression model is built for predicting each variable X_i given all the other data variables $X_j : 1 \leq j < i$ that precede it in the variable ordering (we provide an ordering from a true generating model for the purposes of this evaluation), the group indicator Z, and interactions of Z with each of the data variables X_j. Non-binary variables were handled by using multinomial logistic regression for the target and binary coding for input variables. The largest value of λ at which a given predictor becomes nonzero can then be used as a score of how useful that predictor is for predicting X_i. Hence, for each X_i we can use the largest λ that corresponds to a nonzero coefficient in the logistic model for Z or an interaction with Z as the score for seeing a difference in the distribution of X_i across groups.

4.2 Data and Experimental Setup

Since in real-world data the differences between groups of data are not known in advance, for the evaluation we generated pairs of data groups from known distributions that are based on real-world data. We chose to learn networks from which to generate data because publicly available BN models are overwhelmingly diagnostic, meaning that they often contain many hidden variables, whereas we would like to have a ground-truth model that directly relates observed variables to each other. We picked data where all variables are categorical, since the BD score is designed for BNs that represent multinomial distributions. In this evaluation we used the *balance-scale, car, hayes-roth,* and *nursery* datasets available from the UCI Machine Learning Repository [1]. We learned a BN from the data for each of these sets, which is referred to as the "original BN" in the following description of the data-generation process.

We ran 72 blocks of tests, where each block is characterized by a data source (one of the UCI Datasets), a type of perturbation, the number of perturbations, and the number of samples per group. Each block consists of 20 group pairs, where each pair consists of a group of samples generated from the original BN of the data source and a group of samples generated from a perturbed BN of a data source (a different perturbed BN is obtained for each group pair). The perturbed BN was obtained by performing perturbations to the original BN. There were two categories of perturbations: parametric perturbations and structural perturbations. A parametric perturbation was performed by uniformly randomly

Table 1. Table of AUCs obtained from 72 blocks of tests. The first column indicates the data source for each block, the second column indicates whether the perturbation introduced was structural (Struct.) or parametric (Param.), and the third column indicates the number of perturbations. AUCs that were statistically significantly higher at the $\alpha = 0.05$ level are shown in bold.

			O_i AUC	λ AUC	p-value	O_i AUC	λ AUC	p-value	O_i AUC	λ AUC	p-value
balance-scale	Param.	1	**0.8931**	0.7031	0.0074	**0.9444**	0.7981	0.0303	0.9563	0.8056	0.0542
		3	**0.8303**	0.6457	0.0007	**0.7895**	0.6675	0.0336	**0.8936**	0.7319	0.0024
		5	**0.9038**	0.7217	0.0003	**0.8780**	0.7733	0.0248	**0.8973**	0.7827	0.0131
	Struct.	1	0.9956	0.9788	0.1481	0.9981	0.9888	0.2029	1.0000	0.9981	0.3850
		3	0.9868	0.9836	0.7843	0.9964	0.9804	0.1088	0.9992	0.9892	0.1684
		5	0.9825	0.9721	0.4884	0.9958	0.9812	0.1509	0.9921	0.9975	0.4761
car	Param.	1	**0.6587**	0.5033	0.0282	**0.7171**	0.5744	0.0008	0.7221	0.6477	0.0604
		3	**0.7544**	0.6296	0.0026	**0.7981**	0.6595	$< 10^{-4}$	**0.8260**	0.7136	0.0001
		5	**0.7540**	0.6149	$< 10^{-4}$	**0.7567**	0.6867	0.0265	**0.8079**	0.7209	0.0018
	Struct.	1	0.9229	0.8525	0.1168	0.9367	0.9096	0.6049	0.9788	0.9442	0.0696
		3	0.8272	**0.8952**	0.0439	0.8739	0.8920	0.6019	0.9606	0.9572	0.8760
		5	0.7774	**0.8891**	0.0034	0.8695	0.9340	0.0593	0.9043	0.9538	0.1347
hayes-roth	Param.	1	0.7256	0.6944	0.6718	0.7750	0.7375	0.5904	0.6713	0.6275	0.5563
		3	**0.7648**	0.5889	0.0012	**0.7210**	0.5990	0.0277	0.6973	0.5978	0.0634
		5	0.7560	0.6766	0.1211	0.7490	0.7088	0.4394	0.7331	0.6830	0.2590
	Struct.	1	0.7763	**0.8844**	0.0401	0.8081	**0.9137**	0.0047	0.8344	**0.9238**	0.0058
		3	0.8814	0.8998	0.6295	0.9387	0.9026	0.2959	0.8666	0.9131	0.2554
		5	0.8546	**0.9479**	0.0137	0.9214	0.9505	0.1106	0.9136	**0.9674**	0.0297
nursery	Param.	1	0.6234	0.6153	0.9283	0.6644	0.6247	0.6983	**0.8263**	0.6931	0.0499
		3	0.6460	0.5845	0.2978	**0.7179**	0.5596	0.0035	0.6833	0.5852	0.0987
		5	0.6156	0.6105	0.9226	0.6149	0.5776	0.4796	**0.7198**	0.5755	0.0032
	Struct.	1	0.5897	**0.7984**	0.0035	0.7781	0.8469	0.2932	0.8534	0.8372	0.7410
		3	0.7686	0.8148	0.2443	0.8487	0.8527	0.8924	0.9251	0.8895	0.2596
		5	0.8142	0.8326	0.5419	0.8125	0.8345	0.4145	0.9270	0.8919	0.1333
			500 samples per group			**1000 samples per group**			**5000 samples per group**		

selecting a variable X_i to perturb, selecting for it a conditional distribution $X_i|\pi_{ij}$ to perturb, and then replacing its probability mass vector with a permutation of itself. A structural perturbation was performed by randomly (with probability 1/2) deciding whether to remove or add an arc, and then selecting a random arc to add (or remove) from the existing (or absent) arcs in the network. A node (variable) is considered perturbed by a structural perturbation only if an arc into the node is added or removed.

We provide the ordering of the variables in the generating model to the logistic regression method so that it may take advantage of that information. We do not provide this information to our method in the tests reported in Table 1.

4.3 Results

Table 1 shows areas under receiver operating characteristic curves (AUC) of perturbation detection obtained using the posterior odds O_i as compared to AUC's obtained using the λ-based score from lasso-regularized logistic regression for data group pairs generated from the respective data sources. The table also shows the p-value for a two-tailed test of the difference between the AUCs of the two methods, based on [6]. Of a total of 72 blocks of tests, in 53 the O_i AUC is higher than the λ AUC. At the $\alpha = 0.05$ significance level, the O_i AUC's are statistically significantly better than the λ AUC's in 21 test blocks, whereas the O_i AUC is statistically significantly worse than the λ AUC in only eight test blocks. The p-value of a two-sided paired Wilcoxon signed rank test on the AUCs is less than 10^{-4}, supporting that the overall better performance of O_i is not due to chance.

Every case where the the posterior odds performs statistically significantly worse than the regression-based method is a case of a structural perturbation, and we suspect that this is because perturbed structure is more difficult to recover with no order information. In a different series of tests where we provided order information to the posterior odds based method, of a total of 72 blocks of tests, in 62 the O_i AUC was higher than the λ AUC. At the $\alpha = 0.05$ significance level, the O_i AUC was statistically significantly better than the λ AUC in 43 test blocks, and worse in only one block.

As is typical for statistical methods, we see better performance for data with more samples as well as for lower-dimensional data. The results also suggest that structural differences are easier to detect than parametric ones. We believe that this is because a structural difference reflects a more substantial distributional difference than a simple parametric one, since it can be expressed as a collection of parametric differences in a network containing the removed or added arcs. Overall, our experiments show consistently good AUC for the O_i score over the various generated group pairs.

5   Discussion

We introduced a novel variable-based approach for identifying statistical differences across a pair of groups. Evaluation of the approach on simulated data showed good performance compared to a logistic lasso baseline. The data used in the evaluation is low-dimensional because the logistic lasso baseline scales poorly to many dimensions. The most computationally demanding step in our approach is learning the three network structures. Consequently, our method scales to more dimensions to the extent that the BN structure learning algorithm used with it does. Any structure search strategy that maximizes a Bayesian Dirichlet score is a good fit for our method.

For Bayesian networks with Bayesian Dirichlet priors, we showed how to compute the posterior odds that a given variable has different distribution across the two groups, as well as the posterior odds that the two groups are different overall. The property that enables this is parameter independence in the BD framework. This approach can be applied to other models as well. The distribution of a variable in the BN formulation is simply a grouping of finer-level model parameters. Hence, any model that has similar groupings of parameters in a framework where parameter independence holds can be used with this approach.

Identification of variable-level differences across groups of multivariate data is useful in many application areas. The method presented here considers differences over the sets of relationships that are present in the MAP models constructed for modeling the groups as independent vs. identical. Particularly, for settings in which the typical approaches in practice tend to be univariate analyses and ad-hoc exploration of relationships that are suspected to be important *a priori*, we present a more systematic approach.

Acknowledgments. This research was supported by grant IIS-0911032 from the National Science Foundation and grant T15 LM007359 from the National Library of Medicine.

References

1. Bache, K., Lichman, M.: UCI machine learning repository (2013). http://archive.ics.uci.edu/ml
2. Bay, S.D., Pazzani, M.J.: Detecting group differences: mining contrast sets. Data Min. Knowl. Disc. **5**(3), 213–246 (2001)
3. Chickering, D.M.: Learning Bayesian networks is NP-complete. In: Fisher, D., Lenz, H.-J. (eds.) Learning from Data. Lecture Notes in Statistics, vol. 112, pp. 121–130. Springer, Heidelberg (1996)
4. Cooper, G.F., Herskovits, E.: A Bayesian method for the induction of probabilistic networks from data. Mach. Learn. **9**(4), 309–347 (1992)
5. Daly, R., Shen, Q., Aitken, S.: Learning Bayesian networks: approaches and issues. Knowl. Eng. Rev. **26**(2), 99–157 (2011)
6. DeLong, E.R., DeLong, D.M., Clarke-Pearson, D.L.: Comparing the areas under two or more correlated receiver operating characteristic curves: a nonparametric approach. Biometrics **44**, 837–845 (1988)
7. Friedman, J., Hastie, T., Tibshirani, R.: Regularization paths for generalized linear models via coordinate descent. J. Stat. Softw. **33**(1), 1–22 (2010)
8. Heckerman, D.: A tutorial on learning with Bayesian networks. In: Jordan, M.I. (ed.) Learning in Graphical Models, pp. 301–354. MIT Press, Cambridge (1999)
9. Heckerman, D., Geiger, D., Chickering, D.M.: Learning Bayesian networks: the combination of knowledge and statistical data. Mach. Learn. **20**, 197–243 (1995)
10. Koivisto, M., Sood, K.: Exact Bayesian structure discovery in Bayesian networks. J. Mach. Learn. Res. **5**, 549–573 (2004)
11. Novak, P.K., Lavrač, N., Webb, G.I.: Supervised descriptive rule discovery: a unifying survey of contrast set, emerging pattern and subgroup mining. J. Mach. Learn. Res. **10**, 377–403 (2009)
12. Silander, T., Myllymaki, P.: A simple approach for finding the globally optimal Bayesian network structure. In: Dechter, R., Richardson, T. (eds.) Proceedings of the Twenty-second Annual Conference on Uncertainty in Artificial Intelligence (UAI 2006), pp. 445–452. AUAI Press (2006)
13. Spirtes, P., Glymour, C.: An algorithm for fast recovery of sparse causal graphs. Soc. Sci. Comput. Rev. **9**(1), 62–72 (1991)
14. Yuan, C., Malone, B., Wu, X.: Learning optimal Bayesian networks using A* search. In: Proceedings of the 22nd International Joint Conference on Artificial Intelligence (IJCAI 2011), pp. 2186–2191. Helsinki, Finland (2011)

Automatically Discovering Offensive Patterns in Soccer Match Data

Jan Van Haaren[✉], Vladimir Dzyuba, Siebe Hannosset, and Jesse Davis

Department of Computer Science, KU Leuven, Celestijnenlaan 200A,
3001 Leuven, Belgium
{jan.vanhaaren,vladimir.dzyuba,jesse.davis}@cs.kuleuven.be

Abstract. In recent years, many professional sports clubs have adopted camera-based tracking technology that captures the location of both the players and the ball at a high frequency. Nevertheless, the valuable information that is hidden in these performance data is rarely used in their decision-making process. What is missing are the computational methods to analyze these data in great depth. This paper addresses the task of automatically discovering patterns in offensive strategies in professional soccer matches. To address this task, we propose an inductive logic programming approach that can easily deal with the relational structure of the data. An experimental study shows the utility of our approach.

Keywords: Sports analytics · Spatial data · Strategy detection

1 Introduction

Michael Lewis' book *Moneyball* [11] tells the story of Oakland A's General Manager Billy Beane who relies on statistics to build a competitive baseball team despite a tight budget. In recent years, his work has been an example for many other ball sports like basketball, football, and soccer. While several aspects of baseball games can be analyzed in a rather straightforward way, this is much harder for more continuous sports where players can freely move around the pitch. As a result, it can be challenging to quantify the performances of individual players and teams as a whole.

Since simple statistics (e.g., the number of shots on target in soccer) fail to capture the complex interactions among players, companies have started developing tracking technology that captures the location of both the players and the ball at a high frequency (e.g., [16–18,20]). These positional data do not only tell *how often* a particular event happened in a match but also *when*, *where*, and *how*. While many professional sports clubs have access to large volumes of performance data, the valuable information that is hidden in these data is only used to a limited extent in their decision-making process. What is missing are the computational methods to analyze these data in greater depth.

In this paper, we propose the task of automatically discovering patterns in offensive strategies in professional soccer matches. More specifically, we are interested in revealing which interactions among players (e.g., a pass from one zone

© Springer International Publishing Switzerland 2015
E. Fromont et al. (Eds.): IDA 2015, LNCS 9385, pp. 286–297, 2015.
DOI: 10.1007/978-3-319-24465-5_25

of the pitch to another zone) are most likely to lead to goal attempts. The low-scoring and continuous nature of soccer matches makes this a challenging task. To address this task, we propose an inductive logic programming approach that can easily deal with the relational structure of the data.

The contributions of this paper are as follows:

- We propose using **advanced data mining algorithms** to analyze positional sports data. Most of the techniques that have been proposed to date are statistical and cannot easily deal with the relational nature of these data.
- We present an **inductive logic programming approach** to automatically discover patterns that frequently appear in successful offensive strategies.
- We perform an **empirical study** on a large volume of soccer matches.

2   Related Work

This section provides an overview of the related work on supervised knowledge discovery and sports analytics. The relevant background on inductive logic programming, which is the core of our approach, is provided in Sect. 4.

Knowledge Discovery. The problem addressed in this paper is an instance of supervised descriptive rule discovery [8]. A common variant of this problem is subgroup discovery [5]. Although early variants already supported multi-relational data [22], the data are typically merged into a single table before applying subgroup discovery algorithms [10]. By contrast, inductive logic programming techniques allow us to work directly with the relational (logical) representation of data. This is important for our task, where we want to capture both spatial and temporal patterns as well as interactions among groups of players. An alternative perspective on relational data mining relies on database theory [7].

Sports Data Analysis. The amount of available data about various sports is constantly increasing, most importantly tracking data and event data [14]. Within soccer, the analysis of tracking data focuses on discovering individual or collective movement patterns, e.g., spectral clustering of trajectories [6], strategy analysis with occupancy maps [12], or formation analysis via minimum entropy partitioning [1]. Gyarmati et al. use event data to discover motif patterns in pass sequences [4]. Most of the research studies large datasets encompassing multiple teams or even leagues, whereas we focus on a single team, with the ultimate goal to improve its performance.

3   Dataset

Through our collaboration with a Belgian soccer club, we obtained play-by-play data for 70 soccer matches in the 2013/2014 and 2014/2015 seasons. The dataset consists of 59 matches in the Belgian Pro League, nine matches in the

UEFA Europa League and two matches in the Belgian Cofidis Cup. The data were collected by data provider Prozone [18]. We first discuss the structure of the data and then introduce additional hierarchical information to enrich the dataset.

3.1 Structure of the Data

The data for each match is provided as an XML file which consists of three parts: a *match sheet* with information on the players and managers, a *sequence of events*, and *tracking data* for all players as well as the ball. While the first two parts are available for all matches, the third part is only available for 10 Jupiler Pro League and 4 UEFA Europa League matches.

The match sheet contains each player's name, position on the pitch, jersey number, and team. In addition, it also specifies which players were starters and which players were substitutes.

The sequence of events contains roughly 2,600 events per match. Over 40 different types of events are recorded. The most frequent events include passes between players, players running with the ball, players receiving a ball, players shooting towards goal, players fouling another player, players crossing the ball, and players clearing the ball. Furthermore, events exist to mark the start and end of each half as well as yellow cards, red cards, and substitutions.

The following information is available for each event: the type of the event, the players that are involved, a timestamp, the start location of the event, and the end location of the event if applicable. Depending on the type of event, additional information is available such as the body part involved (e.g., foot or head), type of play (i.e., open or set play), or whether or not a shot was blocked.

3.2 Hierarchical Information

Since we prefer more general patterns to very specific patterns, we enrich the dataset with hierarchical information about both the pitch and the players. This information groups together parts of the pitch and players that fulfill a similar role and hence can be treated in a similar way. As a result, this information facilitates generalizing from very specific to more general knowledge.

We divide each half of the pitch into ten zones resulting into twenty different zones as is shown on the right side of Fig. 1. Assuming the team of interest always plays from left to right, we define a hierarchy as follows. We group together zones 1 to 4 as the *penalty area*, zones 5 to 7 as the *area around the penalty area*, and zones 8 to 10 as the *midfield*. The division is identical for the defensive and offensive half of the pitch.

Similarly, we group together players that play in a similar position. We define four groups of players for the team of interest: *goalkeepers*, *defenders* (i.e., center backs, full backs, wing backs, and sweepers), *midfielders* (i.e., defensive midfielders, central midfielders, attacking midfielders, and wing midfielders), and *attackers* (i.e., wingers, supporting strikers, and strikers).

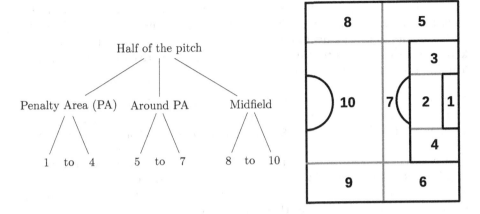

Fig. 1. Each half of the pitch is divided into ten zones, which we group together into three bigger areas. Zones 1 to 4 are the *penalty area*, zones 5 to 7 the *area around the penalty area*, and zones 8 to 10 the *midfield*. The division is identical for the defensive and offensive half of the pitch.

4 Background

This section provides the relevant background on first-order logic, inductive logic programming [13], and the inductive logic programming system Aleph [19].

4.1 First-Order Logic

First-order logic (FOL) is commonly used as representation language for relational data. In this paper, we consider a subset of FOL, where the alphabet consists of only three symbols. *Constants* start with a lower-case letter and refer to specific objects (e.g., a player p_i). *Variables* start with an upper-case letter and range over multiple objects (e.g., Players). *Predicates* represent relations between objects (e.g., a pass $Pass(p_i, p_j)$).

Using these three symbols, we can define the following four constructs: *atoms* $p(t_1, ..., t_n)$, where the t_i are constants or variables; *literals*, which are atoms or their negations; *clauses*, which are disjunctions over finite sets of literals; and *definite clauses*, which are clauses containing precisely one positive literal. Definite clauses are often written in implication form $B \implies H$, where B is a conjunction of literals and H is a single literal. A *definite program* is a finite set of definite clauses. Definite programs form the basis of logic programming. We assume all variables to be universally quantified.

4.2 Inductive Logic Programming and Aleph

Inductive logic programming (ILP) [3] is a well-known framework for learning models, in the form of definite programs, from relational data. ILP offers the benefits of being able to directly model important relationships and it also facilitates incorporating domain knowledge into the learning process. Informally, ILP attempts to learn a definite program that, in combination with background knowledge, can be used to distinguish positive and negative examples. The ILP learning task can be defined as follows:

Given: A target predicate T, background knowledge BK, a non-empty set of *positive* examples E+ of T, and a set of *negative* examples E− of T.
Learn: A set of definite clauses S such that $BK \wedge S \models E^+$ and $BK \wedge S \not\models E^-$.

It is often not possible to ensure $BK \wedge S \not\models E^-$ in practice. Hence, this condition is relaxed and clauses in S are permitted to cover some negative examples.[1] The goal in the relaxed setting is to achieve a balance between the number of positive and negative examples that each clause covers.

In this paper, we employ the widely-used Aleph ILP system [15,19,21]. Aleph applies a two-step approach to learn a clause. In the *saturation* step, the system first selects a random positive example, called the seed example, and finds all facts in the background knowledge that are true for this example. It forms a clause where the body is the conjunction of all these facts and the head is the target predicate. This is the most-specific clause (i.e., the bottom clause) that covers the seed example. In the *search* step, the system performs a top-down search over clause bodies that generalize the bottom clause. The key idea is that a subset of the facts can be used to explain the seed example's label and that this explanation is likely to apply to other examples as well.

5   Approach

This section introduces our ILP approach to automatically discover patterns that frequently appear in successful offensive strategies. We explain how we pre-process the data and learn the clauses.

5.1   Pre-processing the Data

As explained in Sect. 3, the dataset consists of one long sequence of events for each match. We split each sequence into a number of *phases*, each of which is a subsequence of related events. A phase typically starts with a goal kick or a throw-in and ends when the ball goes out of play or a foul is made. We only consider passes, crosses, set pieces and shots, and discard all other events. We also only consider phases in which the team of interest is *dominant*, which is when its players are involved in at least half of the events. Although this rarely happens, both teams can be seen as the dominant team in the same phase. However, this is not a problem since we are only looking at the team of interest.

---

[1] By cover, we mean that a clause, in combination with BK, can be used to derive that the target predicate T is true for a given example.

Building Examples. In our setting, we define *positive* examples as phases during which the team of interest attempts a shot, and we label all other phases as *negative* examples. Thus, the target predicate is shot(Phase), which denotes whether the team attempted a shot in a phase Phase. In the background knowledge, we represent each phase as a set of ground facts using four predicates. The pass(Phase, Player$_1$, Player$_2$, Zone$_1$, Zone$_2$) predicate denotes that in a phase Phase a player Player$_1$ in zone Zone$_1$ passed the ball to Player$_2$ in zone Zone$_2$. Similarly, the cross(Phase, Player$_1$, Player$_2$, Zone$_1$, Zone$_2$) and set_piece(Phase, Player$_1$, Player$_2$, Zone$_1$, Zone$_2$) predicates denote crosses and set pieces. For positive examples, we discard all events following a shot.

Adding Background Knowledge. We add the hierarchical information about both the pitch and the players as background knowledge (see Sect. 3.2). What follows are two examples of such clauses for the pass predicate.

$$\text{pass}(\text{Ph}, \text{pl}_1, \text{pl}_2, Z_1, Z_2) \implies \text{pass}(\text{Ph}, \text{pMidfielder}, \text{pAttacker}, Z_1, Z_2) \quad (1)$$

$$\text{pass}(\text{Ph}, P_1, P_2, z_2, z_7) \implies \text{pass}(\text{Ph}, P_1, P_2, \text{zPenaltyArea}, \text{zMidfield}) \quad (2)$$

Assuming player pl$_1$ is a midfielder and player pl$_2$ is an attacker, Eq. 1 denotes that if pl$_1$ passes the ball to pl$_2$, then also a midfielder passes the ball to an attacker. Assuming zone z$_2$ belongs to the penalty area and zone z$_7$ belongs to the midfield (see Fig. 1), Eq. 2 denotes that a player who passes the ball from z$_2$ to z$_7$ also passes the ball from the penalty area to midfield.

As a practical optimization akin to view materialization in databases, we specify the background knowledge in this way rather than by introducing additional predicates.

5.2   Learning the Clauses

The Aleph system supports many different learning modes and search strategies [19]. We apply the induce_max search strategy. In contrast to the default search strategy, this strategy uses each positive example as a seed example. While slower, it produces a larger set of clauses that are potentially of interest to the user. However, this is a natural choice when doing exploratory data mining as our goal is to generate interesting clauses as opposed to learning a very compact predictive model, which is the traditional goal of ILP.

Since we are interested in as many potentially interesting clauses as possible, we run Aleph with as few restrictions as reasonably possible. We set the maximum number of literals per clause (i.e., clauselength) to 5, the minimum number of positive examples covered (i.e., minpos) to 5, the maximum number of negative examples covered (i.e., noise) to 25, and the minimum precision of acceptable clauses (i.e., minacc), which is the ratio between the number of positive examples covered and the total number of examples covered, to 5 %.

We sort the learned clauses in descending order according to their m-estimates [2,9], which are smoothed versions of their precisions.

6   Experimental Study

In this section, we present the dataset as well as the different experimental setups, define the research questions, and discuss the experimental results.

6.1   Dataset and Experimental Setups

After pre-processing the raw data as described in Sect. 5, the dataset contains 3,803 examples (phases), including 526 (13.8%) positive examples (shots), and 26,338 ground facts in total, including 24,786 passes (94.1%), 1,063 crosses (4.0%), and 489 set pieces (1.9%). An average example consists of 6.93 ground facts, including 6.52 passes, 0.28 crosses, and 0.13 set pieces. Furthermore, there are 34 constants corresponding to the players of the team of interest.

We investigate the performance of the proposed approach in five setups: discovering spatial patterns with and without hierarchical information, player interaction patterns with and without hierarchical information, and the combined setup with the hierarchical information, in order to evaluate the utility of each type of background knowledge.

6.2   Research Questions

In this experimental study, we address the following three research questions:

- **Q1: Do the learned clauses capture the relevant regularities?** The ultimate goal of the analysis is to describe succesful offensive actions of the team. We quantify the capacity of the proposed approach to accomplish this by computing the average m-estimate of the top-ten clauses.
- **Q2: Does the hierarchical knowledge improve the quality of the learned clauses?** One motivation for using ILP is its ability to represent relational data such as the player and zone hierarchies in a natural way. We investigate whether the addition of the hierarchies improves the quality of the learned clauses.
- **Q3: Do the learned clauses describe meaningful patterns?** The purpose of this work is to discover patterns that help the team understand what works well and what does not work well in terms of creating goal-scoring opportunities. Therefore, we qualitatively analyze the discovered patterns.

The proposed approach is meant to facilitate offline performance analysis, e.g., between matches or even seasons. Therefore, it is not necessary to produce instant results. Nevertheless, for the sake of completeness, we report running times for each setup. All experiments are run on a single core of a Linux machine with an Intel Xeon E5645 CPU running at 2.40 GHz and 128 Gb of RAM. We allow Aleph to run for 48 h in each setup.

6.3   Results and Discussion

We first address Q1 and Q2 by comparing the five setups using statistics on the sets of discovered clauses. We then address Q3 by evaluating the utility of the clauses for the first four setups from a performance analysis point of view.

Table 1. For each setup, we report the number of clauses returned by Aleph, the maximum and average m-estimate of the precision [9] for the top-ten clauses, and the runtime. Adding hierarchical information barely improves the quality of the clauses in the spatial setup, whereas it considerably improves the quality of the clauses in the player interaction setup. In the setup marked by (⋆), Aleph exceeds the runtime threshold of 48 h. Hence, we compute the m-estimate on the intermediate output.

Setup	Hierarchy	Rules	m-est. of prec. (top 10)		Time (min.)
			Maximum	Average	
Spatial		276	0.7396	0.6638	1.15
	✓	323	0.7396	0.7065	441.76
Player interactions		91	0.7396	0.4855	2.95
	✓	257	0.7396	0.6606	2,761.64
Combined		426 (⋆)	0.6374	0.6138	2,880.00

Quantitative Analysis (Q1 and Q2). Table 1 contains an overview of the experimental results. We expect that adding hierarchical information allows Aleph to find clauses of higher quality. We observe a considerable improvement in terms of average m-estimate in the player interaction setup, while this increase is rather modest in the spatial setup. However, the runtime cost of adding hierarchical information is substantial since the search space becomes much larger. In the player interaction setup, Aleph still manages to explore the whole search space and to generate high-quality candidate clauses in terms of m-estimate, which it fails to accomplish in the combined setup.

Qualitative Analysis (Q3). Table 2 presents the top-three clauses in terms of their m-estimates for discovering spatial patterns both with and without hierarchical information. These settings have two of their three top-ranked clauses in common (i.e., clauses A and B). Clause A describes a situation where the ball is passed between two players in the left defensive zone (d5), from the defensive midfield (d10) to the right offensive wing (o9), and between two players in the offensive midfield (o10). Clause B describes a situation where the ball is passed between two players in the right defensive zone (d6) and from the defensive midfield (d10) to both the left defensive wing (d8) and the left offensive wing (o8). Both clauses suggest that the team is particularly successful at creating goal attempts when moving the ball from one flank of the pitch to the other.

Clause D, which leverages the hierarchical information, describes a situation where the ball is passed from the area around the defensive penalty area (dAPA) into the defensive penalty area (dPA), from the right defensive zone (d6) to the right defensive wing (d9), and from the offensive midfield (o10) to the central offensive area around the penalty area (o7). This pattern most probably depicts a counter-attack following a set piece from the opponent.

Table 3 presents the top-three clauses in terms of their m-estimates for discovering player interaction patterns both with and without hierarchical information. These settings have only one of their three top-ranked clauses in common

Table 2. Top-three clauses in terms of their m-estimates for discovering spatial patterns with and without hierarchical information. For each clause, we report the total number of examples covered and the number of positive examples covered.

	Clause (C)	$|C|$	$|C^+|$
	Without hierarchy		
A	pass(d10, o9) ∧ pass(d5, d5) ∧ pass(o10, o10)	5	5
B	pass(d10, d8) ∧ pass(d10, o8) ∧ pass(d6, d6)	5	5
C	pass(d10, o9) ∧ pass(d5, d8) ∧ pass(o10, o7) ∧ pass(o9, o10)	5	5
	With hierarchy		
D	pass(d6, d9) ∧ pass(dAPA, dPA) ∧ pass(o10, o7)	5	5
A	pass(d10, o9) ∧ pass(d5, d5) ∧ pass(o10, o10)	5	5
B	pass(d10, d8) ∧ pass(d10, o8) ∧ pass(d6, d6)	5	5

Table 3. Top-three clauses in terms of their m-estimates for discovering player interaction patterns with and without hierarchical information. For each clause, we report the total number of examples covered and the number of positive examples covered.

	Clause (C)	$|C|$	$|C^+|$
	Without hierarchy		
A	pass(p1, p21) ∧ pass(p8, p18)	5	5
B	pass(p18, p9) ∧ pass(p2, p18)	6	5
C	pass(p2, p26) ∧ pass(p3, p1)	8	5
	With hierarchy		
A	pass(p1, p21) ∧ pass(p8, p18)	5	5
D	pass(att, att) ∧ pass(mid, att) ∧ pass(mid, def) ∧ pass(p4, p16)	5	5
E	pass(def, att) ∧ pass(def, mid) ∧ pass(opp, p2) ∧ pass(p8, opp)	7	6

(i.e., clause A). Clause A describes a situation where the goalkeeper (p1) passes the ball to a central defender (p21) and an attacking midfielder (p8) passes the ball to an offensive wing midfielder (p18). This pattern makes sense from a performance point of view as both p8 and p18 are generally considered key players and responsible for creating a large number of goal-scoring opportunities.

Clause B describes a situation where an offensive full back (p2) passes the ball to an offensive wing midfielder (p18) and the latter player passes the ball to another wing midfielder (p9). This pattern makes sense as well as p2 has had a foot in many goals scored by the team of interest. Clause C describes a similar pattern involving a goalkeeper (p1), a central defender (p3), an offensive full back (p2), and a central midfielder (p26).

Clauses D and E leverage the hierarchical information about player roles as they include both specific players (e.g., p4 and p16) and positions (e.g., mid and att). Clause D describes an attack over the left wing involving both an offensive full back (p4) and an offensive wing midfielder (p16), while clause E describes a situation where an offensive full back (p2) intercepts a pass from an

Table 4. Top-three clauses in terms of their weighted relative accuracies for discovering spatial patterns with hierarchical knowledge. For each clause, we report the weighted relative accuracy and m-estimate. These clauses are more general and less pure than the top-ranked clauses according to m-estimate for the same setup.

	Clause (C)	$|C|$	$|C^+|$	WRAcc	m-est.
A	pass(oMF, oMF) $\wedge$ pass(oMF, oPA) $\wedge$ pass(oPA, oAPA)	62	18	0.025	0.275
B	pass(o4, o7)	43	15	0.024	0.324
C	set_piece(dAPA, dPA)	51	16	0.024	0.295

opponent (opp) and an attacking midfielder (p8) attempts a possibly risky pass that is briefly intercepted or touched by an opponent.

Alternative Qualitative Analysis (Q3). We observed that the top-ranked clauses according to m-estimate are markedly specific. Therefore, we compare these clauses with the top-ranked clauses in the same set of clauses according to *weighted relative accuracy*, which is a common quality measure that aims to balance rule coverage and specificity:

$$WRAcc(C) = \frac{|C|}{|E|} \cdot \left(\frac{|C^+|}{|C|} - \frac{|E^+|}{|E|} \right)$$

Table 4 presents the top-three clauses in terms of $WRAcc$ for discovering spatial patterns with hierarchical knowledge. These patterns have a substantially higher coverage, while their m-estimates are much lower. In the same setup, the average m-estimate for the top-ten clauses was 0.707. This contrasts with Op De Beéck et al. [15], where in a similar setting, the coverage of the top-ranked clauses according to m-estimate ranges from 30 to 90 examples. This suggests that different quality measures could reveal different patterns in a dataset. Therefore, if the initial results are unsatisfactory from the domain perspective, ranking the clauses with another quality measure is a reasonable next step.

Clause A describes an attack through the middle, where the ball is passed between two players in the offensive midfield (oMF), from the offensive midfield to the offensive penalty area (oPA), and from the offensive penalty area to the area around the offensive penalty area (oAPA). Clause B describes a pass from the right side of the offensive penalty area (o4) to the area in front of the offensive penalty area (o7). Clause C describes a set piece from the area around the defensive penalty area (dAPA) into the defensive penalty area (dPA). Hence, this clause describes a situation where a counter-attack results in a goal-scoring opportunity. These tactical patterns are different from the patterns in Table 2.

7   Lessons Learned

This paper investigated the task of automatically discovering recurring patterns in successful offensive strategies in soccer matches. More specifically, we aimed to reveal both spatial (e.g., a pass from one zone to another) and player interaction (e.g., a pass from one player to another) patterns that are likely to lead to goal attempts. We presented an inductive logic programming approach for this task and demonstrated it is suitable on data from professional soccer matches.

While undertaking this study, we learned the following lessons. First, it is possible to apply inductive logic programming to the task of revealing recurring patterns in soccer match data. It provides the advantages of coping with the relational nature of the data in a straightforward way. Furthermore, it produces interpretable results, which facilitates debugging the data as well as analyzing the results. Second, the discovered patterns make sense from a soccer perspective and are interesting to a domain expert. However, taking the next step forward would require the full tracking data (i.e., the positions of the players and the ball at regular intervals) as this will allow for more fine-grained analysis. Fortunately, this type of data is becoming commonplace. Third, selecting the most interesting clauses is difficult as there is no natural metric or heuristic for this task and a human domain expert is still needed to assist in the interpretation.

In the future, we wish to further expand our current approach. We want to take the order of the events as well as the positions of the players and the ball into account. We also want to account for the differences in playing style of the opponents. Furthermore, we wish to develop a tool that visualizes the discovered patterns (e.g., on a soccer pitch as partially shown in Fig. 1). This would help to communicate the patterns in a more intuitive way to a domain expert.

Acknowledgments. Jan Van Haaren is supported by the Agency for Innovation by Science and Technology (IWT). Vladimir Dzyuba is supported by the Research Foundation Flanders (FWO) by means of the project "Instant Interactive Data Exploration". Jesse Davis is partially supported by the Research Fund KU Leuven (OT/11/051), EU FP7 Marie Curie Career Integration Grant (#294068) and FWO-Vlaanderen (G.0356.12).

References

1. Bialkowski, A., Lucey, P., Carr, P., Yue, Y., Sridharan, S., Matthews, I.: Identifying team style in soccer using formations learned from spatiotemporal tracking data. In: Proceedings of the Workshop on Spatial and Spatio-Temporal Data Mining, pp. 9–14 (2014)
2. Cestnik, B.: Estimating probabilities: a crucial task in machine learning. In: Proceedings of the 9th European Conference on Artificial Intelligence, vol. 90, pp. 147–149 (1990)
3. Džeroski, S., Lavrač, N.: An introduction to inductive logic programming. In: Džeroski, S., Lavrač, N. (eds.) Relational Data Mining, pp. 48–73. Springer, Heidelberg (2001)
4. Gyarmati, L., Kwak, H., Rodriguez, P.: Searching for a unique style in soccer (2014). arXiv:1409.0308
5. Herrera, F., Carmona, C., González, P., del Jesus, M.: An overview on subgroup discovery: foundations and applications. Knowl. Inf. Syst. **29**(3), 495–525 (2011)

6. Knauf, K., Brefeld, U.: Spatio-temporal convolution kernels for clustering trajectories. In: Proceedings of the Workshop on Large-Scale Sports Analytics (2014)
7. Knobbe, A.J.: Multi-Relational Data Mining. Ph.D. thesis, Utrecht University (2004)
8. Kralj Novak, P., Lavrač, N., Webb, G.: Supervised descriptive rule discovery: a unifying survey of contrast set, emerging pattern and subgroup mining. J. Mach. Learn. Res. **10**, 377–403 (2009)
9. Lavrač, N., Džeroski, S., Bratko, I.: Handling imperfect data in inductive logic programming. Adv. Inductive Log. Program. **32**, 48–64 (1996)
10. Lavrač, N., Cestnik, B., Gamberger, D., Flach, P.: Decision support through subgroup discovery: three case studies and the lessons learned. Mach. Learn. **57**(1–2), 115–143 (2004)
11. Lewis, M.: Moneyball: The Art of Winning an Unfair Game. W. W. Norton & Company, New York (2004)
12. Lucey, P., Oliver, D., Carr, P., Roth, J., Matthews, I.: Assessing team strategy using spatiotemporal data. In: Proceedings of the 19th International Conference on Knowledge Discovery and Data Mining, pp. 1366–1374 (2013)
13. Muggleton, S., De Raedt, L.: Inductive logic programming: theory and methods. J. Logic Program. **19**, 629–679 (1994)
14. Mutschler, C., Ziekow, H., Jerzak, Z.: The DEBS 2013 grand challenge. In: Proceedings of the 7th International Conference on Distributed Event-based Systems, pp. 289–294 (2013)
15. Op De Beéck, T., Hommersom, A., Van Haaren, J., van der Heijden, M., Davis, J., Lucas, P., Overbeek, L., Nagtegaal, I.: Mining hierarchical pathology data using inductive logic programming. In: Holmes, J.H., Bellazzi, R., Sacchi, L., Peek, N. (eds.) AIME 2015. LNCS, vol. 9105, pp. 76–85. Springer, Heidelberg (2015)
16. Opta Sports. http://www.optasports.com. Accessed 24 July 2015
17. PlayfulVision. http://www.playfulvision.com. Accessed 24 July 2015
18. Prozone. http://www.prozonesports.com. Accessed 24 July 2015
19. Srinivasan, A.: The Aleph Manual. Machine Learning at the Computing Laboratory. Oxford University, Oxford (2001)
20. STATS' SportVU. http://www.stats.com/sportvu. Accessed 24 July 2015
21. Vavpetič, A., Lavrač, N.: Semantic subgroup discovery systems and workflows in the SDM-toolkit. Comput. J. **56**(3), 304–320 (2013)
22. Wrobel, S.: An algorithm for multi-relational discovery of subgroups. In: Komorowski, J., Zytkow, J. (eds.) PKDD 1997. LNCS, vol. 1263, pp. 78–87. Springer, Heidelberg (1997)

Fast Algorithm Selection Using Learning Curves

Jan N. van Rijn[1]([⊠]), Salisu Mamman Abdulrahman[2], Pavel Brazdil[2],
and Joaquin Vanschoren[3]

[1] Leiden University, Leiden, The Netherlands
j.n.van.rijn@liacs.leidenuniv.nl
[2] University of Porto, Porto, Portugal
{sma,pbrazdil}@inescporto.pt
[3] Eindhoven University of Technology, Eindhoven, The Netherlands
j.vanschoren@tue.nl

Abstract. One of the challenges in Machine Learning to find a classifier and parameter settings that work well on a given dataset. Evaluating all possible combinations typically takes too much time, hence many solutions have been proposed that attempt to predict which classifiers are most promising to try. As the first recommended classifier is not always the correct choice, multiple recommendations should be made, making this a ranking problem rather than a classification problem. Even though this is a well studied problem, there is currently no good way of evaluating such rankings. We advocate the use of Loss Time Curves, as used in the optimization literature. These visualize the amount of budget (time) needed to converge to a acceptable solution. We also investigate a method that utilizes the measured performances of classifiers on small samples of data to make such recommendation, and adapt it so that it works well in Loss Time space. Experimental results show that this method converges extremely fast to an acceptable solution.

Keywords: Algorithm selection · Meta-learning · Subsampling

1 Introduction

When presented with a new classification problem, a key challenge is to identify a classifier and parameter settings that obtain good predictive performance. This problem is known as the *Algorithm Selection Problem* [13]. Since many classifiers exist, all containing a number of parameters that potentially influence predictive performance, this is a challenging problem. Performing a cross-validation evaluation procedure on all possible combinations of classifiers and parameters (e.g., using a grid search) is typically infeasible, as this would take too much time. The field of *meta-learning* attempts to solve this by learning from prior examples. Typically, a set of classifiers is recommended based on the performance on similar datasets.

The meta-learning method SAM [8] identifies similar datasets based on the *learning curves* of classifiers trained on them, and recommends the classifier that

E. Fromont et al. (Eds.): IDA 2015, LNCS 9385, pp. 298–309, 2015.
DOI: 10.1007/978-3-319-24465-5_26

performs best on these similar datasets. Although the results are convincing, it does not take into account some important aspects of algorithm selection. First, it only recommends the single best classifier, rather than a ranking of candidates. Second, it does not take the training time of the models into account. Indeed, in practical applications there is typically a budget (e.g., limited time or a maximum number of cross-validation runs) within which a number of classifiers can be evaluated. As such, the meta-learning method should be evaluated on how well it performs within a given budget.

Our contributions are the following. We extend the aforementioned technique so that it produces a ranking of classifiers and takes into account the run times of classifiers. Furthermore, we study the performance of this method in Loss space [9], taking into account both predictive accuracy and spent time. We will argue that Loss Curves as presented in [9] are biased, and propose the use of Loss Time Curves, as presented in [6]. Finally, we compare the method against a range of alternative methods, including a rather strong baseline that recommends the classifier that performed best on a small sample of the data [4]. Although our proposed technique dominates the baseline methods, the results suggest that this 'Best on Sample' approach has been mistakenly neglected in the literature.

2   Related Work

Meta-learning aims to learn which learning techniques work well on what data [16]. A common task, known as the Algorithm Selection Problem [13], is to determine which classifier performs best on a given dataset. We can predict this by training a meta-model on meta-data comprised of dataset characterizations, i.e., *meta-features* [2], and the performances of different classifiers on these datasets. The same meta-features can be computed on each new dataset and fed to the meta-model to predict which classifiers will perform well.

Hence, the Algorithm Selection Problem is reduced to a Machine Learning problem. Meta-features are often categorized as either simple (number of examples, number of attributes), statistical (mean standard deviation of attributes, mean skewness of attributes), information theoretic (class entropy, mean mutual information) or landmarkers [11] (performance evaluations of simple classifiers). Many meta-learning studies follow this approach [14, 15, 17, 20, 21].

However, meta-feature based approaches have some intrinsic limitations. First, it is hard to construct a meta-feature set that adequately characterizes the problem space [7]. Second, the most successful meta-features, landmarkers, can be computationally expensive, limiting the options [11]. Finally, because not all classifiers run on all datasets, or take prohibitively long to do so, the meta-dataset usually contains many missing values, complicating the classification task.

In order to overcome these problems, Leite and Brazdil [7,8] identify similar data sets based on partial learning curves. A learning curve is an ordered set of performance scores of a classifier on data samples of increasing size [12]. In this particular method, a *partial* learning curve is computed, using small samples, to measure how similarly algorithms behave on two data sets. As such, running classifiers on these samples is rather cheap.

Alternatively, the `Best on Sample` method uses the performance estimates of classifiers on a small sample and recommends the classifiers which perform best on this sample, in descending order [10]. Prior work is inconclusive about its performance. The authors of [10] suggest that this technique should be used as a baseline method in meta-learning research. The authors of [4] show that this information is not useful as a landmarker. Indeed, it has been correctly observed that learning curves sometimes cross, i.e., one classifier can outperform another on a small data sample, but can be surpassed when trained on the whole dataset [7]. However, this happens less often as the sample size increases, making this method quite reliable when using the right sample size, as we will show in Sect. 4.

The datasets, learning curves and all results of our experiments are made publicly available on OpenML [19], for the purposes of verifiability, reproducibility and generalizability. OpenML is an experiment database [18] that enables the reproduction of earlier results for verification and reuse, and makes much larger studies (covering more classifiers and parameter settings) feasible. Moreover, experiment databases allow a variety of studies to be executed by a database look-up, rather than setting up new experiments.

3   Methods

The method we propose extends the method as defined by [8] in two ways. First, it recommends a ranking of classifiers, rather than just a single best classifier. Second, it can take arbitrary evaluation measures into account, such as run time. It attempts to rank classifiers in order of performance on a given dataset d_{new}.

We consider a set A of classifiers, a_m ($m = 1, 2, 3, \ldots, M$). We also consider a set D of datasets, d_n ($n = 1, 2, 3, \ldots, N$), on which we have information on the performance of the classifiers in A (d_{new} is not in D). The size of dataset d_n is denoted as $|d_n|$. Let $P_{m,n,s}$ and $P'_{m,n,s}$ denote the performance of classifier a_m on dataset d_n, for a given evaluation measure (e.g., predictive accuracy), using a sample size of s; $P_{m,n,\Omega}$ denotes the performance of classifier a_m on the full dataset d_n.

Let S be the set of data samples, of increasing size $s_t = 2^{5.5+0.5 \times t}$ with $t = (1, 2, 3, \ldots, T)$, and T being a parameter set by the user such that $1 \leq T \leq \lfloor \log_2 |d_n| \rfloor$. The samples follow a geometric increase, as suggested in [12]. When using a higher value for T, larger samples are calculated, presumably yielding more accurate estimates at the expense of higher run times.

The distance between two datasets d_i and d_j can be determined using the following function [7]:

$$dist(d_i, d_j, a_p, a_q, T) = \sum_{t=1}^{T} (P_{p,i,s_t} - P_{p,j,s_t})^2 + \sum_{t=1}^{T} (P_{q,i,s_t} - P_{q,j,s_t})^2 \quad (1)$$

This distance function is related to the Euclidean distance. It gives a measure of how similar two datasets are, based on the learning curves of the two classifiers. Other work suggests a distance function that measures the Manhattan distance between learning curves, but experiments show that the difference in performance between these variants is minuscule [8].

Using either of these distance functions, k nearest datasets can be identified, and from the performance of both classifiers on these datasets we can predict which of the two will perform better on the new dataset. Controversially, it has been remarked that as the number of used samples increases, the performance of this technique decreases [7]. The authors of [7] speculate that the learning curves on the nearest datasets are still not similar enough, and propose *Curve Adaptation*, a technique that can adapt retrieved curves to the learning curves on the new dataset. In order to adapt a learning curve of classifier a_p on dataset d_r to dataset d_i, all points of the prior learning curve are multiplied by a coefficient:

$$f(d_i, d_r, a_p, T) = \frac{\sum_{t=1}^{T}(P_{p,i,s_t} \times P_{p,r,s_t} \times s_t^2)}{\sum_{t=1}^{T}((P_{p,r,s_t})^2 \times s_t^2)} \tag{2}$$

Another optimization that could potentially improve performance is the *Smaller Sample* technique. As not all datasets are of the same size, it is possible that a retrieved dataset has a bigger size than the new dataset, which might give an unfair advantage for slow learners. In that case it might be beneficial to use the performance of the classifier at a sample size close to the full size of the new dataset.

Algorithm 1 shows the method in detail. It requires the new dataset as input, and values for parameters k (number of similar datasets to retrieve) and T (number of samples to use to build the partial learning curve), and boolean parameters indicating whether to use the Curve Adaptation and Smaller Sample technique. The while-loop starting on line 3 identifies the most promising classifier left in A (lines 4–29), appends this classifier to the final ranking R (line 30) and removes it from the pool of remaining classifiers to rank.

To find the most promising classifier, we set a_{best} first to a random classifier left in A. We will compare it against all a_{comp} (competing) classifiers left in A (for-loop on line 5). On line 6 we retrieve a set D of datasets on which we have recorded performance results for both classifiers (recall that d_{new} is not amongst those). Line 9 uses Eq. 1 to retrieve the nearest dataset. Lines 12–15 show how Curve Adaptation shifts the retrieved learning curve to the partial learning curve, using Eq. 2. Lines 16–18 show how the Smaller Sample option utilizes learning curves of a size close to the size of the new dataset. The classifier that performed best on the retrieved dataset (line 19) gets a vote, and the dataset is removed from the pool of available datasets. This is repeated k times, for the k nearest datasets. The classifier that has most votes is marked as a_{best}, and will be compared against the next competitor a_{comp} in the following loop iteration. Note that the algorithm potentially utilizes two different evaluation scores, denoted by P and P', but these can also be the same. The scores of one evaluation measure are used for identifying similar datasets and Curve Adaptation (i.e., the one denoted by P); the scores of the other evaluation measure are used for selecting an appropriate classifier (i.e., the one denoted by P'). This is useful because not all evaluation measures are suitable for both tasks.

Algorithm 1. Pairwise Curve Comparison (PCC)

Require: d_{new}, $k \in \mathbb{N}^+$, $T \in \mathbb{N}^+$, $CurveAdaptation \in \{0,1\}$, $SmallerSample \in \{0,1\}$
  1: Initialize A as a set of all classifiers
  2: Initialize R as empty list
  3: **while** $|A| > 0$ **do**
  4:    $a_{best} \leftarrow$ Arbitrary element from A
  5:    **for all** $a_{comp} \in A : a_{comp} \neq a_{best}$ **do**
  6:       Initialize D as the set of all datasets on which a_{best} and a_{comp} were ran
  7:       $votesBest = votesComp = 0$
  8:       **while** $votesBest + votesComp < k$ **do**
  9:          $d_{sim} \leftarrow \arg\min_{d_i \in D} dist(d_{new}, d_i, a_{best}, a_{comp}, T)$
 10:          $coeff_{best} = coeff_{comp} = 1$
 11:          $samp \leftarrow \Omega$
 12:          **if** $CurveAdaptation = 1$ **then**
 13:             $coeff_{best} \leftarrow f(d_{new}, d_{sim}, a_{best}, T)$
 14:             $coeff_{comp} \leftarrow f(d_{new}, d_{sim}, a_{comp}, T)$
 15:          **end if**
 16:          **if** $SmallerSample = 1$ **and** $\lfloor \log_2 |d_{new}| \rfloor < \lfloor \log_2 |d_{sim}| \rfloor$ **then**
 17:             $samp = \lfloor \log_2 |d_{new}| \rfloor$
 18:          **end if**
 19:          **if** $coeff_{best} \times P'_{best,d_{sim},samp} > coeff_{comp} \times P'_{comp,d_{sim},samp}$ **then**
 20:             $votesBest \leftarrow votesBest + 1$
 21:          **else**
 22:             $votesComp \leftarrow votesComp + 1$
 23:          **end if**
 24:          $D \leftarrow D - d_{sim}$
 25:       **end while**
 26:       **if** $votesBest < votesComp$ **then**
 27:          $a_{best} \leftarrow a_{comp}$
 28:       **end if**
 29:    **end for**
 30:    $R \leftarrow R + a_{best}$
 31:    $A \leftarrow A - a_{best}$
 32: **end while**
 33: **return** R {Ranking of classifiers in decreasing order}

Because we arbitrarily select the order in which classifiers are considered, the ranking will not always be the same (the meta-algorithm is unstable). However, classifiers that perform consistently better on similar datasets will always be ranked above their inferior competitors. Furthermore, the meta-algorithm has a start up time, as it needs to build the partial learning curves. In Sect. 4 we will see that this is only a fraction of the run time of large datasets.

The original method as proposed in [8] selects classifiers based on their predictive accuracy on similar datasets, but instead of predictive accuracy any measure can be used for this selection. Because we want to include run times in our experiments, we propose to use $A3R$, which combines predictive accuracy and run time [1]. $A3R$ compares the run times and accuracy of two classifiers on a dataset, so it could be used directly into methods that work based on pairwise comparisons. However, in order to make it useful for methods that do not compare classifiers pairwise, and allow a fair comparison in our experiments, we define a slightly adapted version of the measure:

$$A3R'^{d_i}_{a_p} = \frac{SR^{d_i}_{a_p}}{\sqrt[r]{T^{d_i}_{a_p}}} \tag{3}$$

where $SR^{d_i}_{a_p}$ is the predictive accuracy (success rate) of classifier a_p on dataset d_i, $T^{d_i}_{a_p}$ is the run time of classifier a_p on dataset d_i and r is a parameter controlled by the user, influencing the importance of time. Indeed, a lower value results in a higher emphasize on time. The higher the $A3R'$ score, the more suitable the classifier is on the combination of accuracy and run time.

4 Experiments

To evaluate the meta-algorithm, we selected 53 classifiers and 39 data sets from OpenML [19]. The classifiers come from Weka 3.7.12 [5], and include (but are not limited to) Decision Trees, Bayesian Networks, Support Vector Machines, Bagging, and Boosting. The data sets have between 540 and 48,842 observations, and between 5 and 241 attributes. All classifiers are run on all data sets.

Figure 1 shows how the average training time of all classifiers increases as the sample size increases. There seems to be a linear relation between the run time and sample size. The drop can be explained by a subset of high-dimensional data sets, which take longer to train but contain only 2,000 observations.

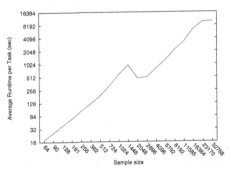

We will use two strong baseline methods to compare our method to. **Best on Sample** runs all classifiers using a given sample size, and ranks the classifiers in the order of perfor-

Fig. 1. Average training time of all classifiers per task per sample

mance on that sample [10]. The **Average Rank** ranks the classifiers in the order of their average rank on previously seen datasets, and has proven to be quite accurate [3,9]. Although comparing the methods also against a meta-feature based approach seems interesting, configuring the latter takes much time, giving an unfair advantage to the sample based approaches.

Section 4.1 describes an experiment that focuses solely on predicting the best classifier; here we attempt to reproduce the results obtained by [8] using a larger meta-dataset. In Sect. 4.2 we show how the meta-algorithm performs when predicting a ranking of classifiers. Section 4.3 describes our main contribution, novel experiments incorporating both accuracy and run times, yielding significant improvements over the baseline methods.

4.1   Predicting the Best Classifier

In the first experiment we aim to establish how well the meta-algorithm performs when the task is to recommend the best available classifier. A recommendation is considered correct if there was no statistically significant difference between the absolute best classifier and the recommended classifier, as is done in, e.g., [8]. It uses predictive accuracy as the evaluation measure to identify similar datasets and select the best classifier. Our proposed method has several parameters. Most importantly, T (number of samples used) and k (number of nearest data sets to be identified). Furthermore, we seek to explore the effect of Curve Adaptation (CA) and the newly proposed Smaller Sample technique (SS) by comparing instances having this option enabled against instances without.

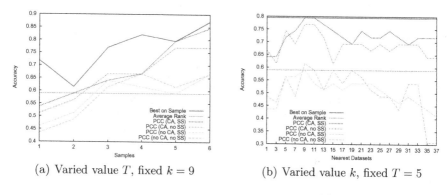

(a) Varied value T, fixed $k = 9$ (b) Varied value k, fixed $T = 5$

Fig. 2. Performance on predicting the best classifier.

Figure 2(a) shows the effect of varying the number of (increasingly large) samples when computing the partial learning curve. It can be seen that using more samples results almost consistently in better performance, as was expected. There are some drops in performance, which can probably be attributed to characteristics of the specific data sets used (e.g., dimensionality). Figure 2(b) shows the effect of varying the number of nearest neighbours, using odd numbers. Average Rank remains constant, as it does not use samples nor identify nearest datasets. Setting k around 9 seem very suitable in this case, but presumably this depends on the size of the meta-dataset. Setting this value too low might lead to instable behaviour, whereas setting it too high might result in including many data sets which are not similar enough.

Both figures show similar trends. Best on Sample dominates the other techniques in most of the cases, even though this method is rather simple. Furthermore, both Pairwise Curve Comparison instances using Curve Adaptation (CA) outperform the instances without Curve Adaptation. Smaller Sample (SS) also seems to improve the prediction quality, although the difference is less prominent. In all, both Best on Sample and Pairwise Curve Comparison obtain very reasonable performance, advising a (statistically) best or equally good classifier in more than 85 % of the cases.

4.2 Ranking of Classifiers

In many meta-learning applications it is not enough to simply predict the single best classifier. When the recommended classifier does not perform well enough, an alternative should be at hand. Rather than recommending a single classifier, a ranking should be created, ordering the classifiers on their likelihood of performing well on the dataset. This way, the user can make an informed decision about which models to try based on the available time and resources. The standard approach to evaluate such a ranking is to compute the Spearman Correlation Coefficient [17]. However, it has a drawback: it penalizes every wrongly ranked classifier equally, whereas we typically do not care about incorrect ranked classifiers after the best one has been identified.

An alternative approach is to use Loss Curves as done in, e.g., [9]. The authors define *loss* as the difference in accuracy between the current best classifier and the global best classifier. In order to find the global best classifier on a dataset, we evaluate all classifiers on this dataset in a certain order, for example by going down a ranking. A Loss Curve plots the obtained loss against the number of classifiers that have been tested. The goal is to find a classifier that has a low loss in relatively few tests. Usually, this is repeated over many data sets and the average Loss Curve is reported. Similarly to ROC Curves for which commonly an Area Under the ROC Curve is calculated, we also can calculate the *Area Under the Loss Curve*, in which low values are preferred over high values. Although this measure is less informative than the Loss Curve itself, it can be used to show certain trends, e.g. the effect of an algorithm parameter.

Figure 3(a) plots the Area Under the Loss Curve against the number of samples. Using more (larger) samples typically results in an improved Area Under the Loss Curve score for Best on Sample and Pairwise Curve Comparison instances using Curve Adaptation. Again, Average Rank remains constant, and there seems to be no improvement for Pairwise Curve Comparison instances without Curve Adaptation. Figure 3(b) shows the Loss Curves. In order not to overload the figure, we only include the baselines and the Pairwise Curve Comparison instance using both Curve Adaptation and the Smaller Sample option. The Best on Sample technique again dominates the other techniques.

Loss Curves assume that every test will take the same amount of time, which is not realistic. For example, Multilayer Perceptrons take longer to train than Naive Bayes classifiers. Therefore, it is better to use *Loss Time Curves*, which plot the average loss against the time needed to obtain this loss. It describes how much time is needed on average to converge to a certain loss (lower is better). The faster such curve goes to a loss of zero, the better the technique is. They have been used before in the Optimization literature [6].

Figure 4 shows the results of the same experiment in Loss Time space. Figure 4(b) shows the Loss Time Curve, scaled to the part where the average loss is lower than 10 %. Compared to Fig. 3(b), it shows that while Pairwise Curve Comparison needs more tests to converge to an acceptable loss, it does so in less time. However, the results for other values of T (number of tests), shown in Fig. 4(a), are less conclusive. Controversially, adding samples does not

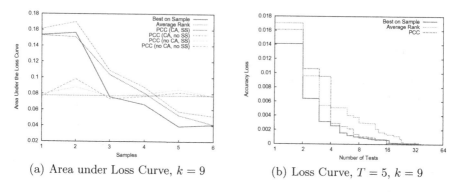

(a) Area under Loss Curve, $k = 9$ (b) Loss Curve, $T = 5$, $k = 9$

Fig. 3. Performance of ranking of classifiers in Loss space.

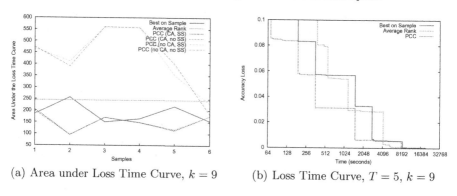

(a) Area under Loss Time Curve, $k = 9$ (b) Loss Time Curve, $T = 5$, $k = 9$

Fig. 4. Performance of ranking of classifiers in Loss Time space.

lead to better results in Loss Time space. The reason for this is that none of the involved methods are taking training times into account when building a ranking.

4.3   Incorporating Run Times

Next, our aim is to involve run times in the classifier selection process and establish that this improves the performance of the meta-algorithm in Loss Time space. One way of doing so can be trading off accuracy and speed. Naively ranking the classifiers in the order of run times yields bad results. Therefore, we adjust `Pairwise Curve Comparison` to compare and select classifiers based on their $A3R'$ scores, as introduced in Sect. 3. Both baseline methods are adjusted in a similar way. Similar datasets are still identified using learning curves based on predictive accuracy scores (recall that the meta-algorithm potentially uses different evaluation measures to identify similar datasets and select classifiers).

Figure 5(a) compares the ranking obtained by `Pairwise Curve Comparison` using $A3R'$ against all methods building the ranking based solely on accuracy. As expected, the gain in performance is eminent. `Pairwise Curve Comparison`

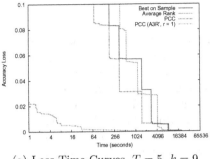
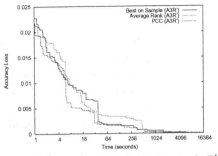

(a) Loss Time Curves, $T = 5$, $k = 9$ (b) Loss Time Curves, $T = 5$, $k = 9$, $A3R'$

Fig. 5. Classifier ranking performance in Loss Time space using the $A3R'$ criterion.

using $A3R'$ converges to an acceptable loss level orders of magnitude faster than the baselines, because it is the only technique that takes run times into account.

In order to make a more fair comparison, we also adjust the baseline techniques in a straightforward way, such that these also rank the classifiers based on $A3R'$ rather than accuracy. Figure 5(b) shows the results of the same experiment run with the baselines incorporating $A3R'$. Indeed, the $A3R'$ criterion is useful in these methods as well, all reducing the accuracy loss drastically faster than before. However, the `Pairwise Curve Comparison` method still dominates the other techniques, though the differences are smaller.

Finally, $A3R'$ has a parameter r that allows users to control the importance of accuracy and run times. Increasing the value of r decreases the importance of run times when selecting classifiers. We track the effect of this parameter in Loss space and Loss Time space. Figure 6(a) shows that the methods emphasizing accuracy converge to a low loss in few tests, since they focus on classifiers that are probably good, but potentially slow. However, Fig. 6(b) shows that they do not converge faster in Loss Time space. Evaluating faster methods earlier clearly pays of, especially if there is limited time to select a classifier.

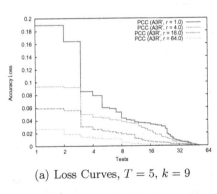
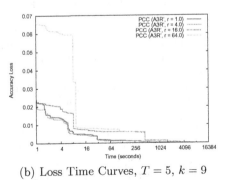

(a) Loss Curves, $T = 5$, $k = 9$ (b) Loss Time Curves, $T = 5$, $k = 9$

Fig. 6. Performance of `Pairwise Curve Comparison`, varying values for r.

5   Conclusion

This paper addresses the problem of algorithm selection under a budget, where multiple algorithms can be run on the full data set until the budget expires.

We have extended the method presented in [8] such that it generates a ranking of classifiers, rather than just predicting the single best classifier, and evaluated it using a much larger amount of classifiers. Interestingly, a simple and elegant baseline method called Best on Sample outperformed this method in our experiments, selecting good classifiers in fewer tests. However, when tested in a more realistic setting where the budget is time, rather than a number of tests, and using a novel selection criterion, $A3R'$ (which trades off accuracy and run time), the newly proposed method outperformed all baselines. This suggests that it is very suitable for algorithm selection applications with a limited time budget.

Another contribution of this work is the use of Loss Time Curves to study meta-learning algorithms which, to the best of our knowledge, have not been previously used in the meta-learning literature. Future work will focus on adapting other meta-learning techniques with the $A3R'$ criterion and/or evaluating them in Loss Time space, as this might lead to even more valuable insight.

Acknowledgments. This work is supported by grant 600.065.120.12N150 from the Dutch Fund for Scientific Research (NWO).

References

1. Abdulrahman, S.M., Brazdil, P.: Measures for combining accuracy and time for meta-learning. In: Meta-Learning and Algorithm Selection Workshop at ECAI, 2014, pp. 49–50 (2014)
2. Brazdil, P., Gama, J., Henery, B.: Characterizing the applicability of classification algorithms using meta-level learning. In: Bergadano, F., De Raedt, L. (eds.) ECML-94. LNCS, vol. 784, pp. 83–102. Springer, Heidelberg (1994)
3. Brazdil, P.B., Soares, C.: A comparison of ranking methods for classification algorithm selection. In: Lopez de Mantaras, R., Plaza, E. (eds.) ECML 2000. LNCS (LNAI), vol. 1810, pp. 63–74. Springer, Heidelberg (2000)
4. Fürnkranz, J., Petrak, J.: An evaluation of landmarking variants. In: Working Notes of the ECML/PKDD 2000 Workshop on Integrating Aspects of Data Mining, Decision Support and Meta-Learning, pp. 57–68 (2001)
5. Hall, M., Frank, E., Holmes, G., Pfahringer, B., Reutemann, P., Witten, I.H.: The WEKA data mining software: an update. ACM SIGKDD Explor. Newsl. **11**(1), 10–18 (2009)
6. Hutter, F., Hoos, H.H., Leyton-Brown, K., Murphy, K.: Time-bounded sequential parameter optimization. In: Blum, C., Battiti, R. (eds.) LION 4. LNCS, vol. 6073, pp. 281–298. Springer, Heidelberg (2010)
7. Leite, R., Brazdil, P.: Predicting relative performance of classifiers from samples. In: Proceedings of the 22nd International Conference on Machine Learning, pp. 497–503. ACM (2005)
8. Leite, R., Brazdil, P.: Active testing strategy to predict the best classification algorithm via sampling and metalearning. In: ECAI, pp. 309–314 (2010)

9. Leite, R., Brazdil, P., Vanschoren, J.: Selecting classification algorithms with active testing. In: Perner, P. (ed.) MLDM 2012. LNCS, vol. 7376, pp. 117–131. Springer, Heidelberg (2012)

10. Petrak, J.: Fast subsampling performance estimates for classification algorithm selection. In: Proceedings of the ECML-00 Workshop on Meta-Learning: Building Automatic Advice Strategies for Model Selection and Method Combination, pp. 3–14 (2000)

11. Pfahringer, B., Bensusan, H., Giraud-Carrier, C.: Tell me who can learn you and i can tell you who you are: Landmarking various learning algorithms. In: Proceedings of the 17th International Conference on Machine Learning, pp. 743–750 (2000)

12. Provost, F., Jensen, D., Oates, T.: Efficient progressive sampling. In: Proceedings of the Fifth ACM SIGKDD International Conference on Knowledge Discovery and Data Mining, pp. 23–32. ACM (1999)

13. Rice, J.R.: The algorithm selection problem. Adv. Comput. **15**, 65118 (1976)

14. van Rijn, J.N., Holmes, G., Pfahringer, B., Vanschoren, J.: Algorithm selection on data streams. In: Džeroski, S., Panov, P., Kocev, D., Todorovski, L. (eds.) DS 2014. LNCS, vol. 8777, pp. 325–336. Springer, Heidelberg (2014)

15. Rossi, A.L.D., de Leon Ferreira, A.C.P., Soares, C., De Souza, B.F.: MetaStream: a meta-learning based method for periodic algorithm selection in time-changing data. Neurocomputing **127**, 52–64 (2014)

16. Smith-Miles, K.A.: Cross-disciplinary perspectives on meta-learning for algorithm selection. ACM Comput. Surv. (CSUR) **41**(1), 6 (2008)

17. Sun, Q., Pfahringer, B.: Pairwise meta-rules for better meta-learning-based algorithm ranking. Mach. Learn. **93**(1), 141–161 (2013)

18. Vanschoren, J., Blockeel, H., Pfahringer, B., Holmes, G.: Experiment databases. Mach. Learn. **87**(2), 127–158 (2012)

19. Vanschoren, J., van Rijn, J.N., Bischl, B., Torgo, L.: OpenML: networked science in machine learning. ACM SIGKDD Explor. Newsl. **15**(2), 49–60 (2014)

20. Vilalta, R., Drissi, Y.: A perspective view and survey of meta-learning. Artif. Intell. Rev. **18**(2), 77–95 (2002)

21. Wolpert, D.H.: Stacked generalization. Neural Networks **5**(2), 241–259 (1992)

Optimally Weighted Cluster Kriging
for Big Data Regression

Bas van Stein[✉], Hao Wang, Wojtek Kowalczyk, Thomas Bäck,
and Michael Emmerich

Leiden Institute of Advanced Computer Science, Leiden University,
Niels Bohrweg 1, Leiden, The Netherlands
{b.van.stein,h.wang,w.j.kowalczyk,t.h.w.baeck,
m.t.m.emmerich}@liacs.leidenuniv.nl

Abstract. In business and academia we are continuously trying to model and analyze complex processes in order to gain insight and optimize. One of the most popular modeling algorithms is *Kriging*, or *Gaussian Processes*. A major bottleneck with Kriging is the amount of processing time of at least $O(n^3)$ and memory required $O(n^2)$ when applying this algorithm on medium to big data sets. With big data sets, that are more and more available these days, Kriging is not computationally feasible. As a solution to this problem we introduce a hybrid approach in which a number of Kriging models built on disjoint subsets of the data are properly weighted for the predictions. The proposed model is both in processing time and memory much more efficient than standard Global Kriging and performs equally well in terms of accuracy. The proposed algorithm is better scalable, and well suited for parallelization.

Keywords: Kriging · Gaussian Processes · K-means · Clustering · Big-data · Regression

1 Introduction

Regression as supervised learning is an important tool for analysis of data sets and as sub goal for further optimization or gaining knowledge about the data sets and their underlying processes. There are many kinds of regression algorithms: parametric models, which are easy to interpret but may lack expressive power to model complex functions, *Regression Tree* based methods like *Random Forests* [3] or *Gradient Boosted Decision Trees*, which lack the advantage of interpretation [7] but have more expressive power. There are also more complex algorithms like *Neural Networks*, or *Extreme Learning Machines* [15], that are able to model very complex functions but are usually not easy to work with in practice. And last but not least there are kernel-based methods such as *Support Vector Machines, Radial Basis Functions* and *Kriging* [16]. These kernel based algorithms are flexible and easy to work with, but are computationally expensive.

© Springer International Publishing Switzerland 2015
E. Fromont et al. (Eds.): IDA 2015, LNCS 9385, pp. 310–321, 2015.
DOI: 10.1007/978-3-319-24465-5_27

Kriging is a stochastic interpolation/regression approach, which originates from geostatistics [16] and originally targets exploration problems in mining. It has been widely used in spatial interpolation and regression tasks. Note that the Kriging method is also called *Gaussian Process Regression* [21] in the machine learning literature. In addition to generating predictions, Kriging also provides the expected mean squared error of point estimates, so-called *Kriging variance*. The Kriging variance is of significant importance because it is typically used to measure the uncertainty of the predictions, but in this paper, it also serves to find an optimal weighting scheme to combine multiple independent Kriging models.

Notation. Through this paper, we shall use n, k, d to denote the size of the data points, the number of clusters and dimensionality, respectively.

A major problem with Kriging, is the complexity of training the model, which requires solving a dense linear system of size $n \times n$, which takes $O(n^3)$[1]. Even more time is required when estimating the hyper-parameters. The algorithm also takes $O(n^2)$ memory, which might be a bottleneck in big data sets as well. In this paper a new algorithm is proposed, *Optimally Weighted Cluster Kriging* (OWCK), as an answer to this complexity problem. Using a clustering method we divide the possible big data set into k much smaller data sets, on each data set a Kriging model is being trained and the results from each model are combined to create a predictor in an optimal way. Using this method we can achieve a theoretical speedup of k^2 (k is the number of clusters), and when executing on a parallel system with k CPU's, we can improve that further to almost k^3. The memory required by the algorithm is reduced by factor k^2.

In Sect. 2 a brief introduction to Kriging is given. Then, in Sect. 3 relevant research is reviewed and in Sects. 4 and 5, our method and the results from our experiments are presented and discussed. Finally, a conclusion is drawn and suggestions for further research are made.

2 Kriging

Kriging is based on the assumption that the function to be approximated is the realization of a Gaussian Random Field with known (or estimated) covariance structure [22]. Based on the this assumption, Kriging interpolates function values at unknown points from observed function values. Normally, the Kriging model is trained on some input vector $\mathbf{X} = \{\mathbf{x}_1, \ldots, \mathbf{x}_n\}$ and the corresponding target values $\mathbf{y} = \{y(\mathbf{x}_1), \ldots, y(\mathbf{x}_n)\}$. Kriging estimates the output at unknown data samples by modeling the response values as a realization of a random process y, which is a sum of a mean function $\mu(\cdot)$ and a centered Gaussian process ε,

$$y(\mathbf{x}) = \mu(\mathbf{x}) + \varepsilon(\mathbf{x})$$

The centered Gaussian process ε is a stochastic process, which is completely defined by providing a prescribed covariance function $k(\cdot, \cdot)$ [21]:

---

[1] There are asymptotically faster algorithms for inverting a matrix. e.g. Strassen's $O(n^{2.807})$ and Stothers $O(n^{2.373})$.

$$k(\mathbf{x}, \mathbf{x}') = \mathrm{Cov}[\varepsilon(\mathbf{x}), \varepsilon(\mathbf{x}')] = \mathbb{E}[\varepsilon(\mathbf{x})\varepsilon(\mathbf{x}')].$$

A common choice of $k(\cdot, \cdot)$ is the Gaussian covariance (also known as squared exponential):

$$k(\mathbf{x}, \mathbf{x}') = \prod_{i=1}^{d} \exp\left(-\theta_i(x_i - x_i')^2\right), \tag{1}$$

where θ_i's are called *hyper parameters*, which are either predetermined or estimated through model fitting. When the mean values $\mu(\cdot)$ are assumed to be constant but need to be estimated, the method is called *Ordinary Kriging* (OK). In OK, the joint distribution of the (uncertain) outcome $y^t(\mathbf{x}^t)$ at a target point $\mathbf{x}^t$ and the observations $\mathbf{y}$ is Gaussian. In addition, for given $\mathbf{X}$ and μ it holds:

$$\begin{bmatrix} y^t \\ \mathbf{y} \end{bmatrix} \Big| \mu, \mathbf{X}, \mathbf{x}^t \sim \mathcal{N}\left(\mu \mathbf{1}_{n+1} \begin{bmatrix} c & \mathbf{c}^T \\ \mathbf{c} & \boldsymbol{\Sigma} \end{bmatrix} \right), \tag{2}$$

where

$$c = k(\mathbf{x}^t, \mathbf{x}^t), \quad c_i = k(\mathbf{x}^t, \mathbf{x}_i), \quad \boldsymbol{\Sigma}_{ij} = k(\mathbf{x}_i, \mathbf{x}_j),$$

and $\mathbf{1}_{n+1}$ represents a column vector of length $n+1$ that contains only 1's.

By introducing a non-informative uniform prior distribution on μ, the *posterior* conditional distribution of y^t can be calculated by marginalizing μ out. Without any derivations, the posterior distribution for OK is again Gaussian [11]:

$$y^t | \mathbf{y}, \mathbf{X}, \mathbf{x}^t \sim \mathcal{N}\left(m(\mathbf{x}^t), s^2(\mathbf{x}^t) \right) \tag{3}$$

$$m(\mathbf{x}^t) = \left[\mathbf{c} + \left(\frac{1 - \mathbf{c}^T \boldsymbol{\Sigma}^{-1} \mathbf{1}_n}{\mathbf{1}_n^T \boldsymbol{\Sigma}^{-1} \mathbf{1}_n} \right) \mathbf{1}_n \right]^T \boldsymbol{\Sigma}^{-1} \mathbf{y} \tag{4}$$

$$s^2(\mathbf{x}^t) = c^2 - \mathbf{c}^T \boldsymbol{\Sigma}^{-1} \mathbf{c} + \frac{(1 - \mathbf{c}^T \boldsymbol{\Sigma}^{-1} \mathbf{1}_n)^2}{\mathbf{1}_n^T \boldsymbol{\Sigma}^{-1} \mathbf{1}_n} \tag{5}$$

The posterior mean function is used as the predictor while the posterior variance is the so-called Kriging variance.

3   Relevant Research

The high computational complexity of Kriging is not an unnoticed problem in the world of data analysis and modeling. Several modifications and algorithms are already proposed. One of the most intuitive and "simple" algorithms is *Nearest Neighbour Kriging* [8], where we train a Kriging model using only k neighbours of the point we want to predict. The disadvantage of such an algorithm is that we need to train a model for each record we want to predict. Another disadvantage is that the accuracy suffers greatly when not enough neighbours are being used.

Another modification to Kriging is the approximation of the covariance matrix with a sparse precision matrix by *Hartman, L. and Hössjer, O.* [12]. In this paper they use *Gaussian Markov Random Fields* (GMRF) on a reasonable dense grid to exploit the computational benefits of a Markov field while keeping the formula of Kriging weights. This method reduces the complexity for simple and ordinary Kriging, but might not always be efficient with universal Kriging. Another algorithm, focused especially on data sets with scattered data points uses fast matrix-vector products to reduce the training complexity [18].

Several other attempts have been made to divide the Kriging model in submodels [6,19], each solution for different domains. In [6], a *Bagging* [2] method is proposed to increase the robustness of the Kriging algorithm, rather than speeding up the algorithms training time. In [19], a partitioning method is introduced to separate the data points into local Kriging models and combine the different models using a distance metric.

While previously mentioned work has some similarities to what is proposed in this paper, the weighting and clustering methods being used in previous mentioned work seems to be far from optimal.

4   Optimally Weighted Cluster Kriging

As mentioned before, Kriging suffers from high computation time as the number of sampling points gets high. In this section, we will propose an algorithm that is suitable for efficiently processing big data sets while maintaining much of the ideas of Kriging. The basic idea of the new algorithm is to cluster the data set and build independent Kriging models for each part of the data. The value of an unknown point is predicted as a linear combination of the predictions from all the Kriging models. In addition, an optimal weights setting for the linear combination exists and is calculated. We therefore call the newly proposed algorithm *Optimally Weighted Cluster Kriging*.

4.1   Clustering the Data Set

In the first step, the input data samples $\mathbf{X}$ should be separated into several clusters (k clusters here), which can be represented by a set of tuples:

$$\{(\mathbf{X}_l, \mathbf{y}_l)\}_{l=1}^k, \quad [\mathbf{X}_1^T, \mathbf{X}_2^T, \ldots, \mathbf{X}_k^T]^T = \mathbf{X}, \quad [\mathbf{y}_1^T, \mathbf{y}_2^T, \ldots, \mathbf{y}_k^T]^T = \mathbf{y}$$

where $\mathbf{y}$ is again the vector containing all of the observed response values. Note that l is the label identifying the clusters. We also use $\{n_l\}_{l=1}^k$ to denote the size of each cluster. Within cluster l, all the input data samples can be represented as:

$$\mathbf{X}_l = [\mathbf{x}_{l_i}]_{i=1}^{n_l}, \quad \text{and} \quad \mathbf{y}_l = [y_{l_i}]_{i=1}^{n_l}.$$

In order to cluster the training data for our local models, a clustering algorithm that gives roughly equal sized parts is preferred. This lead us to choosing two algorithms: *K-means* clustering, and Random clustering. In Random clustering we divide the data points at random in k groups by assigning each data point to an alternating label, with *K-means* we use the K-means clustering algorithm to divide the training data into k ($< n$) clusters using the *Forgy* [9] method. k random data points are picked as the initial centroids of the clusters. Next, each data point is assigned to the cluster with the least Euclidean distance, after assigning a data point to a cluster, the cluster's centroid is updated and the process is repeated several times. The algorithm minimizes the within-cluster sum of squares (Eq. 6):

$$\arg\min_{S} \sum_{i=1}^{k} \sum_{x \in S_i} ||x - \mu_i||^2, \tag{6}$$

where S is the set of clusters, n is the number of data points and μ_i is the mean of the points in S_i. Note that the within-cluster sum of squares takes only $O(nk)$ execution time.

Our hypothesis is that using K-means clustering, the Kriging models trained on each cluster have a high accuracy due to the assumed "local" neighbourhood of the training data. With Random clustering, we hypothesize that each model is equally fitted, since each data set has roughly the same structure. Using random clustering we assume that the weighted combination will be more robust than normal Global Kriging.

4.2 Kriging Model on Clusters

The next step is to fit a Kriging model for each of the clusters. The procedure is the same as described in Sect. 3 except that each Kriging model has its own distinct data set. The Kriging formula for each cluster can simply be obtained by adding the cluster label l to the data set and all the parameters (e.g. μ) in Eq. 2. On cluster l, the joint distribution of the response-values to predict the observed data is:

$$\begin{bmatrix} y^t \\ \mathbf{y}_l \end{bmatrix} \Big| \mu_l, \mathbf{X}_l, \mathbf{x}^t \sim \mathcal{N}\left(\mu_l \mathbf{1}_{n_l+1}, \begin{bmatrix} c_l & \mathbf{c}_l^T \\ \mathbf{c}_l & \mathbf{\Sigma}_l \end{bmatrix} \right) \tag{7}$$

$$c_l = k_l(\mathbf{x}^t, \mathbf{x}^t), \quad \mathbf{c}_{l_i} = k_l(\mathbf{x}^t, \mathbf{x}_{l_i}), \quad \mathbf{\Sigma}_{l_{ij}} = k_l(\mathbf{x}_{l_i}, \mathbf{x}_{l_j}).$$

Note that the covariance function is also indexed by l due to the fact that we might choose a different covariance function for each cluster. The predictive conditional distribution can be expressed as:

$$y^t | \mathbf{y}_l, \mathbf{X}_l, \mathbf{x}^t \sim \mathcal{N}\left(m_l(\mathbf{x}^t), s_l^2(\mathbf{x}^t) \right) \tag{8}$$

The formula above is exactly the same as Eq. 3 except that the posterior mean and variance are labeled by l. We choose the Gaussian covariance function (Eq. 1) for all the Kriging models on the clusters. The hyper-parameters in the covariance function are fitted by Maximum Likelihood Estimation (MLE) [21]. In our algorithm, the *Cobyla* [20] algorithm is used to solve the maximum likelihood estimation task. The *nugget* parameter that specifies the amount of noise expected, is set to 0.01 in our experiments but can be set differently depending on the data.

4.3   Weighting Distribution

In order to combine multiple Kriging models, trained on different clusters of data, a straightforward method is to use a weighting distribution to model how much "trust" should be put on the prediction from each cluster. By using cluster indicator variable C, the weighting vector $\mathbf{w}$ can be written as:

$$\mathbf{w} = \{p(C = l) = w_l\}_{l=1}^k, \quad \sum_{l=1}^k w_l = 1, \quad w_l \geq 0,$$

which is non-negative and satisfies the normalization property. Unlike the weights in the Gaussian mixture model [13], the weighting distribution $\mathbf{w}$ depends on the target data sample $\mathbf{x}^t$. The optimal setting of $\mathbf{w}$ is discussed in the following sections.

4.4   Prediction Using All the Kriging Models

We will show how to make the overall prediction using all the Kriging models by combining the predictions from each of them. The background assumption is that the Gaussian Processes (behind the Kriging models) on the clusters are mutually independent from each other, which is reasonable due to our clustering procedure. Our approach is to first obtain the joint distribution of $y^t(\mathbf{x}^t)$ and $\mathbf{y}$. Actually, it is the joint distribution conditioning on $\mathbf{X}, \mathbf{x}^t$ and $\mathbf{y}$. We omit the conditional symbols in the following for simplicity. By applying the total probability with respect to the cluster indicator variable C, we have:

$$p(y^t, \mathbf{y}) = \sum_{l=1}^k p(y^t, \mathbf{y}|C = l)p(C = l)$$

$$= \sum_{l=1}^k p(y^t, \{\mathbf{y}_i\}_{i=1}^k|C = l)p(C = l)$$

$$= \sum_{l=1}^k p(y^t, \mathbf{y}_l|\{\mathbf{y}_i\}_{i\neq 1}, C = l)p(\{\mathbf{y}_i\}_{i\neq l}|C = l)p(C = l)$$

Due to the fact that $y^t, \mathbf{y}_l$ are conditionally independent of $\{\mathbf{y}_i\}_{i\neq l}$ given $C = l$, the equations above can be further simplified to:

$$p(y^t, \mathbf{y}) = \sum_{l=1}^k p(y^t, \mathbf{y}_l|C = l)p(\{\mathbf{y}_i\}_{i\neq l}|C = l)w_l$$

$$= \sum_{l=1}^k p(y^t, \mathbf{y}_l)\left(\prod_{i\neq l} p(\mathbf{y}_i)\right)w_l$$

The product inside of the sum is again due to the independence. Now we perform the conditioning on $\mathbf{y}$ and omit the cluster indicator variable C:

$$p(y^t|\mathbf{y}) = \frac{p(y^t, \mathbf{y})}{p(\mathbf{y})}$$

$$= \sum_{l=1}^{k} p(y^t, \mathbf{y}_l) \frac{\prod_{i \neq l} p(\mathbf{y}_i)}{\prod_{i=l}^{k} p(\mathbf{y}_i)} w_l$$

$$= \sum_{l=1}^{k} p(y^t|\mathbf{y}_l) w_l \tag{9}$$

Note that each of the conditional distributions inside of the summation is exactly the same as the Gaussian conditional distribution obtained from the corresponding cluster. Finally the distribution of y^t conditioning on $\mathbf{y}$ can be obtained by combining Eqs. 8 and 9:

$$y^t|\mathbf{y} \sim \mathcal{N} \left(\sum_{l=1}^{k} w_l m_l(\mathbf{x}^t), \sum_{l=1}^{k} w_l^2 \sigma_l^2(\mathbf{x}^t) \right) \tag{10}$$

Equation 10 suggests that the overall prediction is simply the weighted average of the prediction from each cluster while the prediction mean square error (variance) is also the weighted average of variance from each cluster, where the weight is squared.

4.5 Optimal Weighting

Equation 10 also suggests that an optimal weighting distribution exists and can be obtained by minimizing the variance of the weighted average. Thus, by putting all the variances into the diagonal of a matrix $\mathbf{Q} = \mathrm{diag}(\sigma_1^2, \ldots, \sigma_k^2)$, the optimal weighting $\mathbf{w}^*$ is the solution to the following optimization problem:

$$\text{minimize:} \quad \mathbf{w}^T \mathbf{Q} \mathbf{w} \quad \text{subject to:} \quad \sum_{l=1}^{k} w_l = 1, \quad w_l \geq 0, \quad l = 1, \ldots, k.$$

This quadratic programming problem can be immediately solved by the method of Lagrangian multipliers [1]. The optimal weights setting is:

$$\mathbf{w}^* = \frac{\mathbf{Q}^{-1} \mathbf{1}_k}{\mathbf{1}_k^T \mathbf{Q}^{-1} \mathbf{1}_k}, \tag{11}$$

Equation 11 gives the optimal setting of the weighting distribution for our approach. Note that matrix $\mathbf{Q}$ is invertible if and only if the conditional variances of the prediction (diagonal elements) are not zero, which is guaranteed because the prediction is not performed on any of the data samples.

4.6 Pseudo Code

In Algorithm 1 an outline of the algorithm is presented. Any algorithm can be used to create the clusters for training the models, though to gain maximal speedup the clusters should be of the same size. In the prediction phase a method *Optimise Weights* is used. This method uses the predicted mean squared errors from the Kriging models in order to find an optimal weighting distribution per prediction.

Algorithm 1. Optimally Weighted Cluster Kriging

Given: A data set X_{train} and X_{test} with records $x_1, \ldots, x_n$, a target attribute y and the number of clusters k
Initialization:
$Clusters = k - MEANS(X_{train}, k)$

for all $Cl_i \in Clusters$ **do**
   $Models[i] = Kriging.train(Cl_i)$
end for
$Predictions_{final} = []$
for all $x_i \in X_{test}$ **do**
   $Predictions = []$
   $MSE = []$
   for all $model_i \in Models$ **do**
      $Predictions[i], MSE[i] = model_i.predict(x_i)$
   end for
   $Weights = Optimise Weights(MSE)$
   $Predictions_{final}[i] = WeightedSum(Predictions, Weights)$
end for
return $Predictions_{final}$

---

5   Experimental Setup and Results

We assessed the performance of *Optimally Weighted Cluster Kriging* (OWCK) on several known benchmark functions from the *DEAP* [10] Python package: *Rastrigin, Rosenbrock, Ackley, Himmelblau, H1, Schwefel, Schaffer,* and *Diffpow*. On these functions, Ordinary Kriging and OWCK were tested. The reason to use Ordinary Kriging is due to its applicability and simplicity. Both k-means and Random partitioning are used in the experiments. For each experiment the number of data samples ranges from 1000 to 10.000 records, in two and five dimensions. Five-fold cross validation is used on each of these runs, effectively using 4/5 of the data samples as training set and 1/5 as test set. The results shown are the averaged results from the five folds.

In the Tables 1 and 2 the R^2 scores of the functions in 2 dimensions are presented. The number of the clusters tested here are $4, 8, 16, 32, 64$. For each column, the entries are shaded in different levels of gray depending on their value. The best scores in each column are the most dark, the lower scores are more light.

In Tables 3 and 4 the results from the same algorithms on 5 dimensional functions are shown.

In Fig. 1 the execution time per algorithm is shown for the Rastrigin function. Note that 4/5 of the data was used for training and 1/5 for predicting in the

Table 1. Accuracy score of each algorithm (R^2) on the benchmark functions in 2 dimensions with a dataset of size 1.000.

	h1	Ackley	Himmel.	Diffpow	Rosenb.	Rast.	Schaffer	Schwefel
OK	0.254	0.920	1.000	1.000	1.000	0.547	0.352	0.170
4 Random	0.229	0.480	1.000	1.000	1.000	0.547	0.354	0.158
8 Random	0.216	0.433	1.000	0.803	1.000	0.546	0.354	0.136
16 Random	0.207	0.447	0.829	0.519	1.000	0.543	0.356	0.137
32 Random	0.213	0.465	0.709	0.531	0.996	0.540	0.355	0.132
64 Random	0.239	0.524	0.717	0.544	0.882	0.530	0.358	0.140
4 K-means	0.311	0.932	1.000	1.000	1.000	0.541	0.400	0.177
8 K-means	0.272	0.936	1.000	1.000	1.000	0.525	0.403	0.476
16 K-means	0.149	0.936	1.000	1.000	1.000	0.515	0.376	0.629
32 K-means	0.111	0.930	0.999	0.998	1.000	0.499	0.306	0.468
64 K-means	−1.364	0.895	1.000	0.997	1.000	−0.085	0.052	−0.054

Table 2. Accuracy score of each algorithm (R^2) on the benchmark functions in 2 dimensions with a dataset of size 5.000.

	h1	Ackley	Himmel.	Diffpow	Rosenb.	Rast.	Schaffer	Schwefel
OK	0.519	0.940	1.000	1.000	1.000	0.543	0.401	0.582
4 Random	0.453	0.929	1.000	1.000	1.000	0.543	0.352	0.196
8 Random	0.370	0.919	1.000	1.000	1.000	0.543	0.350	0.192
16 Random	0.297	0.589	1.000	1.000	1.000	0.543	0.350	0.171
32 Random	0.249	0.449	1.000	1.000	1.000	0.543	0.351	0.142
64 Random	0.229	0.455	0.887	0.578	1.000	0.542	0.351	0.135
4 K-means	0.528	0.942	1.000	1.000	1.000	0.561	0.403	0.549
8 K-means	0.580	0.944	1.000	1.000	1.000	0.540	0.407	0.956
16 K-means	0.528	0.945	1.000	1.000	1.000	0.577	0.410	0.718
32 K-means	0.550	0.945	1.000	1.000	1.000	0.664	0.410	0.938
64 K-means	0.561	0.942	1.000	1.000	1.000	−1.744	0.280	0.936

Table 3. Accuracy score of each algorithm (R^2) on the benchmark functions in 5 dimensions with a dataset of size 5.000.

	h1	Ackley	Himmel.	Diffpow	Rosenb.	Rast.	Schaffer	Schwefel
OK	0.488	0.943	0.999	1.000	1.000	0.539	0.405	0.534
4 Random	0.537	0.942	0.997	0.999	0.999	0.539	0.405	0.438
8 Random	0.511	0.939	0.994	0.997	0.998	0.539	0.401	0.356
16 Random	0.464	0.936	0.987	0.995	0.995	0.538	0.396	0.185
32 Random	0.310	0.927	0.972	0.990	0.990	0.535	0.387	0.133
64 Random	0.175	0.225	0.902	0.980	0.981	0.467	0.201	0.111
4 K-means	0.557	0.942	0.997	0.999	0.999	0.539	0.404	0.634
8 K-means	0.530	0.940	0.995	0.998	0.997	0.538	0.402	0.706
16 K-means	0.467	0.936	0.987	0.995	0.994	0.535	0.392	0.450
32 K-means	0.359	0.924	0.963	0.987	0.981	0.514	0.323	0.318
64 K-means	0.324	0.820	0.912	0.965	0.949	0.399	0.257	0.237

Table 4. Accuracy score of each algorithm (R^2) on the benchmark functions in 5 dimensions with a dataset of size 10.000.

	h1	Ackley	Himmel.	Diffpow	Rosenb.	Rast.	Schaffer	Schwefel
OK	0.606	0.950	1.000	1.000	1.000	0.531	0.435	0.635
4 Random	0.561	0.950	0.999	0.999	1.000	0.529	0.428	0.171
8 Random	0.543	0.948	0.997	0.999	0.999	0.529	0.427	0.156
16 Random	0.516	0.947	0.994	0.997	0.998	0.528	0.425	0.218
32 Random	0.465	0.943	0.986	0.995	0.996	0.526	0.422	0.155
64 Random	0.367	0.935	0.971	0.990	0.991	0.523	0.416	0.109
4 K-means	0.619	0.950	0.999	1.000	1.000	0.529	0.427	0.554
8 K-means	0.547	0.949	0.997	0.999	0.999	0.530	0.428	0.801
16 K-means	0.524	0.948	0.993	0.998	0.997	0.528	0.421	0.668
32 K-means	0.433	0.940	0.979	0.994	0.990	0.523	0.365	0.621
64 K-means	0.361	0.878	0.948	0.980	0.970	0.444	0.340	0.374

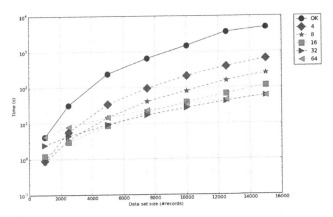

Fig. 1. Execution time per cluster size for the Rastrigin function in 5 dimensions. Using an Intel Core i7-4910MQ CPU 2.90 GHz, 8 cores and 32 GB of main memory. Running on one core.

Figure. To gain maximum benefit from the OWCK algorithm, we can process each cluster on a different thread (on a different CPU core), speeding up the algorithm linearly in the amount of cores.

6   Conclusions and Further Research

In this paper a novel algorithm which creates multiple small Kriging models and combines these models using an optimally weighting method is presented. It is shown that the Optimally Weighted Cluster Kriging model outperforms Ordinary Kriging in both execution time and accuracy. The number of clusters that should be used depends a lot on the size of the dataset and partly on the nature of the dataset as well. When a dataset with n points is split into k clusters of roughly equal size, our method reduces both the required execution time and memory by factor k^2. Moreover, the algorithm can be parallelized, providing yet another speedup factor that is linear in the number of workers. In practice, it pushes the limits of applicability of Kriging from thousands to millions of data points.

For further research several extensions and generalizations can be made to improve the algorithms accuracy. One could look for example for different clustering methods. An interesting candidate is *Mixture of Gaussians* [17], where each point has a probability to belong to a certain cluster. Using these probabilities we may derive new weighting schemes that might perform better. The method used for comparing the different Kriging algorithms can be expanded by using a comparison framework as proposed in [5], as well as comparison with a few other recent Kriging variations [4,14]. Moreover, the nugget of the Kriging model plays an important role in training the model and has a big effect on the accuracy of the models, in further research we should exploit a way to optimize the nugget parameter for both the Ordinary Kriging model as well as for the cluster models.

References

1. Boyd, S., Vandenberghe, L.: Convex Optimization. Cambridge University Press, New York (2004)
2. Breiman, L.: Bagging predictors. Mach. Learn. **24**(2), 123–140 (1996)
3. Breiman, L.: Random forests. Mach. Learn. **45**(1), 5–32 (2001)
4. Bui, T.D., Turner, R.E.: Tree-structured Gaussian process approximations. In: Ghahramani, Z., Welling, M., Cortes, C., Lawrence, N.D., Weinberger, K.Q. (eds.) Advances in Neural Information Processing Systems 27, pp. 2213–2221. Curran Associates Inc. (2014). http://papers.nips.cc/paper/5459-tree-structured-gaussian-process-approximations.pdf
5. Chalupka, K., Williams, C., Murray, I.: A Framework for Evaluating Approximation Methods for Gaussian Process Regression, pp. 1–18 (2012). arXiv preprint arXiv:1205.6326
6. Chen, T., Ren, J.: Bagging for Gaussian process regression. Neurocomputing **72**(7–9), 1605–1610 (2009)
7. D'Ambrosio, A., Aria, M., Siciliano, R.: Accurate tree-based missing data imputation and data fusion within the statistical learning paradigm. J. Classif. **29**(2), 227–258 (2012)
8. Emmerich, M.: Single-and multi-objective evolutionary design optimization assisted by Gaussian random field metamodels. Ph.D. thesis, FB Informatik, TU Dortmund (2005)
9. Forgy, E.W.: Cluster analysis of multivariate data: efficiency versus interpretability of classifications. Biometrics **21**, 768–769 (1965)
10. Fortin, F., Michel, F., Gardner, M.A., Parizeau, M., Gagné, C.: DEAP: evolutionary algorithms made easy. J. Mach. Learn. Res. **13**, 2171–2175 (2012)
11. Ginsbourger, D., Le Riche, R., Carraro, L.: Kriging is well-suited to parallelize optimization. In: Tenne, Y., Goh, C.-K. (eds.) Computational Intel. in Expensive Opti. Prob. ALO, vol. 2, pp. 131–162. Springer, Heidelberg (2010)
12. Hartman, L., Hössjer, O.: Fast kriging of large data sets with Gaussian Markov random fields. Comput. Stat. Data Anal. **52**(5), 2331–2349 (2008)

13. Hastie, T., Tibshirani, R., Friedman, J.: The Elements of Statistical Learning: Data Mining, Inference, and Prediction. Springer Series in Statistics. Springer, New York (2001)
14. Hensman, J., Sheffield, U., Fusi, N., Lawrence, N.: Gaussian processes for big data. In: Proceedings of UAI, vol. 29, pp. 282–290 (2013)
15. Huang, G., Wang, D.H., Lan, Y.: Extreme learning machines: a survey. Int. J. Mach. Learn. Cybern. **2**(2), 107–122 (2011)
16. Krige, D.G.: A statistical approach to some basic mine valuation problems on the Witwatersrand. J. Chem. Metall. Min. Soc. S. Af. **52**(6), 119–139 (1951)
17. Lindsay, B.: Mixture models: theory, geometry, and applications. In: Conference Board of the Mathematical Sciences: NSF-CBMS Regional Conference Series in Probability and Statistics, Institute of Mathematical Statistics (1995)
18. Memarsadeghi, N., Raykar, V.C., Duraiswami, R., Mount, D.M.: Efficient kriging via fast matrix-vector products. In: 2008 IEEE, Aerospace Conference, pp. 1–7. IEEE (2008)
19. Nguyen-Tuong, D., Seeger, M., Peters, J.: Model learning with local Gaussian process regression. Adv. Rob. **23**(15), 2015–2034 (2009)
20. Powell, M.J.D.: A direct search optimization method that models the objective and constraint functions by linear interpolation. In: Gomez, S., Hennart, J.-P. (eds.) Advances in Optimization and Numerical Analysis, pp. 51–67. Springer, Boston (1994)
21. Rasmussen, C., Williams, C.: Gaussian Processes for Machine Learning. Adaptative Computation and Machine Learning Series. University Press Group Limited, New Era Estate (2006)
22. Stein, M.L.: Interpolation of Spatial Data: Some Theory for Kriging. Springer Science & Business Media, New York (1999)

Slower Can Be Faster: The iRetis Incremental Model Tree Learner

Denny Verbeeck[1][(✉)] and Hendrik Blockeel[1,2]

[1] Department of Computer Science, KU Leuven, Leuven, Belgium
{denny.verbeeck,hendrik.blockeel}@cs.kuleuven.be
[2] Leiden Institute of Advanced Computer Science, Leiden University,
Leiden, The Netherlands

Abstract. Incremental learning is useful for processing streaming data, where data elements are produced at a high rate and cannot be stored. An incremental learner typically updates its model with each new instance that arrives. To avoid skipped instances, the model update must finish before the next element arrives, so it should be fast. However, there can be a trade-off between the efficiency of the update and how many updates are needed to get a good model. We investigate this trade-off in the context of model trees. We compare FIMT, a state-of-the-art incremental model tree learner developed for streaming data, with two alternative methods that use a more expensive update method. We find that for data with relatively low (but still realistic) dimensionality, the most expensive method often yields the best learning curve: the system converges faster to a smaller and more accurate model tree.

1 Introduction

Data stream mining is a subfield of data mining that is concerned with analyzing streaming data. There are multiple types of learning tasks in this setting. We here focus on the task of learning a predictive model for the data elements in the stream; that is, given a stream of elements of the form $(\mathbf{x}_i, y_i) \in \mathcal{X} \times \mathcal{Y}$, learn a model $M : \mathcal{X} \to \mathcal{Y}$ that predicts y from $\mathbf{x}$. This task is identical to standard predictive learning, except for one additional constraint: each data element can be looked at only once (and briefly). This setting is ubiquitous in the context of "big data"; for instance, sensors produce large amounts of data at a high pace, and often these data must be analyzed online.

There has been a significant amount of work on adapting several types of data mining methods to the stream context. Commonly, methods that construct predictive models are adapted such that they become incremental: that is, they start with an initial model and update their model each time a new data element is observed. Ideally, the model learned in this way converges to the model that would be learned if all data were stored in a database and, next, a regular learner were used. The incremental learner has the advantage that some model is available at any point in time, well before all data have arrived.

© Springer International Publishing Switzerland 2015
E. Fromont et al. (Eds.): IDA 2015, LNCS 9385, pp. 322–333, 2015.
DOI: 10.1007/978-3-319-24465-5_28

Ideally, the update step is computationally light enough that it can be performed in the time interval between the arrival of two data elements. If this is not the case, then the learner has to skip elements that arrive before it is ready to handle another input, which may slow down learning. However, more efficient update methods may result in lower-quality updates, which may lead to more updates being needed to achieve the same model quality. Moreover, a more expensive update does not necessarily result in skipped instances: as long as it finishes before the next example arrives, the overall learning time is not affected, only the idle time between instances is reduced.

Based on these considerations, we investigate incremental model tree learners. Ikonomovska et al. [5] have proposed an incremental model tree learner, FIMT, that can be considered the state of the art in model tree learning from streaming data. In this paper, we propose two alternative model tree learners for streaming data, iRetis and iMauve. Both methods use the same approach for keeping statistics and deciding the best time to split the tree compared to FIMT. However they employ a more complicated split heuristic and model update mechanism, which should enable these methods to choose splits more intelligently. We experimentally evaluate how they compare to FIMT. We find that, for relatively low-dimensional data, the most complicated update method often gives the best learning curve: it converges faster to simpler and more accurate model trees.

Section 2 discusses related work and describes FIMT in detail. Section 3 describes the modifications that yield iRetis and iMauve. Section 4 reports on experiments, and Sect. 5 concludes.

2   Background and Related Work

A decision tree is a rooted tree where each internal node contains a test and has one child for each outcome of the test. In the machine learning context, such a tree can be used as a predictive function: instances are sorted down the tree based on their test outcomes, and the leaf they end up in contains the prediction. Trees that make numerical predictions are called regression trees. While regression trees often contain a constant prediction in each leaf, variants exist that have a linear model in the leaf; these are called model trees [7]. A model tree defines a piecewise linear function.

Most decision trees learners learn the tree top-down [2,8]. They determine which test should be at the root of the tree by evaluating all possible tests on the whole dataset, choosing the best one (according to some heuristic), and splitting the data according to this test. They then repeat the procedure for the child nodes, and so on until leaves are obtained.

The above assumes access to the whole data set at any time. Incremental learners do not require this: they start with an empty model, and update this model each time they see a new example. By definition, they need to decide on which test to put in a node before seeing the whole dataset. But a test that seems optimal at this time may later turn out not to be. There are three ways of dealing with this: (1) choose a test that may yet turn out to be non-optimal, and repair the tree afterwards if necessary (by restructuring it or simply discarding part of the tree and learning it anew); (2) wait until there is enough statistical evidence to make it highly unlikely that the chosen test will turn out non-optimal later on; or (3) simply accept that a non-optimal tree is learned.

In their seminal work on VFDT ("very fast decision tree learner"), Domingos and Hulten [3] advocate the second approach. Using so-called Hoeffding bounds, they characterize under which conditions there is sufficient statistical evidence that the test that seems optimal at this point is equal to the one that would seem optimal when looking at the whole dataset. Since VFDT, multiple tree learners have adopted the use of Hoeffding bounds; these are called Hoeffding tree learners. It is in this seam of work that Ikonomovska et al. [5] have introduced Fast Incremental Model Trees (FIMT), an algorithm that incrementally learns model trees from streams, using Hoeffding bounds. As our work builds on it, we describe FIMT in detail in the following section.

2.1   FIMT

Like VFDT, FIMT starts off with an empty leaf, reads the examples from the stream as they arrive, and gradually splits leaves (turning them into an internal node) when there is sufficient evidence that the proposed split is optimal. To this aim, it keeps some statistics in each leaf, and for each incoming example the corresponding leaf is determined and its statistics updated. Sufficient statistics must be kept, taking into account that not only the tree structure, but also the linear model in the leaves must be learned incrementally. As the statistics are not expected to differ significantly between consecutive examples, FIMT considers a new split only once every N_{min} examples.

Splitting. FIMT assumes numerical input attributes and uses tests of the form $X_i < c$ with X_i an input attribute and c a threshold; c is also called a "split point". FIMT first finds the best split point for each attribute, and then ranks these attributes according to the Standard Deviation Reduction (SDR) measure, which for a split of S into S_L and S_R is defined as:

$$SDR(S, S_L, S_R) = sd(S) - \frac{N_L}{N} sd(S_L) - \frac{N_R}{N} sd(S_R), \tag{1}$$

$$sd(S) = \sqrt{\frac{1}{N} \left(\sum_{i=1}^{N} (y_i - \overline{y})^2 \right)} = \sqrt{\frac{1}{N} \left(\sum_{i=1}^{N} y_i^2 - \frac{1}{N} \left(\sum_{i=1}^{N} y_i \right)^2 \right)} \tag{2}$$

Equation (2) shows the SDR can be computed efficiently and incrementally, by maintaining the sum of (squared) y values and the number of data points.

FIMT considers the ratio of the SDR values for the two best candidate splits, $r = SDR_1/SDR_2$, with SDR_1 the best and SDR_2 the second best SDR value. FIMT uses the Hoeffding probability bound [4] to state with confidence $1 - \delta$

that the sample average $\bar{r}$ over the N values for r, which have range R, is within distance ϵ of the true average:

$$\epsilon = \sqrt{\frac{R^2 \ln(1/\delta)}{2N}}. \tag{3}$$

With confidence $1 - \delta$, the upper bound of the true average of r is $\bar{r} + \epsilon$. If this upper bound is below 1, the true average of r is below 1 (and c_a is the best split) with confidence $1 - \delta$, and the split is applied.

FIMT builds an Extended Binary Search Tree (E-BST) for the values of each attribute to efficiently maintain the necessary statistics for split quality calculations. The tree structure of an E-BST is like a regular BST, but each node maintains two arrays of statistics; one for attribute values less than or equal to the node value, and one for attribute values greater than the node value. A BST structure allows for $O(log(n))$ average insertion time, and $O(n)$ worst case insertion time. When a leaf node of the regression tree is split, its E-BST structure is discarded, and two new structures are instantiated for the children of that node.

Leaf Models. FIMT maintains a linear perceptron without activation function in each leaf of the model tree. If each data point has m attributes, the linear model will hold a weight vector $\mathbf{w}$ of length $m + 1$, and the prediction $\hat{y}$ for a data point $\mathbf{x}$ is calculated as follows:

$$\hat{y} = w_0 + \sum_{i=1}^{m} x_i w_i \tag{4}$$

The weights are updated with each arriving example using the Delta (a.k.a. Widrow-Hoff) rule:

$$w_i \leftarrow w_i + \eta \left(\hat{y} - y\right) x_i', \quad i = 1, \ldots, m \tag{5}$$

with $x_i' = (x_i - \bar{x}_i)/(3\sigma_i)$ a normalized version of x_i; $\bar{x}_i$ and σ_i are the mean and standard deviation of attribute i. This update procedure has time complexity $O(m)$, which makes it very suitable for dealing with high-speed data streams; furthermore, the Delta rule is known to converge even if the data points do not represent a straight line.

3   The iRetis Algorithm

The learning algorithm we propose is similar to FIMT, except for two important points. First, while FIMT finds the split that maximally reduces standard deviation, like M5 [7], our method tries to minimize the *residual* variance after learning a linear model in both subtrees, which makes more sense into model tree learning setting (but is also computationally more complex). Second, while

FIMT gradually approaches the optimal regression line using perception learning, our approach at each point in time computes the least-squares regression function for the data seen until then. Again, this is computationally more complex, but may enable the learner to reach comparable levels of accuracy with fewer required observations. We next discuss these differences in more detail.

3.1   The Mauve and Retis Heuristics

The quality measure of FIMT's splitting criterion is based on standard deviation reduction. Even if the observed data points are perfectly linear, the SDR will be non-zero, which indicates that splitting a leaf node can improve the overall model. Vens et al proposed a splitting criterion based on regression called Mauve [10]. The Mauve heuristic inspects the standard deviation of the *residuals* after performing linear regression, rather than the attribute values. A simple linear regression (i.e., using one predictor variable) is performed, using as predictor the attribute for which a split is being considered. A model is built for the leaf node as well as the two hypothetical children that arise from the split. As a result, the splits chosen by Mauve are better adapted to the fact that the leaves will contain linear models, not constants.

By expanding the statistics that are kept in the E-BST structure with the sum of attribute values x_j, the sum of squared attribute values x_j^2 and the sum of the product of attribute and target values $x_j y$, it is possible to calculate the residual standard deviation for simple regression on attribute j at any time. Let e_i be the residual for example i and $\bar{e}$ be the residual mean. The residual standard deviation in a leaf model l is:

$$RSD(l) = \sqrt{\frac{1}{N} \sum_{i=1}^{N} (e_i - \bar{e})^2}. \tag{6}$$

Since Mauve considers simple regression, the model expression for an attribute x_j will be of the form $\hat{y} = a + bx$. Using the substitution $e_i = \hat{y}_i - y_i$ in Eq. (6), the residual standard deviation becomes:

$$RSD(l) = \sum_i y_i^2 - \frac{1}{N} \left(\sum_i y_i \right)^2 - \frac{\left(\sum_i x_i y_i - \frac{1}{N} \sum_i x_i \sum_i y_i \right)^2}{\sum_i x_i^2 - \frac{1}{N} \left(\sum_i x_i \right)^2} \tag{7}$$

Since this method considers only the split attribute in its regression, it is possible that some components of the target function will not be modeled. We can extend the Mauve heuristic to multiple linear regression. In that case we are effectively using the RETIS heuristic [6]. We will refer to this algorithm as iRetis. In this case, the residual for an example i can be written as:

$$e_i = \beta_0 + \beta \mathbf{x}_i - y_i. \tag{8}$$

Substituting the new definition of the residual in Eq. (6), we get the following expression for the residual standard deviation RSD and residual variance $RVar$, using complete linear regression in m attributes:

$$RVar(l) = \frac{1}{N} \left(\sum_i (\beta\mathbf{x}_i)^2 + \sum_i y_i^2 - 2\sum_i (\beta\mathbf{x}_i y_i) \right)$$

$$- \frac{1}{N^2} \left(\left(\sum_i \beta\mathbf{x}_i \right)^2 + \left(\sum_i y_i \right)^2 - 2\sum_i y_i \sum_i \beta\mathbf{x}_i \right)$$

$$RSD(l) = \sqrt{RVar(l)} \tag{9}$$

From this equation we can deduce the statistics we need to keep in order to calculate the residual standard deviation incrementally. The most obvious statistics are the number of observed data points N, the sum of y values and the sum of squared y values. The term $\beta\mathbf{x}_i$ can be expanded to $\sum_{j=1}^{m} \beta_j x_{i,j}$. By re-arranging the sums we observe

$$\sum_i \beta\mathbf{x}_i = \sum_j \beta_j \sum_i x_{i,j},$$

revealing the need to keep track of the sums of attribute values. Finally we observe the term $\sum_i (\beta\mathbf{x}_i)^2$. By expanding the term $\beta\mathbf{x}_i$ as above we get:

$$\sum_i (\beta\mathbf{x}_i)^2 = \sum_i \left(\sum_j (\beta_j x_{i,j})^2 + 2\sum_{j<k} \beta_j x_{i,j} \beta_k x_{i,k} \right).$$

This last equation shows the need to keep track of the sum of squares of attribute values, and the sums of the products of all combinations of attribute values.

The amount of statistics kept for each split is $\frac{m^2}{2} + 3m + 3$. Like FIMT, these statistics are kept in an E-BST structure. There is one such structure for each attribute. Every E-BST grows by one node with each data point. This brings the total amount of statistics kept during algorithm execution to $mn(\frac{m^2}{2} + 3m + 3)$. This is a higher count than just storing each data point, however this structure allows us to immediately calculate the residual standard deviation reduction for every split, for a complete linear regression. Additionally it allows us to instantiate the weights of the linear models in the child nodes of a split to the least squares estimate immediately. This contrasts with FIMT, where the weights of child nodes are set equal to the weights of the parent node after a split, thus needing additional data points to converge to their new values. After a split is made, the E-BST structure for that attribute is discarded, freeing up the memory it occupied.

3.2 Incremental Linear Regression

While FIMT's perceptron update rule has a low time complexity for a single update, a large number of updates is required for the perceptron to converge. After each split, the amount of data points arriving in the children of that split is halved on average. As the tree grows larger, the individual perceptrons in the leaves observe ever fewer data points, causing them to converge very slowly in later stages of learning. Therefore we propose a method based on linear least squares regression to estimate the weights of the linear models in the leaves. The least squares estimation of the weights is $\hat{\beta} = \left(\mathbf{x}^T \mathbf{x}\right)^{-1} \mathbf{x}^T y$.

The elements of $\mathbf{x}^T \mathbf{x}$ and $\mathbf{x}^T y$ can be updated incrementally, as each data point is observed. Therefore it is possible to have a least squares estimate of the weight vector at any time during learning. It is important to note that the elements of both matrices all appear in the necessary statistics for calculating the residual standard deviation described in the previous section. As a result, there is no need to explicitly keep these matrices in memory.

To acquire this estimate, it is necessary to invert the matrix $\mathbf{x}^T \mathbf{x}$ and multiply it with $\mathbf{x}^T y$. The time complexity of the matrix inversion and matrix multiplication steps is $O(m^3)$. Slightly faster multiplication and inversion algorithms exist, however they are not used here since they only provide an advantage on very large matrices. This time complexity is significantly slower than FIMT's $O(m)$ perceptron update rule. However, for relatively small values of m, this difference might not be troublesome.

4   Experiments

We experimentally compare iRetis, iMauve and FIMT in terms of the size of the induced model tree, the execution speed and accuracy. We investigate the following hypotheses:

i iRetis and iMauve learn smaller trees compared to FIMT,
ii learning smaller trees will not result in loss of accuracy, thanks to the improved splitting heuristic,
iii iRetis and iMauve require fewer data points to reach the same level of accuracy as FIMT, because they choose splits more intelligently and immediately instatiate linear models in the child nodes of a split with the proper least squares estimate.

4.1   Setup

We took eleven datasets from Luís Torgo's collection of datasets [9] and the UCI machine learning repository [1]. Data for the CART dataset is drawn from two distinct hyperplanes, with noise added. We also added a noiseless version of this dataset; iRetis should build a model with zero error on such a dataset.

On each dataset a 10-fold cross-validation was performed. The same folds were used for each algorithm. During training, each algorithm received data samples from the training set in the same order. The results listed in Tables 1 and 2 are the average values over the 10 folds. *The metrics listed are relative to FIMT's performance* (i.e. FIMT's score is 1 for all metrics for all datasets). The plots shown in Figs. 1, 2, 3, and 4 were generated by taking the average RRSE at each evaluation point over the 10 folds.

Table 1. Results for RRSE, Tree Size and runtime. Additionally the number of attributes d and the number of samples N is shown for each dataset.

	d	N	iRetis			iMauve		
			RRSE	Size	Time	RRSE	Size	Time
Friedmann	10	40768	**0.566**	**0.716**	7.619	0.735	0.862	1.198
Lexp	5	4000	**0.471**	**0.688**	8.012	0.875	0.907	1.251
Cal housing	8	20640	1.100	**0.765**	4.508	1.144	1.084	1.106
CART	10	40768	1.033	0.794	1.707	2.401	**0.146**	1.622
Losc	5	4000	**0.637**	**0.847**	4.824	0.697	0.904	1.239
Paraboloid	12	4000	**0.168**	**0.907**	2.166	0.215	1.035	1.269
CARTNoiseless	10	4000	**0.000**	0.365	1.939	11.883	**0.232**	1.565
Ailerons	40	13750	**0.183**	**0.727**	5.087	0.197	1.580	1.032
PoleTelecom	26	15000	**0.279**	**0.586**	4.811	0.501	1.036	1.200
CPU	21	8192	**0.642**	**0.864**	15.173	2.317	1.515	1.115
Physicochemical	9	45730	1.094	**0.734**	5.105	1.052	1.009	1.107
Abalone	8	4177	**0.928**	1.059	4.662	1.094	1.507	1.144
Avg Rank			**1.33**	**1.25**	3	2.42	2.42	2
Avg Rank FIMT			(2.25)	(2.33)	**(1)**	(2.25)	(2.33)	**(1)**

4.2 Results

Table 1 shows the end results for all datasets, as well as the number of attributes and examples in those datasets. The average rank for each algorithm over the datasets is shown at the bottom of the tables. To test the performance of iRetis, we use the Friedman test followed by the Bonferroni-Dunn post-hoc analysis. The null hypotheses in the Friedman test is that all algorithms have equal performance. If the Friedman test statistic is larger than a critical value, determined by the amount of algorithms and the amount of datasets, the null hypotheses can be rejected and we can follow up with the post-hoc analysis. The Bonferroni-Dunn post-hoc analysis defines a critical distance for the average ranks of two algorithms. If the difference in average ranks is more than this critical distance, the difference can be regarded as significant.

The critical value for the Friedman test with 3 *treatments* (the algorithms) on 12 *blocks* (the datasets) is $Q^*_{0.05} = 6.500$ for a confidence level $\alpha = 5\%$. The critical distance at this confidence level is $CD = 0.879$.

For the tree size metric, we calculate $Q = 10.17 > Q^*_{0.05}$, therefore we reject the null hypothesis. Since the differences in average rank of iRetis compared to the other algorithms is greater than CD, we can conclude that iRetis tends to find smaller trees than the others. The difference between iMauve and FIMT is not significant.

In terms of runtime, we observe no differences in rank between the datasets: FIMT is always the fastest, and iRetis is always the slowest. This result is significant at $\alpha = 0.05$.

Table 2. Results for the data stream simulation experiment.

	iRetis				iMauve			
	RRSE	Size	Time	DSR	RRSE	Size	Time	DSR
Friedmann	**0.567**	**0.599**	8.379	0.177	0.734	0.860	1.204	0.000
Lexp	**0.543**	**0.553**	13.857	0.091	0.875	0.907	1.249	0.000
Cal housing	1.072	**0.719**	6.337	0.064	1.143	1.083	1.073	0.000
CART	1.033	0.794	2.826	0.000	2.401	**0.146**	2.582	0.000
Losc	**0.637**	**0.786**	7.516	0.043	0.697	0.904	1.279	0.000
Paraboloid	**0.171**	**0.907**	3.296	0.002	0.215	1.035	1.132	0.000
CARTNoiseless	**0.000**	**0.365**	4.155	0.000	11.883	0.232	2.709	0.000
Ailerons	**0.179**	**0.356**	3.662	0.501	0.198	1.586	1.208	0.000
PoleTelecom	0.740	**0.508**	6.833	0.190	**0.715**	1.047	1.725	0.000
CPU	**0.749**	**0.456**	7.906	0.491	2.074	1.444	1.137	0.001
Physicochemical	1.158	**0.651**	6.135	0.112	1.053	1.006	1.095	0.000
Abalone	**0.946**	1.029	6.587	0.056	1.094	1.507	1.104	0.000
Avg Rank	**1.417**	**1.25**	3		2.33	2.42	2	
Avg Rank FIMT	(2.25)	(2.33)	**(1)**		(2.25)	(2.33)	**(1)**	

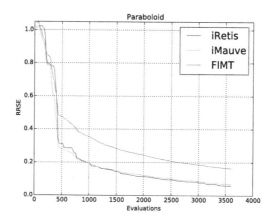

Fig. 1. Results for Paraboloid

We measured accuracy by means of RRSE. The Q-statistic for the RRSE results is $Q = 8.17 > Q^*_{0.05}$. We can reject the null hypothesis. The differences in average rank of iRetis compared to the other algorithms is greater than CD, therefore we can conclude that iRetis converges on more accurate trees than the other systems. The difference between iMauve and FIMT is again not significant.

These results confirm hypotheses i and ii. Figures 1,2,3, and 4 show how test set accuracy (measured by RRSE) evolves with the number of training samples seen by the algorithms. Each point on this plot is the average RRSE over the 10 runs of the algorithm, measured after the corresponding amount of data points

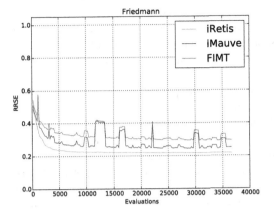

Fig. 2. Results for Friedmann

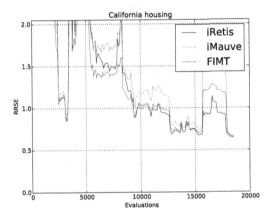

Fig. 3. Results for Cal housing

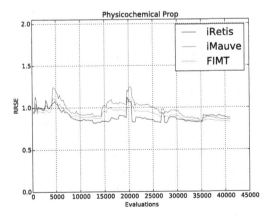

Fig. 4. Results for Physicochemical

observed. Due to space constraints, we cannot show the plots for all datasets tested, but on most datasets, iRetis clearly learns more accurate models from fewer datapoints, as in Figs. 1 and 2. There are some datasets however, where all methods seem to struggle (shown in Figs. 3 and 4), and the difference is less clear.

To further investigate the impact of the longer computation time of iRetis, we have simulated a data stream providing 200 samples per second. This sampling rate was determined by investigating the rate at which iRetis processes samples, and choosing a rate high enough to cause iRetis to drop samples. Here, arriving examples are discarded if the previous example has not yet been fully processed. Table 2 shows the results for this experimental setup. As with the previous experiment, the values for RRSE, tree size an runtime are metrics relative to FIMT. Additionally we included the dropped sample rate (DSR), this is the proportion of samples that was dropped relative to the total amount of samples in the dataset. The Q-values are still larger than $Q^*_{0.05}$ for RRSE, tree size and runtime. Additionally, we observe that the difference in ranks between iRetis and the other approaches is still larger than the critical distance. Keep in mind that the results in Tables 1 and 2 can not be compared directly. The performance of FIMT will be different, and hence the normalization factor is different as well. We conclude that even if samples are dropped during learning, iRetis still finds more accurate trees.

5   Conclusions

We have investigated to what extent incremental model tree learners may benefit from more complex update procedures. To this aim we implemented two variants of the current state-of-the-art system FIMT, called iRetis and iMauve. These use the same EBST structure to manage statistics about the data, and the same Hoeffding bound to decide the best split points, as FIMT, but they use a heuristic based on linear regression (simple for iMauve, multiple for iRetis), and use closed formulas for least-squares regression instead of a perceptron.

Given the more complex splitting heuristic, we expected iMauve to perform better than FIMT. Surprisingly, the average rank for iMauve was slightly worse than FIMT's. However this difference was too small to be of statistical significance, and we can not draw any conclusions.

We found that on datasets with a relatively small number of attributes iRetis builds more compact trees, with comparable or even superior accuracy, compared to iMauve and FIMT. In terms of the number of examples seen, these models are also obtained sooner, even when some examples have to be skipped because they arrive too fast. In other words, slower in terms of computation can still be faster in terms of actual time, under certain realistic conditions such as relatively low dimensionality and allowed computation time between examples in the order of milliseconds or higher.

These results show that updating the model more carefully can pay off, even if it comes at the expense of number of data points that can be observed. More detailed research is needed to identify the conditions under which a more complex update procedure is warranted.

Acknowledgements. DV was supported by the Research Foundation Flanders (FWO-Vlaanderen), projects G.0255.08 and G.0179.10.

References

1. Bache, K., Lichman, M.: UCI machine learning repository (2013). http://archive. ics.uci.edu/ml
2. Breiman, L., Friedman, J., Olshen, R., Stone, C.: Classification and Regression Trees. Wadsworth and Brooks, Monterey (1984)
3. Domingos, P., Hulten, G.: Mining high-speed data streams. In: Proceedings of the Sixth ACM SIGKDD International Conference on Knowledge Discovery and Data Mining, KDD 2000, pp. 71–80. ACM, New York (2000)
4. Hoeffding, W.: Probability inequalities for sums of bounded random variables. J. Am. Stat. Assoc. **58**(301), 13–30 (1963). http://www.jstor.org/stable/2282952?
5. Ikonomovska, E., Gama, J., Džeroski, S.: Learning model trees from evolving data streams. Data Min. Knowl. Discovery **23**(1), 128–168 (2011)
6. Karalič, A.: Employing linear regression in regression tree leaves. In: Proceedings of the 10th European Conference on Artificial Intelligence, ECAI 1992, pp. 440–441. Wiley, New York (1992). http://dl.acm.org/citation.cfm?id=145448.146775
7. Quinlan, J.R.: Learning with continuous classes. In: Proceedings of the Australian Joint Conference on Artificial Intelligence, pp. 343–348. World Scientific, Singapore (1992)
8. Quinlan, J.R.: C4.5: Programs for Machine Learning. Morgan Kaufmann Publishers Inc., San Francisco (1993)
9. Torgo, L.: Regression datasets, September 2014. http://www.dcc.fc.up.pt/~ltorgo/Regression/DataSets.html
10. Vens, C., Blockeel, H.: A simple regression based heuristic for learning model trees. Intell. Data Anal. **10**(3), 215–236 (2006)

VoQs: A Web Application for Visualization of Questionnaire Surveys

Xiaowei Zhang[1]([⊠]), Frank Klawonn[1,2], Lorenz Grigull[3], and Werner Lechner[4]

[1] Helmholtz Centre for Infection Research, Inhoffenstrasse 7, 38124 Braunschweig, Germany
{Xiaowei.Kortum,Frank.Klawonn}@helmholtz-hzi.de

[2] Department of Computer Science, Ostfalia University of Applied Sciences, Salzdahlumer Str. 46/48, 38302 Wolfenbuettel, Germany
f.klawonn@ostfalia.de

[3] Department of Paediatric Haematology and Oncology, Medical University Hannover, Carl-Neuberg Str. 1, 30625 Hannover, Germany
grigull.lorenz@mh-hannover.de

[4] Improved Medical Diagnostics IMD GmbH, Ostfeldstr. 25, Hannover 30559, Germany
werner.lechner@improvedmedicaldiagnostics.com

Abstract. This paper is motivated by analyzing questionnaire data that collected from patients who suffer from an orphan disease. In order to decrease misdiagnoses and shorten the diagnosis time for people who have not been diagnosed yet but already have a long history of health problems, a research project about using questionnaire mode and data analysis methods to predetermine orphan disease has been set up and questionnaires were designed based on experiences from patients who already have a diagnosis.

The main focus of this work is to visualize answering patterns that characterize patients with a specific orphan disease, which questions are most useful to distinguish between certain orphan diseases and how well an answering pattern of a specific patient fits to the general pattern of those patients who share the same disease.

We borrow from the concept of sequence logos, commonly used in genetics to visualize the conservation of nucleotides in a strand of DNA or RNA. Instead of nucleotides, we have possible answers from a question.

Our proposed visualization techniques are not limited to questionnaires on orphan diseases but also can be applied to any questionnaire survey with closed-ended questions for which we are interested in answering characteristics of different groups.

1 Introduction

Questionnaire surveys, which enable researchers to obtain and gather information directly from participants, can be used for measuring participants' knowledge, preferences, attitudes or personal beliefs, also for exploring facts, experiences and present situations [7]. Many questionnaires are using "close-ended

© Springer International Publishing Switzerland 2015
E. Fromont et al. (Eds.): IDA 2015, LNCS 9385, pp. 334–343, 2015.
DOI: 10.1007/978-3-319-24465-5_29

questions". Possible answers of such questions are limited to a categorical or ordinal scale, e.g. the Likert scale (yes/no; satisfied/unsatisfied). Instead, "open-ended questions" offer respondents to express opinions, feelings or suggestions without being influenced by the researcher, which can help to obtain responses that individuals give spontaneously. "Close-ended questions" are often researchers' first choice because they limit the respondent choices to a fixed set of finite alternatives that are offered. The ordered options can not only let respondents easily choose one appropriate position in a series of approval degrees for a questions but also make the statistical analysis of such questionnaires much easier [3,9].

Although a sophisticated statistical analysis of such questionnaires can provide a deeper insight, the domain expert for the questionnaires might not be familiar with the statistical methods and may have difficulties to interpret the results correctly. Therefore, we have developed visualization techniques, called VoQs, which helps domain experts to identify interesting, characteristic and also deviating answering patterns as well as questions of high interest.

Before we describe VoQs in more detail, Sect. 2 reviews the original motivation and background to develop this application. Section 3 introduces the core technology of VoQs followed by preliminary results, including the principal statistics and computational methods used in VoQs. Section 4 presents all functionalities and important characteristics of this application and the visualization aspects with graphical results. Finally, we briefly outline further extensions of VoQs.

2   The Origin of VoQs

The motivation of developing VoQs application originated from questionnaires we had developed for patients who might suffer from an orphan disease. Because rare diseases are often overlooked or misdiagnosed, a clear statement of a final diagnosis and medical treatment is often linked to reviewing the patient's history and the trend of the patient's constitution [6]. For our questionnaires it was of interest to visualize how patients with different orphan diseases differ in their answer patterns, which questions are most useful to distinguish between certain orphan diseases and how well an answering pattern of a specific patient fits to the general pattern of those patients who share the same disease. Although we had already introduced visualization techniques based on multidimensional scaling that helps to discover outliers and could explain how well different diseases could be distinguished [2], these visualizations were still too abstract and provided only an overall view on the data without focus on specific questions.

Individual questionnaires were set up for different groups of orphan diseases, such as bleeding disorders, pulmonological and neuromuscular diseases. Patients data were collected through these anonymous questionnaires, which contain, for instance, information about noticed symptoms, physical constitution in general and specific sports activities. All questions are close-ended with four ordered options from "No" to "Absolutely".

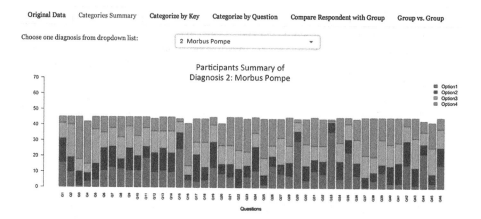

Fig. 1. Data summary of diagnosis 2: Morbus Pompe

As an example, we focus on the questionnaire for neuromuscular diseases. So far, it contains data from 366 persons with 13 different diagnoses (e.g. amyotrophic lateral sclerosis (ALS), Morbus Pompe). To see how much variation the answering pattern of a person from a specific diagnosis shows, one could simply use a bar chart for each question to visualize the absolute or relative frequencies for each possible answer. Figure 1 shows the result for diagnosis 2 (Morbus Pompe). Questions showing a very uniform answer pattern cannot be considered to be characteristic for the corresponding disease, whereas questions for which (almost) all patients choose the same answer might be of more interest – unless people from all other diagnoses also choose the same answer. Such more interesting questions for Morbus Pompe are questions $Q3$ and $Q4$ where patients tend to choose option 4 (Absolutely) or questions $Q29$ and $Q33$ where option 1 (No) is favored.

However, it is quite tedious, to identify these more interesting questions in this simple visualization because one can only see the distribution of answers for each question without emphasizing those that might be of more interest. In order to highlight those questions with a stronger agreement among the patients under the considered group, we borrow ideas from sequence logo and other statistical tests.

3   Involved Statistical Methods

The improved visualization compared to Fig. 1 is shown in Fig. 2. The length of the bars is no longer equal to the number of participants who answered questions. Higher bars indicate a stronger consensus among the answers to the specific question, and colored points at the bottom indicate a significant deviation from a uniform distribution for the corresponding question in the diagnosis. In order to explain how the height of the bar is calculated, and the settings for calculating

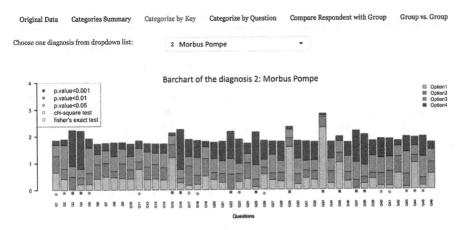

Fig. 2. Diagnosis 2 – Morbus Pompe disease

p-values, we briefly review the concepts of entropy, sequence logos, Chi-square test and Fisher's exact test.

3.1 Entropy

For each question j, we have i possible answers – in our case $i = 4$.

$$Q_j = \{Option_{1,j}, \ldots, Option_{i,j}\}.$$

The relative frequency of option i in question j is denoted $p_{i,j}$. The entropy (see for instance [5]) for the answers to question Q_j is then

$$H(Q_j) = -\sum_i p_{i,j} \cdot \log_2 p_{i,j}.$$

Entropy is a measure of unpredictability of an outcome. The greater the entropy value, the higher the uncertainty of the outcome. If a question has an entropy of zero, this would mean that all patients of the corresponding disease group have chosen the same answer to this question.

3.2 Sequence Logos

Sequence logos, invented by Tom D. Schneider and R. Michael Stephens [8], are usually applied in genetics or proteomics to represent aligned sets of DNA, RNA or protein sequences. It is used to discover conserved patterns in such sequences. In case of DNA sequences, every position would have one of the four nucleotides: A,C,T,G. At each position of a sequence, from which one has multiple samples, it is of interest whether always the same nucleotide occurs – indicating conservation – or whether there is a high variance of nucleotides at this position. Sequence logos display the distribution of the nucleotides by using the letters A,C,T,G as stacks in a bar. The height of the bar chart depends on the entropy w.r.t. A,C,T,G. The lower the entropy, the higher the bar.

In our case, we do not deal with nucleotides but with i possible answers question to instead. We use colored stacked bar charts where each color represents one possible answer to a question. Combined with the case used in this paper, a derivative work of sequence logo consists of stacks of colors. The questions correspond to the sequence. The overall height of each stack in a sequence logo depicts the information content or conservation of the sequence at that position [1], whereas in our case the relative height of each color within the stack reflects the frequency of the corresponding option in the sequence of questions. $R_{sequence}(Q_j)$ defines the height of the bar for question Q_j. We introduce a small correction factor e_n (like a Laplace correction) for the case when no one has chosen an answer.

$$R_{sequence}(Q_j) = \log_2 N - (H(Q_j) + e_n)$$

$$= \log_2 N - \left(\sum_i p_{i,j} \cdot \log_2 p_{i,j} + e_n \right)$$

The height (denoted by $h_{i,j}$) of the color stack of each option at the corresponding position (bar) is determined by multiplying the frequency $p_{i,j}$ by the total information at that question.

$$h_{i,j} = p_{i,j} \cdot R_{sequence}(Q_j)$$
$$= p_{i,j} \cdot [\log_2 N - (H(Q_i) + e_n)]$$
$$= p_{i,j} \cdot \left[\log_2 N - \left(\sum_i p_{i,j} \cdot \log_2 p_{i,j} + e_n \right) \right]$$

3.3   Chi-Square Test and Fisher's Exact Test

Before more rigorous and deeper statistical analysis starts, it is helpful to perform some basic inferential statistical tests like chi-square test and Fisher's exact test to determine whether the answering pattern of one question in one diagnosis deviates significantly from a uniform distribution or the answering patterns of two diagnoses for a specific question differ significantly. Since we are considering frequencies of possible answers of each question with usually more than two options, the chi-square test is an obvious choice to check whether the answering patterns deviate from the uniform distribution or whether two answering patterns differ from each other. However, the chi-square test is an asymptotic test and should only be used for sufficiently large sample sizes. Therefore, we only apply the chi-square test when the sample size – total number of answers to a question – exceeds 40 and when the theoretical absolute frequencies exceed 5 in each considered category. Otherwise, we apply Fisher's exact test by reducing the contingency table to 2×2-table.

We indicate low p-values by colors. Red stands for p-values lower than 0.001, yellow for p-values between 0.001 and 0.01 and green for p-values between 0.01 and 0.05.

For observed data that meet the conditions that mentioned above, the chi-square test is perfect for ascertaining the association between categorical variables [4]. In our case, participants' answer patterns for a specific question in two different diagnoses (x and y) generate a new matrix:

$$mat = \begin{vmatrix} a_x & a_y \\ b_x & b_y \\ c_x & c_y \\ d_x & d_y \end{vmatrix}$$

where entries correspond to frequencies of answers. Then the p-value can be directly calculated by applying the chi-square test.

When the sample size is less than 40 or the expected number of answer in a category is less than 5, Fisher's exact test is used instead. Since Fisher's exact test is designed for 2×2 contingency tables, the participants' answer summary for a specific question needs some further processing before applying Fisher's exact test.

In our case, we have four possible answers in each question. The matrix mat can be organized into four 2×2 contingency tables: mat_1, mat_2, mat_3, and mat_4, each one corresponding to one possible answer against all other possible answers.

$$mat_1 = \begin{vmatrix} a_x & a_y \\ b_x + c_x + d_x & b_y + c_y + d_y \end{vmatrix}, mat_2 = \begin{vmatrix} b_x & b_y \\ a_x + c_x + d_x & a_y + c_y + d_y \end{vmatrix}$$

$$mat_3 = \begin{vmatrix} c_x & c_y \\ a_x + b_x + d_x & a_y + b_y + d_y \end{vmatrix}, mat_4 = \begin{vmatrix} d_x & d_y \\ a_x + b_x + c_x & a_y + b_y + c_y \end{vmatrix}$$

In this way, we obtain four p-values and we finally carry out a correction for multiple testing, i.e. we multiply each p-value with the number of tests – corresponding to the number of possible answers to the considered question.

Different test methods are represented by different shapes of dots. In the bar plot, we use "□" to mark the chi-square test and "○" to mark Fisher's exact test.

4   VoQs - A Functional Data Visualization Application

With the above mentioned visualization principle, various views can be offered to analysis questionnaire data.

By analysis the data set transmitted by users, VoQs supports users check out options probability distribution of each question, observe salient features of identified respondent groups, meanwhile figure out possible internal relationships and differences among data.

In addition to the graphic of summarizing participates number of each diagnosis (Fig. 1), VoQs mainly provides four functions. The main function is to

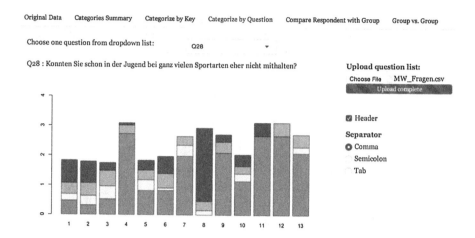

Fig. 3. Compare different diagnoses answer patterns for question 28

display bar charts of different grouping elements based on statistical calculation results. Using the neuromuscular disease questionnaire as an example, one can display the answering pattern for a specific disease as already shown in Fig. 2.

The second function that VoQs provides is to compare all diagnoses answer patterns for any designated question. Figure 3 shows the answer pattern of patients from different diagnoses on question 28. It can be seen that most patients in diagnosis 8 (Morbus McArdle) tend to choose option 4 (Absolutely) while in most other groups option 1 (No) is favored. This means that this question is one relevant indicator to distinguish diagnosis 8 from others.

The third function of VoQs is mapping a particular patient's questionnaire data to any diagnosis in order to check whether the answers of the patient fit to the answer pattern of a specific diagnosis. 46 points on the graph represent the answers the patient selected for each question. Points are positioned in the middle of the color corresponding to the selected answer. Figures 4 and 5 show the answer pattern of patient with diagnosis 2 to the correct diagnosis (Fig. 4) and to another diagnoses (Fig. 5). It is obvious that the patient's answer are more in line with diagnosis 2 than diagnosis 8.

Another function is the comparison of answering patterns for two different diagnoses. Figure 6 shows a comparison between diagnosis 1 (muscular dystrophies, myotonies) and diagnosis 11 (multiple sclerosis). The focus of comparison two different groups will fall on the high peaks of the bar chart. Most interesting are two high peaks for one question with different main colors.

In this case, the answers to the corresponding question are homogeneous within each diagnosis but heterogeneous between two diagnoses. It is also interesting if there is one tall and one short bar in some specific question, which means for one diagnosis patients tend to choose the same answer whereas for the other diagnosis patients show a very heterogeneous answering scheme. In order to obtain a more focused visualization, one can select specific questions restrict

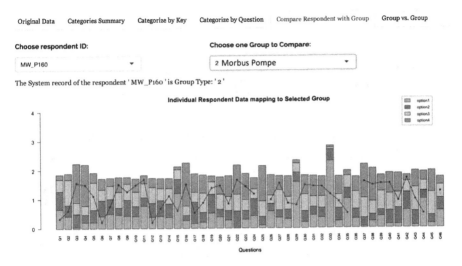

Fig. 4. Patient data mapped to diagnosis 2: Morbus Pompe

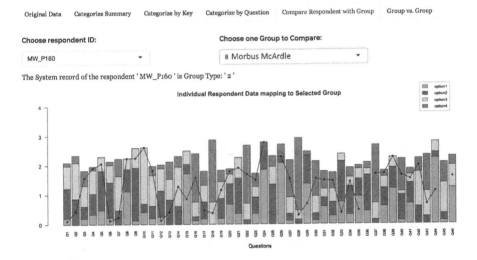

Fig. 5. Patient data mapped to diagnosis 8: Morbus McArdle

to those questions with significant differences as shown in Fig. 7. This web based application is already published in (shiny.improvedmedicaldiagnostics.com).

5   Conclusions and Future Work

VoQs is not limited to this particular area, it can be generally used for every kind of questionnaire with close-ended questions to better understand the answering patterns of certain groups, to identify questions where people from different

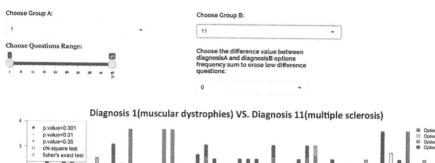

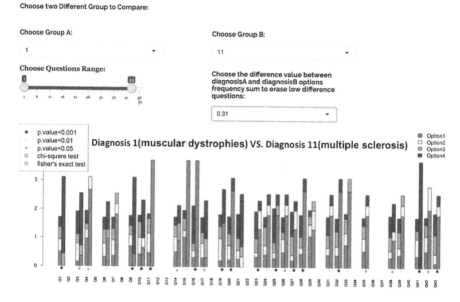

Fig. 6. Compare two diagnoses: Diagnosis 1 vs. Diagnosis 11

Fig. 7. Set the intervals of the graphic

groups typically choose different answers and to discover unusual cases that deviate strongly from usual answering patterns. With the help of VoQs application, researchers can collect important attributes and grouping questions in a more effective way.

In the future, this application will be enhanced with additional features that focus on further complex statistical testing for significant differences and the relevance of combinations of questions.

Acknowledgements. This work is partly funded by the Robert Bosch Stiftung (Germany) and Genzyme GmbH, Germany.

References

1. Crooks, G.E., Hon, G., Chandonia, J.M., Brenner, S.E.: Weblogo: a sequence logo generator. Genome Res. **14**(6), 1188–1190 (2004)
2. Klawonn, F., Lechner, W., Grigull, L.: Case-centred multidimensional scaling for classification visualisation in medical diagnosis. In: Huang, G., Liu, X., He, J., Klawonn, F., Yao, G. (eds.) HIS 2013. LNCS, vol. 7798, pp. 137–148. Springer, Heidelberg (2013)
3. Heiberger, R.M., Robbins, N.B.: Design of diverging stacked bar charts for likert scales and other applications. J. Stat. Softw. **57**(5), 1–32 (2014)
4. Moore, D.S.: Chi-square tests. Technical report, DTIC Document (1976)
5. Paninski, L.: Estimation of entropy and mutual information. Neural Comput. **15**, 1191–1253 (2003)
6. Shire: Rare disease impact report: Insights from patients and the medical community, April 2013. http://www.geneticalliance.org.uk/docs/e-update/rare-disease-impact-report.pdf
7. Sincero, S.M.: Types of survey questions, April 2012. https://explorable.com/types-of-survey-questions
8. Schneider, T.D., Stephens, R.M.: Sequence logos: a new way to display consensus sequences. Nucleic Acids Res. **18**, 6097–6100 (1990)
9. Reja, U., Manfreda, K.L., Hlebec, V., Vehovar, V.: Open-ended vs close-ended questions in web questionnaires. Dev. Appl. Stat. **19**, 159–177 (2003)

Author Index

Abdulrahman, Salisu Mamman 298
Alahakoon, Damminda 229
Amini, Massih-Reza 25, 132
Armant, Vincent 1

Babaki, Behrouz 13
Babbar, Rohit 25
Bäck, Thomas 310
Balikas, Georgios 25
Banerjee, Syagnik 253
Baroni, Alessandro 37
Batista, Gustavo E.A.P.A. 108
Becerra-Bonache, Leonor 49
Belousov, Alexander 61
Berthold, Michael R. 84
Blockeel, Hendrik 49, 322
Bonnevay, Stéphane 120
Borchani, Hanen 72
Brazdil, Pavel 298
Brown, Kenneth N. 1

Clément, Karine 264
Combe, David 181
Cooper, Gregory F. 275

Davis, Jesse 286
De Raedt, Luc 13
Dzyuba, Vladimir 286

Egyed-Zsigmond, Előd 181
Emmerich, Michael 310

Farmer, Michael 253
Fernández, Antonio 72
Fillbrunn, Alexander 84

Galván, María 49
Ganegedara, Thushan 229
Gaussier, Eric 25, 132
Géry, Mathias 181
Gieseke, Fabian 95
Giusti, Rafael 108
Grigull, Lorenz 334
Guns, Tias 13

Hannosset, Siebe 286
Hasnat, Md. Abul 120
Heskes, Tom 95
Horan, John 1

Jacquenet, François 49
Jacques, Julien 120
Joshi, Bikash 132

Kempitiya, Thimal 229
Klawonn, Frank 334
Kottke, Daniel 145
Kowalczyk, Wojtek 310
Krempl, Georg 145
Krijthe, Jesse H. 158

Laclau, Charlotte 170
Langseth, Helge 72
Largeron, Christine 181
Lechner, Werner 334
Loog, Marco 158

Mabub, Nahid 1
Madsen, Anders L. 72
Martínez, Ana M. 72
Masegosa, Andrés R. 72

Nadif, Mohamed 170
Nezvalová, Leona 193
Nielsen, Thomas D. 72
Nijssen, Siegfried 13
Nozari Zarmehri, Mohammad 205

Pahikkala, Tapio 95
Park, Laurence A.F. 217
Partalas, Ioannis 25, 132
Perera, Amal S. 229
Popelínský, Luboš 193

Ralaivola, Liva 132
Rathnasekara, Kevin 229
Rathnayake, Thilina 229
Ratsaby, Joel 61

Rizkalla, Salwa 264
Rönnqvist, Samuel 241
Ruggieri, Salvatore 37

Sáez, Ramón 72
Salmerón, Antonio 72
Sanborn, Randall 253
Silva, Diego F. 108
Simoff, Simeon 217
Soares, Carlos 205
Sokolovska, Nataliya 264
Spiliopoulou, Myra 145
Sverchkov, Yuriy 275

Torgo, Luis 193

Usunier, Nicolas 132

Vaculík, Karel 193
Van Haaren, Jan 286
van Rijn, Jan N. 298
van Stein, Bas 310
Vanschoren, Joaquin 298
Velcin, Julien 120
Verbeeck, Denny 322

Wang, Hao 310
Wijewardena, Maheshakya 229

Zhang, Xiaowei 334
Zucker, Jean-Daniel 264

Printed in the United States
By Bookmasters